Propaganda and Public Relations in Military Recruitment

This book represents the first international investigation of military recruitment advertising, public relations and propaganda. Comprised of eleven case studies that explore mobilisation work in Africa, the Americas, Asia and Europe, it covers more than a hundred years of recent history, with chapters on the First and Second World Wars, the Cold War, and the present day.

The book explores such promotion in countries both large and small, and in times of both war and peace, with readers gaining an insight into the different strategies and tactics used to motivate men, women and occasionally even children to serve and fight in many parts of the world. Readers will also learn about the crucial but little-known role of commercial advertising, public relations and media professionals in the production and distribution of recruitment promotion. This book, the first of its kind to be published, will explore that role, and in the process address two questions that are central to studies of media and conflict: how do militaries encourage civilians to join up, and are they successful in doing so?

It is a multi-disciplinary project intended for a diverse academic audience, including postgraduate students exploring aspects of war, propaganda and public opinion, and researchers working across the domains of history, communications studies, conflict studies, psychology and philosophy.

Brendan Maartens is Lecturer in Communication and Media at the University of Liverpool, UK. He has published on various aspects of military recruitment promotion in Britain and Ireland and has also written about the development of modern media management techniques. At the broadest level, he is interested in how governments and armed forces 'sell' themselves to ordinary citizens and what role private enterprise (and advertising agencies and public relations firms in particular) play in such selling.

Thomas Bivins is the John L. Hulteng Chair in Media Ethics and the head of the Graduate Certificate Program in Communication Ethics in the School of Journalism and Communication at the University of Oregon, US. Before entering academia, he spent six years as a broadcast specialist in armed forces radio and television and has worked in advertising and corporate public relations and as a graphic designer and editorial cartoonist. He is the author of numerous research articles on media ethics and several college texts.

Routledge New Directions in PR & Communication Research
Edited by Kevin Moloney

Current academic thinking about public relations (PR) and related communication is a lively, expanding marketplace of ideas and many scholars believe that it's time for its radical approach to be deepened. **Routledge New Directions in PR & Communication Research** is the forum of choice for this new thinking. Its key strength is its remit, publishing critical and challenging responses to continuities and fractures in contemporary PR thinking and practice, tracking its spread into new geographies and political economies. It questions its contested role in market-orientated, capitalist, liberal democracies around the world, and examines its invasion of all media spaces, old, new, and as yet unenvisaged.

The **New Directions** series has already published and commissioned diverse original work on topics such as:

- PR's influence on Israeli and Palestinian nation-building
- PR's origins in the history of ideas
- a Jungian approach to PR ethics and professionalism
- global perspectives on PR professional practice
- PR as an everyday language for everyone
- PR as emotional labour
- PR as communication in conflicted societies, and
- PR's relationships to cooperation, justice and paradox.

We actively invite new contributions and offer academics a welcoming place for the publication of their analyses of a universal, persuasive mindset that lives comfortably in old and new media around the world.

Strategic Communications in Russia
Public Relations and Advertising
Edited by Katerina Tsetsura and Dean Kruckeberg

Popular Culture and Social Change
The Hidden Work of Public Relations
Kate Fitch and Judy Motion

Propaganda and Public Relations in Military Recruitment
Promoting Military Service in the Twentieth and Twenty-First Centuries
Edited by Brendan Maartens and Thomas Bivins

For more information about this series, please visit: www.routledge.com/ Routledge-New-Directions-in-Public-Relations – Communication-Research/ book-series/RNDPRCR

Propaganda and Public Relations in Military Recruitment

Promoting Military Service in the Twentieth and Twenty-First Centuries

Edited by Brendan Maartens and Thomas Bivins

LONDON AND NEW YORK

First published 2021
by Routledge
2 Park Square, Milton Park, Abingdon, Oxon OX14 4RN

and by Routledge
52 Vanderbilt Avenue, New York, NY 10017

Routledge is an imprint of the Taylor & Francis Group, an informa business

© 2021 selection and editorial matter, Brendan Maartens and Thomas Bivins; individual chapters, the contributors

The right of Brendan Maartens and Thomas Bivins to be identified as the authors of the editorial material, and of the authors for their individual chapters, has been asserted in accordance with sections 77 and 78 of the Copyright, Designs and Patents Act 1988.

All rights reserved. No part of this book may be reprinted or reproduced or utilised in any form or by any electronic, mechanical, or other means, now known or hereafter invented, including photocopying and recording, or in any information storage or retrieval system, without permission in writing from the publishers.

Trademark notice: Product or corporate names may be trademarks or registered trademarks, and are used only for identification and explanation without intent to infringe.

British Library Cataloguing-in-Publication Data
A catalogue record for this book is available from the British Library

Library of Congress Cataloging-in-Publication Data
Names: Maartens, Brendan, editor. | Bivins, Thomas H. (Thomas Harvey),
    1947– editor.
Title: Propaganda and public relations in military recruitment : promoting
    military service in the twentieth and twenty-first centuries / edited by
    Brendan Maartens and Thomas Bivins.
Other titles: Promoting military service in the twentieth and twenty-first
    centuries
Description: London ; New York, NY : Routledge/Taylor & Francis
    Group, 2021. | Series: Routledge new directions in PR & communication
    research | Includes bibliographical references and index.
Identifiers: LCCN 2020028814 (print) | LCCN 2020028815 (ebook)
Subjects: LCSH: Recruiting and enlistment—History—20th century—
    Case studies. | Military service, Voluntary—History—20th century—
    Case studies. | Propaganda—History—20th century—Case studies.
Classification: LCC UB320 .P76 2021 (print) | LCC UB320 (ebook) |
    DDC 355.2/23—dc23
LC record available at https://lccn.loc.gov/2020028814
LC ebook record available at https://lccn.loc.gov/2020028815

ISBN: 978-0-367-33392-8 (hbk)
ISBN: 978-0-429-31962-4 (ebk)

Typeset in Times New Roman
by Apex CoVantage, LLC

Brendan Maartens: To my mother and father, whose care, consideration and encouragement took me from the dockyards to academia.

Contents

Preface	xiii
List of contributors	xv
List of illustrations	xvi
List of abbreviations	xvii

Introduction 1

1 Your country(ies) need you! The case for a global analysis of military recruitment campaigning 3
BRENDAN MAARTENS

'Munitions of the mind': studies of propaganda, recruitment and public opinion 4
Advertising, mass media and the birth of the modern military recruitment campaign 6
Pageantry, iconography and the written word: selling service in the distant past 9
Military recruitment in times of war and peace: an overview of the case studies 11

2 Your media need you! How recruiters use advertising, public relations and propaganda to promote service and allegiance 17
BRENDAN MAARTENS

The art of paying for space: advertising, agencies and advertisements 18
Selling service in news, entertainment and current affairs: the art of propaganda 21
Events, issues and reputation: the public relations of military recruitment 25
Conclusion: reflecting on the process of paying, earning and owning media content 27

viii *Contents*

PART I
Recruitment in an era of total war

31

3 Why Africans in British Empire territories joined the colours, 1914–1918

33

ANNE SAMSON

'A low whisper that vibrated over the empire': recruiting at the outset of the war 34
Agriculture, mining and commerce: the economics of recruitment 35
The 'right sort of man': ethnicity and conscription 36
'A chance to see the world': experiences of enlistment and challenges of recruiting 39
Army bands, public speeches, advertisements and atrocity stories 40
Conclusion 42

4 National aspirations against war fatigue: uses and mechanisms of mobilising propaganda in World War I Greece

48

ELLI LEMONIDOU

Greece, the First World War and the significance of the 'great idea' 49
Channels and content of propaganda in Greece in the early twentieth century 51
The mobilisation of 23 September 1915 53
The mobilisation of 18 April 1917 54
The mobilisation of 22 January 1918 56
Conclusion: from neutrality to participation – recruiting in a divided country 57

5 Winning the battle to lose the war: the *Call to Arms* recruiting campaign in Australia, 1916

61

EMILY ROBERTSON

Recruiting and publicity in Australia in the First World War 62
Conscription, coercion and the Call to Arms *campaign 65*
Recruiting and the slow path to federalism 68
Conclusion: voluntary service, conscription and the shifting tides of public opinion 71

Contents ix

6 It takes a good woman to sell a good war: the use of women in World War I United States propaganda posters 75

THOMAS BIVINS

The great propaganda machine 75
What is propaganda? 76
The Division of Pictorial Publicity 79
Woman as propaganda technique 81
Woman as symbol 82
Protecting angels 86
Conclusions 88

7 'A place for everyone, and everyone must find the right place': recruitment to British civil defence, 1937–44 96

JESSICA HAMMETT AND HENRY IRVING

A 'new chapter'? Establishing the administrative framework 97
'How you can best help your country in a moment of need': the national campaign 99
The 'localisation of recruiting energy': campaigning in towns, boroughs and cities 104
The 'social side' of service: utilising personal and peer-group persuasion 108
A 'rush of volunteers': the significance of war events 110
Conclusion: the importance of national, local and personal pressures 110

PART II
Recruitment at a Time of Cold War 115

8 'It's like a good school, only better': recruiting boys to the British armed forces under the first Attlee government, 1946–50 117

BRENDAN MAARTENS

Government communications, military recruitment and the start of the Cold War 118
The 'product' and the 'sales team': organising the campaigns of 1946–50 120
Having a 'man's time' in military: newspaper advertising and the sale of service 121

x   *Contents*

*Fashioning 'news pegs': press conferences, press releases and
    public exhibitions 124*
*'What lies beyond the horizon'? Visualising military life on the
    silver screen 126*
Reviewing the campaigns of 1946–50: a critical assessment 127

9   **Eastern Europe's reluctant soldiers: recruitment to the armies
    of the Warsaw Pact, 1956–1991**   131
    ROGER R. REESE

*The establishment of the Warsaw Treaty Organization and the
    politics of recruitment 132*
*Pre-conscription ideological indoctrination and military
    training: the Soviet model 133*
*'We will never take up weapons': East Germany as a case study
    in contrasts 136*
*An 'ingrained aversion to all uniforms': youth attitudes towards
    service 138*
*Conclusion: the relationship between service and strife in the
    communist East 142*

10 **'The Army just sees green': utopian meritocracy, diversity,
    and United States Army recruitment in the 1970s**   145
    JESSICA L. GHILANI

*The Gates Commission, the Army, and the beginning of the
    'volunteer' era 147*
'Be all you can be': the N. W. Ayer–Army partnership 149
*'Today's Army wants to join you': utopia in recruitment
    advertising 150*
*Conclusion: idealised simulations in military service in
    recruitment advertising 157*

PART III
Recruitment in the digital age   161

11 **Canadian military public affairs and recruitment in an age
    of social media platforms**   163
    TANNER MIRRLEES

*Canada's foreign policy, the Department of National Defence and
    the Canadian Armed Forces in the twenty-first century 165*
*The Canadian military's public affairs office, militarising media
    events and recruitment advertising 167*

The Canadian Armed Forces' social media platforms, policies and practices 171

Conclusion: Canadian military digital dependence in the age of US platform imperialism 174

12 'Life is wonderful because of the military': People's Liberation Army recruitment campaigns in contemporary China   178

ORNA NAFTALI

From a guerrilla force to a modern army: a history of the People's Liberation Army 179

Volunteers and 'involuntary conscripts': the challenges of recruiting in the twenty-first century 181

Strengthening the 'brand' and the 'packaging': media campaigns in the age of Web 2.0 182

Contributing to 'national rejuvenation': the Chinese conscription video 183

'Fulfil your personal dream of military life': the use of aspirational appeals 185

Conclusion: military recruiting in an era of market liberalism 187

13 The caliphate wants you! Conflating Islam and Islamist ideology in Islamic State of Iraq and Syria recruitment propaganda and Western media reporting   192

HALIM RANE AND AUDREY COURTY

The origins of the Islamic State of Syria and Iraq and its propaganda network 193

'A state for all Muslims': recruiting using Dabiq *and* Rumiyah *195*

Islam, Islamism and the use of religion in mobilisation promotion 198

Giving terrorists the 'oxygen of publicity': Western media reporting 200

Conclusion 202

Conclusion   207

14 Narratives of service, sacrifice and security: reflecting on the legacy of military recruitment   209

BRENDAN MAARTENS

Measuring the impact of campaigns: the factors and effects of enlistment 213

xii   *Contents*

Looking ahead: future avenues of scholarly research 216
Looking ahead: military recruitment in an unstable world 218

Index   223

Preface

The seed of this book, like so many others in the New Directions series, was planted at the International History of Public Relations Conference. An interdisciplinary forum for debate and discussion, this conference considers the whole gamut of public relations (PR) history. The editors of this collection are regular attendees and met in 2017 after delivering separate papers on military recruitment promotion in Britain and the United States. Striking up a conversation in a lift shortly after, they broached the prospect of a future collaboration. A comparative international study involving the US and the UK certainly had potential, not least because the two countries have fought alongside each other (and in the odd case, against one another) at various points over the past two and a half centuries. Yet what of other countries outside the Anglosphere? How was military recruitment organised there? When was the first major recruitment campaign launched, and has the art of campaigning changed much since then?

What follows are some preliminary answers to these questions. The combined effort of thirteen scholars working at different academic institutions around the world, and in one case as an independent researcher, it is the first investigation of military recruitment promotion to consider the subject across time and space. Many books have explored war propaganda, including several that adopt a comparative international approach. This volume considers the work of those tasked specifically with raising troops, doing so through the prism of eleven national or international case studies. Not all of the authors are PR specialists; some are military historians, others scholars of digital communications and others cultural studies academics. What unites them all is a common interest in how governments and armed forces 'sell' military careers and military service to civilian audiences and what implications such selling has for broader understandings of war, conflict and persuasive communications.

Like all edited collections, this book has represented a labour of love, and many deserve credit for its delivery. Kevin Moloney, the editor of the New Directions series, is chief among them. His persistence and patience ensured that this book left the drawing board; it would have remained nothing more than a nice idea otherwise. Jacqueline Curthoys and Guy Loft, commissioning editors who shared responsibility for the project at various points over the past two years, have been xiv *Preface*

equally patient, as has Mathew Ranscombe, their editorial assistant. Next up are two men almost every delegate at the International History of Public Relations Conference will recognise: Tom Watson and Anastasios Theofilou. Sharing the responsibility for organising this conference since its inception in 2009, Tom and Tasos have worked long nights and longer days to ensure that people like us get to talk through all matters PR and much else besides. Last but not least are the authors' many colleagues, friends and family members – too numerous to name here, but without whose support no academic work would see the light of day.

To these people, and to all others who have played a part both large and small in this book, we would like to express our sincere gratitude. To those who read the book, we ask only that any errors, which should hopefully be scarce, are treated as our own.

Contributors

Audrey Courty, Griffith University, Australia
Dr Jessica L. Ghilani, University of Pittsburgh, US
Dr Jessica Hammett, Birkbeck, University of London, UK
Dr Henry Irving, Leeds Beckett University, UK
Dr Elli Lemonidou, University of Patras, Greece
Dr Tanner Mirrlees, University of Ontario Institute of Technology, Canada
Dr Orna Naftali, The Hebrew University of Jerusalem, Israel
Dr Halim Rane, Griffith University, Australia
Dr Emily Robertson, Australian National University, Australia
Professor Roger R. Reese, Texas A&M University, US
Dr Anne Samson, Great War in Africa Association

Illustrations

6.1	'Columbia Calls', designed by Frances Adams Halsted, painted by Vincent Aderente	84
6.2	'The Navy Needs You', James Montgomery Flagg	85
6.3	'Fight or Buy Bonds', Howard Chandler Christy	87
6.4	'In the name of mercy give', Albert Herter	89
6.5	'The Spirit of America', Howard Chandler Christy	90
6.6	'Third Liberty Loan Campaign: Boy Scouts of America', J. C. Leyendecker	91
6.7	*Life* magazine, October 28, 1920, Charles Dana Gibson	92
7.1	*National Service* (London: HMSO, 1939), inside cover. Message from the Prime Minister, January 1939	101
7.2	Imperial War Museum, PST 13380, Goodfellow, 'Air Raid Wardens Wanted' poster (1939)	102
7.3	*The Wardens' Post* (Middlesbrough), Vol. 1, No. 6, May 1940, back page. Tear-out poster to display in windows.	105
7.4	Harpenden and District Local History Society, ARP-5-3	106
7.5	*Air Raid Precautions Gazette* (Doncaster), No. 4, 24 February 1940, p. 15. Auxiliary Fire Service members and friends at a whist drive	109
10.1	'Amy's an Expert in Psychological Warfare'	153
10.2	'Now That You Don't Have to Go'	155
10.3	'Lead the People Who've Joined the Army'	156

Abbreviations

ARP: Air Raid Precautions
AIF: Australian Imperial Force
ADM-PA: Assistant Deputy Minister Public Affairs
BBC: British Broadcasting Corporation
BEA: British East Africa
CAF: Canadian Armed Forces
DND: Canadian Department of National Defense
COI: Central Office of Information
CCP: Chinese Communist Party
CPI: Committee on Public Information
DPP: Division of Pictorial Publicity
DOSAAF: All-Union Voluntary Society for Assistance to the Army, Air
             Force, and Navy
FPWC: Federal Parliamentary Recruiting Committee
FDJ: Freie Deutsche Jungend [Free German Youth]
DDR: German Democratic Republic
GSWA: German South West Africa
GST: Gesellschaft für Sport und Technik [Society for Sport and
             Technology]
ISIL: Islamic State of Iraq and the Levant
ISIS: Islamic State of Iraq and Syria
KAR: King's African Rifles
LCC: London County Council
MOD: Ministry of Defence
NSW: New South Wales
NVA: Nationale Volksarmee [National People's Army]
NATO: North Atlantic Treaty Organization
PLA: People's Liberation Army
PR: public relations
QRC: Queensland Recruiting Committee
RAF: Royal Air Force
SWCSA: Secretary of the State War Council
SRPC: Services Recruiting Publicity Committee

xviii *Abbreviations*

SANLC:	South African Native Labour Corps
UN:	United Nations
USSR:	Union of Soviet Socialist Republics
WTO:	Warsaw Treaty Organization
WAC:	Women's Army Corps
WVS:	Women's Voluntary Services
WWI:	World War I

Introduction

1 Your country(ies) need you! The case for a global analysis of military recruitment campaigning

Brendan Maartens

Abstract

This chapter introduces readers to the topic of military recruitment promotion. Taking a long durée perspective, it shows how public spectacles and cultural artefacts have been used to sell service in armed forces throughout the world and how such things have been combined, in recent years, with persuasive strategies and techniques derived from the modern advertising, public relations and media industries. A fair amount has been written about these developments, with some scholars offering expansive overviews of the many different ways in which civilians are enticed to serve and others charting the use of specific channels of communication, such as posters or films, in large-scale mobilisation efforts. The approach taken in this book, and one called for in this chapter, is different. Focusing on recruitment campaigns as objects of analysis in their own right, it makes a case for studying them nationally and internationally before concluding with an overview of the book's case studies.

What drives people to risk their lives to serve in the military? This question has gripped philosophers, poets, politicians and, of course, soldiers for millennia, and like many recurring problems, it does not lend itself to a straightforward answer. For the pharaoh Thutmose III, wars were supported by his subjects to uphold 'valour, might, and right, to overthrow [the] wretched enemy, [and] to extend the borders of Egypt'.[1] For Aristotle, the 'art of war' was a 'natural art of acquisition . . . an art which we ought to practise . . . against men who, though intended by nature to be governed, will not submit'.[2] A more enlightened view, at least to contemporary eyes, can be found in the Sanskrit epic *Mahābhārata*, which suggests that wars can be supported, if not condoned, so long as they help to maintain civic order, defend a people or its culture or prevent a 'crime' from being committed. Yet, they should only ever represent a last resort. As Vyasa, an important character in and perhaps the actual author of the poem, says:

> success which is won by negotiation and other means is the very best. That which is achieved by producing disunion (among the foe) is indifferent. . . . [S]uccess . . . won by battle is the worst. In battle are many evils, the initial one . . . being slaughter.[3]

Such ideas do not, of course, constitute reliable evidence of *why* people actually serve: that can only be gleaned from combatants themselves, most of whom, in

4 *Brendan Maartens*

antiquity at least, left no written record of their guiding motivations or principles. However, they do provide a valuable insight into the kinds of values and ideals commonly associated with military service, which can sometimes include, paradoxically, compassion, empathy and love. Writing in the third century BCE, the Confucian philosopher Xun Kuang suggested that otherwise benevolent people might be convinced to take up arms out of a sense of 'humanity' and 'loving others':

> It is just such a love of others that causes a hatred of whoever does injury to them. . . . [Wars] are just the means whereby to prohibit violent and aggressive behaviour and to prevent harm to others. . . . Wherever the army of a humane man is, it has an effect like that of a spirit; wherever it travels, it produces transformation.[4]

'Transformations' of a religious kind have featured in the writings of many theologians. About a millennium after Kuang wrote *Xunzi*, in a text attributed to the Islamic scholar Muhammad ibn al-Hasan al-Shaybani, war was described as a means of solidifying religious bonds and extending the reach and influence of Sunni Islam: 'Fight in the name of God and in the path of God. Fight the *mukaffirun* ["ingrates," "unbelievers"]. Do not cheat or commit treachery, and do not mutilate anyone or kill children'.[5] A similar spiritual call to arms can be found in the work of the medieval scholastic Saint Thomas Aquinas, who argued some half a millennium later that 'Christians often make war on unbelievers, not to force them to believe – since even if they conquered them and made them prisoners they would leave them free as to whether they wished to believe – but to prevent them from interfering with the Christian faith'.[6]

For many thinkers of the early modern and modern periods, wars served more instrumental goals. The English economist Thomas Malthus suggested that economic necessity – or a 'bad harvest, and a want or unemployment' – compelled the poorest in society to enlist.[7] The German philosopher Immanuel Kant said citizens consented to military service to 'secure themselves and their country against foreign aggression'.[8] The American statesman Abraham Lincoln, whose life was of course defined by war, claimed individuals signed up for 'want of employment' and 'convenience' but were also drawn by 'patriotism, political bias, ambition, personal courage, [and] love of adventure'.[9] A different perspective, though one shorn of idealism, is found in the writings of Frederick Engels, who lent support to compulsory military service for 'political and not military reasons': trained soldiers, Engels claimed, 'provide protection not so much against the external enemy, as the internal one'.[10]

'Munitions of the mind': studies of propaganda, recruitment and public opinion

A means of justifying and explaining conflict, these ideas, to borrow a phrase from the propaganda historian Philip Taylor, represent 'munitions of the mind' – 'weapon[s] of no less significance than swords or bombs or guns'.[11] This book is about such 'munitions' and in particular those developed by individuals tasked with mobilising populations. All military organisations, including those that relied on conscription, produced some form of persuasive communication to try to motivate men, women and occasionally even children to serve and fight. This communication has been central to the ways in which military service and wars more generally have been imagined, particularly in the twentieth and twenty-first centuries, which represent the primary focus of this volume. Yet it has not received a great deal of scholarly scrutiny. On the contrary, much existing literature, including Taylor's extensive *oeuvre*, focuses on war propaganda in its broadest sense, exploring not just statements of the kind already referenced but plays, poetry and speeches, banners, flags and insignia, cenotaphs and memorials and the entire panoply of modern mass media communications as well.[12]

There are clearly many ways of promoting war and sound reasons for studying these *in toto*. '[H]istory's recruiting sergeants', Taylor reminds us, often operated without official guidance or support, and analysis of their work should not therefore be restricted to the corridors of power or indeed the battlefield.[13] Garth Jowett and Victoria O'Donnell have also drawn attention to the breadth of war propaganda. 'Where there is a communication channel', they claim, 'there is also a potential propaganda medium', and in the contemporary era 'all available forms of communication, from the very effective oral tradition still widely used to the most sophisticated modern electronic systems', are utilised to sell war and service.[14] The past one hundred or so years have attracted a wealth of attention precisely because of the growth of mass media. A recent volume edited by Jo Fox and David Welch, for example, explores how political 'leaders and "spin-doctors", operating largely at the behest of the state, sought to shape popular attitudes' towards conflict and the individuals who participated in it but extends this analysis far beyond the realm of recruitment to topics like pacifism, fine art and human rights.[15]

These studies obviously represent only a fraction of published commentary on military recruitment, with the subject also explored in the literature on wartime mobilisations, which tends to focus on the logistical challenges of raising hundreds of thousands of troops in a given nation or region;[16] in writing on specific media, such as posters, films and television;[17] and in occasional quantitative attempts to measure the efficacy of campaigning.[18] Each type of investigation can tell us something important about the nature of military recruitment. Studies of war propaganda in its broadest sense, for example, reveal the kaleidoscopic array of appeals that prospective recruits are exposed to in times of conflict and, in so doing, demonstrate the extent to which many societies, both past and present, have been or currently are militarised. Explorations of specific media accomplish a similar task, albeit in relation to a single communications channel, and thus provide a degree of scholarly detail that is often lacking in more general surveys. Studies of mobilisation document the many steps that governments and armed forces take when implementing large-scale recruitment campaigns, while investigations of effects seek to answer the all-important question of whether such campaigns actually *work*.

Some contributors to this book have produced research that falls into one of these categories, and the work that they and others have published has done

6 Brendan Maartens

much to advance current understandings of the relationship between recruitment, communications and public opinion. Each approach, however, has limitations. Expansive studies of war propaganda often elide official and unofficial promotion, affording an equal degree of prominence to each type of appeal even if only one was actually sponsored by official actors. Casting a long line rather than a wide net, explorations of specific media benefit from depth rather than breadth, but since recruitment campaigns typically involved coordinated appeals carried across a range of media simultaneously, they are not well suited for the task at hand. Studies of mobilisation, the preserve of military rather than media historians, tend to relegate the question of persuasion to the margins, focusing instead on the technicalities of enrolment and the consequences it has for individuals and societies as a whole. Studies of impact, finally, do place some emphasis on persuasion and its role in shaping behaviour but often in a fairly simplistic attempt to draw causal correlations between campaigns and concomitant fluctuations in enrolment rates.

Advertising, mass media and the birth of the modern military recruitment campaign

The approach taken in this book is different. Focusing primarily on recruitment campaigns organised at specific moments in time with the intention of enrolling large numbers of volunteers into armed forces or civil defence services or socialising conscripts into military service, it explores not just the impact (or lack thereof) of such campaigns on public opinion but the institutions and individuals that organised them, the tactics and strategies they developed, and the appeals and exhortations they produced. This approach is not, it is worth noting, unique. In an important monograph published in 2009, Beth Bailey investigated the role of advertising and market research in the creation of the all-volunteer Army in the United States in the 1970s, and the corollary attempt, to quote one high-ranking officer serving at the time, to make military service appear 'more enjoyable, more professionally rewarding, and less burdensome in its impact on our people and their families'.[19] In shorter but no less significant studies, Nicholas Hiley showed how newspapers, films and posters were used to sell service to the British Army before and during the Great War and how professionalism, monetary rewards and enjoyment also formed part of recruiters' repertoire, albeit in peacetime, not wartime.[20]

Similar findings have been unearthed beyond the Anglosphere, albeit in studies that only briefly touch on recruitment promotion. During the 1912–13 Balkan Wars, the Ottoman Empire used newspapers, religious ceremonies, theatre productions, stamps and greeting cards to promote enlistment in and support of its armed forces.[21] At the start of the Second World War, the Swedish government, though nominally committed to a policy of neutrality, established a *Finlandskommittén*, or Committee for Finland, to raise volunteers for the latter's war with Russia in 1939–40. Also making use of print media, recruiters on this committee produced newspaper advertisements and posters to promote service, portraying

Your country(ies) need you! 7

the Swedes and Fins as kin with a common Scandinavian ancestry and the war as a fight for Nordic Independence or (to quote one poster) 'För Nordens Frihet'.[22] More recently, the Sri Lankan government, engaged in a long-running struggle against Tamil separatists in the north and east of the country, hired the Colombo branch of Leo Burnett Solutions, a global advertising chain, to boost army recruitment. The outcome of this collaboration was *Lion Cubs in Paradise* (2000), a major newspaper and television advertising campaign that depicted military service, to quote one scholar writing on the topic of militarisation, as a mélange of 'camaraderie, preparedness for unexpected challenges, and strength' but tellingly showed no scenes of actual conflict.[23]

These campaigns were all sanctioned by governments and either produced by them or by agents working on their behalf. They were comprised of two main types of promotion: exhortations delivered interpersonally without the aid or indeed encumbrance of mediation and appeals carried in and across a range of media. As we shall see, the first type of promotion has formed part of recruiting drives for a very long time, but the second only really became a realistic possibility in the twentieth century, which is sometimes referred to as humanity's 'most violent century'[24] and was certainly the period in which mass media in their modern guises emerged. Described by Marshall Poe as an age of *Homo Lector, Homo Videns* and *Homo Somnians*,[25] the twentieth century ushered in the mass-circulation newspaper and national radio and television broadcasting. The 'communications revolution' that such technology heralded was recognised by scholars as early as the 1960s[26] and was only accelerated by the invention in 1991 of the World Wide Web, which was initially conceived of as a means of sharing 'information' but quickly metamorphosed into a much more grandiose platform for the exchange of ideas, entertainment and promotion and for social networking.[27]

Like propagandists, recruiters worked with whichever media were available to them at the times in which they operated. Yet they also routinely drew inspiration from another class of hidden persuader: the commercial advertising expert. Such inspiration was reflected in the character of the appeals recruiters developed, which imbibed what Hiley has called the 'basic grammar of opinion control' furnished by commercial advertising[28] and in the institutional interactions and exchanges that underpinned their work. Today, distinctions are often drawn between propaganda, ostensibly a product of the state, and advertising, a child of commerce. Yet such distinctions often break down when exploring military recruitment. Both advertisers and recruiters shared a common currency, campaigns, and both made use of the same mediated and interpersonal appeals when exhorting the public. The very word 'campaign' and its continental variants[29] typifies the parallels between the two activities: used initially to describe military engagements on a field of battle, it became part of the nomenclature of advertising in the late nineteenth century, when more targeted, strategic methods of promotion emerged and when advertising agencies began to offer such methods as part of planned client services.[30]

Armed forces throughout the world became clients of such agencies, and this book explores some of the campaigns that grew out of this marriage of military

8   Brendan Maartens

and commercial promotion. It also considers some campaigns organised wholly or predominantly by political entities that used techniques of persuasion that were developed within the commercial realm. Both geographically and chronologically ambitious, it analyses recruitment drives organised on four continents from 1914 until the present day. Most chapters focus on armed forces of one kind or another, but one considers recruitment for a series of civil defence services that put recruits' lives at risk but did not compel them to take up arms. Most case studies investigate the recruitment of men, who have historically made up the lion's share of combatants,[31] but some explore the mobilisation of women or exhortations that used women in an attempt to convince men to sign up, while others consider the enlistment of children, a group with an unfortunate history of frontline service.[32] Some case studies consider recruitment conducted in times of peace, but others explore campaigns waged in wartime, and while some of these wars were 'total' in the sense that they required the mobilisation of the entire resources of a given nation or people, others were 'limited' in that they did not require large-scale mobilisation efforts. Most case studies, finally, consider recruitment for established nation-states, but one considers mobilisation work for a disputed or 'unofficial' state in present-day Iraq and Syria.

There are problems with casting such a wide net. The cultural distance separating First World War Greece (Chapter 4), for example, from present-day China (Chapter 12) is so great that one might question the wisdom of including analyses of both countries in the same volume. The short length of each chapter, meanwhile, which amounts to no more than 7,000 words, footnotes included, also limits what each contributor is able to say about their respective country or countries, and obviously precludes any form of comprehensive, long-term historical analysis of either the national or the international scenes. Last but not least, despite several earnest attempts to secure case studies from Central and South America, those regions receive no direct coverage here, which ensures that this book is not entirely global in scope.[33]

Nevertheless, in bringing together case studies from so many different parts of the globe, it does move beyond the narrow national purviews that have characterised much scholarly writing on military recruitment to date. Each of the case studies also showcases original research, with none recycling material from existing published work and two, on British Africa (Chapter 3) and Eastern Europe (Chapter 9), exploring recruitment campaigns waged in a range of countries simultaneously. All told, upwards of thirty nations are discussed in ten case studies, not counting material considered in the final case study, which explores the global recruitment work of *Dā'ish* or the Islamic State of Iraq and the Levant (Chapter 13).

By exploring military recruiting across time and space, this book seeks to make some tentative observations about the nature of the practice. Were similar appeals used to encourage civilians to serve in different countries, regions and periods? And if so, what does this tell us about military service in particular and war and conflict more generally? Do recruiters deploy different kinds of exhortations in times of war and peace, and if so what does this reveal about the processes of preparing civilians for service? These questions are of fundamental importance to studies of politics, international relations and war, and some preliminary answers to them will be sketched out in the conclusion of this volume (Chapter 14). Before then, however, it is worth saying something about the origins of military recruitment campaigns, the historical forces that have given rise to them and the institutions and individuals that have shaped them.

Pageantry, iconography and the written word: selling service in the distant past

A central contention of this volume is that military recruitment promotion was not developed in isolation but rather grew out of existing methods of persuasion and customs of exhortation. We have already mentioned the 'grammar' of commercial advertising, but another important antecedent was military pageantry and iconography. Armed forces have organised spectacles to promote service and allegiance for a long time. In many of the great civilisations of antiquity, wars and the individuals who waged them were celebrated in elaborate public ceremonies and commemorated in objects imbued with mystical or mythical meanings. In ancient Mesopotamia, stelae, rectangular stone monuments inscribed with images and text, were used to honour victories on the field of battle, ward off future foes and celebrate gods, kings and queens.[34] In the thirteenth century BC, Ramesses II memorialised the Egyptian victory over the Hittites by ordering the carving of 'lengthy compositions . . . in a propaganda campaign of unprecedented proportions . . . on the walls of all the major temples'.[35] From the eighth century BC until their demise as regional powers, Greek city-states used 'great temples, monumental sculptures and other edifices' to signify their military prowess,[36] and at the height of the Roman Empire, paintings, statues, pottery, vexilla, busts and coins were used to glamorise martial endeavour, with foreign conquests routinely re-enacted on the sands of the Colosseum.[37]

Such artefacts were designed to make wars seem both natural and inevitable and associated the generals, emperors and empresses who waged them with early cults of personality.[38] Demonstrating 'growing sophistication in the art of persuasion', to quote one recent scholarly survey,[39] they projected an image of rulers and the deities to whom they often paid deference as central to the act of war. The class dynamics that underpinned this process are worth highlighting. Wars may have been started by elites, but ordinary people invariably bore their main brunt.[40] Earning their acquiescence or forcing their compliance was a prerequisite of large-scale conflict and a matter, to quote the Greek philosopher and general Xenophon, of making soldiers 'stronger in soul [than] their enemies'.[41] Whether leaders were successful at doing so is of course an open question, but they certainly made repeated attempts to cultivate *esprit de corps* among their subjects and also offered them rewards, in the form of money, land or political status, in exchange for service. From antiquity to the early Middle Ages, landowning was in fact central to military recruitment in both Europe and the Near East.[42]

The Crusades, which brought these two regions into internecine conflict over a three-century period beginning in 1096, witnessed a spate of recruiting activities spearheaded by priests and *khaṭībs* who used sermons to provide moral instruction to congregations.[43] Such sermons were usually delivered in churches and mosques, where worshipers may also have encountered intricate tapestries and

10 *Brendan Maartens*

mosaics depicting scenes of famous battles and victories. Muslims and Christians were also, however, enticed to serve with hand-written *fada'il* literature and papal bulls, including the *quantum praedecessores* bull issued by Pope Eugenius III to launch the Second Crusade in the twelfth century.[44] Promising 'remission of and absolution from sins' on 'so holy a journey', this bull was promoted by the French abbot Bernard of Clairvaux, who embarked on what one historian has called a 'preaching tour' of western Europe in an attempt to drum up enthusiasm for war.[45] Today, such a decree would no doubt receive wide coverage across a range of media, but in medieval times, it could only be communicated from person to person, and often only verbally because most people could not read or write. A literate clerical class was thus essential for communicating it to lay audiences and to mobilisation *tout court*.

Here it is worth saying something about the importance of language in its spoken and written forms. The capacity to record one's thoughts with symbols – to write – is more than 5000 years old.[46] The development of papyrus in Ancient Egypt and paper in Han China revolutionised the practice, replacing stone, clay or ivory transcription with cheaper plant-based alternatives, which allowed documents to be produced and circulated with much greater frequency. The invention of the printing press some millennia later marked another milestone. Before then, documents had to be painstakingly copied by hand and were expensive to produce and hard to come by for this reason. The shift from script to print in the early modern era allowed for the mechanical reproduction of written text. Dramatically increasing the speed at which documents could be created, it boosted the rate at which they could be consumed, lowered their cost of production further and encouraged the development of new types of documents, including an array of printed ephemera associated with the periodical press.[47]

Such media, which catered to a burgeoning reading public that was 'more dispersed . . . atomistic and individualistic' than its listening counterpart,[48] furnished recruiters with new tools of persuasion and allowed them to persuade without having to be physically present in front of readers. Satirical fiction and military treatises were, for example, used to sell service in eighteenth-century France, with republicans and royalists alike using pamphlets to raise volunteers during the revolutionary period of 1789–99.[49] In China some decades later, forces loyal to Hong Xiuquan, a Christian convert who founded the Taiping Heavenly Kingdom in the south-east of the country, also printed literary tracts as part of recruiting drives for their revolt against the Qing Dynasty in 1851.[50] More than 10,000 kilometres away at around the same time, Union and Confederate forces commissioned posters to promote voluntary service in the early stages of the American Civil War, with editors of the popular periodical *Harper's Weekly* organising their own private, pro-Union recruitment drive using a series of cartoons.[51]

Taken as a whole, these practices were clearly important examples of military recruitment promotion. Yet they appear to have been carried out on a relatively modest scale and restricted, for the most part, to specific regions or localities. It was not until the end of the nineteenth century, when the newspaper became a truly mass medium, that recruitment promotion became a definitively *national*

Your country(ies) need you! 11

phenomenon. By 1900, recruiters could distribute appeals to hundreds of thousands of people simultaneously, reaching them whenever they found time – in the mornings, at lunch or in the evenings – to read. By 1914, that number had grown to millions, at least in the industrialised West, with the then relatively new medium of film affording additional opportunities. These developments transformed mobilisation but did not spell the end of the spectacles that had been associated with it for millennia. Public displays of martial might could, on the contrary, be mediated in ways that gave them greater exposure and could also be *combined* with persuasive communication carried in and across a range of media. The next chapter will review the different strategies and tactics used by recruiters to get content into mass media, but before that, a brief overview of this book's case studies will be given.

Military recruitment in times of war and peace: an overview of the case studies

This book has been divided into three parts, the first of which considers enlistment in times of total war. A great deal has been written about recruitment during the world wars, which are usually regarded as turning points or 'landmarks' in the development of twentieth-century society.[52] Yet the case studies featured in this volume explore countries or topics that have received little scholarly scrutiny. In the opening chapter, Anne Samson investigates recruiting practices in Africa in British Empire territories. Colonised in the years leading up to the Great War, the people of these territories were compelled to support the Allied war effort by providing raw materials, labour and, of course, soldiers. Some of the strategies used to entice them to serve, such as public meetings, martial bands, posters and newspapers, were also deployed in Britain.[53] Yet the experience of service differed markedly between the two places. In certain territories, black Africans (as opposed to those of European descent) appear to have been physically captured by recruiters and forced into service or indentured labour, an act of press-ganging that has not received the opprobrium it clearly deserves.

The three chapters that follow Samson's timely intervention also consider recruitment during the Great War, but in different parts of the world. In Chapter 4, Elli Lemonidou considers the unusual case of Greece, a country that remained neutral for much of the war but swung its support behind the Allies in 1917 following a period of internal strife that almost spilled over into civil war. Examining three separate mobilisation campaigns waged in 1915, 1917 and 1918, Lemonidou shows how newspapers, books, pamphlets and word-of-mouth communication were used to boost enlistment and how the Greek experience both reflected and diverged from the broader European experience of the conflict. A major recruitment campaign organised in Australia in 1915–16 represents the focus of Chapter 5. Emily Robertson, its author, shows how public meetings, door-to-door canvassing and a postal poll were used to try to convince Australians to volunteer. Yet she also considers the broader impact this campaign had on public opinion at a time when Australian attitudes towards the war were beginning to harden.

12 Brendan Maartens

Focusing on another campaign waged some 15,000 kilometres away, Tom Bivins explores the work of the American Committee on Public Information, set up to promote US involvement in the war in 1917. Like equivalent British organisations, this Committee has been subject to a fair amount of historical criticism, but Bivins explores an aspect of its work that is less well-known: the use of women, both real and mythical, in pictorial propaganda. Showing how such figures were used to symbolise the American nation, Bivins reveals the role that they played in promoting ideals of freedom and self-determination within the parameters of traditional (that is, patriarchal) gender roles.

The final chapter in Part I, the sole Second World War case study in this book, is also the only piece that explores recruitment of civil defence personnel. Co-authored by Jessica Hammett and Henry Irving, it considers pre-war and wartime recruitment work, taking Britain as its case study. Recruiters here used newspaper advertisements, leaflets, recruiting rallies, radio broadcasts, posters and films to sell service in civil defence forces, but Hammett and Irving also make use of eyewitness testimony to investigate public responses to promotion. Their findings are noteworthy, indicating that global events and pressure from community peers often played a greater role in encouraging individuals to join up than official exhortations.

Part II moves away from the total wars of the first half of the twentieth century to the Cold War of the second. Unlike the 'hot' conflicts of earlier years, the principle actors in this war, the US and the Union of Soviet Socialist Republics, did not engage in any direct conflict, though they did sanction a series of devastating proxy wars in Africa, Asia and Central and South America. They also maintained broader strategic alliances with other nations, embodied in institutions like the North Atlantic Treaty Organization, which represented much of the capitalist West, and the Warsaw Treaty Organization (WTO), which served part of the communist East. Roger Reese explores recruitment for the latter organisation in a chapter boasting both geographical and chronological breadth. To date, little has been written on recruiting tactics in Warsaw Pact countries, a void Reese seeks to fill with a wide-ranging analysis of the steps taken to socialise conscripts into service, including the use of pre-service educational programmes, posters and newspapers and the organisation of sporting activities and competitions. Similar strategies were, incidentally, used to recruit soldiers on the other side of the Iron Curtain, but the types of *appeals* often differed, with WTO recruiters placing a primacy on ideals of national unity, socialist pride and collective sacrifice, while recruiters in Europe and North America typically pandered to ideologies of individualism and materialism.

Chapters by Brendan Maartens and Jessica Ghilani on the UK and US respectively explore how such ideologies were communicated in recruitment campaigns in the late 1940s and early 1970s. Though both countries feature in Part I, they are examined in markedly different ways in Part II, with Maartens exploring attempts to recruit minors into active positions in the British Army, Navy and Air Force in the run-up to the Korean War and Ghilani investigating recruitment of women,

African Americans and Latinos into the US Army towards the end of the Vietnam War. Each country witnessed similar appeals, with American and British recruiters repeatedly stressing the 'qualifications' and 'skills' that new recruits acquired when serving and how they could be put to use on return to civilian life. Yet there were also important differences, with recruiters in America making an effort to incorporate the values and principles of the burgeoning Civil Rights and feminist movements into their campaign messaging and their counterparts in Britain portraying service as akin to a 'school' that allowed teenage boys to continue their education while serving in an armed force of their choosing.

Part III considers military recruitment in the present day and places some emphasis on the use of digital media. Beginning with Tanner Mirrlees's Canadian case study, it shows how such media have changed how recruiters operate and how prospective recruits are targeted using networked communication. Canada has received considerably less attention in studies of war propaganda and military recruitment than the US, and Mirrlees shows how its Department of National Defence uses platforms like YouTube, Facebook and Twitter to sell service and how it complements such work with promotion carried on traditional media – specifically television and film. In an equally important contribution on China, Orna Naftali investigates an array of People's Liberation Army recruiting materials that appear on Weibo and WeChat but also explores the increasing use of private expertise, in the form of (civilian) public relations practitioners, media consultants and commercial advertisers, in mobilisations.

The last chapter in Part III considers recruitment for an organisation unlike any other featured in this volume: ISIS. A quasi-official state that came into being in 2014 following the mergers of several radical Islamist factions in Iraq and Syria, ISIS occupies a unique place in this book's narrative because it recruited predominantly outside its borders for soldiers who either travelled to serve within Iraq and Syria or fought on behalf of the self-proclaimed caliphate in Europe or elsewhere. Halim Rane and Audrey Courty, the co-authors of this chapter, make several intriguing points about ISIS's recruiting strategies, showing how the organisation used multiple languages in its online magazines and videos to reach diverse national audiences and how they conflated the religion of Islam with armed insurrections.

Notes

1 Cited in Rory Cox, 'Expanding the History of the Just War: The Ethics of War in Ancient Egypt', *International Studies Quarterly* 61, no. 2 (2017): 374.
2 Cited in Peter Garnsey, *Ideas of Slavery from Aristotle to Augustine* (Cambridge: Cambridge University Press, 1996), 113.
3 Cited in Valerie Morkevicius, 'Hindu Perspectives on War', in Howard Hensel (ed.), *The Prism of Just War: Asian and Western Perspectives on the Legitimate Use of Military Force* (Farnham: Ashgate, 2010), 176.
4 Cited in David Graff, 'The Chinese Concept of Righteous War', *Prism of War*, 201.
5 Cited in John Kelsay, 'Hindu Perspectives on War', *Prism of War*, 122.
6 Cited in Hensel, 'Christian Belief and Western Just War Thought', *Prism of War*, 46.

14   *Brendan Maartens*

7 Cited in Philip Taylor, *Munitions of the Mind: A History of Propaganda from the Ancient World until the Present Day*, 3rd ed. (Manchester: Manchester University Press, 2003), 7.
8 Cited in Deborah Avant, 'War, Recruitment Systems and Democracy', in Elizabeth Kier and Ronald Krebs (eds.), *War's Wake: International Conflict and the Fate of Liberal Democracy* (Cambridge: Cambridge University Press, 2010), 239.
9 Cited in Mark Neely, *Lincoln and the Triumph of the Nation: Constitutional Conflict in the American Civil War* (Chapel Hill: North Carolina University Press, 2011), 192.
10 Frederick Engels, 'Can Europe Disarm?', in Barrie Selman (trans.), *Karl Marx and Frederick Engels: Collected Works, Vol. 27. Engels: 1890–95* (London: Lawrence & Wishart, 1990), 371–2.
11 Taylor, *Munitions of Mind*, 5.
12 See, for example, Susan Brewer, *Why America Fights: Patriotism and War Propaganda from the Philippines to Iraq* (Oxford: Oxford University Press, 2009); Mark Connelly et al. (eds.), *Propaganda and Conflict: War, Media and Shaping the Twentieth Century* (London: Bloomsbury, 2019); Valerie Holman and Debra Kelly (eds.), *France at War in the Twentieth Century: Propaganda, Myth and Metaphor* (New York: Berhan, 2000); Barak Kushner, *The Thought War: Japanese Imperial Propaganda* (Honolulu: Hawaii University Press, 2006); Richard Miller, *Fighting Words: Persuasive Strategies for War and Politics* (New York: Savas Beatie, 2010); Michael Sanders and Philip Taylor, *British Propaganda During the First World War, 1914–18* (London: Macmillan, 1982).
13 Taylor, *Munitions of Mind*, 12.
14 Garth Jowett and Victoria O'Donnell, *Propaganda and Persuasion*, 6th ed. (London: Sage, 2015), 231–3.
15 Jo Fox and David Welch, *Justifying War: Propaganda, Politics and the Modern Age* (London: Macmillan, 2012), 1.
16 See, for example, Peter Beattie, 'Raising the "Pagan Rabble": Wartime Impressment and the Crisis of Traditional Recruitment, 1864–1870', in *The Tribute of Blood: Army, Honor, Race, and Nation in Brazil, 1864–1945* (Durham: Duke University Press, 2001), 38–63; Mehmet Beşikçi, *The Ottoman Mobilization of Manpower in the First World War: Between Voluntarism and Resistance* (Leiden: Brill, 2012); Stephen Conway, 'The Mobilization of Manpower for Britain's Mid-Eighteenth-Century Wars', *Historical Research* 77, no. 197 (2004): 377–404; John Gooch, 'A Policy for Defence', in *Army, State and Society in Italy: 1870–1915* (New York: Palgrave, 1989), 18–35.
17 James Aulich, *War Posters: Weapons of Mass Communication* (London: Thames & Hudson, 2007); Nancy Bernard, *U. S. Television News and Cold War Propaganda, 1947–1960* (Cambridge: Cambridge University Press, 2003); Tricia Goodnow and James Kimble (eds.), *The 10c War: Comic Books, Propaganda and World War II* (Jackson: Mississippi University Press, 2017); Keith Somerville, *Radio Propaganda and the Broadcasting of Hatred: Historical Development and Definitions* (Basingstoke: Palgrave, 2012); Richard Taylor, *Film Propaganda: Soviet Russia and Nazi Germany*, 2nd ed. (London: IB Tauris, 1998).
18 Most of these studies consider the case of America. See Paul Sackett and Anne Mavar, *Evaluating Military Advertising and Recruiting: Theory and Methodology* (Washington: National Academies Press, 2004); Ofer Shtrichman, Rami Ben-Haim and Moshe Pollatschek, 'Using Simulation to Increase Efficiency in an Army Recruitment Office', *Interfaces* 31, no. 4 (2001): 61–70; P. L. Brockett et al. 'Alternative Statistical Regression Studies of the Effects of Joint and Service Specific Advertising on Military Recruitment', *Journal of the Operational Research Society* 55, no. 10 (2004): 1039–48.
19 General William Westmoreland, cited in Beth Bailey, *America's Army: Making the All-Volunteer Force* (Cambridge, MA: Harvard University Press, 2009), 51–2.
20 Nicholas Hiley, 'Sir Hedley Le Bas and the Origins of Domestic Propaganda in Britain 1914–1917', *European Journal of Marketing* 21, no. 8 (1987): 30–46 and '"Kitchener

Wants You" and "Daddy, What Did You Do in the Great War?": The Myth of British Recruiting Posters', *Imperial War Museum Review* 11 (1997): 40–58.

21 Eyal Ginio, 'Mobilizing the Ottoman Nation during the Balkan Wars (1912–1913): Awakening from the Ottoman Dream', *War in History* 12, no. 2 (2005): 160.

22 Martina Sprague, *Swedish Volunteers in the Russo-Finnish Winter War, 1939–1940* (Jefferson: McFarland, 2010), 56, 64, 69.

23 Neloufer De Mel, *Militarizing Sri Lanka: Popular Culture, Memory and Narrative in the Armed Conflict* (New Delhi: Sage, 2007), 73.

24 For a wide-ranging discussion of this concept, see Ian Kershaw, 'War and Political Violence in Twentieth-Century Europe', *Contemporary European History* 14, no. 1 (2005): 107–23.

25 Marshall Poe, *A History of Communications: Media and Society from the Evolution of Speech to the Internet* (Cambridge: Cambridge University Press, 2011).

26 Ohio State University, for example, hosted a televised debate on the topic of the 'Communication Revolution' in 1960. It was attended by the Canadian media theorist Marshall McLuhan, among others. 'The Communications Revolution', Marshall McLuhan Speaks: www.marshallmcluhanspeaks.com/panel/1960-the-communications-revolution/ (accessed 3 January 2020).

27 For a useful overview of key developments in Britain, France, Germany, Japan and the United States, see Jane Chapman, *Comparative Media History* (Cambridge: Polity Press, 2005).

28 Hiley, 'Sir Hedley', 30.

29 The French *campagne*, Italian *campagna*, Portugese *campanha* and Spanish *campana* also possess the military connotations of the English 'campaign'.

30 Liz McFall, *Advertising: A Cultural Economy* (London: Sage, 2004), 156.

31 The Amazons, a tribe of warrior women from the ancient world, are perhaps the most well-known example of female combatants. Yet they were by no means the only women to serve on front lines. Julie Wheelright, *Sisters in Arms: Female Warriors from Antiquity to the New Millennium* (New York: Bloomsbury, 2020).

32 One of the most disturbing examples of recruitment of child soldiers can be traced to Tsarist Russia, where Jewish children were forcibly enlisted in the Army as Cantonists. Larry Domnitch, *The Cantonists: The Jewish Children's Army of the Tsar* (Jerusalem: Devora, 2003).

33 One of the few studies on military recruitment in Latin America is authored by Monica Rankin, *Mexico, La patria Propaganda and Production during World War II* (Lincoln: Nebraska University Press, 2010).

34 Pietro Mander, 'War in Mesopotamian Culture', in K. Ulanowski (ed.), *The Religious Aspects of War in the Ancient Near East, Greece, and Rome* (Leiden: Brill, 2016).

35 Jacobus Van Dijk, 'The Amarna Period and the Later New Kingdom (c.1352–1069 BC)', in I. Shaw (ed.), *The Oxford History of Ancient Egypt*, 2nd ed. (Oxford: Oxford University Press, 2003), 289.

36 Jowett and O'Donnell, *Propaganda and Persuasion*, 60. The Parthenon boasted a 16-meter-long frieze that celebrated those slain defending Athens from Persian invaders, raising the 'heroic dead into the realm of immortal fame'. William Tyrrell and Frieda Brown, *Athenian Myths and Institutions* (Oxford: Oxford University Press, 1991), 176.

37 Jean Seaton, *Carnage and the Media: The Making and Breaking of News about Violence* (London: Allen Lane, 2005), 56–7.

38 Both during and after his reign, images of Alexander the Great, the general-king who famously never lost a battle, adorned coins, buildings, pottery and art throughout the sprawling expanse of his empire. The Roman general and tyrant Julius Caesar enjoyed similar fame during and after his lifetime.

39 David Welch, *Propaganda: Power and Persuasion* (London: British Library, 2013), 4.

40 One is reminded here of Jean Paul Sartre's aphorism, in his play *Devil and the Good Lord* (1951): 'When the rich wage war, it's the poor who die'.

16 *Brendan Maartens*

41 Welch, *Propaganda and Persuasion*, 4.
42 Leif Petersen, *Siege Warfare and Military Organization in the Successor States (400–800 ad): Byzantium, the West and Islam* (Leiden: Brill, 2013), 54.
43 Osman Latiff, *The Cutting Edge of the Poet's Sword: Muslim Poetic Responses to the Crusades* (Leiden: Brill, 2018), 38–9.
44 Christoph Maier, *Crusade Propaganda and Ideology: Model Sermons for the Preaching of the Cross* (Cambridge: Cambridge University Press, 2000), 4.
45 Thomas Asbridge, *The Crusades: The War for the Holy Land* (London: Simon & Schuster, 2012), 218; Jonathan Phillips, *Defenders of the Holy Land: Relations Between the Latin East and the West, 1119–1187* (Oxford: Oxford University Press, 2011), 79.
46 Steven Fischer, *The History of Writing* (London: Reaktion, 2001).
47 *Relation aller Fürnemmen und gedenckwürdigen Historien* is generally regarded as the first newspaper and appeared in Strasburg, the same city that bore witness to Guttenberg's printing press.
48 Elizabeth Eisenstein, *The Printing Revolution in Early Modern Europe*, 2nd ed. (New York: Cambridge University Press, 2005), 105.
49 Valerie Mainz, *Days of Glory? Imaging Military Recruitment and the French Revolution* (London: Macmillan, 2016), 4–5.
50 Rudolf Wagner, 'Operating in the Chinese Public Sphere: Theology and Technique of Taiping Propaganda', in C. Huang and E. Zurcher (eds.), *Norms and the State in China* (Leiden: EJ Brill, 1993), 123.
51 William Thompson, 'Pictorial Propaganda and the Civil War', *The Wisconsin Magazine of History* 46, no. 1 (1962): 23.
52 Arthur Marwick, 'Introduction', in Arthur Marwick (ed.), *Total War and Social Change* (London: Macmillan, 1988), x.
53 Brendan Maartens, 'The Great War, Military Recruitment and the Public Relations Work of the Parliamentary Recruiting Committee, 1914–1915', *Public Relations Inquiry* 5, no. 2 (2016): 169–85.

2 Your media need you! How recruiters use advertising, public relations and propaganda to promote service and allegiance

Brendan Maartens

Abstract

How have recruiters used modern methods of communication – media – to promote service in and allegiance towards armed forces and civil defence organisations? This question is more difficult to answer than one might at first suspect. There is great variety both in the number of communication channels utilised by recruiters and in the different uses to which such channels can be put. Newspapers, for example, can endorse service in articles, opinion pieces or editorials, but they can also host paid announcements – advertisements. Some media texts, furthermore, can be produced by recruiters, while others require special creative or technical expertise that only external agents possess. To complicate matters, scholars continue to debate the terminology used to define persuasive communications, a debate that this chapter will avoid because it opens up the semantic equivalent of a can of worms. What it will do, instead, is give a sense of the many devices and techniques utilised by recruiters during the twentieth and twenty-first centuries and a framework for conceptualising such promotional endeavours. It will also show how technological and institutional changes have expanded the means and methods of military recruitment during a very volatile period in human history.

The study of persuasive communication began in Ancient Greece in the fifth century BC. Corax and Tisias may have written the first essays on the topic,[1] though Aristotle can lay claim to the most notable. For Aristotle, *peithō* (persuasion) was tied inextricably to language and more precisely, *rhēthorikē* (rhetoric): an individual's capacity to convince others of a position or point of view.[2] In his time, such convincing was done through the spoken and written word. Yet neither Aristotle nor his contemporaries could have foreseen the dramatic growth of communications channels in the millennia that followed or the accompanying development of new types of persuasion (including visual) that spawned new ways of thinking about the phenomenon and new terminology for describing it. First deployed by the Catholic Church to spread the faith in the seventeenth century, the word 'propaganda' assumed its modern pejorative overtone in the wake of the First World War. 'Puff', 'puffing' and 'puffery' surfaced in the eighteenth century but were used to describe commercial rather than religious persuasion,[3] and were joined by 'advertising', 'publicity', 'public relations', 'spin' and 'strategic communication'.

18   *Brendan Maartens*

Sometimes used interchangeably, sometimes defined in opposition to one another, these terms can cast scholars into deep conceptual waters. To avoid getting caught in the current, this chapter will move away from questions of semantics to a discussion of practice. Its primary goal is to give a sense of the different ways in which recruiters used media to promote enlistment, and it does so by offering readers a framework for classifying such promotion that can make it easier to understand. This framework has been used before, in studies of corporate communication and the 'promotional mix' that underpins it,[4] and might seem like a strange bedfellow for an analysis of military recruitment. Yet it has some utility for the task at hand, partly because it can shed light on the different elements that make up many large-scale recruitment campaigns and partly because recruiters often turned to the commercial world when seeking inspiration for their campaigns and, in so doing, adopted persuasive tactics and techniques that were rooted in corporate rather than governmental communications.

At the core of the framework lies a simple proposition: there are three ways of generating media content. The first, and in many respects the most straightforward, is to create the media oneself. This might entail, for example, printing a pamphlet or setting up a website. The second and third involve getting material into *someone else's* media, either by paying for the privilege, which is sometimes described as advertising, or by convincing a proprietor, editor or producer to include such material without paying: a matter, we might say, of public relations. Military organisations, as a general rule, do not possess the expertise required to master all three methods, which is why many have hired commercial firms to work on their behalf or employed individuals with experience of working in or with the media to work for them, in uniform. Little is known about such processes of outsourcing and internalising expertise, even in studies that place interactions between the military and the media at their core,[5] but they have been central to the public presentation of armed forces for generations.

This chapter will give a sense of how such presentational work was managed, the tactics and strategies that underpinned it and the institutions and individuals responsible for it. Beginning with a discussion of paid promotion – advertising – it will introduce readers to the different types of advertisements found in print, film, broadcast and digital media and the role of commercial agencies in planning and developing such content. It will then turn to owned promotion – what might be called, for the sake of brevity, propaganda – and consider how films, newsreels, radio and television broadcasts and a plethora of digital platforms and applications are used to sell service in the military. The last section will consider practices associated with earned content – PR – and their place in promoting military service. Taken together, these sections provide some much-needed context to this book's eleven case studies and also demonstrate the centrality of media to modern recruitment campaigns.

The art of paying for space: advertising, agencies and advertisements

Much of the existing commentary on paid promotion has concerned corporate communications or what the American intellectual historian Jackson Lears called

Your media need you! 19

'commercial fables-stories . . . [which] have been both fabulous and didactic, [which] have evoked fantasies and pointed morals, [and which] have reconfigured ancient dreams of abundance to fit the modern world of [consumer] goods'.[6] Advertising is primarily about buying and selling goods and services, but other 'fables-stories' were told – and sold. Using the same devices and techniques and working with the same media, governments and armed forces created their own genre of promotional communication which did not sell anything in the conventional sense of the word. Indeed, while corporations looked to advertising to boost or maintain market share, armed forces used it to tempt men, women and even minors to sign up. They 'sold' themselves, in a manner of speaking, and did so in ways that have garnered little sustained scholarly scrutiny.

One of the reasons so little attention has been given to this particular type of advertising is the complexity of the industry that produces it. When we discuss advertising, we are not just discussing advertisements, the means of selling products, services or employment opportunities, but the agencies that produce them and the clients (or 'advertisers' to use industry parlance) that pay for them. We are also, however, discussing the media in which advertisements appear and the relationships that emerge between such media and agencies and advertisers. The 'advertising tripartite', as it has come to be known,[7] has been central to the business of advertising for more than a century, but it has attracted little attention in studies of military recruitment, which often reduce discussions of advertising to discussions of advertise*ments*, not the institutional interactions or exchanges that shape them. This has lent an air of superficiality to some accounts, which consider the end product of the advertising process – the advertisements themselves – but not the work that goes on behind them.

The study of advertising is made additionally complex by the profusion of advertising forms within and across media and by the impact of new technology on such forms and media. Forms should not be confused with media. The poster, for example, is a single medium, but it can be hand illustrated or printed, full-colour or black and white, illustrated or photographic, or textual or visual (or a combination of the two). Variation in composition and design is matched by variation in messaging, with some appeals or 'archetypes' appearing time and again across multiple countries and periods, though not necessarily with the same outcomes.[8] In this volume, Tom Bivins (see Chapter 6) explores several archetypes that were central to promoting recruitment in posters during the Great War, including the use of guilt to shame men into joining up and the use of patriotism to inspire them to do so. Yet these were not the only archetypes used during this war, and nor were posters the only medium deployed by recruiters.

The newspaper, the world's first mass medium, played host to a range of advertising during and after 1914–18 and, like the poster, has given rise to its own advertising forms. The most notable are classifieds – short written announcements that usually appear as discrete items within columns – and display advertisements – combinations of visual and textual appeals that typically occupy a larger part of a given page. The technology used to produce the imagery (or 'art' to defer once again to industry parlance) in display advertising has changed significantly over

20 *Brendan Maartens*

the past two centuries. The first display advertisements were cast in dreary shades of black and white, but colour reproduction made an appearance by the mid-nineteenth century, with photography surfacing around the same time (and beginning, like illustration, as a monochromatic form before colour was introduced to the medium in print later on).[9]

While the technology used to create and display advertising in newspapers has changed, the method of getting them into print has not and involves paying an editor or proprietor to run an announcement over the course of one or several days. Agents have been offering such services from the late-eighteenth century onwards,[10] buying slots in publications and selling them back to clients for a fee (known in the industry as 'space brokerage') and designing the wording of appeals ('copywriting'). After the introduction of display advertising in the nineteenth century, agencies also began to offer services in graphic design and photography, which, together with copy, make up the 'creative' component of the advertising craft.[11]

Such creativity lies at the heart of all advertising, but agencies also need to know which publications to target and conduct research to allow them to do so. Such research entails exploration of the customers of products and services *and* the audiences of specific media, the objective being to match the two things together to better target one's appeals. Firms that specialised in all three types of work – space brokerage, creative development and market research – became known as 'full-service' agencies, and their capacity to do all of the work required to advertise effectively has brought them major clients in the corporate and governmental sectors.[12]

The emergence of the full-service agency represented a landmark moment in the history of advertising and consumer culture more generally. Agencies became centres and sources of expertise, with promotion viewed as an objective-driven, target-orientated activity that entailed the development of coordinated *campaigns* rather than single messages or appeals. These campaigns had become multi-media affairs by the turn of the twentieth century, with many agencies specialising not just in newspaper advertising but in poster and leaflet production as well. By the turn of the twenty-first century, print media had been joined by film, broadcast and digital, affording new opportunities for advertisers and novel advertising forms.

Film, for example, spawned the propaganda film, which advertised the work of a specific studio; the commercial film, which advertised consumer goods and durables; and the trailer, which advertised films themselves.[13] Radio gave rise to sponsored programmes, financed by advertisers but typically produced by agencies; theme songs, which associated products, services or brands with specific tunes; and jingles, an amalgamation of non-musical verse advertising and non-broadcast sheet music.[14] Television also witnessed sponsored programmes and its own version of the jingle, the commercial, which initially amounted to 'little more than a radio message with pictures' but had become a proper moving-image form by the 1950s, at least in countries that possessed recognised commercial networks.[15] The internet, finally, generated its own eclectic array of advertising, such as pop-ups and skyscrapers, which disrupt audiences' viewing experiences, banners, which are embedded into the body of webpages, and search advertising, which is in some senses a reworking of the newspaper classified.

Clearly, not all of these forms lend themselves to military recruitment. However, many do and are explored in several subsequent chapters. Jessica Hammett and Henry Irving (see Chapter 7), for example, consider how posters and newspapers were used to boost recruitment to British civil defence services before and during the Second World War. Jessica Ghilani (see Chapter 10), explores a mixture of magazine and television advertising in the US in the early 1970s, focusing on the Army, the largest of that country's fighting forces. North of the border some forty years later, Tanner Mirrlees (see Chapter 11) examines how cinema and television commercials were used for similar purposes by the Canadian Armed Forces.

In all three cases, external agencies – W. S. Crawford in London, N. W. Ayer in New York and Ogilvy in Montreal – were hired to handle the advertising, and a similar public–private partnership can be witnessed elsewhere in countries not featured in this book. Kenny & Co., which might have been Ireland's first full-service agency, used newspaper advertising to promote recruitment to the British armed forces in 1918,[16] while in India a hundred years later, Grey Global worked for the Indian Army, producing a mixture of television commercials, online videos and posters that portrayed service in this force as a 'life less ordinary'.[17]

Such campaigns have attracted little attention in studies of war propaganda or commercial advertising, a shortcoming this book seeks to rectify. No attempt, furthermore, has been made to compare recruitment campaigns across time and space, a topic that will be addressed in this book's final chapter. Before then, we shall consider another type of promotion.

Selling service in news, entertainment and current affairs: the art of propaganda

While recruiters could, and frequently did, turn to advertising agencies to handle paid promotion, they could also produce their own media content. Film represented an important means of doing so and was used for recruiting purposes as early as 1900, when the British Army commissioned a series of shorts entitled *Army Life; or How Soldiers Are Made*. Combining 'actuality footage of cavalry, artillery and infantry at exercise' with 'staged scenes of soldiers joining up',[18] these films would likely have been a novelty to most cinemagoers. Yet by the end of the First World War, quasi-factual shorts depicting scenes of enrolment, training and service had become an established cinematic genre, and by the end of the Second, audiences had become accustomed to ambitious, feature-length productions that dramatised war and service and portrayed soldiers, sailors and pilots as proverbial saviours of the nation.[19]

There are substantive differences between such films and the 'paid' kind mentioned already. To get a commercial into a cinema, a recruiter needed to pay for its inclusion in a programme. To get a film into a programme without paying, they needed to convince an exhibitor to screen it, and to do so, they required content that excited or interested audiences. Whether short or long or fictional or factual, the film they produced, in other words, needed to be *entertaining* as a matter of course, and filmmakers were the ideal people to ensure it was. The American Office of War Information worked with several Hollywood studios on scores of propaganda films during the Second World War. Some of these productions were transparently propagandistic, but many contained propaganda messages 'casually and naturally introduced into the ordinary dialogue',[20] thereby selling service implicitly rather than explicitly.

Newsreels also played host to such implicit promotion. A selection of topical items held on a single reel of film, they were usually shown before feature screenings and formed part of the overall viewing experience for most cinema audiences in the first half of the twentieth century.[21] Their value as a propaganda tool was recognised quickly. In Hungary in 1919, for example, officials of the short-lived Soviet Republic commissioned the *Vörös Riport Film* (or Red Newsreel) to help raise troops for military deployments abroad.[22] During the Spanish Civil War, 'propaganda newsreels' became central to the 'Republican mobilisation effort'.[23] In China towards the end of that country's much longer civil war, communist party filmmakers produced *The War of Self-Defence, First Report* (1947), one of several productions that lent 'propaganda support' for People's Liberation Army recruitment campaigns[24] and a precursor to the more recent productions explored by Orna Naftali in this book (see Chapter 12).

Like actuality films, newsreels were valued for recruiting purposes because they did not *seem* to openly 'sell' anything. Their currency was not persuasion but news and the supposedly impartial information it conveyed, and recruiters learned to capitalise on this by portraying enlistment, the armed forces and their activities as a form *of* news. Newsreels gave them one means of doing so, but they could also turn to radio and produce their own broadcast items or programmes. In the early 1940s, Latin American airwaves were flooded with 'thousands of hours' of content that portrayed support of the Allied war effort as a pre-requisite for 'significant economic rewards at the war's end'.[25] Some fifty years later, in one of the grimmest recorded uses of radio for recruiting purposes, Radio Television Libre des Mille Collines, an ostensibly independent broadcaster that had ties to governing Hutu elites, used 'racist, violent and hate-filled messages' to turn Hutus against Tutsis during the Rwandan genocide.[26]

Only the naïve consider news impartial and value free, and recruiters' exploitation of it attests to the manner in which propaganda often took on the form and appearance of 'information'.[27] The same point can of course be made about content intended ostensibly to entertain. In the early 1940s, the US Army sponsored talkies hosted by the celebrity Bob Hope and worked with the drinks manufacturer Coca-Cola on *Victory Parade of Spotlight Bands* (1941–6), a long-running series which featured performances from the nation's top bands at various military installations throughout the country.[28] These shows were designed to promote the national war effort, but similar work continued after 1945 on radio and television, with *The Big Picture* (1951–64), for instance, exploring topics like weapons development, sports and foreign affairs. It was produced using footage captured by the Army's Signal Corps' Pictorial Service.[29]

Your media need you! 23

Governments elsewhere also turned to television to promote recruitment. Following construction of the Berlin Wall, officials in the German Democratic Republic, one of the nations considered by Roger Reese in his wide-ranging study on recruitment in Warsaw Pact countries (see Chapter 9), made concerted efforts to cultivate support of military service among 'wayward [male] youths', with Deutscher Fernsehfunk, the national broadcaster, using fictional crime thrillers like *Blaulicht* (1959–68) to offer rosy portrayals of military figures.[30]

Given its provenance, it would be tempting to regard *Blaulicht* as a form of communist state 'propaganda' that can be juxtaposed with the capitalist commercial 'entertainment' broadcast in the West at the same time.[31] Yet this would miss the point. Recruiters on either side of the Iron Curtain turned to news, current affairs and entertainment because these things did not *appear* to 'sell' anything. In that regard, they differed from paid advertising, which was usually easy to recognise because of the form it took or when (or where) it appeared in a given medium. Film commercials, for example, were traditionally screened before features and considerably shorter in length, while classified advertisements were often relegated to the end of newspapers or magazines. Audiences could recognise these devices as promotion because of this, but the same principle did not apply to broadcasts like *The Big Picture Show*, which was described by one recruiter as a 'telementary' that provided a valuable 'public service' to the US Army.[32]

Towards the end of the twentieth century, several technological advances created new opportunities for recruiters that are worth highlighting here. The growth of cable and satellite transmission were among them, and they changed the television landscape inexorably. More channels emerged, and more networks began to broadcast across national boundaries, encouraging the development of a 'globalised media culture that substantially diminish[ed] national differences in media systems'.[33] The creation of the World Wide Web in 1991 added fuel to the fire, linking individuals and institutions via wired connections and computers, and subsequently handheld devices and Wi-Fi, to a veritable 'global village'.[34] Constantly evolving in response to technological advances, this 'village' has been identified with all manner of cultural transformations and allowed military organisations to create their own websites.

The US Air Force may have created the world's first, airforce.com, sometime in 1997 or 1998. It did so, according to Brigadier General Peter Sutton, commander of the force's recruiting service from 1998 to 2000, because the internet represented a 'revolutionary tool for meeting our recruiting . . . objectives'. Such 'web recruiting' entailed the deployment of '"e-recruiters"' to 'handl[e], by quick e-mail response . . . web-based leads', the creation of 'micro-sites within our web site, which streamlined the navigation process', the application of Flash animation software and 'audio banners and "web-mercials"' to make the user experience more interactive and immersive, and the use of 'live web casts' to reach prospective recruits remotely.[35] (airforce.com remains online to this day, and to visit it is an experience in its own right. The home page contains a full-screen, high-definition video that runs in a continuous loop until visitors scroll down or select a tab from a list of options on the right. Taking the form of a montage, this video boasts scenes of recruits sky-diving, rockets launching and drones flying anchored by a slogan, 'AIM HIGH', superimposed onto the centre of the screen in bold white lettering. Elsewhere, visitors are invited to explore the Air Force's 'mission' and 'lifestyle' and to play a game, the *Airman Challenge*, that conflates the act of serving with gaming.[36])

Web recruiting can take many forms, and unlike traditional media can be directed at audiences dispersed across the globe. Most nations do not permit the recruitment of foreign soldiers, but the terrorist organisation ISIS did, and Halim Rane and Audrey Courty (see Chapter 13) explore how it used online magazines to promote recruitment in 2014–17. These magazines did not boast the slick production values of sites like airforce.com, but they had other advantages. They could be produced using inexpensive desktop publishing software and distributed at little cost using internet forums and social media networks. For an organisation that was acutely reliant on foreign recruits, this method of producing and distributing content was ideal.

Social media platforms, which began to dominate online communication in the second decade of the web, have been used extensively by military organisations in recent years. At the time of writing, the Philippine government, for instance, maintains TeamAFP, an official Twitter account that represents all three branches of the country's armed forces and has more than 50,000 followers.[37] The armed forces of Iran do something similar with an Iran Military Facebook page, currently followed by over 170,000 individuals.[38] Such pages are not standalone sites but gateways to other parts of the web, with Iran Military, for example, directing users to the website of Ayatollah Ali Hosseini Khamenei. This website contains its own material relevant to recruiting, including an article entitled 'The Armed Forces are the Fortress of the People', which, repeating the words of Khamenei, claims 'the Islamic Republic of Iran Army is not merely a provider of machinery, experience, science and skill . . . [but] an exhibition of Islamic values . . . the fortress of the masses of the people'.[39]

Spreading promotion across multiple websites allows recruiters to target civilians in different ways. The French Army, for example, hosts hundreds of videos on its Armee de Terre YouTube channel, 1699 posts (mostly photographs) on Instagram, a large quantity of audio-visual, visual and textual content on Facebook, and more than 13,000 tweets on Twitter.[40] Each of these accounts directs visitors to the official French Army website, sengager.fr, whose title plays on the French verb *s'engager*, meaning to enlist or to commit, and whose primary goal is to direct visitors to an online application form. Like airforce.com, sengager.fr seeks to achieve this goal by profiling existing personnel, by dramatising war and service and by giving prospective recruits an indication of the 'Recruitment Path' they could take if they signed up.[41]

These platforms are also significant, however, because they typically allow users to contribute their own content to pages. Users can do so by liking or writing about a post or by sharing content they view on an official military account with their friends and acquaintances. Social networks are governed by such 'many-to-many' exchanges and differ from print, film and broadcast media for this reason, at least in theory.[42] Encouraging people with similar interests and values to come together to form groups, they may be powerful conduits for persuasion, since 'connected people', as Charles Kadushin has argued, 'tend to have an effect on one another'.[43] They are also, of course, popular with young people, a key recruiting demographic.

Events, issues and reputation: the public relations of military recruitment

A third and final source of expertise that recruiters can draw on, and one that they have used in one form or another for well over a hundred years, is public relations. PR, as noted, can be regarded as a means of earned promotion, and those who practise it use a range of devices and techniques to ensure that their appeals are heard.

Perhaps the most important, and certainly the most striking, are events. As the first chapter demonstrated, governments and armed forces have organised public spectacles for a very long time. Such spectacles, however, took on a novel character in the twentieth and twenty-first centuries because they could be (and frequently were) used to generate additional *media* coverage that extended their reach and therefore potential impact beyond any specific locality.

The Nuremburg Rallies stand out as quintessential examples of such mediated spectacles. Consisting of assemblies, demonstrations and exhibitions, they involved what one contemporary observer called 'expert staging, elaborate use of flags, manuals of arms, a sham battle, marching, rousing short speeches, singing, and impressive ritual'. Combined with annual press receptions that ensured each rally was reported widely in newspapers, newsreels and radio broadcasts, such events were 'brought home to people in all parts of Germany'.[44]

They were not the only ostentatious displays of military might that took place in Europe between the wars. The British hosted their own major rally in 1939 to launch a long-running recruitment campaign for civil defence (see Chapter 7), while scores of smaller 'mass political rituals' were witnessed in Spain during the 1936–39 Civil War. Such rituals, according to one historian, acted as 'mechanisms with which to generate social meanings', with some organised by conservative groups boasting an explicitly religious character that associated the 'death cults . . . [of] '"fallen" heroes and martyrs' with the 'mystique of combat'.[45]

The post-war era did not spell the end of such spectacles. On the contrary, military organisations around the world continue to use them to generate media coverage by promoting the prestige of service. They do so using naval reviews, at which dignitaries and members of the public can watch fleets perform maritime manoeuvres, fly-overs, which afford a similar experience from the air, and live-fire exercises, which involve large assemblies of ground troops. Japan's Self Defence Force is one of the many armed forces that has utilised them to aid recruitment in recent years. Maintaining an Information Division that employs almost a thousand staff, its public relations officers have organised annual military training exercises at the foot of the (photogenic) Mount Fuji and public 'voyage experiences' on navy ships.[46]

Described by one sociologist as a form of mass-spectator militarism,[47] these events share some similarities with the commercial publicity stunt. The American showman P. T. Barnum is usually credited with pioneering this particular type of event and suggested in his 1855 memoirs that he used them to keep his 'name before the public'. Barnum achieved this by combining visual spectacles like an elephant ploughing a lawn adjacent to a railway with 'novel advertisements and unique notices [press releases] in newspapers',[48] merging earned and paid promotion adroitly before distinctions between such types had been made. Yet he also used acts, like uniformed processions and marching bands, drawn directly from the military world. While Barnum's stunts (or 'humbug' as he called them) were intended to make money and not raise volunteers, recruiters in his native America also monetised one particular type of event that became popular at the turn of the last century: the military festival. Attracting thousands of paying spectators, these festivals showcased marksmanship, infantry and cavalry drills and wall scaling. Boasting similar carnivalesque qualities to the commercial publicity stunt, they were, nevertheless, much grander in scale and deeply militaristic and nationalistic.[49]

Recruiters have organised other types of events that are less ostentatious but still significant. In my own case study (see Chapter 8), I explore the use of Schoolboys' Exhibitions, a special type of event aimed at schoolchildren in Britain in the years following the Second World War. Smaller than rallies, processions, reviews and festivals, these exhibitions were nonetheless important sources of promotion, not least because they allowed recruiters to speak directly to prospective recruits at special stalls set up for the purpose.

Recruiters also host press conferences, though these are designed, as their name suggests, to cater to journalists, not potential recruits, and represent 'pseudo-events' in the sense in which Daniel Boorstin once deployed the term: any 'happening . . . [whose] occurrence is arranged for the convenience of the reporting or reproducing media . . . [and whose] success is measured by how widely it is reported'.[50] The goal of a press conference, and pseudo-events more generally, is to generate coverage in the news media, and to do so, recruiters require some knowledge of news cycles, values and selection protocols. They also need an understanding of how events are reported in the media, how they are used to construct broader narratives about topical issues or controversies and how organisations can exploit such reportage.

Journalists possess a better grasp of these processes than most and are often hired by military organisations to act as press officers or spokespersons for this reason. Yet while recruitment may represent one of their primary duties, they are also tasked with the more granular work of building reputation. To do so effectively, they require knowledge of military procedure and protocols and a capacity to nurture relationships with a range of stakeholders over many years. This type of work does not, in contrast to paid promotion, lend itself to outsourcing. Indeed, while an advertising campaign can be planned, launched and executed in the space of a few months, the task of building relationships with journalists and the public as a whole is ongoing and typically entails the development of a reservoir of *in-house* expertise. This expertise is often sourced from special units or divisions embedded within armed forces, such as the Israeli Defence Force's Spokesperson's Unit, which has been operating since 1948.[51]

As their name suggests, press officers are tasked with liaising with the press, a job that can be made considerably easier if the journalists they interact with are sympathetic to their cause or organisation. In Greece during the First World War, the close links that many newspapers shared to the two main political factions of the day allowed recruiters, representing one faction, to promote military service. The ultimate goal of this work, as Elli Lemonidou (see Chapter 4) has shown, was to influence public debates and discussions via the media and to do so (as with certain types of owned promotion) using the vernacular of news.

Recruiters working in Africa during the same war might have followed a similar process, but in many places, no newspapers were produced or distributed. They therefore chose more direct methods, combining word-of-mouth appeals delivered through intermediaries like tribal chiefs with military bands and public oratory. These strategies ensured the recruiting message would be heard, at least to those who listened, but this does not, as Anne Samson has shown in her study (see Chapter 3), necessarily mean that they were more effective.

Emily Robertson also explores interpersonal appeals in her First World War Australian case study (see Chapter 5), though recruiters here established local recruiting committees and distributed postal appeals to try to boost enlistment. Sent directly to householders, the appeals were designed to solicit information from prospective recruits, who were asked to attest their willingness to serve by completing a form and posting it back to a local committee, whose agents visited the houses of those who responded positively to the call to arms. Many recruiters in Australia were volunteers, not serving soldiers, and local committees comprised individuals who held prominent positions in their respective communities. Such a 'civilianisation' of recruitment was not restricted to Australia or the First World War.[52] In Cuba in the 1980s, for instance, officials at the Servicio Militar Voluntario Femenino (or Women's Voluntary Military Service) turned to civil society groups like the Federación de Mujeres Cubanas (Federation of Cuban Women) to promote the benefits of service to members.[53]

Whether they are tribal chiefs or village elders, public officials or small-business owners, or journalists or local volunteers, there are clearly advantages to using intermediaries to promote service. They give the impression that support of enlistment has grown organically from within society and not just from on high and suggest that ordinary people are willing to serve. Whether this made them more effective than paid or owned forms of promotion is another question, and one that will be dealt with separately in the final chapter of this book.

Conclusion: reflecting on the process of paying, earning and owning media content

Three key developments shaped military recruitment in the twentieth and twenty-first centuries: the growth of mass and digital media, the maturation of

28 *Brendan Maartens*

the advertising industry, and the emergence of public relations as a recognised profession. Recruiters, as we have seen, responded to each of these developments in kind: paying for advertisements in print, broadcast and digital media, earning coverage in a variety of news and entertainment media and producing and distributing their own media content modelled on existing genres or forms. If there was great variety in their uses of media, there was also, however, great diversity in the character of recruiting appeals, a topic that has not yet been explored in this book but will be considered in the case studies that follow and in the conclusion (see Chapter 14) as well. Before then, it is worth making one final point about the relationship between the media and recruitment: this chapter has barely scratched the surface, and more work needs to be done to test the validity of the ideas presented here, especially in parts of the world, such as Asia and South America, that have received very little scholarly attention.

Notes

1 James Price Dillard and Michael Pfau, 'Introduction', in *The Persuasion Handbook: Developments in Theory and Practice* (Thousand Oaks: Sage, 2002), ix.
2 Aristotle, *On Rhetoric: A Theory of Civic Discourse*, trans. George Kennedy, 2nd ed. (Oxford: Oxford University Press, 2007), 37.
3 Liz McFall, *Advertising: A Cultural Economy* (London: Sage, 2004), 155.
4 Thomas O'Guinn, Chris Allen, Richard Semenik and Angeline Scheinbaum, *Advertising and Integrated Brand Promotion*, 7th ed. (Stamford: Cengage, 2015), 284.
5 James Der Derian, for example, devotes an entire book to America's 'military-industrial-media-entertainment complex' but reserves no space for the role of commercial advertising or public relations firms in such a 'complex'. *Virtuous Wars: Mapping the Military-Industrial-Media-Entertainment Network*, 2nd ed. (New York: Routledge, 2009).
6 Jackson Lears, *Fables of Abundance: A Cultural History of Advertising in America* (New York: Basic Books, 1994), 2.
7 Winston Fletcher, *Powers of Persuasion: The Inside Story of British Advertising* (Oxford: Oxford University Press, 2008), 2.
8 Pearl James, 'Introduction: Reading World War I Posters', in Pearl James (ed.), *Picture This: World War I Posters and Visual Culture* (Lincoln: University of Nebraska Press, 2009), 19.
9 On the history of print advertising, see James Norris, *Advertising and the Transformation of American Society, 1865–1920* (New York: Greenwood, 1990); Gillian Dyer, 'The Origins and Development of Advertising', in *Advertising as Communication* (London: Routledge, 2009), 11–32; Mark Tungate, 'Pioneers of Persuasion', in *Adland: A Global History of Advertising* (London: Kogan, 2007), 1–32.
10 In the UK at least. McFall, *Advertising*, 110–11; Terence Nevett, 'London's Early Advertising Agents', *Journal of Advertising History* 1, no. 12 (1977): 15–18.
11 For a useful overview of the role of creativity in advertising, see Sean Nixon, 'The Cult of Creativity: Advertising Creatives and the Pursuit of Newness', in *Advertising Cultures: Gender, Commerce, Creativity* (London: Sage, 2003), 74–92.
12 The Madison Avenue agency J. Walter Thompson was something of a pioneer in this regard. See Stefan Schwarzkopf, 'Discovering the Consumer: Market Research, Product Innovation, and the Creation of Brand Loyalty in Britain and the United States in the Interwar Years', *Journal of Macromarketing* 29, no. 1 (2009): 8–20; Tungate, *Adland*, 25.
13 The tripartite structure of the industry, with producers, distributors and exhibitors each sponsoring their own forms of advertising, complicates this history somewhat. Keith

Hamel, 'From Advertisement to Entertainment: Early Hollywood Film Trailers', *Quarterly Review of Film and Video* 29, no. 3 (2012): 269–70.

14 Timothy Taylor, 'The Depression and the Rise of the Jingle', in *The Sounds of Capitalism: Advertising, Music, and the Conquest of Culture* (Chicago: Chicago University Press, 2012), 65–100.

15 Paul Rutherford, *The New Icons? The Art of Television Advertising* (Toronto: Toronto University Press, 1995), 11.

16 Brendan Maartens, 'For "Common Christianity": War, Peace and the Campaign of the Irish Recruiting Council, 1918', *The English Historical Review* (forthcoming).

17 Grey Global, 'Indian Army Campaign' (undated): http://brasil-pt.grey.com/amea/work/key/indian-army-campaign/id/6692/ (accessed 17 January 2020).

18 Simon Mackenzie, *British War Films 1939–1945: The Cinema and the Services* (London: Hambleton, 2001), 2.

19 For a useful overview war films, see John Garofolo, 'War Films in an Age of War and Cinema', in D. Cunningham and J. Nelson (eds.), *A Companion to the War Film* (Oxford: Wiley, 2016), 36–55.

20 Clayton Koppes and Gregory Black, *Hollywood Goes to War: How Politics, Profits and Propaganda Shaped World War II Movies* (Berkeley: University of California Press, 1990), 64.

21 Cinemagazines, which made an appearance by the 1930s, devoted more time to news items and were closer, in that sense, to the topical television news broadcasts that eventually supplanted them in the post-war era. Ciara Chambers, Mats Jönsson and Roel Vande Winkel, 'Introduction', in *Researching Newsreels: Local, National and Transnational Case Studies* (Cham: Palgrave, 2018), 1–14.

22 Bob Dent, *Painting the Town Red: Politics and the Arts During the 1919 Hungarian Soviet Republic* (London: Pluto, 2018), 93.

23 Filipe Ribeiro De Meneses, *Franco and the Spanish Civil War* (London: Routledge, 2001), 116.

24 Mathew Johnson, 'Propaganda and Censorship in Chinese cinema', in Y. Zhang (ed.), *A Companion to Chinese Cinema* (Chichester: Blackwell, 2012), 165.

25 Such propaganda was actually produced in America. Joy Hayes, *Radio Nation: Communication, Popular Culture, and Nationalism in Mexico, 1920–50* (Tucson: University of Arizona Press, 2000), 3.

26 Keith Somerville, *Radio Propaganda and the Broadcasting of Hatred: Historical Development and Definitions* (Basingstoke: Macmillan, 2012), 199.

27 Marshall Soules, *Media, Persuasion and Propaganda* (Edinburgh: Edinburgh University Press, 2015), 65–6.

28 Michele Hilmes, *Radio Voices: American Broadcasting, 1922–1952* (Minneapolis: Minnesota University Press, 1999), 232–3.

29 Anonymous, 'Big Picture to Initiate New Distribution Plan in September', *Recruiting Journal of the United States Army* 12, no. 8 (1959): 21.

30 Heather Gumbert, 'Coercion and Consent in Television Broadcasting: The Consequences of August 1961', in *Envisioning Socialism: Television and the Cold War in the German Democratic Republic* (Ann Arbor: Michigan University Press, 2014), 105–34.

31 Heather Gumbert, 'Split Screens? Television in East Germany, 1952–89', in K. Führer and C. Ross (eds.), *Mass Media, Culture and Society in Twentieth-Century Germany* (Basingstoke: Palgrave, 2006), 147.

32 Anonymous, 'Big Picture', 21.

33 Daniel Hallin and Paolo Mancini, *Comparing Media Systems: Three Models of Media and Politics* (Cambridge: Cambridge University Press, 2004), 282.

34 For a wide-ranging review of the history of the web, both as an object of study and as a historical resource, see Niels Brügger and Ian Milligan (eds.), *The Sage Handbook of Web History* (London: Sage, 2019).

30 *Brendan Maartens*

35 U. S. Congress, Senate, Committee on Armed Services, *Department of Defense Authorization for Appropriations for Fiscal Year 2001 and the Future Years Defense Program*, 105th Congr., 2nd sess., 2000, 88.
36 U. S. Air Force, 'Home', 'Mission', 'Play the Airman Challenge'. airforce.com: www.airforce.com; www.airforce.com/mission; www.airforce.com/airmanchallenge/?_ga=40016710.1572601322 (accessed 2 November 2019).
37 Armed Forces of the Philippines, 'Team AFP'. Twitter.com: https://twitter.com/teamafp?lang=en (accessed 2 November 2019).
38 Armed Forces of Islamic Republic of Iran, 'Iran Military'. Facebook.com: www.facebook.com/Iranian.Military/ (accessed 2 November 2019).
39 Khamenei Iran, 'The Armed Forces are the Fortress of the People', Khamenei.ir: http://english.khamenei.ir/news/6647/The-Armed-Forces-are-the-fortress-of-the-people (accessed 2 November 2019).
40 These figures were accurate at the time of access: 2 November 2019. See Armee de Terre, 'Home Page', YouTube.com: www.youtube.com/armeedeterre; Armee de Terre, 'Home Page', Instagram.com: www.instagram.com/armee2terre/; Armee de Terre, 'Home Page', Facebook.com: www.facebook.com/armee2terre; Armee de Terre, 'Home Page', Twitter.com: https://twitter.com/armeedeterre
41 Armee de Terre, 'Home Page', sengager.fr: www.sengager.fr/ (accessed 2 November 2019).
42 Some scholars have suggested that the 'mass' logic of traditional media has begun to permeate the online social space. See, for example, Paolo Gerbaudo, 'Populism 2.0: Social Media Activism, the Generic Internet User and Interactive Direct Democracy', in D. Trottier and C. Fuchs (eds.), *Social Media, Politics and the State: Protests, Revolutions, Riots, Crime and Policing in the Age of Facebook, Twitter and YouTube* (New York: Routledge, 2015), 67–87.
43 Charles Kadushin, *Understanding Social Networks: Theories, Concepts, and Findings* (Oxford: Oxford University Press, 2012), 9.
44 Sinclair, 'The Nazi Party Rally at Nuremburg', *Public Opinion Quarterly* 2, no. 4 (1938): 575, 582.
45 Eduardo Gonza Lez Calleja, 'The Symbolism of Violence during the Second Republic in Spain, 1931–1936', in C. Ealham and M. Richards (eds.), *The Splintering of Spain Cultural History and the Spanish Civil War, 1936–1939* (Cambridge: Cambridge University Press, 2005), 35–6.
46 Sabine Frühstück and Eyal Ben-Ari, '"Now We Show It All!" Normalization and the Management of Violence in Japan's Armed Forces', *The Journal of Japanese Studies* 28, no. 1 (2002): 18–20.
47 Michael Mann, 'War and Social Theory: Into Battle with Classes, Nations and States', in C. Creighton and M. Shaw (eds.), *The Sociology of War and Peace* (Basingstoke: Macmillan, 1987), 67.
48 P. T. Barnum, *The Life of P. T. Barnum: Written by Himself* (London: Sampson Low, 1855), 176, 157.
49 Roger Possner, *The Rise of Militarism in the Progressive Era, 1900–1914* (Jefferson: MacFarland & Co., 2009), 52–4.
50 Daniel Boorstin, *The Image: A Guide to Pseudo-Events in America* (New York: Vintage, 1992), 11.
51 Clila Magena and Ephraim Lapid, 'Israel's Military Public Diplomacy Evolution: Historical and Conceptual Dimensions', *Public Relations Review* 44, no. 2 (2018): 287–98.
52 Britain, the country to which the Australian government pledged allegiance, also played host to recruiting committees and a national postal poll. See Brendan Maartens, 'The Great War, Military Recruitment and the Public Relations Work of the Parliamentary Recruiting Committee, 1914–1915', *Public Relations Inquiry* 5, no. 2 (2016): 169–85.
53 Radio Marti Research Department, *Cuba Annual Report: 1988*. Office of Research and Policy. Voice of America: United States Information Agency (New Brunswick: Transaction, 1991), 228–9.

Part I

Recruitment in an era of total war

3 Why Africans in British Empire territories joined the colours, 1914–1918

Anne Samson

Abstract

The First World War extended to four German territories in Africa: Togoland, Cameroon, South West Africa and East Africa, whilst British troops were diverted during the war years to Egypt and Somaliland for actions against the Senusi. In addition, men and women from the white settler colonies enlisted for service in Europe. Initially, each campaign had its own recruitment strategy localised to immediate demands and pre-war conditions. However, from late 1915 into 1917, recruitment for service elsewhere in Africa and for Europe saw different strategies employed, and as a complete anomaly, troops who had fought for the enemy in East and West Africa were recruited into British forces in the last years of the war. Using local newspapers and official correspondence where possible, supplemented with archival-based secondary material, this chapter compares the various recruiting strategies across the sub-Sahara African campaigns and the European recruitment drives in the years 1914–1918. The study allows attitudes towards empire and service to be discerned and emphasises the diversity of the British Empire across Africa in its achievement of a common goal.

Africa is a continent of diversity to which the varied experiences of the British Empire territories in the 1914–18 war lay testimony. Compared with literature examining British recruitment, little attention has been given to recruitment practices in Africa.[1] Moreover, where discussion of recruitment in Africa has taken place within wider campaign, regimental and force histories, it has invariably centred on conscripting carriers and labourers who did not, as a general rule, engage in actual conflict. Texts by Geoffrey Hodges, Melvin Page and Albert Grundlingh are the most well known in this regard.[2]

This chapter provides a comparative analysis of military recruiting practices throughout British Africa, thereby demonstrating that the African black, white, Indian and Arab experience was far more complex than hitherto believed. Initially, standing or existing military contingents, police and other para-military forces including rifle clubs and the Preventive Service in Gold Coast, were used for service, the men having enlisted voluntarily.[3] There was thus no immediate need for recruits when war broke out in August 1914. However, as the captured territories of Togoland (28 August 1914), South West Africa (9 July 1915) and

34   *Anne Samson*

Cameroon (26 March 1916) fell under military occupation from their respective surrenders through to the allocation of mandates, and as the war progressed in Europe and dragged on in East Africa until late November 1918, additional manpower was needed.

While the scale of mobilisation work remained small when compared to the recruiting campaigns in Europe, North America and parts of Asia, it had profound social and economic consequences. On the African continent, while there was no immediate need to mass-recruit soldiers, the demand for labour and medical services ensured that civilians, male and female and of all ethnic backgrounds, were involved. The nature of the territory, the type and length of time under British occupation and the duration of the local campaigns contributed to how people reacted, with tailored recruitment initiatives, including conscription and commandeering,[4] being undertaken. Internal unrest in various territories and longstanding nationalist movements in Egypt and Somaliland which flared up further impacted the limited manpower available in a continental theatre regarded by Britain as secondary.

'A low whisper that vibrated over the empire': recruiting at the outset of the war

Recruitment of soldiers across Africa began in earnest in 1915: February in West Africa, July in South Africa. Before that, it had generally been 'business as usual' in terms of men enlisting despite the demands of war and the mainstay Imperial Garrison forces having been sent back to Europe. With the existing forces thought to be sufficient, administrators having little intention to escalate tensions in Africa, there was no reason to change systems and processes.

This led initially to recruitment being discouraged in some territories as men spontaneously rushed to join the colours in fear of all being over before long. In South Africa, offers to raise white units for service in Europe were declined,[5] as were offers by Indians and the Coloured community to serve anywhere within the empire.[6] In Southern Rhodesia (Zimbabwe), public meetings were held in September 1914, white men giving their names to form 'one Rhodesian troop for service, if necessary, anywhere in the Empire'.[7] The First Rhodesia Regiment was to serve in German South West Africa, leading the legislative council to approve a second contingent of 500 men in October 1914.[8] A. E. Capell recalled his force enlisted 'just because England called, not articulately, but in a low whisper that vibrated over the Empire, a fervent and trustful "S.O.S."'.[9] They had 'No thought of gain, recompense, remuneration – for they joined at Imperial rates, "the noble sum of thirteen-pence per day"'.[10] The regiment consisted of British South African Police who filled officer roles supplemented with men from the Southern Rhodesia Volunteers. From these, men were handpicked to form a machine gun unit and scouts. Lack of shipping meant the contingent was kept in abeyance, undertaking training and leave, until early March 1915, when it left for East Africa.[11] When the contingent was disbanded in July 1917 due to lack of available reinforcements, the men themselves would become reinforcements to the various

Union troops overseas. Unhappy, the men sought transfer or discharge to re-enlist with other units.[12]

In British East Africa (BEA; Kenya), settlers rushed to join the colours as news of the war filtered through the country by newspaper and telegraph, visitor and trader. Despite the governor's reluctance to involve his colony in the conflict, two settler corps were formed, many with previous military experience, while scout corps were raised from resident South African Boers, Arabs and Somalis and from 'some of the wilder tribes'. The men were well known by their commanders, who personally recruited their forces.[13] Men who did not enlist were asked to form local defence units. As the local protectorate and colonial forces were under command of the Colonial Office rather than the War Office, many in civil service, doctors, veterinary specialists and the transport department, were given military commissions often in addition to their civilian role and 'organised to meet the new situation'.[14]

In contrast to other African territories, the legislative committee in BEA was forced by the settlers, in March 1916, to introduce conscription in the colony, whites to serve in the armed forces and blacks as labour.[15] The latter was implemented first, the former only once all alternatives had been explored. While administrators were reluctant to involve too many people of colour in the war, for fear of upsetting existing social hierarchies, the increased need for white men to serve in Europe meant that eventually from late 1916, the King's African Rifles (KAR) would be expanded and select men from West Africa brought across to fight in East Africa.

This was not the complete picture, for although recruitment in some areas was discouraged, it needed to be encouraged in others. Labour was needed to assist with military invasions in West and South Africa in 1914 and in East Africa from early 1916.

Agriculture, mining and commerce: the economics of recruitment

Recruitment, military and labour, took different forms. In common with European recruitment, local cultural and political conditions had to be considered. Where recruits were to serve and with whom determined when and to what extent certain ethnic groups were recruited and into what roles. The idea of martial races was prevalent at the time, resulting in certain groups being favoured as soldiers over others who made better labourers.[16] The policy of 'divide and rule' was common: whilst units consisted of men from the same group or region, they were sent to serve amongst people they did not know to prevent fraternisation and to better enforce control.[17] All had white officers, mostly Britons.

The struggle for resources between commerce and the military was similar in the metropole and the African territories. Men were needed on farms and in other employment to sustain and maintain the military forces, resulting in conflict between government departments over manpower. In Africa, many such as the Gold Coast Ashanti were 'too obsessed with their cocoa farms to enlist for Military Service',[18] and payment for working on the mines was more lucrative than joining the armed forces, where the risk to life was similar. Economic demands thus put pressure on military recruitment, each territory responding according to local priorities. In contrast, the Transvaal Chamber of Mines and other employers, paid bonuses to Union employees who served in East and Central Africa and in Europe with the Overseas Expeditionary Force.[19] Jobs were held open for their return.[20] When it became evident that men were reluctant to enlist for German South West Africa (GSWA), mine recruiting agencies were employed, which resulted in men who signed up to work on the mines providing six months' labour service to the government's war effort.[21] As in Europe, white women in Cape Town offered white feathers to men they felt should be serving. When Portugal officially entered the war (March 1916), the South African mine labour recruiters helped recruit carriers 'at a price', while direct recruitment 'was successfully thwarted by the minor officials of the companies "farming" the various parts of the country'.[22] Many of these had German sympathies and business interests.

The 'right sort of man': ethnicity and conscription

Initially, men of all ethnicities voluntarily joined the forces, military and labour, for adventure, employment, to get away from restrictive family and community obligations.[23] South Africa proved exceptional when a section of the population rebelled at the decision to invade GSWA, which led to notifications being issued instructing all men to report with their rifles for registration; failure to indicate willingness to support the government resulted in imprisonment.[24] Across the continent, as news of the harsh conditions filtered back, fewer men chose to enlist, making compulsion necessary, especially for labour purposes.[25]

Even where conscription was prevalent, conditions varied. Missionary groups, realising conscription was inevitable, volunteered to serve as coherent units allowing them to organise themselves as they saw best. Thus, Bishop Weston of Zanzibar's carrier contingent and the Western-educated Kikuyu Missions were trained before they took to the field, resulting in fewer losses than those pressed into immediate service.[26]

Hodges identified four phases of war-time carrier recruitment in East Africa: 'part compulsory, part voluntary' at the outbreak of war; conscription using the 1915 Native Followers Recruitment Ordnance; 'mass levy' between March and August 1917, when there was a shortage of fit men; and a return to 'part compulsion, part voluntary'.[27] 'Part compulsory, part voluntary' best describes recruitment across the continent for most of the war years.

Compulsory labour was not unknown. It was the only way to ensure railway and construction projects were completed and enticed men to earn money to pay taxes.[28] The need to feed the armies in Africa and Europe led to increased demands on agriculture, which put military conscription in conflict with local demands. Men could avoid military conscription while in civilian employment, although employers could re-assign employees to military labour, which some did. All men were paid for their services, the amount varying by the time, manner and place of recruitment and where they served. Comments by veterans about not being paid at the end of the war suggests a lack of understanding of Western systems and the impact of decisions men made on enlisting and being registered. Invariably there was some unscrupulous practice.[29]

Commandeering took place in all theatres, particularly amongst the African black population. However, compared with other recruitment methods, it features little in British primary source documents until the later stages of the various campaigns. Reports of commandeering in West Africa dominate around German Cameroon, suggesting the German forces tended to prefer this method of obtaining manpower.[30] Significantly, coercion dominates West African secondary literature, but there is little or no mention of recruiting or complaints of commandeering in the press. The papers, edited and managed by the West African elite, professed loyalty while complaining of lack of independence and self-government.[31] The wealthier coastal residents preferred to support the war effort financially, suggesting issues of recruitment and coercion were class based, affecting those in the interior who were less powerful. As in West Africa, status was important. Kikamba preferred employment as soldiers to that as carriers,[32] while the more educated Swahilis and Muslims expected preferential treatment.

Other than for Cameroon, there is hardly mention of soldiers being coerced. An unwilling soldier was ineffective and could be detrimental to the unit as a whole, as the Officer Commanding Gold Coast commented on recruiting men from the Northern Territories: some were 'dull and stupid', while others were 'dissatisfied and wanted to return home'. Investigation revealed they did not want to be soldiers but rather carriers employed for at most a year. Because of their 'grievance', they 'would never have made efficient soldiers'. He preferred having his force under strength than filled with 'the wrong type of recruit'.[33] Gambia was also concerned about the 'right sort of man' as 'several bambaras' recruited had to be discharged, being incapable of performing military duties.[34]

Ethnic balance and mix further impacted recruitment, putting strain on certain groups. In Sierra Leone, there could be no more than 50 per cent Mandis. They were easily raised, however, raising the equivalent of Timini recruits would be difficult, as men were not forthcoming.[35] Ashanti recruits were sent to Cameroon to replace non-commissioned officers and those whose contracts were due to end.[36] In all territories, permission was eventually granted for troops to be raised from ethnic groups not usually called on for military service, each forming their own company.[37]

Coercion increased when district political officers were under pressure. Soon after war broke out, the number of administrators reduced by 30 per cent, and the workload increased.[38] Added to this, the military demanded quick results, as men had to undergo medicals and training before being transported to the relevant theatre or front.

Mass media as experienced in the industrialised West was a limited option. Limited literacy in English or regional black languages such as Kiswahili and great distances between villages meant it was pointless advertising for carriers, labourers and porters in the press. Instead, colonial administrators were briefed before meeting local chiefs and headmen to explain the needs and situation. These men then undertook to supply the required number of recruits.[39] Where necessary,

38 *Anne Samson*

groups such as the Asante were shamed into supplying recruits; all conscripted.[40] In West Africa, men not liked by the chief and his elders, seen as troublemakers or whose families were not well regarded were forced to enlist.

Recruitment for the South African Native Labour Corps (SANLC) followed labour officers meeting with local chiefs or leaders who called meetings, which the officer addressed. Whilst some volunteered, others were volunteered including chiefs' sons tasked to report on conditions before the chief permitted additional enlistment.[41] The SANLC were contracted for a year through the South African Department of Native Affairs. White officers with experience of managing black labour were placed in command; not all were of a conciliatory disposition. The actual time the men served, longer than their contracts stipulated, along with the sinking of the transport ship SS *Mendi* in 1917, which saw more than 600 lives lost, black and white, resulted in South Africa suspending labour recruitment for service in Europe. Similarly, deaths on the troopship *Aragon* impacted recruitment for those serving in East Africa.

In south-east and central Africa, when recruits dried up, tax defaulters were arrested and imprisoned to induce others to seek employment.[42] When men were urgently needed to defend Kasama, prisoners especially released from gaol by all accounts willingly helped defend the territory.[43] For short distances, and in keeping with many traditional roles, women and children were frequently recruited as carriers, supplementing the dearth of male labour.

Some chiefs blamed absent administrators for the ensuing cruelty, whilst some administrators physically punished chiefs in front of their people or had them replaced for not delivering the expected quotas, thereby diminishing the status of chiefs.[44] In general, however, both the Colonial and War Offices deplored conscripting soldiers and labour for fear this would lead to trouble,[45] but they had little control over outlying areas, where their administrators were seen to hold all the power and command of the communication channels.[46] There were exceptions. With pressure mounting, the Northern Rhodesia administrator hoped 'a little pressure', not defined, would be 'sufficient to persuade very many without great opposition'.[47] When few from Koinadugu enlisted, district commissioners were instructed to 'catch recruits'.[48] On occasion, in East Africa men were obtained through nocturnal raids or by paying headmen a fee per recruit, while in the field, men were recruited directly by the military without reference to administrators, reference being made to 'press gangs'.[49] As the British forces began to converge, the condition of carriers from the north deteriorated, resulting in more labourers preferring agricultural work.[50] To ease pressure on British territories, many carriers conscripted by the Germans were subsumed into British service when captured. British impressment occurred when carriers were urgently needed for Togoland, the latter then providing labour for service in the Cameroon campaign.[51]

Attempts were made to prevent labour abuse. In 1915, 'the employment of natives to assist in labour recruitment' was prohibited.[52] In BEA, a labour system developed under the auspices of John Anderson and Oscar Watkins to ensure some parity and fairness. Despite appeals, the military did not always adhere to procedures, leading to men not being paid, as there was no evidence of their having done the work.[53]

'A chance to see the world': experiences of enlistment and challenges of recruiting

In Europe, British forces all spoke English. However, in Africa, there were a myriad of local languages, necessitating officers who could communicate accordingly or use translators.[54] Suitable white officers, preferably with previous experience of working with African troops, had to be sourced from the War Office, as many on leave in England when war broke out were instructed to France and could not be released.[55] The Army Council appealed to volunteers amongst those training to serve in Europe:[56] 'A circular came from Brigade HQ asking for volunteers, W[arrant] O[fficer]s and N[on] C[ommissioned] O[fficer]'s to go to Africa to serve with the KAR's. . . . It was quite voluntary: my family were against my going but I thought it a chance to see the world'.[57]

Obtaining and training new recruits became problematic where there were no 'old' soldiers who could speak the local language[58] and consequently did not understand the culture they were working in. Other concerns affecting the number of voluntary recruits were insufficient officers in general and a shortage of arms and stocks of clothing.[59] To overcome some of the issues, Gold Coast recruits serving overseas were promised protection of their wives and contributions to family member funerals.[60] However, administrative indecision led to fewer recruits than hoped for without pressure being applied, while shipping delays resulted in desertions as men tired of waiting. Men feared going to strange lands by boat, especially those from the interior who had never seen a huge expanse of water.[61] Thus, when 760 men enlisted between November 1916 and May 1918 as drivers for service in East Africa, 'mostly untrained, and from the coastal region,' they were rapidly shipped before the cocoa season began to prevent desertions, despite rates of pay being good.[62]

Garrisoning conquered territories required an occupying force. Recruiting rank and file generally provided little problem; on occasion, recruits were forthcoming from the conquered territory itself in the form of police units. The challenge was sourcing white officers, as the men would perform better and be less disruptive if they had officers they knew. Rostered leave for those on contracts and contracts terminating provided further complications.[63] Colonial status impacted the use of regiments and thus recruitment, especially when Nigerian Governor Lugard accused the Sierra Leone regiment of inappropriate behaviour. Jealousy between troops existed as those from Sierra Leone were paid more.[64] Civil servants enlisting left rural areas with little or no civil administration, causing power vacuums, resulting in chaos and reduced social control. Newspaper advertisements to obtain replacements failed.[65]

Maintaining local security was a further consideration. It was expected that 60 per cent of Gambia Company would volunteer for service in East Africa during 1916. However, as they were the only military company in Gambia, the

40 *Anne Samson*

government was reluctant to release them.[66] Sierra Leone too was constrained in sending troops to East Africa. In 1917, the director of recruiting enlisted men from Gold Coast and Nigeria to maintain force numbers and for potential use in other theatres following the announcement that the campaign in East Africa was all but over.[67] This contrasted with the 1916 cohort of Gold Coasters, who were sent under orders to East Africa rather than volunteers; they were the men selected from existing units and felt to be the most suitable for service 'overseas'. In 1914 the Gold Coast Regiment consisted of 41 per cent recruits from the Northern Territories and 59 per cent from outside, mainly French territory. By 1918, only 5 per cent of recruits came from French territories,[68] the result of French recruiting for service in Europe, attempts by others to avoid enlisting and a reluctance by Britain to return French refugees who were employed on road works, construction and the mines.[69]

Luck of the draw determined who was called to provide labour. Existing infrastructure played an important role as seen in Northern Rhodesia. Distances between villages were great and the terrain often difficult to travel. Communities that had contact with the administration were invariably closer to roads and other colonial infrastructure and became the first port of call when recruitment in urban centres failed. Expansion of the KAR occurred mainly in Northern Rhodesia, the police forming the core of the new regiments. During 1916 and 1917, in Nyasaland, military recruiters focused on Bemba villages, who negotiated higher rates of pay having had previous military and policing experience.[70] In Nigeria, the police were instructed to assist in recruiting, conditions there seeming harsher than other West African territories, yet desertions were lower than for Gold Coast. Recruitment in Nigeria, however achieved, was successful, with the regiment being over establishment by 28 February 1915 after losses had been accounted for.[71]

Army bands, public speeches, advertisements and atrocity stories

Conscription and coercion had mostly occurred in rural and more remote areas. In contrast, a variety of recruitment strategies were used in urban centres.

A military presence, such as a base or training camp, led to higher recruitment than elsewhere. When the military base at Zouaragou closed on the men going to Cameroon, the number of recruits in the interior of Gold Coast declined. To improve recruitment, it was suggested the base be re-opened,[72] while in Sierra Leone, some enlistment continued to 'let the natives see that recruiting has not stopped altogether'.[73] News of military successes further spurred recruitment. Similarly, in East Africa, as it became apparent that the Germans were being pushed out of their territory, recruitment and desertions to British forces increased.[74]

Army bands played their part. When Sierra Leone met its quota of recruits for service in Cameroon, the result of recruiting bands, 'many [from Ronietta] walked from Moyamba to Freetown – a distance of about 80 miles in the hope of being engaged'.[75] In January 1917, with good pay offered and knowing the recruiters led to 'a good class of carrier' being recruited despite the hardships of carriers in Cameroon. The bands would march through a town attracting a crowd. How the message about where to enrol or sign up at these events has not yet materialised but presumably leaflets or pamphlets were handed out. Speeches were made informing observers of the benefits of signing up. Fundraising events had a similar impact or role in encouraging able-bodied men to enlist. The recruitment rally, where ministers of religion and politicians held public meetings to motivate enlistment and answer questions, were popular in South Africa. On occasion these were preceded or at least held on the same day as the band performing. There are few adverts in newspapers announcing these events, suggesting local posters, notice boards and church announcements informed people of their taking place. Some events were likened to electioneering.

The main need for recruits came with South Africa's decision in July 1915 to send troops to central and East Africa and Europe once the GSWA campaign ended and men were demobilised. This was in keeping with the 1912 Defence Force Act, which only permitted volunteers to serve outside the Union. With the increased need for armed white volunteers, a recruitment bureau was set up at Kya Rosa in Pretoria under CP Crewe and depots located in the main centres where men could enlist directly.[76] This being the Union army's first military engagement, much of the support network needed to be put in place, resulting in administrators, skilled and unskilled labour having to be sourced for a myriad of reasons.

The opportunity to serve in Europe as a South African contingent arose before that of East Africa. In anticipation of the latter, a register was opened for men to indicate their preferred theatre, and some were prompted not to enlist too hastily, as a 'better' opportunity was foreseen.[77] This allowed South Africans, not comfortable directly supporting Britain or with the more disciplined way of fighting, to have a suitable outlet. Men with a greater affinity for the Union selected to serve in 26th Air Squadron and the South African Expeditionary Forces, which served in Europe and East Africa. Others preferred British regiments because of previous or family links.

From mid-1915, in urban areas, notification of recruitment meetings, conditions of service and other necessary information were given in the press. From 1917, direct appeals for pilots and motorcycle riders featured.[78] A limited number of posters encouraging recruitment for Europe were produced, especially in South Africa.[79] In West and South Africa, where out-spoken sections of the population were not in favour of the war, the West African coastal elites and South African Boers or more nationalist Afrikaner, it was safer to keep recruitment drives as low key as possible. Instead, reliance was placed on the emotional reporting of German atrocities to encourage recruitment, especially in the Union, which had experienced two months' civil war over whether to support Britain in its war against Germany.

As the allies became more dominant, so adverts became bolder. The exception was the pro-empire English press, managed by mining magnates, which consistently called for the government to do more. Groups such as the Indian Congress and African People's Organisation representing the South African Coloured

42   *Anne Samson*

community used the press to make known their offers to raise men to act as stretcher bearers and soldiers respectively – up to 500 men each. These prompts occurred as early as 1914, but the offers were only accepted in late 1915 and into 1916. While some decisions were politically motivated, not using Indian and Coloured men to appease the growing white nationalist population, there were, in the early days of the war, practical considerations. None of the territories had sufficient weapons and uniforms or even instructors to cope with mass recruitment drives.

Overall, the press played little role in recruiting in Africa. Word of mouth was the biggest recruiter, no doubt encouraged by the payment of 'bringers money', as it was known in West Africa, providing the recruit was still in the army after six months.[80] Where possible, officers were handpicked, following which they would use their networks to obtain men to fill the ranks. This ensured a loyalty and cohesion early on, which was important for getting into the field quickly. South African mounted units required that men had their own horses and rifles, as these were in limited supply in the Union Defence Force. In East Africa, local civilian leaders called friends and others to join them in defending the territory and Uganda Railway leading to units such as Arnoldi's Scouts, Wavell's Arabs and the Skin Corps. As the war progressed, these units were brought under more formal control in the East Africa Mounted Rifles. To bring the Northern Rhodesia forces up to strength, an 'experienced officer' was tasked with obtaining the services of ex-policemen and reserves. However, low rates of pay hindered obtaining greater reserves, it being noted that men 'are not coming forward in the same way as they did in the past', the drive to enlist being reduced because the 'martial instincts of the [Awemba and Angoni] are dying out'.[81] Similarly, word of mouth discouraged labour recruitment across the continent. In 1914, when news spread that soldiers' fatigues had reduced to an acceptable level at Kumasi, Gold Coast, recruitment improved and desertions reduced.[82]

In both East and West Africa, accounts exist of the 'enemy' changing sides and fighting or serving with the British. In West Africa, the local police in Cameroon were recruited to help maintain law and order under the British Government, whilst in East Africa, captured German askari took up arms against their German masters in preference to being carriers or remaining in prison.[83] In this way, the 6th battalion KAR came into being under the command of Phillip Pretorius, a South African hunter specially recruited by the British War Office and Admiralty to track down the SS *Königsberg* despite the South Africans initially believing him a spy.[84] Carriers who proved brave fighters in the field could transfer to the KAR.[85] European-educated men were allocated roles with responsibilities such as mess and store supervisors or medical services, leading to disappointment when some did not receive medals for their service.[86]

Conclusion

The diversity of the African continent, different ethnic groups, anthropological beliefs, martial race theories and how the territory was colonised all impacted

Why Africans joined the colours 43

how recruitment was undertaken and how successful it was. The men who enlisted did so for the same reason those in Europe did: adventure, economic necessity, sense of obligation, patriotism or pressure by others. Only BEA officially implemented conscription, instigated by the settlers rather than the government, partly to encourage labour for their farms but also to do their bit for 'King and country'. For GSWA, South Africa recruited rebels using registration of rifles as a means of conscription rather than official policy.

Recruitment success was variable. At the time, the press highlighted achievements, as did Charles Lucas, who wrote about Africa's involvement in the post-war years.[87] However, subsequent commentators have demonstrated that recruitment initiatives were not as effective as initially thought.[88] Recruitment was most successful where communities offered their services. Some had to lobby government to serve, namely the Indian Stretcher Bearer Corps and Cape Corps. Bishop Weston in Zanzibar and the Kikuyu Missionaries were challenged to raise contingents, while others raised contingents, Bailey's Sharp Shooters and the Sportsman's Regiment, knowing they would be accepted for political and economic reasons. In Gold Coast, the Omanhene of Akim Abuakwa and the Konor of Manya Krobo offered financial inducements for men in the Eastern Province to enlist,[89] while existing regiments which proved themselves in the field, such as the Gold Coast Regiment and Transvaal, Scottish attracted recruits. Conversely, recruitment proved difficult amongst groups previously denied opportunities to serve, such as the Sierra Leone Krio, while the Masaai changed their allegiance based on the most lucrative offer.[90]

With few exceptions, most forces in and from Africa were constantly understrength due to poor recruitment or miscalculation of reserves.[91] To encourage recruitment, public meetings and tours were undertaken by prominent officials, including religious leaders,[92] while press reports 'percolated to the general public through informal processes of dissemination of information between the illiterate masses and the literate group'.[93] When circumstances mitigated against sufficient volunteers coming forward, conscription of some sort was implemented, resulting in different experiences within colonial territories and across the continent.[94] In contrast to European theatres, West and East Africa saw German askari and carriers enlist with British contingents, in keeping with the general African practice of allegiance to the perceived strongest leader rather than to a country or specific government.[95]

While most government or legislative motivation for participating in the war was preservation of empire, for some communities, it was to preserve their identity or position in society, such as the whites on the Northern Rhodesia border who felt serving under black officers was unacceptable,[96] or to obtain political recognition, as expressed by the Indians and Cape Coloureds in South Africa and the Ewe in West Africa.[97] Others enlisted or supported the war effort for fear of German colonial rule.[98] Some whites resident in Africa and a few African blacks resident in England preferred service in Europe.[99]

In West Africa especially, the removal of district officers for war work led communities to assume the whites had left, creating a power vacuum, and chiefs, who

44 Anne Samson

were not well respected, came under threat. This led to unrest, most notably in Zouaragou in 1916 and Bolgatanga in 1917.[100] In contrast, Freetown experienced a reduction in crime, while agriculture suffered.[101]

Wartime recruitment, for both military and civilian labour purposes, opened the interior and areas not previously known for supplying labour, while ideas of martial race theory were challenged.[102] Official structures and processes were introduced, enabling more rigorous labour recruitment and management of taxes after the war. Not all were popular, as protesters of the *kipende* demonstrated in BEA during 1919.

Researching this chapter has highlighted the gaps in our knowledge of African recruitment and preparation for war. Existing literature has been generalised to cover the whole of Africa and the colonial period. While coercion and compulsion have dominated the First World War narrative to date, it was one of multiple recruitment methods, and while acknowledged to be the most ruthless, it was by no means the dominant form of recruitment. Where and when men were forced to serve, desertion numbers were high. The military recognised the need to have willing recruits, as did administrators who understood the people they worked with and governed, whilst others, new or on the career path, were only concerned with getting the job done, irrespective of the long-term consequences. The challenge today is the lack of access to original material in the form of indigenous African views, as many who served were unlettered in the European sense, and officers and few others recorded their experiences. Where oral histories have been recorded, these were done after the Second World War, possibly clouding recollections of what happened in the First. In territories previously colonised by Germany and then one of the allies, discerning between the practices of the two, where accounts do exist, is difficult – the white man, irrespective of origin, was the white man, some distinguish but not all, the result being that the behaviour specific to one group may well have been generally attributed. With no veterans alive to question and clarify, drawing more solid conclusions might never be possible, and invariably the extremes dominate the mundane and 'usual practice'. This is not to excuse ruthless or unequal treatment but rather to highlight the complexity and diversity of experience across the continent.

Notes

1 The first detailed study of British recruitment was published in 1970, with the most comprehensive published at the end of the following decade. See Roy Douglas, 'Voluntary Enlistment in the First World War and the work of the Parliamentary Recruitment Committee', *Journal of Modern History* 42, no. 4 (1970): 564–86; Peter Simkins, *Kitchener's Army: The Raising of the New Armies* (Barnsley: Pen & Sword, 2007 [1989]).

2 Geoffrey Hodges, *Kariakor: The Carrier Corps: The Story of the Military Labour Forces in the Conquest of German East Africa 1914–1918* (Nairobi: University of Nairobi, 1999); Melvin E. Page, *The Chiwaya war: Malawians and the First World War* (Colorado: Westview, 2000); Albert Grundlingh, *Fighting Their Own War: South African Blacks and the First World War* (Johannesburg: Raven, 1987).

3 Kwame O. Kwarteng, 'World War 1: The Role of the Gold Coast and Asante towards the British Victory', in D. V. N. Y. M. Botchway & K. O. Kwarteng (eds.), *Africa*

and the First World War: Remembrance, Memories and Representations after 100 Years (Newcastle upon Tyne: Cambridge Scholars, 2018), 26, 32–3; James G. Willson, *Guerillas of Tsavo: An Illustrated Diary of a Forgotten Campaign in British East Africa 1914–1916* (James Willson, 2012); Peter Roger Charlton, *Cinderella's Soldiers: The Nyasaland Volunteer Reserve* (Rickmansworth: GWAA, 2018); Sandra Swart, 'A Boer and His Gun and His Wife Are Three Things Always Together: Republican Masculinity and the 1914 Rebellion', *Journal of Southern African Studies* 24, no. 4 (1998): 737–51.

4 Commandeer means to seize (men or goods) for military service.

5 South African National Archive (SANA): GG 599 9/59/1–3 War 1914 Occupation of German South West Africa Expeditions; Arrangements on; Transport for.

6 Gulam Vahed, '"Give Till It Hurts": Durban's Indians and the First World War', *Journal of Natal and Zulu History* 19 (2001): 41–60.

7 *Rhodesia Herald*, 3 September 1914, 20; SANA: GG 599 9/59/17.

8 A. E. Capell, *The 2nd Rhodesia Regiment in East Africa* (Uckfield: Naval & Military, 2009), 1.

9 Ibid.

10 Ibid.

11 Ibid., 3, 5.

12 Ibid., 100–1.

13 C. P. Fendall, *The East African Force 1915–1919: An Unofficial Record of Its Creating and Fighting Career: Together with Some Account of the Civil and Military Administrative Conditions in East Africa before and during That Period* (London: HF & G Witherby, 1921), 26.

14 Fendall, *East African Force*, 26–8.

15 Anne Samson, *Britain, South Africa and the East Africa Campaign 1914–1918: The Union Comes of Age* (London: Tauris, 2005), 56.

16 Myles Osborne, *Ethnicity and Empire in Kenya: Loyalty and Martial Race among the Kamba* (Cambridge: Cambridge University Press, 2014).

17 T[he] N[ational] A[rchives], London: CO 445/35 37974 Ashantis – Enlistment in Gold Coast Regiment.

18 Ibid.

19 SA General Order 772, 12 October 1915.

20 *The Mafeking Mail*, 31 January 1917.

21 *Rhodesian Herald*, 3 September 1914; Samson, *East Africa*, 111, 115.

22 Fendall, *East African Force*, 99.

23 Hodges, *Kariakor*, 9–10.

24 SANA: GG 559 9/59/28; P. J. Pretorius, *Jungle Man: Mtanda Batho, Hunter and Adventurer, the Autobiography of Major PJ Pretorius* (Bela Bela: Dream Africa, 2013), 298.

25 Osborne, *Kikamba*, 76.

26 John Lonsdale, 'Kikuyu Christianities', *Journal of Religion in Africa* 29 (1999): 213.

27 Hodges, *Kariakor*, 35, 72.

28 Elspeth Huxley, *Red Strangers* (London: Penguin, 1999).

29 Hodges, *Kariakor*, 36; Bodleian Library: MS 5469/1 file 1 Hodges interviews.

30 George Njung, *Soldiers of Their Own: Honour, Violence, Resistance and Conscription in Colonial Cameroon during the First World War*, PhD dissertation (Ann Arbor, MI: University of Michigan, 2016).

31 Wilson Jeremiah Moses, *The Golden Age of Black Nationalism, 1850–1925* (Hamden, CT: Archon, 1978).

32 Osborne, *Kikamba*, 77.

33 TNA: CO 445/35 52634 Ashantis – Enlistment in Gold Coast Regiment.

34 TNA: CO 445/35 20182 Gambia Recruiting. 'Bambara' are a West African people of the Mandé ethnic group.

35 TNA: CO 445/35 8615 WAFF Recruiting; CO 445/35 11878 Sierra Leone Recruiting.

46 *Anne Samson*

36 TNA: CO 445/35 37974 Ashantis – Enlistment in Gold Coast Regiment.
37 TNA: CO 445/35 52634 Ashantis – Enlistment in Gold Coast Regiment; Marciana M. Kuusaana, 'Impact of the First World War on Labour Recruitment in the North of the Gold Coast (Ghana)', in Botchway & Kwarteng (eds.), *Africa and the First World War*, 82; Hodges, *Kariakor*, 41–2; Grundlingh, *Fighting*.
38 Kuusaana, 'Impact of the First World War on Labour Recruitment in the North of the Gold Coast (Ghana)', 82.
39 Hodges, *Kariakor*, 41–2; Grundlingh, *Fighting*.
40 Kwarteng, 'World War 1', 34; Akurang-Parry, 'African Agency', 156.
41 Grundlingh, *Fighting*, 67.
42 Page, *Chiwaya*, 33.
43 Charlton, *Cinderella's Soldiers*.
44 Kuusaana, 'Labour Recruitment', 85–6; David Killingray, 'Repercussions of World War I in the Gold Coast', *The Journal of African History* 19, no. 1 (1978): 41–2.
45 Killingray, 'Repercussions', 49; Cole, 'Sierra Leone and World War 1' (PhD Thesis, SOAS, University of London, 1994), 109; Edmund J. Yorke, *Britain, Northern Rhodesia and the First World War: Forgotten Colonial Crisis* (London: Palgrave, 2015), 271 fn130.
46 Osborne, 78; Cole, 'Sierra Leone', 121.
47 Yorke, *Northern Rhodesia*, 270–1 fn118.
48 Ibid.
49 Hodges, *Kariakor*, 39, 66, 114.
50 Ibid., 37.
51 Killingray, 'Repercussions', 47.
52 Yorke, *Northern Rhodesia*, 46, 50, 268 fn64.
53 Bodleian Library: MS 5469/3 Hodges collection, Oscar Watkins report.
54 For an insight into Africa's ethnic and linguistic diversity, see 'A Fascinating Color-Coded Map of Africa's Diversity': www.vox.com/2015/11/10/9698574/africa-diversity-map (accessed 6 December 2019).
55 TNA: CO 445/35 8615 WAFF Recruiting; CO 445/35 11878 Sierra Leone Recruiting; CO 445/35 14277 Nigeria Recruitment of natives for WAFF; Cole, 'Sierra Leone', 59.
56 TNA: CO 445/36 42364 Nigerian Overseas contingent; Kwarteng, 'World War 1', 38.
57 Bodleian Library, Western Manuscripts: MSS Afr s. 1715 (144) WG Hughes, f.6.
58 Cole, 'Sierra Leone', 102–5, 111–15.
59 TNA: CO 445/35 20182; Killingray, 'Repercussions', 47; Kwarteng, 'World War 1', 38.
60 Kwabena O. Akurang-Parry, 'African Agency and Cultural Initiatives in the British Imperial Military and Labour Recruitment Drives in the Gold Coast (Colonial Ghana) during the First World War', in Ashley Jackson (ed.), *The British Empire and the First World War* (London: Taylor & Francis, 2017), 160.
61 Killingray, 'Repercussions', 43; Cole, 'Sierra Leone', 109.
62 Killingray, 'Repercussions', 48.
63 TNA: CO 445/36 19325 Officering the WAFF after conclusion of the Cameroon campaign.
64 Cole, 'Sierra Leone', 60.
65 Yorke, *Northern Rhodesia*, 66–7.
66 TNA: CO 445/36 32704 Gambia Service in East Africa.
67 Cole, 'Sierra Leone', 58.
68 Killingray, 'Repercussions': 46 fn36.
69 Killingray, 'Repercussions', 39–59.
70 Yorke, *Northern Rhodesia*, 80.
71 TNA: CO 445/35 14277 Nigeria Recruitment of natives for WAFF.
72 TNA: CO 445/35 17955 Gold Coast Recruiting.
73 Cole, 'Sierra Leone', 54–5.

74 Michelle R. Moyd, *Violent Intermediaries: African Soldiers, Conquest, and Everyday Colonialism in German East Africa* (Athens: Ohio University, 2014), 147.

75 Cole, 'Sierra Leone', 54–5.

76 Pretorius, *Jungle Man*, 294.

77 Samson, *East Africa*, 100.

78 *Rand Daily Mail*, from August 1914; *The Mafeking Mail*, 29 January 1917; Akurang-Parry, 'African Agency', 151, 156; South African National Defence Force Document Services: OC Records 18, 12 July 1918.

79 Art.I[imperia] W[ar] M[useum] PST 12330; Art.IWM PST 12329; Art.IWM PST 12319.

80 TNA:CO 445/35 8615 WAFF Recruiting; CO 445/35 11878 Sierra Leone Recruiting; CO 445/35 14277 Nigeria Recruitment of natives for WAFF; Cole, 'Sierra Leone', 53–4, 63.

81 Wright, *Northern Rhodesia Police*, 97.

82 TNA: CO 445/35 17955 Gold Coast Recruiting.

83 Pretorius, *Jungle Man*, 432.

84 Pretorius, *Jungle Man*.

85 Osborne, *Kikamba*, 77.

86 IWM: Sound recordings 28924–28927, Gerald Rillings interviews with Kikamba.

87 G. T. W. Hodges, 'African Manpower Statistics for the British Forces in East Africa 1914–1918', *The Journal of African History* 19, no. 1 (1978): 101–16.

88 Akurang-Parry, 'African Agency', 162–3.

89 Killingray, 'Repercussions', 50.

90 Cole, 'Sierra Leone', 79–80.

91 Samson, *East Africa*, 114.

92 Cole, 'Sierra Leone', 62–3.

93 Akurang-Parry, 'African Agency', 155, 158, 162.

94 Hodges, *Kariakor*, 14.

95 Supported by Moyd, *Violent Intermediaries*.

96 Yorke, *Northern Rhodesia*, 81.

97 Kwarteng, 'World War 1', 48.

98 Akurang-Parry, 'African Agency', 154 quoting *The Nation*, 27 May 1915.

99 Frederick Njilima, Malawi, Royal Artillery; Bulaya or Samson Jackson, Zambia, 9 London Regiment; Krio FS Dove, Sierra Leone, Tank Corps; Krio Patrick Freeman, Sierra Leone.

100 Kuusaana, 'Impact', 82–3.

101 Cole, 'Sierra Leone', 29.

102 Cole, 'Sierra Leone', 74–5; Osborne, *Kikamba*.

4 National aspirations against war fatigue

Uses and mechanisms of mobilising propaganda in World War I Greece

Elli Lemonidou

Abstract

Mobilisation campaigns during the First World War in Greece had to consider the (often conflicting) impact of three distinctive factors: the still-dominant idea of fulfilling national aspirations, the war fatigue shared by large parts of the population and the sharp division in domestic politics over the role of the country in the Great War. In this chapter, I examine how these factors influenced efforts by Greek governments to persuade citizens about the importance of serving their country, as well as how authorities used specific vectors of propaganda (such as press and other kinds of publications) for that purpose.

The history of Greece in the First World War is a case of great historiographical interest. Under many aspects, it mirrors the experience of many combatant nations during the war, while at the same time, it possesses many important differences that make it a unique case study which is difficult to approach and understand in depth. This finding applies not only to the international public – the general histories of the war include only a few occasional references to Greece, mainly in the context of the Macedonian Front or, in recent years, in studies about the neutral countries in the war[1] – but also for Greeks themselves, for whom 1914–18 (even in its domestic dimension) remains, for a variety of reasons, a largely unknown page of European and national history.

The same can be said about one of the most intriguing aspects in the history of that war, which regards the use of propaganda to manipulate public opinion and, in a broader sense, to serve political, military and diplomatic objectives in all countries affected by the war. Academic research has stressed in various ways the importance of the First World War in the development of this phenomenon, within the broader context of the expansion of mass communication that had already begun in the second part of the nineteenth century.[2] Among other things, the First World War is inextricably linked to the golden age of the Greek press, which constituted the main (but not exclusive) vector of informing and influencing public opinion before the emergence of broadcast media in later decades.[3]

In the field of propaganda, as it will be shown, the case of Greece is characterised by many peculiarities, which put the country in a somewhat singular position, even when compared to other countries that remained neutral temporarily or throughout the war. Regarding mobilisations, we will see that the role of propaganda was much less oriented (in comparison to other war-afflicted countries) to inspiring people to enrol in the army and participate in the war. However, the three mobilisation decrees during the war set the pace for a wide range of propaganda initiatives focused on the central question about the participation (or not) of Greece in the war and the arguments used by supporters of both sides.

Aiming to shed light on the communicative aspects of the three mobilisation campaigns that took place in Greece during the First World War, this study begins with a general overview of Greek society, communication and propaganda. A detailed presentation of the three recruitment campaigns will follow, focusing on their common and distinctive features and stressing the overall singularity of the Greek case. No less than four different factors (compulsory military service, accumulated fatigue after the victorious but exhausting experience of the 1912–13 Balkan Wars, the persistence and various interpretations of the decade-long aspiration to expand the Greek state and the division in the domestic political scene over the attitude Greece should take in the war) influenced the discourse about joining the army and eventually participating in the war.

Greece, the First World War and the significance of the 'great idea'

Even in the wake of the massive wave of events that marked the hundredth anniversary of the outbreak of the First World War, Greek involvement in this enormously important event of world history remains relatively unknown outside of scholarly circles. From an international perspective, the major historical narratives concerning the war have traditionally been dominated by the history and memory of the Western Front, with other fronts receiving much less attention. As reasonable as this may be, this trend (without being the sole reason) has perpetuated the lack of knowledge about what was happening in other parts of Europe and the world at that time, even if those 'remote' developments in the Balkans or the Middle East were an integral part of the same universal conflict.

Creating inclusive narratives of the war in its entirety, through the horizontal examination of similar phenomena on more than one front, has been a major question for academic research in recent decades. In the particular case of Greece, the limited interest in the First World War is linked to many factors, most notably the overshadowing of the event by later, highly traumatic pages of Greek history, such as the defeat in the Greek–Turkish War of 1922 and, to an even greater extent, the entire 1940s, marked by the occupation of the country during the Second World War and the painful civil conflict that followed.[4] A careful look at the history of Greece during the First World War, however, proves that this is an extremely important, as well as very complicated page in the history of twentieth-century Greece.[5]

Taking into account the latest historiographical trends, which increasingly emphasise the need for a coherent examination of First World War events with local or regional conflicts in the years immediately preceding and following that war, it can be claimed that for Greece, the Great War effectively started with the two Balkan Wars of 1912–1913. Greece emerged victorious from those wars in both military and diplomatic terms, having achieved the most significant territorial expansion since the creation of the modern Greek state in 1830. It was the culmination of the long-standing aspiration (called 'The Great Idea') to integrate all neighbouring Ottoman areas into a new Greek state. This vision had dominated political and public discourse in Greece since the late nineteenth century. Consequently, the outbreak of war in 1914 found the country in a state of collective satisfaction after the successful outcome of the Balkan Wars.

There was, however, much scepticism about the subsequent steps to be taken in pursuit of the Great Idea (despite important territorial gains, significant areas remained out of state borders) but also on the immediate management of certain open issues, such as those concerning Greek-inhabited areas in the newly established Albanian state as well as the treatment of the Greeks of Asia Minor by the Ottoman regime. In this context, a dilemma arose almost immediately regarding Greece's approach to the Great War. Officially, Greece declared neutrality, a position largely dictated by the need to attend to clear signs about the position of the country's two main rivals in the region, namely the Ottoman Empire and Bulgaria. In practice, this position fully served the interests of Germany, which counted on (and very soon secured) the Ottoman Empire's participation in the Central Powers' camp. In the first period of the war, however, Greek neutrality did not conflict with the interests of the Entente, which used active diplomacy to secure the best possible alliances to serve its interests in the region.[6]

A few months after the beginning of the war, two different trends in Greek leadership regarding the country's attitude in the war began to emerge. King Constantine, supported by a strong core of the military leadership, embraced the choice of neutrality, arguing, inter alia, that the Greek army was insufficiently prepared to engage in a very demanding military confrontation with uncertain benefits for Greece. One should not also ignore the strong pro-German feelings nurtured by the king himself and many among the members of his staff, who showed great confidence in the strength of the German Army, considering that it would be impossible to lose the war. On the other hand, Prime Minister Eleutherios Venizelos was in favour of Greece joining the Entente camp, believing that only through this path would Greece have the chance to secure the maximum possible territorial gains in future peace negotiations. Although the first serious incident of the two men's discord had occurred in early 1915, with Venizelos's first resignation following his disagreement with the king over the feasibility of Greece's participation in the Dardanelles campaign, the turning point came in the autumn of the same year, after Bulgaria entered the war on the side of the Central Powers and the Allied Army (or 'Armée d'Orient') landed in Thessaloniki.[7]

The biennium 1915–1917 can be described as one of the most dramatic periods in modern Greek history due to the escalation of tension in the domestic front as a result of the rupture between Venizelos and Constantine, widely known as the 'National Schism'.[8] In the autumn of 1916, Eleutherios Venizelos formed, with the support of Entente, a separate government, which controlled a significant part of the Greek state. In December, Athens witnessed bloody scenes that resembled

National aspirations against war fatigue 51

a civil conflict. During the biennium, the country repeatedly suffered violations of its neutrality, through the overt interventions of the Allied forces that had camped in Thessaloniki and through the German-Bulgarian advance in eastern Macedonia in the summer of 1916. These events exacerbated discord between the two rival factions in Greece, with each side accusing the other of treason. Entente pressure on Constantine culminated in late 1916 and early 1917 in a series of ultimatums and a naval blockade that caused serious problems in supplying the country with food. The coordinated action of the Allies, coupled with some favourable developments on the international diplomatic scene, resulted in the removal of Constantine in June 1917, paving the way for Venizelos to return to power and for the country to enter the war on the side of the Entente.[9]

For all the great difficulties encountered during the first months of his new rule, Venizelos managed to establish a solid army that played a substantial part in the decisive victories of the Allies in the final stage of the war on the Macedonian front. This development, marked by the capitulation of Bulgaria, is considered a pivotal moment in both symbolic and material terms in the defeat of the Central Powers. Despite the wounds suffered throughout the war, Greece tried to make the best out of its contribution to the Allied victory during the Peace Conference in Paris, temporarily achieving a settlement favourable to its interests in the Treaty of Sevres (1920).[10] However, this treaty was never implemented on the field because of radical changes in the political, military and diplomatic scene regarding Asia Minor and the subsequent defeat of the Greek army in the Greek–Turkish war in 1922.

Channels and content of propaganda in Greece in the early twentieth century

Before proceeding to the specific examination of the use of propaganda in the context of World War I campaigns in Greece, it is appropriate to consider the general framework of informing and disseminating ideas in the country during the period under consideration. This reveals the options available to the opinion leaders of the time and the landscape of ideas and perceptions in which they were trying to communicate their messages.

The case of Greece is not isolated from that of many European countries, for which the First World War is inextricably linked to the absolute primacy of the press.[11] There are, of course, major divergences because of the country's small size and its relatively short history as an independent state. The Ottoman past left several structural deficiencies in the country, which struggled for a long period of time to modernise its infrastructure and economy. Particularly noteworthy was the slow pace of urbanisation, which resulted in a large part of the population living in rural areas during the First World War. As a consequence, involvement in armed conflicts caused great upheaval in Greek society.

Greece had nevertheless experienced a remarkable expansion of its press sector since the last decades of the nineteenth century. During this period, the first professional efforts were made to create newspapers focused on information, which subsequently became an essential feature of daily urban life.[12] The newspaper

52   *Elli Lemonidou*

boom owes much to the rise of public literacy, but it was also rooted in techno-logical advancements that improved the production process and accelerated the flow of information. The first 10 years of the twentieth century were particularly significant in Greece's press history due especially to the appearance of several important newspapers, which subsequently would become an integral part of Greek public life for decades to come.

The main obstacle to the smooth functioning of the press as a forum of pub-lic dialogue has always been the close association of newspapers with political entities or factions, which impeded the development of independent papers. This partisan journalism, dictated by the will of the publishers and their political con-nections, would have a decisive role in 1914–18.[13]

Another important channel was the publication of books or small booklets, as well as articles in literary reviews. Even if the total number of these publications was rather limited and their readership not very broad, their importance for public debate should not be overlooked. In these texts, in fact, all the new ideological trends appeared in a more articulated way than in the newspapers, while their readership – for example, school educators or high-ranking officials – often acted as transmitters and propagators of these ideas. In the same category, we can clas-sify a number of clubs or associations, which had been a very important part of public life during the last decades of the nineteenth century, retaining a smaller though still notable role in the 1910s. In general, intellectuals and the educated public who had direct access to intellectuals' speeches and writings constituted, despite their heterogeneity, a small but very influential group in Greek society. This gave them a high degree of authority and contributed to the easier penetra-tion and wider acceptance of the ideas they mediated.

Last but not least, and a very important factor, was the content of public discourse. In this regard, we must emphasise the absolute dominance, for many decades, of one single topic in both political and intellectual discourse in the country: the already-mentioned Great Idea. From the second half of the nineteenth century until 1922, this issue was central to many public interventions by any available means. The very essence and purpose of that collective aspiration was hardly ever questioned during this period. The only thing that changed, from time to time, was the content that each speaker or writer gave to the Great Idea and the means to achieve it, as well as the positive or negative assessment of the role played by some politicians in this context. In this way, the national question became a privileged field for the formulation of noble declarations and for sharp criticism of political opponents.

Just before the beginning of World War I, the debate on the Great Idea had reached a very particular moment. Greece's huge territorial gains in the Balkan Wars had created a totally new basis for discussion about the strategy to be under-taken in the future. Celebratory references in the press (in which the two future rivals in the National Schism, Venizelos and Constantine, were almost equally praised) appeared together with more sceptical texts on the management of the new reality, emphasising the need to fully integrate new areas and make careful steps to acquire additional territory. The outbreak of war in the summer of 1914 put an abrupt end to this transitional phase. Greece had to decide on its position in the Great War, which created at the same time opportunities and dangers for the national cause. Opinion makers responded immediately to this new reality, creating a new framework for public dialogue in Greece.[14]

The mobilisation of 23 September 1915

Greece was one of many countries that had introduced conscription for a large majority of the male population before the war. Conscription had been used periodically in Greece since the late nineteenth century but was introduced as an explicit provision of the Hellenic Constitution in 1911.[15] Consequently, the question of recruiting voluntary soldiers was never raised inside the country, though the need to promote morale, cohesiveness and discipline among conscripted servicemen was nevertheless essential. Taking this into consideration, it becomes particularly important to examine in each of the three campaigns the degree of responsiveness of the call to arms, the perceptions that were formed for each such decision and, of course, the modalities and arguments used to ensure the successful enforcement of each decision.

The first mobilisation during the war was declared on 23 September 1915, under the pressure of a similar move initiated by Bulgaria a few days earlier. Even if the mobilisation was supported by both Constantine and Venizelos, disagreement over its interpretation and consequences caused a rift between the two men in the following days. On a first level, the campaign had a preventive and defensive character, given the suspicion about the stated goals of the Bulgarian mobilisation. However, it became quickly the subject of sharp political confrontation. The royal side insisted that the mobilisation was not going to change Greece's choice of neutrality. On the contrary, Venizelos tried to link the mobilisation of the Greek army with the situation in the Balkans and the immediate threat of a Bulgarian attack on Serbia. It was claimed that, in such a case, Greece should support Serbia on the basis of an agreement signed by the two countries in 1913.[16] In order to cover the deficit of the Serb military forces provided by the agreement to be present on the border with Bulgaria, which Serbia was not able to satisfy at that moment, a proposal was made to ask for Entente assistance. This demand essentially paved the way for the arrival of the Allied military corps in Macedonia, a move that brought Venizelos much closer to fulfilling his aspiration for Greece's participation, under the best possible terms, in the Entente alliance. Coexistence with the king became then virtually impossible; almost simultaneously with the arrival of the English and French troops in Thessaloniki, Venizelos was forced to resign.[17]

It can be said, therefore, that the mobilisation of September 1915 had very particular characteristics. Its very substance was soon undermined by political and diplomatic interests, at a time when alliances and the balance of power on the Balkan Peninsula were rapidly changing. At the military level, moreover, the difficulties encountered in implementing the measure were significant due to organisational and budgetary problems. It is no coincidence, therefore, that historiographical research over the years has dealt less with the details of the event and

54   *Elli Lemonidou*

much more with its consequences – the mobilisation is just seen as the first link in a chain of decisive developments in domestic political life closely connected to Greece's role in the war.

On a purely communicative level, the message accompanying the call to arms was simple and referred to the need for Greece to respond to Bulgarian actions and confirm its military readiness, in case there would be a direct threat to Greek territory. It appears that there was, on a first level, a consensual acceptance of this message by both Venizelists and Royalists, as evidenced by newspapers close to either of the two sides on the day following the announcement of the mobilisation.[18] The same papers transmitted a climate of restrained enthusiasm in the streets of Athens upon hearing the news. This cannot be compared with the much-discussed pro-war spirit that prevailed in some Western European countries in the beginning of the First World War and not even with an emblematic case of war enthusiasm in later history of Greece (mobilisation against the Italian invasion in October 1940). Although the present status of research does not allow drawing definitive conclusions about the real situation in the country as a whole, it seems that the majority of citizens understood why they were called to arms and were prepared to fight, if necessary, against the Bulgarians. Civil and military authorities, therefore, did not have to undertake any particular campaign to secure popular consensus.

On the contrary, much more complex and demanding were the efforts to allure public opinion after the Venizelos–Constantine rupture. From that point on, a relentless 'war' began between the two sides, mainly through columns in party-biased newspapers, defending Venizelos's pro-Entente stance on one side or the neutrality adopted by the king while denouncing the role of the Allied forces in Thessaloniki on the other. The autumn of 1915 brings in action, for the first time with such intensity during the war, the networks of organized propaganda, focusing on the needs of each of the rival factions in Greece. Such networks were supported, to a lesser or greater extent, by the leading forces of the Great War coalitions outside Greece. There is, therefore, a great paradox: a mobilisation which, by itself, was rather insignificant, as far as the subject of this study is concerned, proved to be the fuse for the gradual expansion of the propaganda phenomenon in Greece, setting the agenda and the main arguments that would be dominant in the public sphere for some years. The 1915 mobilisation remained in force as a negotiating weapon for the Greek state until June 1916, when it was suspended under pressure by the Entente, in the dramatic aftermath of the surrender of Fort Rupel to the German-Bulgarian troops.[19]

The mobilisation of 18 April 1917

The second Greek mobilisation took place in April 1917 and is also characterised by many particular features. At the time of the decree, the National Schism was a definitive reality, following the establishment of the Provisional Government of Thessaloniki in the fall of 1916. Shortly afterwards, the bloody incidents of December in Athens further aggravated the tension. The gap between the two sides appeared to be unbridgeable. While the Central Powers did not decide to launch a general offensive against the Allied positions in Macedonia, the Entente forces were escalating their pressure towards the royal government of Athens, which would eventually lead to the overthrow of Constantine. Even though in the ranks of the Entente there was no uniform attitude towards the pro-Venizelist movement in Thessaloniki, Great Britain and France, which had an active presence in Macedonia, welcomed the formation of the Provisional Government. They could now count on a friendly structure of power in the area where they had camped, and they showed willingness to provide all possible support in order to consolidate its prestige in the areas under its control.

The creation of a strong and reliable army was seen from the outset as a matter of utmost priority for the Venizelist side; however, the realisation of such plans encountered many difficulties. The first deterrent was the financial strains of the regime and its total dependence on foreign aid – it is no coincidence that the general mobilisation order in the areas controlled by the regime could only be issued when a part of the promised support was sent to Thessaloniki. To tackle the problem, Venizelos tried, without success, to secure the support of wealthy Greek communities abroad. A second difficulty arose from the supportive feelings for the king that existed in a part of the population and were particularly detectable in the military. Finally, the factor of fatigue from the accumulated burden of the Balkan Wars and the first – unnecessary, as it turned out in practice – mobilisation of 1915 should not be underestimated.[20]

Taking all this into account, but also having experienced the diminished enthusiasm for joining the movement in several areas since the fall of 1916, Venizelos arranged, at the time of general mobilisation, to pass through his own propaganda networks two clear messages: the first one hinted at the purely patriotic nature of military mobilisation, whose sole purpose was to halt the Bulgarian advance in Greek territory; the second was a rather moderate approach to the king, with the emphasis on his readiness to work with him again under certain conditions. This last argument was of particular importance, because one of the main concerns in the ranks of ordinary citizens and officers regarded a possible contestation of the royal institution as a whole (and not only of Constantine) by Venizelos; rival propaganda rushed to exploit this fear. The pro-royal camp also sought to build on the population's reluctance to engage in a new war, openly accusing Venizelos for his 'pro-war' and 'adventurous' attitude.[21]

Even if Venizelos did use his friendly press to pass on the messages related to the mobilisation, there is another factor that has to be taken in consideration in this case: as the areas controlled by the provisional government were almost entirely provincial, with many islands among them, the appeal to the population passed to a large extent through the networks of local officials and opinion makers created by Venizelos, a particularly popular figure in regions recently incorporated into the Greek state.[22] However, under the influence of all the factors mentioned earlier, in several cases, the recruitment was met with reluctance or even active resistance from the local population, forcing the provisional government to resort to violence and other coercive measures.[23]

The difficulties encountered by the regime in this process, despite the careful discourse of its leader and the purposeful use of propaganda tools, can be viewed as a precursor to what would happen about a year later, in the third mobilisation during the war. It was now clear that the patriotic message alone was not enough

56   *Elli Lemonidou*

to encourage the population to rally around the idea of serving their country, while the poison of National Schism had penetrated deep into Greek society, preventing the development of any project that could easily be perceived (and denounced) as an arbitrary and unilateral action of the other side.

The mobilisation of 22 January 1918

The third mobilisation in Greece during the First World War can be considered the most important one, as it involved the whole country – and not just a specific part of it, as in the case of the provisional government in 1917 – and, above all, was directly linked to the country's active involvement in the war, contrary to the pre-emptive character of the 1915 general mobilisation. It is also the most well-known and discussed in Greek historiography, mainly because of the serious obstacles recruiters faced and the repressive measures they ultimately took to overcome these difficulties. This dimension introduces the 1918 mobilisation into the general question about the refusal to engage in warfare, which was observed during the last period of World War I hostilities and has become one of the major issues of scholarly interest worldwide in the last decades.[24]

The mobilisation was declared by the government of Venizelos, who had returned to the duties of prime minister in June 1917, following the removal of King Constantine. The domestic political change sealed Greece's formal entry into the war by the Entente camp. Venizelos had every reason and interest in wanting the country to participate as quickly and effectively as possible in the Allied forces. Having, since the outset of the war, his eyes firmly focused on post-war peace negotiations, he believed that an active involvement of Greece in a possible Allied victory would substantially strengthen the future negotiating position of the country. However, this desire was not easy to fulfil in the short term. Venizelos had already encountered difficulties in recruiting the population in areas that were theoretically under his complete control and where he was, in any case, very popular. By the time of his return to the prime minister's office, the unresolved problems had multiplied: the country was in dire financial straits and still struggling to heal the wounds left by the long Allied blockade. A significant part of the population, especially in the cities, had been severely affected by the impact of this blockade on economic life, especially on the supply chain. In addition, Greece had to cope with the trauma of the National Schism and its dramatic consequences. Even after Constantine's removal and exile to Switzerland, his supporters in Greece remained active and blamed Venizelos at any opportunity for all the suffering the country was facing.[25]

In this context, Venizelos had to wait several months and focused on seeking funds abroad to complete the military organisation of the forces recruited by the provisional government of Thessaloniki before the conditions were considered right to resort to general conscription. The decree was issued on 22 January. To ensure its successful outcome, all available means were used, such as the pro-Venizelist press, thriving due to the supremacy of the party leader, clubs, civic associations and intellectuals loyal to the regime, as well as local networks of influence. Texts and posters of the time include references to Venizelos's leading figure, defamation of both the former king and the Central Powers, as well as invocations of atrocities performed against the Greeks in the previous years. This campaign was aimed at the patriotic feeling of the Greeks, but it also clearly took into account the strong popularity still enjoyed by Constantine, attempting to deconstruct it through evidence and arguments, which focused mainly on the responsibility of the royal side for the Bulgarian advance and occupation of Eastern Macedonia in 1916.[26]

Venizelos was, however, confronted with the phenomenon of war weariness, which had been exacerbated by the hardships of 1916–17 and public reluctance to participate in the war but mainly by the profound flaws in national unity caused by the National Schism. Royal propaganda made the most of this situation in order to provoke what we might call a war of attrition towards Venizelos. Organised either directly by Constantine and his close connections in Switzerland, where the former king now resided, or from circles adhering to him in Greece, the anti-Venizelist campaign created many obstacles aimed at minimising the people's fighting spirit. From the perspective of royal propaganda, participation in the war was a personal challenge of Venizelos rather than a national strategy. In the most extreme cases, this contributed to the outbreak of incidents of disobedience and indiscipline in the first period after mobilisation. Faced with the visible risk of completely losing control of the situation and failing in his aspirations to create a reliable army – an explicit commitment to his allies – Venizelos resorted to measures of violent suppression against rebels in the military.[27] At the same time, he followed a policy of persecuting political opponents, many of whom were forced into exile. The substantial rebuilding of the army was one of the main gambles won by Venizelos in his struggle to impose his will in the domestic field, while he also continued his intense diplomatic efforts. Among other things, he decided to organize from a new base the pro-Greek propaganda network abroad, aiming to strengthen the image of the country in view of post-war settlements.[28]

The third and decisive mobilisation led to the formation of an effective Greek military force, which had a significant contribution to the Allied victory on the Macedonian Front in September 1918. Although Venizelos tried to use propaganda weapons to ensure the success of recruitment, he essentially lost the communications war, because his political opponents succeeded in penetrating important parts of Greek society with their own countervailing messages. This made it necessary to impose strict military discipline and political persecution. Thus, the architect of an organised system of promoting Greek interests abroad temporarily lost the battle of public opinion at home. This serves as the ultimate proof of the complex and unstable character of propaganda initiatives, especially as they were orchestrated in Greece and elsewhere in 1918.

Conclusion: from neutrality to participation – recruiting in a divided country

An overview of the three general mobilisation efforts that took place in Greece during the First World War and the communication strategies associated with them confirms the great importance of the subject, the specific features of the Greek case, as well as the significant difficulties that exist for its in-depth study and codification. Greece is characterised by the almost exclusively domestic character of propaganda aims and argumentation, but also for the very interesting fact that a series of rather unimpressive mobilisation campaigns in various moments of the war have served as turning points for the emergence of important propaganda campaigns inside the country.

From the preceding analysis it becomes clear that each of the three recruitment drives had very specific characteristics. The 1915 decree could be described as a tactical move, more symbolic than material. The campaign of 1917 had a structural character, as it primarily served the aim of the revolutionary government to create a military force from scratch, and the 1918 mobilisation was the only purely warlike venture, serving the purpose of Venizelos (agreed with the Allies and explicitly formulated inside the country) to offer the greatest possible contribution to the Macedonian Front.

Three decisions, so different as far as their targeting and their potential are concerned, were inevitably characterised by a diversified field in terms of communication strategy and management. The conditions of 1917 and, to a bigger extent, those of 1918 were much more pressing for the formation of strong military forces than the 1915 preventive mobilisation. On the other hand, public opinion appeared to be much more prepared to accept the rightfulness and feasibility of such a move in 1915, in comparison to the divided and troubled Greek society in the last two years of the war.

There is a very special connection between the three mobilisations and the way in which they were conducted, as well as with the general phenomenon of propaganda in Greece during the war. The actions undertaken to promote the purposes of each of the mobilisations had by themselves a relatively limited scope and impact. In other words, the case of Greece cannot be compared with some countries where extensive and sophisticated campaigns took place designed to persuade citizens about the importance of participating in the war effort. It is obvious that compulsory military service in Greece played a key role in that direction. However, especially in the cases of 1915 and 1918, the general mobilisation decrees were the first link in the chain that led to an outburst of propaganda activities in the country, reflecting the absolute rupture between the two opposing camps of Greek political life.

Concerning the channels and the typology of propaganda (as a whole and in the specific cases of mobilisations) during the period under review, we see the dominant role of newspapers (with a striking use, as in other European countries, of images, despite the limited technical means of the time) and, to a lesser extent, other print material. Traditional structures of influence, especially in small provincial communities, were also preserved. Given the broader ideological climate of the period, it is also interesting to note that the concept of defending the homeland against specific enemies was thoroughly invoked in the calls to arms. References to great national aspirations were rather rare in this context, while the broader international framework of after-war visions was totally absent. A third dimension, partially linked with mobilisation, concerns the extent of propaganda and the introduction of organised forms in its conduct throughout the war, with the decisive involvement of foreign powers and their supporters in Greece, adding an innovative element to Greek public life.

Finally, if we try to put the Greek case within the broader European context, we certainly have to mention many particular features, which largely reflect the overall singular position of Greece in the panorama of First World War history, as a country that experienced one year of official neutrality (until the fall of 1915), one year of full involvement in the hostilities (after June 1917) and an intervening two-year period during which the boundaries between participation and non-participation were blurred. On the other hand, key aspects of the cultural history of war throughout Europe are present in the Greek example: the centrality of the national press, the rapid development of organised propaganda, the great importance of the home front, and cases of indiscipline and war fatigue (like in other countries, but under completely different conditions) in the last two years of war. This conclusion offers crucial arguments for the increasing research interest in First World War Greece and other cases that have hitherto remained marginal in general historical narratives of the war. Studying them will help create a much more accurate and comprehensive history of strategies and instruments used in the call to arms, as well of the ways in which societies lived the experience of a universal war, both in and out of the battlefields.

Notes

1 Samuël Kruizinga, 'Neutrality', in *The Cambridge History of the First World War*, Vol. 2, *The State*, ed. Jay Winter (Cambridge: Cambridge University Press, 2014), 542–75; Elli Lemonidou, 'Une neutralité inflammable ou quand tous désiraient la Grèce en tant qu'alliée', in Ineke Bockting, Béatrice Fonck and Pauline Piettre (eds.), *1914: neutralités, neutralismes en question* (Bern: Peter Lang, 2017), 109–19.

2 Anne Rasmussen, 'Mobilising Minds', in Jay Winter (ed.), *The Cambridge History of the First World War*, Vol. 3, *Civil Society* (Cambridge: Cambridge University Press, 2014), 390–417.

3 Jean-Noël Jeanneney, *Une histoire des médias. Des origines à nos jours* (Paris: Seuil, 2000).

4 Elli Lemonidou, 'La Première guerre mondiale des Grecs: une guerre oubliée', in Elli Lemonidou (ed.), *Cent ans après: la mémoire de la Première Guerre mondiale / One Hundred Years after: The Memory of the First World War* (Athens: École française d'Athènes, 2018), 187–99.

5 See the reference works by George B. Leon [Leontaritis], *Greece and the Great Powers, 1914–1917* (Thessaloniki: Institute for Balkan Studies, 1974) and *Greece and the First World War. From Neutrality to Intervention, 1917–1918* (New York: Boulder, 1990).

6 Leon, *Greece and Great Powers*, 19–20, 129–32; Christos Theodoulou, *Greece and the Entente, August 1, 1914–September 25, 1916* (Thessaloniki: Institute for Balkan Studies, 1971), 30–8, 100–1; Elli Lemonidou, *La Grèce vue de France pendant la Première Guerre mondiale, entre censure et propagandes*, Unpublished PhD (Paris: Paris-Sorbonne (Paris IV), 2007), 21–33, 47–54.

7 Ibid., 38–41, 54–60.

8 Giorgos Th. Mavrogordatos, *1915: O Ethnikos Dihasmos (1915: The National Schism – in Greek)* (Athens: Patakis, 2015).

9 Leon, *Greece and Great Powers*, 396–489; Yannis Mourélos, *L'intervention de la Grèce dans la Grande Guerre (1916–1917)* (Athènes: Institut français d'Athènes, 1983); Lemonidou, *La Grèce*, 190–248.

60　*Elli Lemonidou*

10　Ibid., 354–63, 409–40; Dimitri Kitsikis, *Propagande et pressions en politique interna-tionale. La Grèce et ses revendications à la Conférence de la Paix (1919–1920)* (Paris: PUF, 1963).

11　William Mulligan, *The Origins of the First World War* (Cambridge: Cambridge University Press, 2017), 136–79.

12　Nasi Balta, 'I exeliksi ths eidhseografias stis ellinikes efimerides ton 19o aiwna (1830 k.eks.)', ('The Evolution of Newswriting in the Greek Newspapers in the 19th Century, from 1830 Onwards', – in Greek), in Loukia Droulia (ed.), *O ellinikos typos. 1784 ews shmera. Istorikes kai theoritikes proseggiseis* (*Greek Press from 1784 until Nowadays: Historical and Theoretic Approaches*). Proceedings of an International Conference. Athens, 23–25 May 2002 (Athens: National Foundation of Research, Institute of Modern Greek Research, 2005), 65–70.

13　Despoina Papapdimitriou, 'O typos kai o dihasmos', ('The Press and the National Schism', – in Greek), in Thanos Veremis and Gioula Goulimi (ed.), *Eleutherios Venizelos. Koinwnia – oikonomia – politiki stin epohi tou* (*Eleutherios Venizelos: Society-Economy-Politics in his era*) (Athens: 'Gnwsi', 1989), 425–34.

14　Thanos Veremis, 'Apo to ethniko kratos sto ethnos dihws kratos. To peirama ths Organwshs Kwnstantinoupolews', ('From the National State to the Nation without State: The Experiment of the Constantinople Organization', – in Greek), in Thanos Veremis (ed.), *Ethniki taytotita kai ethnikismos sti Neoteri Ellada* (*National Identity and Nationalism in Modern Greece*) (Athens: MIET, 1999), 27–52.

15　Dimitris Malesis, *Htta – Thriamvos – Katastrophi. O stratos sto ellhniko kratos apo to 1898 ews to 1922* (*Defeat-Triumph-Catastrophe. The Army in the Greek State from 1898 to 1922* – in Greek) (Thessaloniki: Epikentro, 2017), 64.

16　Frank Maloy Anderson and Amos Shartle Hershey, *Handbook for the Diplomatic History of Europe, Asia, and Africa 1870–1914* (Washington: Government Printing Office, 1918), 441–3; Édouard Driault, *Histoire diplomatique de la Grèce*, Vol. 5 (Paris: PUF, 1926), 118–21; Lemonidou, *La Grèce*, 18–22.

17　Elli Lemonidou, 'Propaganda and Mobilizations in Greece during the First World War', in *Propaganda and the First World War*, ed. Troy Paddock (Leiden: Brill Publishers, 2013), 274–9.

18　See the front pages and editorials of *Patris, Empros* and *Skrip* on 24 September 1915. Please note: all newspaper publication dates are based on the Julian calendar used in Greece until 1923.

19　Lemonidou, *La Grèce*, 38–45, 171–88.

20　Ibid., 190–201, 296–317.

21　Lemonidou, 'Propaganda and Mobilizations', 279–82.

22　For a vivid account of how mobilization pursued its goals in the Greek island of Lesvos, see the novel of Stratis Myrivilis, *Life in the Tomb*, trans. Peter Bien (Hanover, NH: University Press of New England, 1977).

23　Hellenic Army General Staff, Army History Directorate (= HAGS, AHD), *A Concise History of the Participation of the Hellenic Army in the First World War 1914–1918* (Athens: Army History Directorate, 1999), 103–4.

24　Pierre Renouvin, 'L'opinion publique et la guerre en 1917', *Revue d'histoire moderne et contemporaine* 15 (January–March 1968): 14–17. Jean-Jacques Becker, 'L'opinion publique française en 1917', *Historiens et Géographes* no. 315 (July–August 1987): 1499–505, id., *1917 en Europe. L'année impossible* (Bruxelles: Complexe, 1997).

25　Lemonidou, *La Grèce*, 321–9.

26　Ibid., 330–41.

27　Hellenic Army General Staff, Army History Directorate (= HAGS, AHD), *A Concise History of the Participation of the Hellenic Army in the First World War 1914–1918*, 157–8.

28　Lemonidou, 'Propaganda and Mobilizations', 286–9.

5   Winning the battle to lose the war

The *Call to Arms* recruiting campaign in Australia, 1916

Emily Robertson

Abstract

Promotional activities concerning recruiting in Australia during the Great War had unique salience due to the fact that voluntary recruiting was maintained throughout the conflict. The 1916 Call to Arms campaign, which has been under-examined by historians, occupies an important position in the story of voluntary recruiting, as it was the last major campaign to take place before Australia was politically divided by two failed conscription plebiscites. The campaign was both successful and unsuccessful: while it attracted the promised extra 50,000 men to join the Australian Imperial Force, the tactics employed served to alienate other potential recruits and marked the beginning of heated debates about conscription that overshadowed recruiting until the close of the war.

In early 1916, councillors at a meeting of the Blaxland Shire in rural New South Wales (NSW) were considering the logistics of a federal campaign to raise 50,000 men to serve in the Australian Imperial Force (AIF). The scheme, which required volunteer members of the local recruiting committee to personally meet and interrogate men who had refused to join, caused concern. Councillor Burgess complained of having to chase up local men: 'they want to send us out as a lot of cadgers [beggars]'. He was particularly troubled about being involved in a scheme that would force him to confront his neighbours. Councillor Nicholls condemned the organisation of the campaign, stating, '"These folk couldn't build fowl houses"'.[1] The scheme, which was officially known as the *Call to Arms* campaign, was controversial and ushered in a period of bitterness and deep division that lasted until the end of the war. Autocratic and poorly organised on the federal level, the campaign employed techniques that one contemporary journalist described as 'almost coercion'.[2] Yet despite the negative publicity the campaign attracted at the time, it was also a remarkable success, reaching the target of 50,000 recruits.[3] At the local level, campaigners enthusiastically approached recruits with a range of campaigning techniques, from recruiting meetings to route marches. The campaign was also significant in that it was integral to establishing bureaucratic systems that allowed the voluntary system to limp through the remaining years of the war.

62   Emily Robertson

Despite its success in raising 50,000 extra men, the campaign has been regarded by some historians as a failure. 'If it was the purpose of the *Call to Arms* appeal to apply pressure to those who had so far refused service', Bart Ziino has written, 'then it was certainly a failure'.[4] Joan Beaumont has noted that the campaign 'was counterproductive' and was regarded as 'veiled conscription' by its opponents.[5] This was a significant issue, because the campaign ushered in a very challenging period in Australian history, in which the country became polarised between those who wanted to maintain voluntary recruiting and those who wanted to introduce conscription. The *Call to Arms* is significant therefore not just in terms of its short-term success but also as a lens through which to examine the developing schisms that emerged in Australia over the issue of conscription.

It is also a particularly unusual campaign to examine in terms of the complexities of marketing recruiting in a period of near-total war. This chapter is a case study that examines both the power and the limits of persuasion: where men had the capacity and willingness to join, they did. Where they did not have the ability or interest in enlisting, they ignored the call. In simple marketing terms, the recruiting 'product' being promoted in the *Call to Arms* had a limited appeal to the range of eligible men in Australia, and following this successful campaign, the 'pool of willing recruits', as Ziino observed, 'had essentially dried up'.[6] The sharp decline in recruiting numbers following the campaign suggest that while it was successful in attracting the large number of remaining willing recruits, the 'product' of voluntary recruiting simply did not appeal to others.

For some of those who were hesitant about enlisting, the tactics and messaging of the campaign pushed them into becoming actively resistant. The abrasive style and disorganisation of the campaign (which included repeated breaches of privacy of those who refused to enlist) served only to alienate them further. *Call to Arms* exacerbated the growing hostility within the labour movement towards the conflict and paved the way for the brutal conscription plebiscites of 1916 and 1917. It marked the beginning of open conflict in Australian discourse about whether or not a voluntary recruiting system was sufficient.

Essentially, recruiters won a battle only to lose the broader war, ushering in a period of division, paranoia and anger from which Australia was only to partially recover after the war ended. It also represented the last phase in which a large number of Australians embraced voluntary recruiting before the cost of the war became widely apparent.

Recruiting and publicity in Australia in the First World War

Why Australian men enlisted during the First World War remains a topic of debate amongst Australian historians. As Peter Stanley has noted, 'who knows why many men and women went to war? No one asked them, and when they expressed a view it may have been . . . from individual motives too complex to be subsumed under the rhetoric of nation'.[7] More problematically for scholars of propaganda, there was no measurement taken of the efficacy of publicity campaigns. We have evidence of reasons for individuals joining in J. N. I. Dawes and L. L. Robson's book, *Citizen to Soldier: Australia before the Great War, Recollections of Members of the First AIF*, which was based on correspondence with men about their reasons for enlistment. This book tracked the varied reasons Australian men chose to risk their lives at war through correspondence of veterans which had been collected in the 1960s. 'Nation, empire, money and family' were 'constantly recurring motives' in the letters Dawes and Robson received.[8] Bill Gammage, too, in his book, *The Broken Years*, discerned patterns in reasons for enlistment, including a sense of outrage at the behaviour of the German military.[9] While this information is useful and interesting, it does not relate directly back to the recruiting campaigns of the war. As Leanne Green has pointed out, 'there was no measuring instrument of effectiveness for war publicity during the First World War' in Great Britain. Nor was there such an instrument in Australia.[10]

In the case of the *Call to Arms* campaign, however, we can correlate recruiting numbers with a specific recruiting drive. What is novel about the *Call to Arms* campaign is that there were no other complicating factors (such as the news of the defeat at Gallipoli) to explain the rise in enlistments, and there is convincing quantitative evidence that the *Call to Arms* campaign had a positive impact on recruiting numbers. In December 1915, just before the campaign began in earnest, total enlistments across Australia in December were 9119. By the end of January 1916, enlistments had more than doubled to 22,101 men. While the number of men enlisting declined over the next few months, both February and March saw the continuation of a large flow of men into the recruiting depots (18,508 and 15,597, respectively).[11]

Factors such as improvements in pension arrangements for the recruiting spikes in January to March can be discounted, as pensions for soldiers' dependents were not increased until late May 1916, well after the increase in enlistments. The amendment to the War Pensions Bill was important, as rates for permanent disability were raised by 50 per cent and may have had a role in attracting more married men to the AIF than had previously been the case.[12]

What is beyond dispute is that the numbers of men enlisting increased in the period in the first three months of the *Call to Arms* campaign and sharply decreased afterwards; in July 1916, only 6179 men enlisted. Therefore, while the quantitative data available is not comprehensive, perhaps the main factor that can account for the significant increase in enlistments between January and March 1916 was the *Call to Arms* campaign, which has received little attention from scholars.[13]

What perhaps made the campaign a success was not necessarily the publicity material or techniques employed but the sheer ferocity with which it was approached across Australia. The material itself, using appeals to 'King and Country', duty, and the use of recruiting marches, was not new.[14] There was, however, a more concentrated focus on the use of both returned and actively enlisted soldiers in public events. This, coupled with the mailing of appeal cards to men who were deemed to be eligible across Australia and the widespread reporting in the press, made the campaign omnipresent for a period.

The *Call to Arms* campaign was launched in mid-December 1915. It was an enormous enterprise that required people across the Australian community to act as voluntary recruiters. The former federal director-general of recruiting, Donald Mackinnon, recalled that the campaign led to the creation of recruiting committees 'in almost every town and village throughout the [Australian] Commonwealth'. Cards

64   *Emily Robertson*

were mailed out to eligible men, and any refusals to join the AIF were followed up personally with 'a vigorous canvas' by recruiting bodies.[15] The campaign had been triggered by pressure from the British Army Council to increase their enlistment rate, Beaumont has written, to almost 'fifteen times that promised in August 1914'. *Call to Arms*, which targeted the eligible men that had been identified by the War Census, was based on Lord Derby's original recruiting scheme in Britain.[16]

An important element of the campaign lay not in the publicity material that was produced (i.e. posters and pamphlets) but in its reliance upon the much more ephemeral public relations activities of events and personal engagement with potential recruits. There are only three extant posters in collections relating to the campaign. The small number of posters produced was most likely a result of the small sums of money available from the federal government for producing campaign material. New South Wales produced a simple, text-only poster that appealed to duty and patriotism to both the Empire and Australia.[17] South Australia created a poster of a frowning kangaroo set against the backdrop of soldiers in silhouette wielding bayonets. It asked the viewer if they would 'help us keep that promise' to the British government to provide more men.[18] Victoria was reportedly planning on producing a recruiting poster based on territorial names for battalions, but this poster is not extant in collections.[19]

Given that a wide range of posters have survived from other recruiting campaigns but so few from the *Call to Arms* campaign, it is reasonable to surmise that community events and relationship building were the primary promotional vehicles. Events like recruiting marches and concerts, speeches and face-to-face encounters between recruiters and potential enlistees were held across Australia by both the small local recruiting bodies and state authorities. Thus, while the campaign was federal, smaller organisations had their own ideas about how to best engage local communities.

In February 1916, for example, soldiers who were on leave in the small Queensland town of Maryborough 'requested the recruiting sergeants' conduct a street march. This was in response to the poor showing of enlistments. 'With the Australian flag flying', wrote the reporter for the *Maryborough Chronicle*, 'and to the rat-tata-tat of the kettle drum, they paraded along the main business thoroughfares, singing the soldier's ditty, "Go and get our Dungarees on"'. Three new recruits fell into line in the parade, which, the *Maryborough Chronicle* stated, was 'very encouraging for an initial march'. A march was planned for the following day, and all returned soldiers and those on leave were requested to join.[20]

In the case of Maryborough, the march had been in response to a disappointing enlistment rate. In contrast, in the small city of Richmond in Victoria, a march of new recruits was planned to 'hold up Richmond's example for other districts to emulate'.[21] Community pride combined with community pressure was one of the central means through which the *Call to Arms* message was amplified. Within the community sphere, the coercive element of the top-down organisation of the campaign (for example, the use of the federal census to find the addresses of eligible men) was transmuted into the more intimate pressure of relationship management.

The campaign also drew upon the presence of both returned and serving soldiers. The men who had seen battle were a reasonably new sight in Australia. The first

Winning the battle to lose the war 65

wave of wounded soldiers returned home in July 1915, and others continued to arrive after that. Some ended up in the criminal courts, disturbed by their experiences in the war, and others were brought in to support recruiting.[22] Because wounded men were not a common sight at this phase in the war, recruiting organisers were keen to involve them in campaigns. In organising the metropolitan launch of the *Call to Arms* campaign in December 1915, the secretary of the State War Council of South Australia, Victor H. Ryan, requested that Colonel Sandford, the military commandant, provide the names of wounded returned soldiers in order to address recruiting meetings. They were to be used as a grim kind of military spectacle; in addition to serving members of the AIF participating in a parade, the Secretary also intended for 'a few wounded soldiers . . . to take a seat on the platform'.[23]

The uniform in and of itself was regarded by civilian recruiters as a unique publicity tool that they wanted at their disposal. Ryan also asked for a uniformed Recruiting Sergeant to be present at recruiting meetings 'in order to take the names of Recruits who offer'. The secretary was particularly keen to have uniformed men at as many meetings as possible, as he believed 'that in the Suburban areas especially some special means are absolutely necessary in order to awaken interest in this campaign'.[24] There was a belief that the sight of a man in uniform would make the previously uninterested civilian aware of the importance of the war effort and inspire him to join. This arguably naïve perspective was challenged during the course of the war, as recruiting authorities recognised that men were more likely to be persuaded with improved pay and conditions.[25]

These tactics, combined with the appeal cards and the personal follow-ups from recruiters, ultimately proved to be effective, and by June, the federal government declared that they had attracted the promised 50,000 men. However, the backdrop against which the campaign took place was complex, and this meant that while these community-oriented tactics were successful with some men, they served only to alienate others. This was partly due to poor organisation of the logistics of the campaign and partly due to the manner in which the campaign became tied in with the concept of conscription.

Conscription, coercion and the *Call to Arms* campaign

The *Call to Arms* campaign was the last significant voluntary recruiting campaign to take place before the issue of conscription came to dominate recruiting. Although Australia never adopted conscription during the Great War, the issue eventually overshadowed all recruiting matters after the first failed conscription plebiscite in 1916. As the number of voluntary recruits continued to decline, Prime Minister William Hughes attempted to drive through conscription in a second plebiscite in 1917, which also failed. The conscription campaigns, recalled the director-general of recruiting, 'had created a spirit of direct hostility' which made it very difficult for the voluntary recruiting system to attract recruits.[26] However, while the failed conscription plebiscites wreaked a large amount of political damage – for example, Labour Prime Minister Billy Hughes was expelled from the Labor Party after the first conscription plebiscite – an examination of the *Call to Arms*

66   *Emily Robertson*

campaign demonstrates the issue of conscription was already creating divisions well before the conscription plebiscites.

As Ziino has demonstrated with his analysis of negative responses to the *Call to Arms* forms, conscription was regarded by some men as the ideal solution to the recruiting problem.[27] So too did many who served on recruiting committees. Indeed, the issue of conscription was not new amongst people of influence and was being discussed quite early in the war. In September 1915, a resolution from the Ballina Recruiting Association informed the Federal Parliamentary Recruiting Committee (FPWC) that they had adopted a resolution in favour of compulsory service.[28] In the same month, Gavin Duffy, Secretary of the FPWC, invited federal parliamentarians to assist with speaking at a NSW recruiting campaign. Labour MP Frederick Bamford declined, his reason being that he was 'in favour of conscription, and these appeals for voluntary enlistment are but feeble attempts to dodge the inevitable, appeals which I cannot endorse'.[29]

Given the strength of pro-conscription sentiment that already existed in Australia, it is not surprising that the issue of conscription hovered over the *Call to Arms* campaign from the beginning. In Penshurst, Victoria, politician Walter Manifold stated that the appeal was a test of the voluntary system. Recruiting authorities 'were determined to give the voluntary system every chance, but if men would not come forward voluntarily, other means would have to be employed, as the Federal promise would have to be redeemed'.[30] Amongst the organisers, there was the view that the campaign could provide the organisational capacity to quickly introduce conscription. The Queensland Recruiting Committee (QRC) noted in a letter to the Commonwealth Statistician, George Handley Knibbs, that the completed appeal cards would 'simplify matters in the event of conscription being introduced. We could start calling up any particular group of males at a moment's notice'.[31]

The fear on the part of the working class that the campaign was potentially a ruse to introduce conscription was therefore not entirely unfounded. One day after the campaign was launched, A. D. Jones of the Agricultural Implement Makers called for members of the Trades Hall Council to boycott the cards, stating that 'the new recruiting scheme was disguised conscription'.[32] The Bendigo Trades Council in Victoria also passed a resolution that people should refuse to fill in the cards. The Brisbane Industrial Council responded to the campaign by threatening to 'withdraw its support for the Labour candidate' standing in former Prime Minister Andrew Fisher's seat 'unless the federal government radically amended the scheme'.[33] Through a combination of threats and blandishment, the Labour government managed to silence the unions on the matter. Although the threat to not return the cards was later withdrawn, the early negative response does demonstrate the extent to which the phrasing in the appeal cards could be interpreted as a presage to conscription.[34]

The appeal cards, sent to eligible men throughout Australia, had all of the hallmarks of Prime Minister Hughes's choleric nature – perfunctory, forceful and coercive – and were worded:

> Are you willing to ENLIST NOW? Reply "Yes" or "No."
> If you reply "Yes" you will be given a fortnight's notice before being called up.

> If *not* willing to enlist *now,* are you willing to **ENLIST AT A LATER DATE?** Reply "Yes" or "No," and if willing, state when.
>
> If **NOT WILLING TO ENLIST,** state, the reason why, **AS EXPLICTLY AS POSSIBLE.**[35]

While there were some strong responses within the labour movement to the cards, other elements were less prone to brinkmanship. The *Australian Worker* chose to accept the situation 'with some degree of tolerant resignation', believing that the information contained in the cards would demonstrate either way that conscription was impracticable: if successful, the scheme would 'sound the death knell of conscription'. Alternatively, should the response to the scheme be 'inadequate, its very inadequacy will prove beyond all doubt that a big majority of those directly concerned are against fighting at all – and, therefore, of course, against conscription in any shape or form'.[36]

Objections to the appeal cards were not just based upon concerns about conscription but the general tone of the cards. Their invasive nature inevitably drew 'rude' responses from some potential enlistees. In South Australia, the Secretary of the State War Council (SWCSA) complained to the FPWC that some of the negative replies were 'frivolous and decidedly discourteous, and some cases contemptuous'.[37] In some cases, the men refused to fill out the cards at all. In New South Wales, James H. Catts, Secretary of the State Recruiting Committee, complained to George Pearce, Minister of Defence, that men were destroying the cards and in some cases 'purposely changing their boarding houses from one suburb to another to avoid being communicated with'.[38] In response, the War Precautions Act was extended to place the 'obligation on the person of obtaining the appeal and reply form'. The penalties for non-compliance were escalated to a potential 500 pounds and a period of one year in prison.[39]

The coercive nature of the campaign lay, therefore, not just in the abruptly worded appeal cards but in the manner in which those who failed to reply, or provided 'unsatisfactory' replies, would be followed up. Firstly, 'defaulters' who did not send back a form were asked again to send a reply; if they did not do this, 'failure to comply with this instruction will be followed by prosecution'.[40] This was a problematic threat to make, given that for various reasons (including incorrect addressing of appeal cards), many of the appeal cards were unclaimed. By 21 January 1916, several thousand appeal cards had already been returned to the central Bureau of the Postmaster's Office (colloquially known as the Dead Letter Office).[41] By May, 40,000 unclaimed forms were languishing in a Post Office in Queensland.[42]

The disorganisation of the campaign coupled with threats of prosecution was provocative. At a general level, and even outside of the labour movement, the cards had created 'a great deal of misapprehension'. The *Darling Downs Gazette* noted that while 'the rabid socialist organisations' were concerned the appeal was a gateway to conscription, there were also 'a great many, earnest and most loyal people who have not quite grasped the purport of the scheme that is now being put into operation'.[43]

In Victoria, both conservatives and socialists were disturbed by the way the scheme was to be rolled out. Sir Alexander Peacock, the Liberal Premier, was opposed to the power given to recruiting committees to determine 'whether a man's reasons were satisfactory or not'. He believed that 'any young man of spirit

68   *Emily Robertson*

would resent the method by which the appeal was made'. George Elmslie, the leader of the Victorian Labor Party, was equally concerned, stating that the campaign was 'inquisitorial'.[44] Elmslie did not believe Victoria had behaved in a manner that warranted 'anything savouring of dragooning [coercing]' and believed that the 'wrong method' for gaining reinforcements had been employed.[45]

The large number of negative responses by eligible men had an important impact upon the pro-conscription movement, as it led some within the voluntary recruiting movement to believe conscription was the only answer to the recruiting problem. Halfway through the campaign, recruiters began to actively canvas organisers at both the state and federal levels to introduce conscription. In March 1916, the local recruiting committee of Gawler South Australia wrote to the SWCSA and stated that, 'judging by the unsatisfactory nature of the replies . . . and consequently the failure of the voluntary system of recruiting', conscription needed to be introduced. The local Gawler committee felt that some of the men treated the question of enlistment 'with contempt'.[46] The secretary of the local recruiting committee of Port August agreed with this view, sarcastically describing one man he believed to be evading enlistment as a 'splendid sample'. Other men the committee could simply not 'deal with' as they were trenchantly refusing to join, even after a follow up from the Recruiting Sergeant.[47] Port August's local recruiting committee's view that 'conscription' was 'the only way out' was echoed in multiple letters to the state and federal recruiting bodies.

Pro-conscriptionists also seized upon the fact that some men stated in the appeal cards that they would not enlist until conscription was introduced. In a letter to the FPWC, Western Australia's local recruiting committee in Eastern Freemantle declared the voluntary system a failure:

> the majority of men favour conscription and are prepared [to join] if this came about. . . . The Committee is of the opinion that conscription of single men should be resorted to at once, and married men to follow when necessary in order of the number of their dependents.[48]

'As a principle', Ziino has written, 'conscription offered a way of ensuring that all would be obliged to present themselves', from married men to those 'hiding behind their wealth'.[49] The promise of conscription challenged the voluntary system and made it difficult for recruiters and potential recruits to take the principle of voluntarism seriously. *The Call to Arms* campaign marked the beginning of open, dogged opposition to the voluntary recruiting system, both by those within it and by those outside of it.

Recruiting and the slow path to federalism

Another of the key challenges facing Australian recruiting authorities was not just the vast size of the country and the distances that needed to be traversed but also the fragmented nature of the federal system at the start of the war. Although Australia had federated in 1901, states remained dominant until the war acted as a stimulus for national systems to be developed. Over the course of the conflict, the commonwealth progressively extended its sphere of influence. The first federal income tax was introduced in 1915 along with the formation of the AIF, Australia's first overseas national military force.[50] An efficient national censorship system followed, and eventually a federal recruiting system was implemented.[51]

That the recruiting and propaganda system was dominated by the states at the start of the war is therefore not surprising, as this situation reflected the nature of Australia's federation in its early phase. While Section 51 of Australia's constitution clearly articulated the commonwealth government's areas of responsibility, which included defence, many undefined residual powers remained in the hands of the states; they therefore assumed responsibility for war effort promotion at the outbreak of war.[52]

The most important positive contribution of the *Call to Arms* campaign to the recruiting effort was the establishment of centralised state recruiting bodies that were in direct contact with the FPWC. Donald Mackinnon, who eventually became the head of the federal recruiting system, recalled that the *Call to Arms* campaign had necessitated a strengthening of 'the recruiting movement' through a 'strong Central Executive' in each state, which were either called 'State War Councils' or 'State Recruiting Committees'. Recruiting Sergeants, whose first role was to follow up unsatisfactory replies, were 'employed in great numbers', and smaller local recruiting committees were 'formed in almost every town and village throughout the Commonwealth'. The FPWC took on the role of attempting to coordinate the campaign, although the task was so large and the responsibilities of the individual states so heavy that complete co-ordination was elusive.[53]

Although the FPWC sought to be the 'central committee' in leading and controlling recruiting, and the states were to 'act in conjunction with the Committee in each State', the reality was that the federal government had little control over the material and methods employed by the states. With the exception of two posters published by the FPWC (a large Union Jack poster being the most popular), ephemera, from pamphlets to posters, were produced by states and not the federal government.[54] Indeed, the costs of promotion were largely borne by the states. In August 1915, following the creation of the State Recruiting Committees and War Councils, the acting secretary of the Department of Defence asked if, given the organisations were producing 'specially designed posters and patriotic literature', the federal government could defray their costs by 'providing postage stamps'?[55] Another letter from late October 1916 asked the FPWC to pay for the postage costs of Critchley Parker, who was an independent propagandist (and newspaper owner), to send pamphlets to Queensland. Parker was a very important propagandist for the war effort, as he reprinted and distributed a large amount of atrocity propaganda from Europe.[56]

The discrete budgeting of promotional material by state rather than federal government reflected the limited distribution of information between the bodies about campaign tactics. The lack of a centralised, controlling body meant that states were highly self-contained. As part of the reassessment of the recruiting system from the fallout of the first conscription plebiscite, Professor Ronald G McIntyre,

70 *Emily Robertson*

Chairman of the NSW State Recruiting Committee, observed of the recruiting system, 'At present each State is so far as recruiting is concerned a kind of watertight compartment'.[57]

This lack of centralisation and clear organisation directly impacted the roll-out of the *Call to Arms* campaign in a number of interlinked ways. Communication between states and the federal recruiting authorities was poor, particularly in relation to recruiting numbers, and this led to key messaging becoming confused. Essentially, states were incapable of focusing beyond their own borders. For example, Frank Clarke of the Victorian SWC issued a circular stating that no more recruits were needed – just as the federal campaign was being planned to attract 50,000 more men.[58]

The chaotic nature of the system also meant that confidentiality of the appeal was compromised. This was highly problematic given the increasingly heated environment over the issue of enlistment and 'shirkers'. The FPWC wanted negative responses to bypass the local recruiting committees and go directly to the state recruiting committees again – and war councils, yet the lack of centralised directions (as well as funding), meant that states were not respecting the confidentiality of those who had refused to enlist. In late December, the head of the local recruiting committee in Launceston, Tasmania, caused some issues when he put out a request via the *Examiner* for 'public-spirited citizens with time on their hands' to 'place their services at his disposal'. He stated, 'Obviously it is impossible for me single-handed to deal with so large a number of replies. Nor can the municipal staff, depleted by enlistments as it is, render any help'.[59] This meant that any member of the community would be able to view the cards, some of which had personal information on them. Senator Pearce asked Gavin Duffy, the president of the FPWC, to remind the Tasmanians that as per the instructions, 'the replies are to be treated as strictly confidential'. The minister was aware that the communities the recruiting committees worked in were small and that some people 'for private reasons, prefer not to disclose information relating to their affairs to the local committee'.[60]

In January 1916, Knibbs was forced to again reiterate the importance of confidentiality to the SWCSA. Knibbs pointed out to Ryan that the purpose of confidentiality was 'to allow the answer to be frank, and at the same time to ensure that local personas should not learn anything of the private reasons which prevented persons offering their services for the war'. It had, however, come to his and the prime minister's attention that 'complaints have arisen of betrayal of confidence'. His solution was, given the system was not working for vulnerable respondents, to place the responsibility upon the respondent themselves: the press would broadcast the instruction that people who did not want the local recruiting committee to view their responses to put it 'explicitly on their enlistment appeal paper'.[61]

Ryan replied that while he had put out a notice in the press that the respondents who wanted their privacy protected needed to direct their replies to the state level, he was somewhat confused about how the whole scheme was to work if the local recruiting committees in the large country regions were not able to see the unsatisfactory responses. 'It is not quite clear', he wrote, 'as to what method should be adopted to follow up those unsatisfactory replies from the country centres'.[62] Knibbs responded with the following solution:

> Where, however, confidential information is given which does not appear to furnish adequate reason for the reply, the local committee should, in most cases, be informed that a reply has been received which contains confidential information, and therefore cannot be forwarded, but that the reasons given do not appear adequate and that local investigation is desirable. Further, in some cases it may be necessary, owing to the nature of the confidential information, for you to communicate by letter directly with the person concerned.[63]

In other words, the replies were not in fact confidential, as the local recruiting committees were ultimately authorised and empowered to approach the writers of 'unsatisfactory' replies. Knibbs's apparently blithe lack of awareness of the contradictions inherent in the campaign was yet another organisational blunder. As the campaign wore on, the absurdity of the lost appeal cards, the paranoia about conscription, the lack of confidentiality and the overall poor coordination between local, state and federal groups began to wear away at the voluntary recruiting system. Despite Catts's claim that the 'vigorous propaganda' of the campaign would 'awaken the recalcitrant and the thoughtless', many potential eligible en continued to refuse to join.[64] These men were not interested in what the government was offering, no matter how many marches and speeches were rolled out. Therefore, while it was true that 50,000 men had been raised, it was doubtful that Australia had much more to give in terms of fresh recruits.

Conclusion: voluntary service, conscription and the shifting tides of public opinion

The campaign indicated that the voluntary recruiting system was in trouble.[65] For pro-conscriptionists, *Call to Arms* was therefore a strange success, since it highlighted the inadequacies of the voluntary system. This opened up a dialogue between pro-conscriptionists within the *voluntary* recruiting movement to begin to agitate for change.[66]

The campaign also revealed that whether it was voluntary or compulsory, the business of recruiting was taking an enormous toll on families and businesses. The pressure of the campaign and the pressures created at home when working men left for the war meant that successful recruitment came at a cost to communities. This was particularly the case in rural areas, which were dependent on seasonal labour. In a heated exchange about the *Call to Arms* campaign with the SA SWC, Mr Alfred Townsend of Lameroo, a rural town in South Australia, threatened to resign from his role if adequate pay were not forthcoming.[67] Townsend was the Secretary of the Local Recruiting Committee and had stirred up the ire of the SWCSA by dismissing the Recruiting Sergeant and prematurely declaring the campaign to be over. The war council found Townsend's letter 'distinctly

72 *Emily Robertson*

disrespectful and improper'.[68] In response to its demand for an apology, he supplied an explanation based on his frustration with balancing the goals of the campaign and trying to maintain a business.

He stated that he had successfully recruited all of his staff and his son – 'the mainstay' of his business – into the AIF. The result had been a labour shortage, which meant the remaining workers in his area felt they could demand '50 per cent additional pay'. Townsend could not afford this so resorted to an 'Australian-born German to go on with the work'. The anti-Germanism by that point was so vicious that the worker was 'intimidated' and Townsend 'was boycotted'. Eventually, Townsend had to accede to the original demand of extra pay and was reportedly told by one worker that he 'should not have been so smart at sending men away'. Townsend completed his letter to the South Australian war council with this plea: 'I had given my Son and both he and myself have sacrificed our business connections, and I venture to think that you will agree, that to be penalised by those for whom you are doing it is hard'.[69]

Townsend's letter encapsulates the frustrations and obstacles facing people who were operating within the voluntary recruiting system. Attempting to both run a business and recruit men, his very success in the recruiting arena had damaged him in the business arena. This paradox applied across Australia generally. It is clear that well before the first conscription referendum took place, Australia was suffering under the impositions of the war both in terms of loss of labour and in terms of widening political divisions about what constituted the fairest way for the burden of the war to be shared.

While Australia certainly did not suffer in the same manner that belligerent countries in Europe did, by early 1916, the Australian social fabric was unravelling. With two more years of war ahead, the recruiting system would incur the shocks of two failed conscription referenda, the unmitigated slaughter of Passchendaele, and the negative impact of the collapse of Home Rule on the Irish Australian population. As the working class rebelled in the Great Strikes of 1917 and the Labor Party began to withdraw support for recruiting in 1918, the voluntary system was on the verge of complete breakdown. Had the war continued past November, Australia – which had 'suffered proportionately higher casualties than any other army in the British Empire'[70] – would certainly not have been able to continue to offer up more men.

Notes

1 'Recruiting Scheme for the 50,000', *Democrat*, 8 January 1916.
2 'How Are We to Raise the Next 50,000?', *The Grafton Argus and Clarence River General Advertiser*, 6 December 1915.
3 'Australia's Army', *Bendigo Independent*, 23 March 1916.
4 Bart Ziino, 'Enlistment and Non-Enlistment in Wartime Australia: Responses to the 1916 Call to Arms Appeal', *Australian Historical Studies* 41, no. 2 (2010): 220.
5 Joan Beaumont, *Broken Nation* (Crows Nest, New South Wales: Allen & Unwin, 2013), 148.
6 Ziino, 'Enlistment and Non-Enlistment', 221.
7 Peter Stanley, 'Eloquent Poppies', *History Australia* 10, no. 3 (2013): 283.

8 J. N. I. Dawes and L. L. Robson, *Citizen to Soldier: Australia before the Great War, Recollections of the First AIF* (Melbourne: Melbourne University Press, 1977), 93.
9 Bill Gammage, *The Broken Years: Australian Soldiers in the Great War* (Australia: Penguin Books, 1990 [1974]), 10.
10 Leanne Green, 'Advertising War: Picturing Belgium in First World War Publicity', *Media, War and Conflict* 7, no. 3 (2014): 323.
11 Beaumont, *Broken Nation*, 447–558.
12 'Soldiers' Dependents: War Pensions Amending Bill', *Daily Advertiser*, 20 May 1916.
13 L. L. Robson, *The First AIF: A Study of Its Recruitment, 1914–1918* (Melbourne: Melbourne University Press, 1970), 74. Robson draws a link between the campaign and the rise in recruitment but does not investigate the link in detail. The peak in January–February was perhaps also partially due to the withdrawal from the Dardanelles in early January, but given the lag in reporting this event in Australia, this is not likely to have accounted for the peak.
14 See Peter Stanley, *What Did You Do in the War, Daddy: A Visual History of Propaganda Posters* (Melbourne: Oxford University Press, 1983).
15 Donald Mackinnon, 22 September 1919 to CEW Bean, Historian, Department of Defence, A[ustralian] W[ar] M[emorial Archives], 38 3DRL 6673/168.
16 Beaumont, *Broken Nation*, 147–8.
17 '50,000 men wanted', JH Catts Organising Committee, 1915 [printer not named]. Collection of the State Library of New South Wales.
18 'Australia has promised Britain 50,000 more men', Adelaide [no printer or publisher recorded]. Collection of the National Library of Australia.
19 'Recruiting Campaign: Appeal for 50,000 Men', *Bendigo Independent*, 31 December 1915.
20 *Maryborough Chronicle, Wide Bay and Burnett Advertiser*, 18 February 1916.
21 'Richmond's Army', *Richmond Guardian*, 5 February 1916.
22 Elizabeth Nelson, 'Victims of War: The First World War, Returned Soldiers, and Understandings of Domestic Violence in Australia', *Journal of Women's History* 19, no. 4 (2007): 90.
23 Secretary SWC to Military Commandant, 2nd Military District, 1 December 1915, GRG 32 Series 1 Item 1, S[tate] R[ecords] O[ffice of] S[outh] A[ustralia].
24 Ibid.
25 Donald Mackinnon to C. E. W. Bean, 22 September 1919, AWM, 38 3DRL 6673/168.
26 Ibid.
27 Ziino, 'Enlistment and Non-Enlistment', 217.
28 Minutes meeting FPWC, 22 September 1915, A13886 FPWC.2 N[ational] A[rchives] A[ustralia], Canberra.
29 FW Bamford to Gavin Duffy, 7 September 1915, FWPC. 10 File No 1 [Part 5] NAA Canberra.
30 'The Call to Arms', *Penshurst Free Press*, 5 February 1916.
31 QRC (correspondent unknown) to G. H. Knibbs, Federal Statistician, 23 May 1916, GRG 32 Series 1 Item 1, SROSA.
32 'Federal Recruiting Scheme: Labor Criticisms and Defence Minister', *The Australian Worker*, 16 December 1915.
33 Beaumont, *Broken Nation*, 148–9.
34 Ziino, 'Enlistment and Non-Enlistment', 219.
35 GRG 32 Series 1 Item 1, SROSA.
36 '50,000 and the Rest: A Consideration of Some of the More Sinister Phases of the Recruiting Scheme', *The Australian Worker*, 23 December 1915.
37 V. H. Ryan Secretary of the SA SWC to the Secretary, FPWC, 6 March 1916, GRG32 Series 1 Item 2, SROSA.
38 Catts to Pearce, 20 January 1916, B539 AIF 144/2/1118, NAA Melbourne.
39 Memorandum, Attorney General's Department, 31 January 1916, B539 AIF 144/2/1118, NAA Melbourne.

74 *Emily Robertson*

40 Knibbs to V. H. Ryan, Secretary SA SWC, 6 July 1916, GRG 32 Series 1 Item 1, SROSA.
41 Duffy to Knibbs, 21 January 1916, FPWC.15, NAA Canberra.
42 QRC to Knibbs, GRG 32 Series 1 Item 1, SROSA.
43 'Enlistment Questions', *Darling Downs Gazette*, 28 December 1915.
44 'New Force: The Recruiting Method Criticised by Politicians', *The Bathurst Times*, 2 December 1915.
45 'The Wrong Way: State Labor Leader's Opinion', *The Australian Worker*, 23 December 1915, 7.
46 Secretary Gawler LRC to SWCSA, 13 March 1916, GRG 32 Series 1 Item 2, SROSA.
47 Secretary Port Augusta LRC to SWCSA, 10 March 1916, GRG 32 Series 1 Item 2, SROSA.
48 Secretary, War Council of Western Australia to Secretary FPWC, 9 May 1916, A13886 FPWC.46, NAA Canberra.
49 Ziino, 'Enlistment and Non-Enlistment', 230.
50 Ernest Scott, *Australia During the War* (Sydney: Angus and Robertson, 1936), 481–2.
51 Nicole Moore, *The Censor's Library* (Queensland: University of Queensland Press, 2012), 30.
52 John Connor, Peter Stanley and Peter Yule, *The War at Home* (South Melbourne, Victoria: Oxford University Press, 2015), 6.
53 Mackinnon to Bean, 22 September 1919, 38 DRL 6673/168, AWM.
54 Duffy to Mr H Whiteside, 6 October 1919, A13886 FPWC.57, NAA Canberra.
55 Minute Paper, acting Secretary of Defence, 18 August 1915, A13886 FPWC.6, NAA Canberra.
56 Memorandum, FPWC, 25 October 1915, A13886 FPWC.6, NAA Canberra.
57 Professor Ronald McIntyre to Donald Mackinnon, Director-General of Recruiting, 17 November 1916, B3B/13 A11085, NAA Canberra.
58 Minutes, FPWC, 28 October 1915, A13886, FPWC.2, NAA Canberra.
59 'Examiner', 31 December 1915.
60 Senator George Pearce to Gavin Duffy, 8 January 1916, A13886 FPWC. 20, NAA Canberra.
61 Knibbs to Ryan, 13 January 1916, GRG 32 Series 1 Item 1, SROSA.
62 Ryan to Knibbs, 19 January 1916, GRG 32 Series 1 Item 1, SROSA.
63 Knibbs to Ryan, 21 January 1916, GRG 32 Series 1 Item 1, SROSA.
64 'The New Army', *Daily Telegraph*, 11 February 1916.
65 SA SWC, intended recipient of letter unknown, 10 December 1915, GRG 32 Series 1 Item 1, SROSA.
66 Emily Robertson and Robert Crawford, 'Activist Nation: Australia and the 1916 Conscription Referendum', in Ani Adi (ed.), *Protest Public Relations: Communicating Dissent and Activism* (Abingdon: Routledge, 2019), 35–6.
67 Mr Townsend to SA SWC, 7 March 1916, GRG 32 Series 1 Item 2, SROSA.
68 Ryan to William Mitchell, Chairman, Pinaroo Recruiting Committee, 17 March 1916, GRG 32 Series 1 Item 2, SROSA.
69 Townsend to SWCSA, 19 May 1916, GRG 32 Series 1 Item 1, SROSA.
70 Beaumont, *Broken Nation*, 488.

6 It takes a good woman to sell a good war

The use of women in World War I United States propaganda posters

Thomas Bivins

Abstract

This chapter focuses specifically on the poster campaign of the US Committee for Public Information and its Division of Pictorial Publicity, created by the best-known advertising and magazine illustrators of the period. Their talents were turned into a world-changing form of propaganda incorporating a range of techniques including the manipulation of gendered symbols used to empower women to become active participants both in sending their men off to war and in supporting them once they were serving. A special element of this campaign was its use of the female figure both as a symbol of American nationalism and as an angelic caregiver. This approach encompassed styles from the mythological to the practical, using persuasive techniques ranging from patriotism to guilt. The idea and definition of propaganda are also explored in an effort to fathom its importance in America's war effort and its status as a communicative technique.

After three years of professing neutrality, during which the United States had walked a diplomatic tightrope, attempting to mollify the Germans while tentatively courting the British and their allies, all reasonable options seemed to have vanished. Seeing no other alternatives, President Woodrow Wilson asked Congress for permission to go to war, and on April 6, 1917, Congress officially declared it. As part of his justification for going to war, Wilson framed it as a crusade to 'make the world safe for democracy'.[1] When Wilson appeared before Congress to declare the entry of the United States into a war that had been raging since 1914, the country was woefully unable to provide the desperately needed fresh troops to relieve their exhausted allies on the battlefields of the Western Front. In May 1917, Congress passed the Selective Service Act, creating a draft that registered 24 million men and supplied sixty per cent of the nearly 5 million American men who served during World War I (WWI). The effective propaganda campaign that preceded and supported that move helped establish an acceptance of the draft, the nation's support for its soldiers, and a common sense of purpose behind the country's involvement in the war.

The great propaganda machine

After having promoted American neutrality since 1914, the government now needed a way to convince the public that American participation in the European

76   *Thomas Bivins*

war was both necessary and essential to saving the world for democracy. On April 14, 1917, barely two weeks after war was declared, President Wilson issued Executive Order 2594 establishing the Committee on Public Information (CPI).[2] Their charge was to act as an agency for releasing news of the government, issuing information to sustain morale in the US, administering voluntary press censorship, and later, developing propaganda abroad. Put more bluntly, the CPI would 'take on the task of explaining to millions of young men being drafted into military service – and to the millions of other Americans who had so recently supported neutrality – they should now support war'.[3] After America entered the war, the CPI used every medium available to create enthusiasm for the war effort and enlist public support for America's war aims. They effectively blended advertising techniques with a sophisticated understanding of human psychology, pioneered by Sigmund Freud and others beginning near the end of the nineteenth century. Its efforts represent the first time that a modern government disseminated propaganda on such a large scale.[4]

George Creel, a progressive journalist from Denver and long-time Wilson supporter, was appointed as the CPI's civilian chairman. Creel's stated goal was to coordinate 'not propaganda as the Germans defined it [which he noted had become associated with deceit and corruption], but propaganda in the true sense of the word, meaning the "propagation of faith"'. For him, 'it was a plain publicity proposition, a vast enterprise in salesmanship, the world's greatest adventure in advertising'.[5] As Creel saw it, 'The Committee on Public Information was called into existence to make this fight for the "verdict of mankind", the voice created to plead the justice of America's cause before the jury of Public Opinion'.[6] Nonetheless, throughout all CPI activities ran a thread of propaganda, recognized or not. James Mock and Cedric Larson noted in their 1939 history of CPI's activities, *Words That Won the War*, that Americans had come to associate propaganda as a term with the work of German agents and saboteurs in the United States.[7] At the same time, they point out that Creel was completely aware that what he was promulgating was propaganda, 'and brilliant were the famous Americans working under him, but the mighty propaganda machine of the CPI was his creation'.[8] They also note that even though most of the CPI didn't view the term 'propaganda' as necessarily negative and believed that their messages were 'more truthful than that of other countries and consecrated to a higher cause', the word was still used without 'value-judgment' in much of their correspondence.[9]

What is propaganda?

Propaganda has been studied as long as it has existed as a form of persuasive communication. According to the Oxford Dictionary, the word 'propaganda' dates to the year 1622, when Pope Gregory XV founded a committee of cardinals responsible for foreign mission. The actual term comes from the Latin *congregatio de propaganda fide* or 'congregation for propagation of the faith'.[10] Up until WWI, the term 'propaganda' had not been widely used, and it has been hard to pin down since then. Journalism professor Ralph D. Casey noted in 1944 that the term 'is

It takes a good woman to sell a good war   77

one of the most troublesome words in the English language. To define it clearly and precisely, so that whenever it is used it will mean the same thing to everybody, is like trying to get your hands on an eel. You think you've got it – then it slips away'.[11] Since WWI, propaganda has most often been defined in negative terms involving manipulation – a word which itself has negative connotations. Jowett and O'Donnell define it as 'the deliberate, systematic attempt to shape perceptions, manipulate cognitions, and direct behavior to achieve a response that furthers the desired intent of the propagandist'.[12] And Brunello paraphrases Jacques Ellul in describing modern propaganda as a 'systematic mode of communication within the world of facts deployed to intentionally distort reality'.[13] The *Oxford Dictionary* currently defines propaganda as, 'chiefly derogatory information, especially of a biased or misleading nature, used to promote or publicize a particular political cause or point of view' and traces the origin of this sense of the word 'from the early twentieth century'.[14] Interestingly, the US military, which, in cooperation with the CPI, pioneered tactical propaganda techniques during World War I, currently uses the term 'propaganda' to refer exclusively to *enemy* communications, defining propaganda as: 'Any form of adversary communication, especially of a biased or misleading nature, designed to influence the opinions, emotions, attitudes, or behaviour of any group in order to benefit the sponsor either directly or indirectly'.[15]

However, several modern scholars have attempted to jog the word free from its negative connotations. According to Krystina Benson, propaganda can also

> propagate useful and desirable outcomes for a group propaganda is not inherently evil – it is neutral. For example, in addition to promoting hatred of the enemy, the CPI also propagated awareness campaigns about sexually transmitted diseases and encouraged the donation of clothes to The Salvation Army for those in need.[16]

Harold Lasswell, an early investigator of psychological persuasion, offered one of the first attempts to systematically define propaganda to assure some degree of validity and reliability in studies of the phenomenon. Propaganda, Lasswell wrote, is 'the control of opinion by significant symbols, or, so to speak, more concretely and less accurately, by stories, rumors, reports, pictures, and other forms of social communications'.[17] Perhaps more importantly, Lasswell took a neutral stance on propaganda as inherently neither bad nor good.

> [Propaganda is] no more moral or immoral than a pump handle. Whether specialization in the technique can be justified in one's mind depends upon the conviction that the long-run interest of society in social harmony will be served by expert mobilization of opinion as they have been served by expert litigation.[18]

In essence, Lasswell believed that propaganda should be understood as a *means*: it can be applied towards ends that may be good or evil. And if propaganda is

78   *Thomas Bivins*

best understood as a technique, it is most easily recognizable when its content represents deception or disinformation; however, that judgment can only be made after the fact.

This is completely in line with the earliest recorded investigation into the techniques of persuasion. Aristotle believed that the propriety of rhetoric could be judged by the communicator's intent, the means used in the speech to further the argument, and the accompanying circumstances. He also thought the integration of reason and emotional appeals was acceptable as long as the speaker advocated for the general public good. He defined the art of rhetoric not as the ability to persuade but as 'the ability to see the possible means of persuasion in particular cases'.[19] Aristotle was trying to strengthen political community, which cannot be done without involving people's passions, yet the ability to elevate them is also the ability to degrade them. It is important to note that Aristotle placed no moral value on the techniques of persuasion themselves. He pointed out that they could be used for good or ill, depending entirely on the *intent* of the user. Ultimately, he believed that the potential harmfulness of rhetoric is outweighed by its potential good, later recognized as a utilitarian perspective. Altheide and Johnson in fact argue that propaganda emphasizes an essentially utilitarian conception of truth and information in which truth is subordinated to the service of expediency.[20]

Near the close of *Propaganda and Persuasion*, Jowett and O'Donnell also conclude that 'Propaganda is not necessarily an evil thing'.[21] Ultimately, propaganda must be evaluated, they say, within its own context according to the *players*, the target *audience*, and its *purposes*. Cunningham agrees. He proposes that there is a widespread assumption that propaganda is ethically wrong, while there is a competing view that, in general, propaganda is inherently neutral.[22] Looking at propaganda through the lens of means/ends can help determine both the efficacy and the propriety of propaganda. He notes that

> the propagandist's attitude toward truth is inherently equivocal: He or she will use either truthful information or disinformation depending upon which is most likely to succeed, but the preferred value is truth. . . . That preference, however, is dictated not by the inherent superiority of truth, but because of its utility.[23]

This definition of propaganda clearly highlights the intention of the propagandist and the one-sided, biased nature of the messages, which in turn leads to a common belief that, as Brunello points out, 'The ends, no matter how noble, cannot justify any means in the use of propaganda'. However, upon investigation, this does not seem a universally valid assumption.[24]

So we return to Aristotle's proposal that persuasion, even propaganda, is just a tool, a technique, which, in and of itself, is neutral. The person who uses it and that person's intent will determine the morality of its use, which can be assessed by looking at the means used and the ends sought. A good end does not necessarily justify questionable means, but it does help. For example, if President Wilson's concern that the very survival of democracy was in question was true, that increases the latitude that might be given to the construction of propaganda. Conversely, a morally unjustifiable end cannot be vindicated by ethical means. For example, the violent use of German military aggression on civilian populations (such as Belgium, a neutral country) could not be justified; thus, neither could the German propaganda machine seeking to obfuscate reality via patriotic hysteria. We must use a modicum of caution, however, in judging the validity of both means and ends. If we take too critical a stance regarding the purpose of propaganda, almost nothing can be justified. For example, if we assume that the practice of propaganda naturally subverts personal autonomy or produces, de facto, a society of mindless patriots, then no amount of moral justification will suffice. On the other hand, if we conceive of propaganda as a necessary component of a larger campaign aimed at righteous goals, then we must regard it as also capable of acting appropriately – indeed require it to do so. The question now is, how did that play out in the propaganda materials, especially posters, produced by the CPI during WWI?

The Division of Pictorial Publicity

Historian and archivist George Vogt, referring to the late entry of America into WWI, notes,

> It is easy to surmise that after three years of watching the war in the European theater, achieving a rapid and high level of public involvement would require more than mere heartfelt entreaties. Isolationism was still a significant cultural obstacle, and support of the war made more sense when it came in the form of something familiar.[25]

That something familiar was advertising. The late nineteenth and early twentieth centuries brought a renaissance of advertising and magazine art. As historian Lynn Dumenil observes, 'the burgeoning advertising industry was intimately tied to the production and distribution of images. Businesses turned to posters to sell products and advertise entertainments. . . . A visual revolution was thus already under way by World War I'.[26] And as with commercial advertising, this first effort of American government to use modern advertising techniques in wartime implies that these posters 'must be judged on one level by their ability to sell their "product"'.[27]

Creel eventually created twenty-one divisions devoted to domestic propaganda alone. These divisions included, among others, the News Division, the Film Division, the Advertising Division, the Speakers Division and, importantly for our purposes, the Division of Pictorial Publicity (DPP). Creel noted early on the importance of visuals to the overall communication campaign.

> Even in the rush of the first days . . . I had the conviction that the poster must play a great role in the fight for public opinion. The printed word might not be read; people might choose not to attend meetings or to watch motion pictures,

80 *Thomas Bivins*

but the billboard was something that caught even the most indifferent eye. . . . What we wanted – what we had to have – was posters that represented the best work of the best artists – posters into which the masters of the pen and brush had poured heart and soul as well as genius.[28]

On April 22, 1917, George Creel met with Charles Dana Gibson in New York City, and the Division of Pictorial Publicity of the Committee on Public Information was formally launched. Gibson was one of the most well-known illustrators in America at the time and had been since the end of the preceding century. His work appeared in advertising and in magazine illustration, and he was credited with the creation of the 'Gibson Girl', at once a representation of the 'modern woman' while, at the same time, an iconic version of the 'perfect woman'. Barely a month later, Gibson had taken charge of a committee of artists and illustrators who would form the CPI's Division of Pictorial Publicity. 'It is the greatest opportunity the artists have ever had to serve their country', Gibson observed to the *New York Times*.[29]

The new division under Gibson's command included 279 artists and 33 cartoonists. Among them were such well-known illustrators and artists as N. C. Wyeth, Howard Chandler Christy, Harrison Fisher, Joseph Leyendecker, Edward Penfield, Jessie Wilcox Smith, and James Montgomery Flagg, all of whom were already recognized for their work in advertising and magazine illustration.[30] In conceiving the nature and form of his division's posters, Gibson, who had long been a supporter of America's entry into the war, constantly encouraged his artists to create posters that focused on ideas, not events. 'We must see more of the spiritual side of the conflict and we must illustrate the great aims of this country in fighting this war'.[31] In an interview for the *Philadelphia Record* toward the end of the war, Gibson explained what he was trying to show through his division's work. 'The spirit that will lead a man to put away the things of his accustomed life and go forth to all the hardships of war is not kindled by showing him the facts. . . . We are being purged with fire, and the work of the artist will be to catch the new spirit of the people, to blow on the new flame'.[32] Alexandra Petri says Gibson and his committee undertook to do more than illustrate:

> They sought to inspire. Few set forth the uplifting character of the Progressive war effort in such glowing words and images as Gibson, who proved an ideal – and idealistic – ally in Creel's efforts to enlist the minds and hearts of the American people. . . . Gibson could well appeal to great aims and spiritual elements of conflict because America's war effort had become, in the hands of Creel and other home-front Progressives, not a military but a moral undertaking.[33]

Creel bragged that 'America had more posters than any other belligerent, and, what is more to the point, they were the best. They called to our own people from every hoarding like great clarions, and they went through the world, captioned in every language, carrying a message that thrilled and inspired'.[34] In total, the

It takes a good woman to sell a good war 81

United States produced approximately 20 million posters in less than two years. Creel calculated that over the course of the war, the Division of Pictorial Publicity alone accounted for 1,438 designs for some fifty-eight separate departments and agencies.[35] Not surprisingly, hundreds of those designs contained women, because, as Karima Omar points out, 'By viewing nationalism and its rhetoric through the lens of symbolism, it becomes apparent that nationalism is inherently a gendered experience'.[36]

Woman as propaganda technique

As noted, a propaganda campaign could be more successful if it were couched within an already familiar form, such as advertising. At the turn of the twentieth century, advertising illustrators had begun to explore the boundaries of propriety in advertising in order to garner an increasingly greater market. Images of young, beautiful, 'modern' women, such as the Gibson Girl and the Christy Girl, soon became literal icons of visual selling. Given the talent and marketing success of most of its members, it made sense to the Division of Pictorial Publicity that those same advertising icons might transform easily into propaganda icons. And as Susan Grayzel notes, 'That women were seen as vital to the war can be found in one of the First World War's innovations: propaganda produced by governments specifically to shape public opinion'.[37] Almost immediately, posters began to display images of women.

Women's propaganda roles, especially as depicted on posters, covered a variety of categories. The most common were:

- Allegorical/symbolic images personifying such ideals as Liberty, Victory, and Justice (or broadly representing the nation itself);
- Guardian of the home front, contributing to the war effort through labour, conservation practices and fundraising;
- Ordinary women participating in official activities such as the Motor Corps (including ambulance drives), telephone operators in the Signal Corps, and, most frequently, nurses;
- Female victims of the war, especially prior to America's official involvement and again as the casualty figures rose and tempers flared against the enemy.

Martha Banta points out in *Imaging American Women* that what she sees as the two dominant female types depicted in war posters – the Amazon Warrior and the Protecting Angel – actually converge. She maintains that together, they serve to assert American supremacy while also conveying the nation's ability and desire to protect the weak.[38] Similarly, in one of the earlier analyses of the use of women in WWI propaganda, Michelle Shover, like Banta, organizes image categories of women into two groups, essential symbolic figures and service to the war effort.[39] The latter falls neatly into one of the common categories already listed: ordinary women participating in official activities, especially, nurses – or as Banta refers to them, 'protecting angels'. Because they are related, these two types are the focus here.

82 *Thomas Bivins*

Woman as symbol

Historian David Hackett Fischer, in 'The Many Faces of Miss Liberty', says that, 'Popular as Uncle Sam and Yankee Doodle may have been, the most appealing images of liberty and freedom have always been female'.[40] Or, as Banta notes, 'Once the focus is placed on national allegories, females are the figures that count'.[41] By the nineteenth century, the allegorical figure of Columbia was ubiquitous in both advertising and political images. She was often depicted carrying an American flag or a shield with the national arms, or later, the more martial accoutrements of the Roman goddess Minerva, often including a spear and helmet. Her gown ranged from the classical white of Greek goddesses to the colours of the American flag. Her chapeau, when not helmeted, was either covered in stars and stripes or the solid red of the Phrygian cap given to freed Roman slaves and made popular as a 'liberty cap' during the French Revolution. By the time she reached her zenith in the first decade of the twentieth century, she was one of the most easily recognized emblems of the United States, representing above all the idea of freedom and liberty and the strength and the fortitude of a nation.

Marina Warner, Author of *Monuments and Maidens*, in a 1986 piece for *The New York Times*, pointed out that because allegory is 'an integral part of our common language', no one has ever had difficulty deciphering it.[42] However, some warned then and have suggested since that the use of allegory is not productive in poster design because of its ambiguity. For example, the National Committee of Patriotic Societies, formed in February of 1917, represented dozens of nationalistic organizations dedicated to the mission of preparedness. Its stated mission was to coordinate the work of member societies by compiling publications, issuing bulletins on war work, and facilitating communication with federal agencies. As part of that work, the NCPS developed a series of pamphlets, one of which dealt specifically with printed propaganda: 'How to put in Patriotic Posters the stuff that make people Stop – Look – Act'. In it they advised publicity agents to avoid allegorical imagery in favour of explicit illustrations. Their belief was that the 'common man' could not be motivated by nuance, only by direct messages.[43] Nonetheless, Perlinger and Hacker note that 'although a cultivated audience would surely recognize the exact source of an image, it was not necessary to do so; the general population would respond instinctively to the high diction of the picture and both its overt and subliminal message'.[44]

Michelle Shover holds that 'probably the most anomalous symbolic figure attributed to women in posters was that of the Spirit of War. The women so portrayed were almost always classically, sometimes romantically-draped, heroic figures who project alternately stateliness, sensuality, or furious wrath'.[45] This figure, in various guises yet always recognizable, appeared quickly on posters calling for the enlistment of troops. Although it had been Wilson's original desire to use only volunteers, it soon became clear this would not meet the need. Barely three weeks after war was declared, only 97,000 had volunteered for service. Wilson was forced to accept the recommendations of his Secretary of War to institute a draft. Approximately 2.8 million men were drafted into service by the end of the war, and another 2 million volunteered to serve in the existing branches of the armed forces.[46] According to Murphy and White,

> CPI's domestic efforts during the war met with a high-degree of success: draft registration – the first since the tumultuous call-up of the Civil War – occurred peacefully, bond drives were over-subscribed, and the American population was, generally, supportive of the war effort.[47]

Early posters made frequent use of the traditionally garbed Columbia, usually in either white gown or tri-collared clothing, topped with a liberty cap and often waving an American flag. One of the most ubiquitous posters prior to but in anticipation of America's engagement in the war was 'Columbia Calls' featuring Columbia in a white gown and liberty cap holding a flag and a sword while standing on North America on top of a globe (see Figure 6.1). The poster represents a collaborative effort between its designer Frances Adams Halsted and the artist Vincent Aderente and includes text of a poem by Halsted in the lower right corner. The first line, in the poetic style of the time, reads,

> Awake! ye men from dreams of Peace – Nor sleep when danger's near.
> But fling Old Glory to the breeze – There are no cowards here!

The image of a classically tall and powerful figure with an imposingly large flag captures attention. Although she is armed with a sword, her face doesn't show aggression as much as determination. *The New York Times* announced plans to print 500,000 copies as posters, intending to use the proceeds to establish a home for orphaned children of American soldiers and sailors.[48]

One of the best-known artists of the war, James Montgomery Flagg, recognized more for his image of Uncle Sam urging YOU to enlist than his portrayal of Columbia, nevertheless used the female image quite heavily. He produced almost exactly the same Columbia image for each poster in which she appeared. Whether she is embracing soldiers and sailors or planting seeds in her War Garden, she is uniformly dressed in a gown of stars and stripes, a red liberty cap, and Grecian sandals indicating her classical lineage. In Flagg's 'The Navy Needs You', we see a crowded scene with elements layered in each visual ground (see Figure 6.2). The background is beset by a stormy sky, with a burning Europe in the distance contributing to the heavy cloud layer. In the foreground is a well-to-do young man standing on a wind-blown beach reading a newspaper. Just off to his side with a hand on his shoulder is a young sailor with his other hand gesturing toward the gathering storm. The message on the poster reads, 'The navy needs you! Don't read American history – Make it!' Over the couple's shoulder in the middle ground, mediating the background and foreground, floats an image of Columbia clothed in her standard uniform, with sword and flag in hand, propelled by the addition of angelic wings – her face clearly pleading, even worried. The poster is personalized with the address of the local recruiting station on East Twenty-Third Street in New York City.

Figure 6.1 'Columbia Calls', designed by Frances Adams Halsted, painted by Vincent Aderente

Source: Library of Congress, Prints & Photographs Division, WWI Posters, LC-DIG-ppmsca-50012

It takes a good woman to sell a good war 85

Figure 6.2 'The Navy Needs You', James Montgomery Flagg
Source: Library of Congress, Prints & Photographs Division, WWI Posters, LC-USZC4–8890

86 Thomas Bivins

There was no single formula for depicting the allegorical figure of America. Each artist imbued their images with their personal artistic standards and beliefs. Yet as Charles Dana Gibson forcefully pointed out, imparting the 'spiritual side' of the conflict was of utmost importance. The image changes, and the appeal is varied, but the goal remains the same. Aside from military recruitment, the most frequent appearance of Columbia and Lady Liberty was on posters heavily pushing the purchase of Liberty Bonds. Liberty bonds were first utilized during World War I to support the allied cause. Subscribing to the bonds became a symbol of patriotic duty in the United States and introduced the idea of financial securities to many citizens for the first time. This allowed private citizens to purchase a bond to help support the military effort. After the war, the bond could be redeemed for its purchase price plus interest. The image of Columbia/Liberty, however, did change depending in large part on the artist.

One of the best-known illustrators of the period, Howard Chandler Christy, was already famous for his pre-war images of glamorous young women who came to be known as the 'Christy Girl'. His 'girl' seemed to transition easily into posters without any loss of what had made her popular in the first place – a thinly veiled, almost untouchable, yet inviting sexuality. As Pearl James notes, 'In American World War I posters the sexual appeal common to commercial advertising of that period frequently found its way into the images'.[49] It's not surprising that Christy's posters tended to transform the classical image of Columbia into an image more familiar to modern consumers of advertising. Christy's Liberty Bond posters, especially, move the Columbia figure into a literal erotic zone. In his 'Fight or Buy Bonds' poster, she appears with some of the classic props – a white, Grecian-like gown and a waving American flag. She seems to be leading an army of men marching just behind her with a facial expression that could be both desperate and pleading (see Figure 6.3). This is not surprising given that the third Liberty Bond drive was enacted in April of 1918 after shortcomings of the first two drives. What is most different, however, is that her 'classic' gown is alluringly diaphanous, with her midriff clearly showing through, her breasts plainly focused in the centre of the poster, and her crotch accented by the tuck of her dress. Christy's girl appears frequently in his posters, sometimes eschewing the gown for a man's oversized military uniform with a come-hither invitation to 'join up' on her face. Christy's sexualized version of Columbia even reappears as a nurse on his poster 'The Spirit of America'.

Protecting angels

American nurses had been serving overseas even before the United States officially entered the war. With nearly a million American troops in Europe by the summer of 1918, it was clear they would need more medical assistance. Although the Red Cross was a peacetime organization, President Wilson announced that an appointed War Council would take over its leadership shortly after US involvement began overseas. In order to recruit nurses, the CPI became intimately involved with the Red Cross's publicity campaign, including its extensive poster output. The images used often mimicked the female forms already developed

Figure 6.3 'Fight or Buy Bonds', Howard Chandler Christy
Source: Library of Congress, Prints & Photographs Division, WWI Posters, LC-USZC4–9735

88   *Thomas Bivins*

for other posters, basically young heroines. According to the Red Cross, many of these images were less than accurate; however, these 'romanticized – almost angelic – visions of women appealed to nurses' patriotism and sense of compassion for soldiers on the front line'.[50] This appeal may also have had something to do with a shift from the symbolic version of women to a more realistic version of women's work (see Figure 6.4). Shover points out that '[a]mong all the types of posters the nursing posters are among a small group that show women as the dominant figures for men'. In these posters, the figure of strength is the woman – a literal role reversal. The men, she says, 'are clearly the helpless, appealing figures of sympathy'.[51] Nonetheless, the 'protecting angel' motif continued.

The Spirit of America, created for the American Red Cross, also illustrates an archetypal Christy beauty (see Figure 6.5). In this image, he has melded his diaphanous-gowned Columbia with a Red Cross nurse. The gauzy, transparent nightgown-like frock and the billowing American flag mark her as a sort-of Columbia clone; although her liberty cap has now been replaced with a nurse's cap and a veil (not actually used in the war), or as Rother notes, it is somewhat reminiscent of a nun's habit.[52] Although the giant red cross in the foreground and the printed message make it clear that it's supposed to be for recruiting women, the image sends mixed messages of sexuality and angelic calm.

A beautiful female image, often clutching the US flag or sometimes even dressed in a flag, suggested why the nation was fighting, while other posters explicitly used beautiful women to signify that America's honour was at stake and we needed fighting men to protect it. She often appeared as encouraging or pleading. She gradually changed from the ethereal image of the 'woman in white' to the 'woman in armour' as the CPI grew more forceful and their campaign became almost pure propaganda. And, as the war progressed, the Lady Liberty represented by the original Columbia began to be replaced by the 'new' Lady Liberty – the one that had been erected in New York harbour at the end of the nineteenth century. J. C. Leyendecker's image of a transitional Columbia/Lady Liberty being fully armed by a Boy Scout kneeling at her feet is an example of this change (see Figure 6.6).

Conclusions

While Columbia/Liberty was central to propaganda posters, primarily for recruiting and Liberty Bonds, most of the representations of women perpetuated traditional concepts of appropriate gender roles, especially as homemakers. And although the images of an American goddess may have stirred the blood of patriotism, they also often imparted a mixed message. According to Gomrad,

> She is the girl next door; she is daughter, sister, mother, grandmother, and all the defenceless persons who depend on men to protect them. She is family, home, and everyday life; She is also Lady Liberty and Lady Justice. She is our way of life and the nation itself, which are both in grave danger.[53]

Very briefly, the image of Columbia was revived in aid of the suffrage movement in the US, but it never achieved the prominence it had during WWI. Charles Dana

It takes a good woman to sell a good war 89

Figure 6.4 'In the name of mercy give', Albert Herter
Source: Library of Congress, Prints & Photographs Division, WWI Posters, LC-USZC4–9738

Figure 6.5 'The Spirit of America', Howard Chandler Christy
Source: Library of Congress, Prints & Photographs Division, WWI Posters, LC-USZC4–8369

Figure 6.6 'Third Liberty Loan Campaign: Boy Scouts of America', J. C. Leyendecker
Source: Library of Congress, Prints & Photographs Division, WWI Posters, LC-USZC4–1127

Gibson, the head of DPP, produced very few posters of note during the war, but as a cartoonist, he had drawn a number of *Life* magazine covers prior to America's entry into the conflict utilizing the image of Columbia actively supporting US involvement. His last use of Columbia on a *Life* cover came in October 1920 as a celebration of the passage of women's suffrage (see Figure 6.7). Otherwise, by then, the image of woman as powerful, national symbol had all but disappeared.

Figure 6.7 *Life* magazine, October 28, 1920, Charles Dana Gibson
Source: reproduced from private collection

It is difficult to point to any one cause of her demise. It could be that because of the war and its painful losses, Americans simply became weary of her message of self-sacrifice. They were ready to move on. Other symbols took her place: The Statue of Liberty was less ambiguous, and Uncle Sam seemed to better represent a newfound American power and its global influence. Whatever the reason, she was, for a while, an influential participant in America's massive propaganda campaign for the hearts and minds of her people.

Jowett and O'Donnell laid out a set of points for the analysis of propaganda, most of which apply here. They include the ideology and purpose of the campaign, the context in which it occurs, the structure of the propaganda organization, the audience it is targeted to, and the media it uses – all of which have been discussed here.[54] By all of these measures, the CPI's propaganda campaign was a success, despite the numerous negative reviews following the war by such notables as Walter Lippmann. In his *Preface to Morals*, Lippmann was insistent that propaganda was by nature 'deceptive' and thus evil.[55] What George Creel judged 'a plain publicity proposition' and 'the world's greatest adventure in advertising', Lippmann analyzed as the 'manufacture of consent'.[56] On the one hand, Lippmann believed that the human mind was prone to the allegorical action of imagistic stereotypes, yet he also believed in the ability of reason to eventually transform prejudicial associations into nuanced opinions and representations.[57]

So we are left with a war that changed the shape and direction of the world and a new form of propaganda that seems to have worked yet has left us with a negative view of its current and future applications. If there is a lesson to be had here, it is that since the time of Aristotle, we have been told that the techniques of persuasion are merely tools, neutral in nature yet guided by the will and intent of their users. Columbia is, in the end, only a symbol, and symbols can be and frequently are manipulated. It is up to those who use propaganda as a means of persuasion to privilege morality over efficiency and to justify, not merely rationalize, their actions.

Notes

1 Wilson's War Message to Congress, The World War I Document Archive: https://wwi. lib.byu.edu/index.php/Wilson's_War_Message_to_Congress.

2 Executive Order 2594, April 14, 1917, in The Papers of Woodrow Wilson, ed. Arthur Link, vol. 42 (Princeton, NJ: Princeton University Press, 1966), 59.

3 Christopher B. Daly, 'How Woodrow Wilson's Propaganda Machine Changed American Journalism', Smithsonian.com, April 28, 2017: https://theconversation.com/how-woodrow-wilsons-propaganda-machine-changed-american-journalism-76270.

4 Library of Congress, Posters: World War I Posters, Background and Scope: www.loc.gov/pictures/collection/wwipos/background.html.

5 George Creel, *How We Advertised America: The First Telling of the Amazing Story of the Committee on Public Information That Carried the Gospel of Americanism to Every Corner of the Globe* (New York and London: Harper & Brothers, 1920), 4.

6 Ibid.

7 Cedric Larson and James R. Mock, *Words That Won the War* (New York: Russell and Russell, 1939), 74.

8 Ibid., 236.

94 *Thomas Bivins*

9 Ibid.
10 Oxford Dictionaries, s.v. 'Propaganda': www.oxforddictionaries.com/us/definition/american_english/propaganda.
11 Ralph D. Casey, online at American Historical Association/ AHA History and Archives/ GI Roundtable Series/Pamphlets/EM 2/What is Propaganda?, 1944: www.historians.org/about-aha-and-membership/aha-history-and-archives/gi-roundtable-series/pamphlets/em-2-what-is-propaganda-(1944)/defining-propaganda-ii.
12 Garth S. Jowett and Victoria O'Donnell, *Propaganda and Persuasion*, 5th ed. (Thousand Oaks: Sage, 2012), 7.
13 Anthony R. Brunello, 'A Moral Compass and Modern Propaganda? Charting Ethical and Political Discourse', *Review of History and Political Science* 2, no. 2 (June 2014): 173.
14 *Oxford Dictionaries*, s.v. 'Propaganda'.
15 Headquarters, Department of the Army, Field Manual 3–53: Military Information Support Operations (January 2013), Glossary-10.
16 Krystina Benson, 'The Committee on Public Information: A Transmedia War Propaganda Campaign', *Journal of Cultural Science* 5, no. 2 (2012): 65.
17 Harold D. Lasswell, 'The Theory of Political Propaganda', *American Political Science Review* (1927): 627.
18 Harold D. Lasswell, 'The Function of the Propagandist', *International Journal of Ethics* 38, no. 3 (1928): 264.
19 Mary P. Nichols, 'Aristotle's Defence of Rhetoric', *The Journal of Politics* 49, no. 3 (August 1987): 675.
20 David L. Altheide and J. M. Johnson, *Bureaucratic Propaganda* (Boston: Allyn and Bacon, 1980).
21 Jowett and O'Donnell, *Propaganda and Persuasion*, 367.
22 Stanley B. Cunningham, *The Idea of Propaganda: A Reconstruction* (Santa Barbara, CA: Greenwood Publishing Group, 2002), 132.
23 Ibid., 237.
24 Anthony R. Brunello, 'A Moral Compass and Modern Propaganda? Charting Ethical and Political Discourse', *Review of History and Political Science* 2, no. 2 (June 2014): 183.
25 George L. Vogt, 'When Posters Went to War: How America's Best Commercial Artists Help Win World War I', *Wisconsin Magazine of History* (The State Historical Society of Wisconsin, Winter 2000–2001), 40.
26 Lynn Dumenil, *The Second Line of Defense: American Women and World War I* (Chapel Hill: The University of North Carolina Press, 2017), 201.
27 Vogt, 'When Posters Went to War', 44.
28 Creel, *How We Advertised America*, 133–4.
29 'C.D. Gibson's Committee for Patriotic Posters: Artists Have Been Organized to Help America Win the War by Flooding the Whole Country with Stirring Pictures', *The New York Times*, 20 January 1918: www.nytimes.com/1918/01/20/archives/cd-gibsons-committee-for-patriotic-posters-artists-have-been.html.
30 James P. McNally, 'The Poster Goes to War', Army Heritage and Education Center, 8 November 2007: www.army.mil/article/6032/the_poster_goes_to_war.
31 The New York Times, Gibson.
32 Quoted in, Louis J. F. Moore, 'Win the War: The Poster as Power', *Philadelphia Record* 3 (27 January 1918): 1 *ff.*
33 Alexandra Petri, 'Progressivism's Last Crusade: Raymond Fosdick, George Creel, and the Moral Mobilization of America in World War I', *The Concord Review* 16, no. 3 (Spring 2006): 70.
34 Creel, *How We Advertised America*, 133.
35 'When Posters Went to War', 44.
36 Karima Omar, 'National Symbolism in Constructions of Gender: Transformed Symbols in Post-Conflict States', *Seton Hall Journal of Diplomacy and International Relations* (Winter/Spring 2004): 49.

It takes a good woman to sell a good war 95

37 Susan R. Grayzel, *Women and the First World War* (Harlow: Pearson Education, 2002), 10.
38 Martha Banta, *Imaging American Women: Idea and Ideals in Cultural History* (New York: Columbia University Press, 1987), 559.
39 Michelle J. Shover, 'Roles and Images of Women in World War I Propaganda', *Politics & Society* 5 (1975): 473.
40 David Hackett Fischer, 'The Many Faces of Miss Liberty', in *Liberty and Freedom: A Visual History of America's Founding Ideas* (New York: Oxford University Press, 2005), 233.
41 Banta, *Imaging American Women*, 567.
42 Marina Warner, 'Eternally Female', *The New York Times*, 18 May 1986: www.nytimes.com/1986/05/18/magazine/eternally-female.html?pagewanted=2&pagewanted=print.
43 See especially Leslie Hahner, 'The National Committee of Patriotic Societies and the Aesthetics of Propaganda', *Rhetoric and Public Affairs* 17, no. 1 (2014): 35–65.
44 Elizabeth Perlinger and Barton Hacker, '"The Spirit of Woman Power"': Representation of Women in World War I Posters', in *History of Warfare: A Companion to Women's Military History*, 459.
45 Ibid., 479.
46 Howard Zinn and Anthony Arnove, *A People's History of the United States* (New York, NY: Harper Perennial, 2015), 364.
47 Dennis M. Murphy and James F. White, 'Propaganda: Can a Word Decide a War?', *Parameters: US Army War College* 37, no. 3 (Fall 2007): 19.
48 World War I: American Artists View the Great War, Library of Congress Online Exhibition: www.loc.gov/exhibits/american-artists-view-the-great-war/online-exhibition.html.
49 Pearl James, 'Images of Femininity in American World War I Posters', in Pearl James (ed.), *Picture This: World War I Posters and Visual Cultures* (Lincoln: University of Nebraska Press, 2009), 281.
50 Nicholas Lemesh, 'From the Archives: Red Cross Nurses in World War I', 2015: https://redcrosschat.org/2015/07/10/from-the-archives-red-cross-nurses-in-world-war-i/.
51 Shover, 'Roles and Images of Women in World War I Propaganda', 469.
52 Laura M. Rother, *World War I Posters and the Female Form: Asserting Ownership of the American Woman*, unpublished thesis (John Carroll University, 2003), 48: https://engagedscholarship.csuohio.edu/do/search/?q=rother&start=0&context=2292565&facet=.
53 Mary Ellen Gomrad, *Visual and Verbal Rhetoric in Howard Chandler Christy's War-Related Posters of Women during the World War I Era: A Feminist Perspective*, unpublished thesis (University of Central Florida, 2007), 23.
54 Jowett and O'Donnell, *Propaganda and Persuasion*, 280.
55 Walter Lippmann, *A Preface to Morals* (New York: Macmillan, 1929), 281.
56 Walter Lippmann, *Public Opinion* (New York: Macmillan, 1922).
57 Lippmann, *Public Opinion*, 103.

7 'A place for everyone, and everyone must find the right place'

Recruitment to British civil defence, 1937–44

Jessica Hammett and Henry Irving

Abstract

This chapter analyses the recruitment techniques employed by Britain's civil defence services before and during the Second World War. Recruitment depended upon a combination of national and local efforts, with formal publicity campaigns complemented by more informal methods such as pressure from family and friends. Using a diverse range of sources – recruiting materials, local and national government records, newspaper reports, civil defence magazines, and personal testimony – the chapter analyses the development of recruitment strategies while also exploring some of the motivations for enlistment described by volunteers. It argues that while national and local publicity was crucial for developing an understanding of civil defence roles and duties, it was often personal persuasion or international events that pushed individuals to volunteer.

In June 1940, an editorial in *The Daily Mail* informed readers that every adult in the country should adopt a new motto, 'It all depends on me', continuing: 'in air-raid precautions there will be a place for everyone, and everyone must find the right place'.[1] Civil defence – originally known as Air Raid Precautions (ARP) – offered a wide range of work on the home front, in the air raid warden, firewatch, rescue, first aid, ambulance, decontamination and fire services. The success of recruitment into these roles was frequently praised. The Home Secretary Herbert Morrison, for example, drew a parallel with the military when he told the House of Commons in June 1941 that 'This army of civil defence people, the vast majority of whom are unpaid, volunteer, and spare-time is extraordinarily typical of the character, the spirit, courage, and the grit of the British people, fighting at times with their backs to the wall'.[2]

There are, however, very few historical accounts of recruitment into civil defence. Where this is considered, the focus has fallen on the difficulty of attracting volunteers to a service that was both underfunded and often criticised, with volunteers regularly accused of 'army dodging'.[3] Despite the language of inclusivity used by politicians, Lucy Noakes and Susan Grayzel have shown that representations of civil defence remained deeply gendered, with Noakes revealing how recruitment material was used to maintain gender hierarchies.[4]

This chapter considers the diverse methods used to attract volunteers in this context. Building on the work of Brendan Maartens, who has considered the pre-war national recruitment campaign, and Lucy Allwright, who has provided detailed analysis of civil defence in London, we show that national and local government worked closely together, and that these formal efforts were complemented by persuasion by friends and neighbours as well as international events.[5] Indeed, we argue that informal recruitment methods were not only crucial as a powerful persuasive tool but could also cut across divisions of gender, class and age.

A 'new chapter'? Establishing the administrative framework

Civil defence was a response to the expectation that the bombing of civilians would be central to any future conflict. The First World War had shown the devastating impact of aerial bombardment and convinced authorities of the need to prepare. This process began in 1924 with the establishment of the Committee of Imperial Defence Sub-Committee on Air Raid Precautions but remained secret until 1935. Recruitment, for its part, did not begin until the formation of an air raid wardens' service by the Home Office, which had overarching responsibility for domestic security, in March 1937.

Nonetheless, the proposals put forward in these early plans established a series of principles that endured throughout the war. Structurally, the most important principle was that the responsibility for recruiting and training personnel rested with local authorities, with the government's role limited to legislation, general publicity and the provision of certain equipment. This division of responsibility was designed to reduce the financial and administrative cost of civil defence by avoiding the replication of existing emergency services. As the Home Office explained in its first circular to local authorities in 1934, it expected that schemes would make 'full use of all existing machinery'.[6]

The Air Raid Precautions Act that came into force on 1 January 1938 put this principle into law and marked the start of active, large-scale recruitment.[7] The ARP sub-committee had thought that roles could be filled by seconding local authority employees to civil defence work and making use of existing voluntary organisations like the Red Cross and St John's Ambulance. By 1935, however, it was obvious that such tactics would not produce the numbers required; the air raid wardens service alone was calculated to need no fewer than 250,000 recruits.[8] The tone of this campaign was set by the Home Office's ARP Department, but responsibility for recruitment remained with local authorities. This can be seen clearly in the case of the Women's Voluntary Services (WVS), which was launched in June 1938, initially to encourage women to participate in ARP. The WVS was set up and supported by the Home Office but could only work in areas with the consent of local authorities.[9]

These arrangements were put to the test in September 1938, when Britain's civil defence services were temporarily mobilised in response to the Munich crisis. A review after the Munich Agreement led to a greater degree of centralisation with the appointment of Sir John Anderson as the Lord Privy Seal and de facto Minister of Civil Defence. This role gave Anderson control of the ARP Department, although it transferred partial responsibility for recruitment to the Ministry of Labour (after 1939, the Ministry of Labour and National Service). The trend towards centralisation continued after the outbreak of war, when Anderson was given the joint portfolio of Home Secretary and Minister of Security, retaining control of civil defence until his replacement by Morrison in October 1940. Yet in line with the ARP Act, central designs always depended upon local implementation, whether by individual local authorities or, during 1939, a quasi-autonomous network of National Service Committees.

The objective of the recruitment drive was to appoint a core of full-time paid staff supported by a much larger pool of unpaid, part-time volunteers. While roles in the warden's service required only introductory training, other jobs were highly skilled. The rescue service, for example, was primarily staffed by builders who understood how to safely remove rubble without causing it to collapse. The services required different levels of physical fitness and had varying upper and lower age limits. Women were ineligible for many roles, and the language used to describe the work they and men were expected to perform was clearly gendered. Within first aid, for example, an advertising flyer called for 'Men who are willing to go out into the street in conditions of danger' while women, who 'have always bourn the main burden of caring for the sick and the wounded', were encouraged to join sheltered posts.[10]

It is difficult to determine the number of people actually involved in such services because of the complex division of responsibility for recruitment. Recruitment figures were calculated using self-reported returns from local authorities, which often failed to account for those who dropped out of the services and those who participated without enrolling. Despite limited central auditing, the official history of civil defence determined that the size of the service peaked in December 1943 with 1.85 million members, more than 80 per cent of whom served part-time.[11] However, the wartime Ministry of Information (which was broadly responsible for government publicity) claimed that 1941 was the peak year, with 1.93 million members, while the National ARP Committee suggested that there were up to 3.25 million engaged in 1942.[12] Local-authority statistics suggest that the greatest growth occurred before the war, with 1,208,720 tallied on 31 March 1939.[13] By September 1939, with an estimated 1.6 million enrolments, the Government was confident that it would reach its objective of some 1.8 million members. However, it also understood that this figure hid serious problems of maldistribution between different localities and different services, with vulnerable urban areas often reporting the largest shortfalls.[14] The 'Phoney War' period made these problems worse. In the absence of air raids, there was significant public pressure to reduce spending, and many existing volunteers resigned due to 'boredom, flavoured with unpopularity'.[15] By January 1940, the Ministry of Home Security warned that some services were 'seriously understrength' despite a reduction in targets.[16]

In the debate on the ARP Act, Samuel Hoare (then Home Secretary) had described civil defence as the beginning of a 'new chapter in which the Government and the local authorities and the citizens in this country will all co-operate'.[17] Nonetheless, while the principle of civic voluntarism remained important until civil defence was stood down in May 1945, wartime labour shortages challenged the way it worked in practice. The introduction of 'freezing orders' that prevented personnel from leaving their jobs from June 1940 and the potential for conscription for firewatching under the National Service Act of April 1941 introduced new elements of compulsion, while the inclusion of civil defence in the 1941 Manpower Budget gave the Ministry of Labour the power to direct people to take up part-time civil defence duties.[18] Coupled with a wartime focus on the retention and deployment of existing volunteers, these changes marked the end of official recruitment drives.

The recruitment effort can therefore be regarded in two parts. The first, during 1938–39, focused on mass enrolment for all civil defence services. The second, from 1939 onwards, prioritised specific needs.

'How you can best help your country in a moment of need': the national campaign

The initial challenge facing civil defence recruiters was to explain what ARP measures the government had planned and the role that civilians would play in them. On 14 March 1938, three months after the ARP Act came into force, Samuel Hoare addressed the nation after the British Broadcasting Corporation's (BBC) 9 p.m. news. His broadcast, 'The Citizen and Air Raids', came three days after Anschluss (the annexation of Austria into Germany) and was widely reported in the press. It was the first time that the provisions included in the ARP Act had been shared directly with the public.[19] Hoare trod an awkward line, reassuring listeners that war was not inevitable while attempting to counter criticism that the government had not done enough. Appealing for 1 million volunteers to come forward, he argued that strong preparations made war less likely while stressing that service was a civic duty akin to helping a pedestrian struck by a car. More practically, the broadcast briefly introduced the various services that would make up Britain's passive defences. 'There was', said Hoare, 'a place for everyone who is willing and reasonably fit . . . Each of you must think tonight how you can best help your country in a moment of need'.[20]

These lines of argument would become hallmarks of the national recruitment drive, which sought to both explain the range of jobs that were available and to emphasise that everyone had a responsibility to be 'active citizens' in wartime.[21] As Noakes has shown, propaganda material urged individuals to put collective needs above individual ones and 'be willing to risk their life in defence of their family, their community and their nation'.[22] In 1939, the National Service campaign amplified this message. Anderson explained that he regarded civil defence as a 'service to the community in which all had a part to play', while advertisements stressed that in modern war 'There is no such thing as "they" . . . On "you" rests the safety of yourself and your family'.[23] The message was repeated again in April 1940, when a reduction in funding for full-time staff led to calls for more part-time volunteers:

100 Jessica Hammett and Henry Irving

'It is for the people of the community to provide their own protection . . . for every member of the community who can possibly do so to offer himself [sic] for training'.[24] The success of this rhetoric can be demonstrated by its frequent repetition by civil defence personnel. In the victory edition of a Lewisham civil defence magazine, for example, the chief warden argued that going into peacetime, 'every one of us will be a better citizen, and find happiness in giving service and help to our neighbours'.[25]

'The Citizen and Air Raids' also began a multimedia approach to the recruitment campaign. The appeal was followed by other broadcasts, with Hoare appearing on radio again on 23 May when he encouraged listeners to imagine what an air raid would look like in their own area.[26] It was also accompanied by a press release and a leaflet providing further information about the different services and requirements for enrolment.[27] These activities were initially organised by C. W. G. Eady, the civil servant in charge of the ARP Department, but by summer 1938, the department had set up a small public relations division to oversee a renewed campaign planned for the autumn. While this plan was disrupted by the Munich Crisis, Anderson's appointment ultimately strengthened the government's capacity to undertake publicity work.[28] With extensive experience of government publicity from his time at the General Post Office (GPO), one of Anderson's first acts was to approach Ernest Crutchley, an old colleague and former public relations officer at the GPO, to become his director of publicity. Crutchley, in turn, drafted Alexander Highet, the director of the GPO film unit, as his deputy. Their experience working with print and broadcast media and commercial advertising agencies played a crucial role in the development of the recruitment campaign.[29]

The use of different media reached its apogee during the National Service campaign. This centred on a forty-eight–page handbook that provided information designed to allow people to decide how they could best serve in the event of war (see Figure 7.1). Although not exclusively concerned with civil defence, the guide was deliberately focused on civilian services and positioned as a continuation of earlier appeals.[30] Prime Minister Neville Chamberlain launched the handbook during a broadcast appeal for volunteers on 23 January 1939. The first of 20 million copies were delivered the following morning, with almost every household receiving one by the end of the week.[31] A recruitment rally at London's Royal Albert Hall provided further publicity, and a panel of speakers including cabinet ministers and prominent figures from local government was formed for similar activities outside London. A fortnight later, Crutchley commissioned the advertising agency W. S. Crawford, which had previously worked with the GPO, to undertake a newspaper advertising campaign from 15 February to the end of March.[32] This was supported by a separate poster campaign and the release of a twenty-minute film, *The Warning* (1939), which ended with a call to service from Anderson. The combination of media was deliberate, reflecting Crutchley's and Highet's belief that the approaches would be mutually reinforcing.[33]

The sheer quantity of material produced during the National Service campaign is striking. Alongside the 20 million handbooks posted to householders, four million recruitment leaflets and around 800,000 posters (see, for example, Figure 7.2) were printed for distribution by local authorities. These sat alongside millions

'A place for everyone' 101

Figure 7.1 National Service (London: HMSO, 1939), inside cover. Message from the Prime Minister, January 1939

Figure 7.2 Imperial War Museum, PST 13380, Goodfellow, 'Air Raid Wardens Wanted' poster (1939)

'A place for everyone' 103

more leaflets on practical ARP measures.[34] The scale of these activities overshadowed all other parts of the civil defence recruitment campaign. The newspaper advertising during February and March, for instance, consisted of 118 separate insertions in twenty-five newspapers and cost just under £18,000. To put this in context, the War Office spent £24,000 on army recruitment advertising during the whole of 1938, which had made it the second-largest government spender on publicity after the GPO.[35] We have found only one other example of a campaign for voluntary civil defence service that used national newspaper advertising. It took place at the height of the Blitz, when the Ministry of Home Security sought to bolster the number of people working in demolition squads, and consisted of just three advertisements at the cost of £1,100.[36]

Unlike in previous campaigns, there was also an attempt to gauge the impact of National Service publicity. In April 1939, Dr. A. E. Morgan, a retired academic working with the Ministry of Labour, convinced his superiors to commission the research group Mass-Observation to investigate people's motivations for joining civil defence. Its study of volunteers in Fulham found that the majority of people attributed their decision to one of the forms of publicity included in the campaign, even though their reasons were often imprecise.[37] Those responsible for the campaign had already concluded that the film *The Warning*, which used a mixture of documentary and staged footage to depict a fictional raid on Nottingham, had been the most effective item of publicity. The anecdotal reports they commissioned suggested that 60 per cent of screenings led to an increase in recruitment in the area the film was shown.[38]

It would be wrong, however, to view the campaign as an unequivocal success. Practical difficulties affecting the distribution of publicity material led to complaints from local authorities, and recruiters were left frustrated by what they regarded as a lack of interest from the BBC and newsreel companies. In some cases, the publicity campaign also exacerbated long-standing complaints from recruits about inefficient organisation and the haphazard quality of training available. There were similar problems during the first weeks of the war, when a series of appeals was cancelled after delays caused by printing difficulties and a lack of certainty about recruitment needs.[39]

The decision to hold a second large-scale recruitment rally in the final stages of the National Service campaign was partly a response to the difficulties encountered with print and broadcast media. The event, held in London's Hyde Park, was designed to build an *esprit de corps* among existing recruits while providing a focal point for further recruitment. It culminated with a parade of 20,000 volunteers, who were saluted from a platform by the king and queen.[40] Tens of thousands more civilians turned out to watch the procession, which featured military and civil defence equipment, as well as music from the Brigade of Guards. The organisers estimated that 15,000 attendees enquired about voluntary service, with 500 confirmed civil defence enrolments on the day.[41] A similar technique was revived in 1942, when the government declared 15 November Civil Defence Day. This time, civil defence workers from every area of the country that had been bombed were invited to participate in parade outside St Paul's Cathedral, presided over by

104 *Jessica Hammett and Henry Irving*

the king and queen.[42] In both cases, the national events were designed to galvanise local activity.

The 'localisation of recruiting energy': campaigning in towns, boroughs and cities

The emphasis placed on local experience reflected the importance of local campaigns to civil defence recruitment. At the time of Hoare's 1938 broadcast, the Treasury had warned that it should not set a precedent that would relieve local authorities of their responsibilities under the ARP Act.[43] Although able to provide some additional funding, the planners of the National Service campaign agreed that they should remain in the background: 'The main feature . . . should be the localisation of recruiting energy'.[44] It was for this reason that the campaign was devolved to a network of quasi-autonomous National Service committees, with the Ministry of Labour appointing special officers to liaise between the committees, local authorities and Whitehall. The emphasis on localisation was even evident in the newspaper advertising campaign mentioned earlier, which involved a mixture of national and regional dailies, centred on urban areas with the greatest need for recruits. In Glasgow, where the advertisements were carried by three papers, the campaign was delayed slightly so that it would coincide with a National Service Week held in that city.[45] This approach continued during the war. In September 1939, for instance, the Ministry of Home Security distributed 2.6 million copies of a leaflet purporting to be 'A Message from Your Council', which were sent alongside municipal gas and electricity bills and included blank spaces where local appeals could be overprinted.[46]

This relationship was not one directional. Local initiatives could influence national policy, while national efforts were frequently criticised by the regions. As early as July 1938, the *ARP News*, a commercial magazine established to promote civil defence, reported on complaints from local authorities about red tape and a 'Home Office Lag' in preparations.[47] In London, where the shortfall of volunteers was particularly acute, the London County Council (LCC) sought to force the government into action. In February 1939, Morrison (then leader of the Council) complained to Anderson that the early momentum of the campaign had been lost. Morrison's intervention appears to have tipped the balance in favour of the newspaper advertising campaign, which was formally agreed on the day Anderson responded to his letter.[48] In return, the London County Council agreed to spend £3,000 on a bespoke advertising campaign for the capital, working with W. S. Crawford to ensure a consistent message.[49] The London campaign focused primarily on the Auxiliary Fire Service, reflecting the Home Office's awareness that local authorities were usually best placed to respond to the specific needs in their area. This approach continued during the war, and in summer 1940, it was reported that 'Manchester, Edinburgh, Leeds, Nottingham, Birmingham and Oxford . . . made strenuous appeals for recruits', while Sheffield was 'engaging in special efforts to enrol women'[50] (see Figure 7.3 for an example of local recruitment publicity).

'A place for everyone' 105

Figure 7.3 The Wardens' Post (Middlesbrough), Vol. 1, No. 6, May 1940, back page. Tear-out poster to display in windows.

The autonomy enjoyed by the National Service committees also provided an opportunity to explore alternative channels for publicity. Public meetings, parades and practical demonstrations had been used in some areas before 1939, but the National Service drive encouraged others to follow suit. The LCC incorporated recruitment events into its jubilee celebration, including an ARP display in an exhibition at County Hall and a procession of civil defence workers along the Thames. In Cheltenham, a parade of new civil defence equipment was 'watched by dense crowds' and was reported to have led to a large number of enrolments.[51] While ceremonial occasions like these invoked civic identity, other recruitment techniques drew on informal local allegiances. A particularly high-profile example occurred over the Easter weekend with a series of co-ordinated appeals at football grounds: players and managers encouraged spectators to enrol, and an appeal from Arsenal Football Club was broadcast live on the BBC. County cricket clubs followed suit once the summer season had started.[52]

Local events could also increase the visibility of civil defence by disrupting normal patterns of life. This was most obvious in the use of training exercises as a means of recruitment (see Figure 7.4).[53] The largest of these, like the mock bombing of Nottingham featured in *The Warning*, dramatically introduced civil defence to potential volunteers by showing how it would work in practice. The recruitment value of such exercises was explicitly understood. In May 1938, for instance, the London Fire Brigade granted permission for a vacant building on Kensington High Street to be blown up and set alight specifically 'to encourage ARP volunteers'.[54] Thirteen months later, Anderson attended an exercise in Chelsea, where around 7,500 people took part in the largest pre-war test of civil defence.

Although sometimes treated light-heartedly by participants and observers, these events drew people onto the streets and were regarded as a valuable means of recruitment by publicity specialists and personnel alike.[55] Writing for Mass-Observation, one ARP assistant from Trowbridge, Wiltshire, commented on the response to two demonstrations. The first took place in January 1940, when 'a large percentage of the population of the town turned out', but 'the whole thing

Figure 7.4 Harpenden and District Local History Society, ARP-5-3

Source: Image of Civil Defence Competition, Warden Section, Harpenden, 1944. We thank the Harpenden and District Local History Society for permission to use images from their archives; if anybody believes their copyright to have been infringed, do not hesitate to contact us..

'A place for everyone' 107

[was treated] as being rather a joke'. Two months later, aeroplanes were used, resulting in a markedly different response: 'People came out of their homes to watch – to watch with seriousness and a realisation that it might have been real and that the planes may be going to machine-gun them'.[56]

These parts of the campaign, which were not run on commercial lines, echoed the military recruitment strategies used in Britain at the beginning of the First World War. During that conflict, the War Office recognised the importance of local connections for recruitment and the maintenance of morale at the front. It was for these reasons that it attempted to preserve the regional identities of regiments, and promoted the establishment of locally raised Pals Battalions.[57] As Jay Winter has argued, these strategies 'tapped powerful sentiments of loyalty felt by men, whatever the occupation, to town, county or community'.[58] Local attachment could also be used to promote a connection to the national war effort in the Second World War, as John Hodsoll (Inspector General of Civil Defence) explained to Bristol wardens in January 1940: 'I want them all to feel not only that they are helping to defend their own city, but that they are playing also a most important part in the defence of the country against hostile air attack'.[59]

As at the national level, however, the success of local recruitment campaigns should not be overstated. In August 1940, as local authorities renewed their appeals for volunteers, the *ARP News* lamented that recruitment had been 'left to local councillors who had only the faintest conception of what was wanted'.[60] On their part, many councillors had been left frustrated by the limited impact of their appeals, and the LCC expressed profound disappointment about its newspaper advertising when calculating enrolments in March 1939.[61] Significantly, this led to a further innovation, as the LCC worked with the National Service committee and the ARP Department to organise a house-to-house canvass in various London boroughs during May and June 1939. Canvassers were given copies of the National Service handbook, enrolment forms and specific information about the recruitment needs of local areas. With almost 31,000 enrolments, the canvass was described as 'more effective than anything that had been tried yet'.[62] Those responsible believed that 'the personal approach was the material factor'.[63]

Canvassing could offer solutions to local issues. The *ARP News* reported on problems faced in Poplar, London, over the summer of 1938:

> Poplar Borough Council are taking Air Raid Precautions very seriously, but, unfortunately, the people of Poplar are not. . . . There is a strong pacifist movement in Poplar and it is felt by the authorities that this is probably the cause of the lack of enthusiasm.[64]

The local press did not give any 'help or sympathy', and it was thought that a demonstration 'would only obtain ridicule from the people'. However, following the employment of two canvassers, 480 personnel were recruited in the space of two months.[65]

Other local problems were, however, more difficult to overcome. As the *ARP News* explained, 'more remunerative employment under better conditions is available in civil life', and the financial restrictions on local authorities meant

108 *Jessica Hammett and Henry Irving*

there was no chance of improving wages to 'attract a sufficient number of recruits of the right type'.[66]

The 'social side' of service: utilising personal and peer-group persuasion

The problems that faced national and local recruitment campaigns before and during the war also led recruiters towards informal methods to counter shortcomings. In addition to the personal approach of canvassers, the power of persuasion by a friend, neighbour or family member was recognised by officials. In June 1940, when the Battle of Britain had just begun, William Mabane (Parliamentary Secretary of the Ministry of Home Security) asked existing personnel to use their public spirit to convince friends and neighbours to join up.[67] A year earlier, women had been targeted when asked to assist in recruitment across Britain by encouraging their friends to enlist – a strategy *The Brechin Advertiser* attributed to their 'reputation for volubility'.[68] This method was sometimes used in wider publicity campaigns, as was the case in Hartlepool in October 1938, when each volunteer was asked to find at least one new recruit.[69] An additional motivation was given to air raid wardens in Fulham in July 1940, when the Borough Council prompted a 'friendly rivalry by offering Savings Certificates as prizes'. In response, one warden designed a poster to display on the post door, which read: 'Don't wait. Come right in and sign on for civil defence'.[70] These strategies brought in significant numbers of recruits across class, gender and generation divides, and given the limited financial support for civil defence, it is unsurprising that they were popular.

Social events were essential for creating community within civil defence and for retaining volunteers and could also be used as recruitment tools (see Figure 7.5).[71] An early campaign in Tottenham included 'an interesting and unusual departure from current practice . . . a dance for A.R.P. workers and their friends', attended by 1,500 people.[72] When Turton, near Bolton, met its recruitment target in December 1938, this success was said to be because the 'social side . . . had not been neglected'.[73] And in Plymouth, both during and after the Blitz, wardens were encouraged to invite their friends to social events to aid recruitment and wished 'good hunting'.[74] One respondent to Mass-Observation's Fulham Survey (May-June 1939) noted the draw of social activities when he gave his reasons for volunteering: 'Well the young man next door is an A.R.P. warden and he thought, he and myself being single, we thought it would be rather interesting. He asked me to join'.[75]

Volunteers were also enrolled through their places of work, and employers as well as trade union leaders were asked to support recruitment. Sometimes this was targeted, with medical professionals asked to volunteer for first aid or ambulance work and construction workers directed to rescue. One Fulham Survey respondent said, 'My job is nursing. I have to do it anyway', while a builder responded that 'I tell you one reason, the guvner you see he was in the engineers and he was telling me all about demolition and that and I thought I would prefer it'.[76] For less specialised work, factory bosses were asked to help. At the height of the Blitz in January 1940, Anderson asked employers in Birmingham to support closer

'A place for everyone' 109

Figure 7.5 Air Raid Precautions Gazette (Doncaster), No. 4, 24 February 1940, p. 15. Auxiliary Fire Service members and friends at a whist drive

co-operation to protect factories from air raids. 'In supporting this development', Anderson argued, 'they would not only be making an important contribution to the general efficiency of their defences, but they would also be helping to secure considerable financial economy'.[77] The *ARP News* reported in August 1938 that 'several large industrial undertakings' in Liverpool were helping recruit and train volunteers, with 700 enrolled through the Tate and Lyle sugar factory.[78]

Even without official direction, the persuasion of existing personnel seems to have been crucial for motivating friends, family and neighbours to volunteer. The Fulham Survey includes many accounts of personal influence, including a labourer whose 'children told me to fill in the form', a bank clerk who enrolled 'Simply on the request of the air-raid warden. He suggested that they were short', and a young man who responded 'Actually I didn't have any intention of volunteering. My brother-in-law he volunteered and he said they were very interesting and I went along out of interest and they sort of wangled me into it'. Other respondents volunteered with friends. A factory hand answered that 'my friend at work, she wanted to join and she didn't want to join alone', while another young woman said, 'I don't like to go on my own. Joined up with friend and would go if she did'.[79] Word of mouth continued to play a significant role once the war began, and the *ARP News* reported on the success of recruitment in Portsmouth in mid-1941:

> While no detailed record of the sources from which recruits have been obtained has been kept, repeatedly men and women have come to volunteer because they have been told about the Service by a friend who had just joined and been through the [new casualty training] school.[80]

A 'rush of volunteers': the significance of war events

A final motivating factor which officials had no control over was the tempo of the war, the importance of which was illustrated even before war had been declared. The 'crisis' of September 1938 saw frantic air raid preparations with civil defence personnel distributing gas masks and digging trenches. It also prompted a spike in volunteer numbers, with Mass-Observation's Fulham Survey calculating that the number of civil defence enrolments jumped from around 25 per month in early summer 1938 to a peak of more than 330 in September, before falling back that autumn. The number of enrolments grew to around seventy a month during the National Service campaign, but it seems that a large proportion of Fulham volunteers joined when bombing felt imminent, even if there was only limited recruitment publicity.[81]

This trend was not limited to the capital. Writing in the *ARP News*, one local official wrote about his 'crisis week' experience in a North Yorkshire village:

> I don't know how they got the crowd together but at 8pm that village hall was packed! Not even standing room! They even opened the windows to let the 'overflow' gathering in the playground to hear a word or two. And yet when I addressed a meeting there a fortnight before, there wouldn't be thirty![82]

Indeed, while their figures need to be treated with caution, the Home Office believed that across the United Kingdom, around half a million people joined civil defence at this time.[83]

After the lull of the Phoney War, the experience of aerial bombardment encouraged more volunteers to come forward. Witnessing a female warden working during an alert convinced one man to volunteer in Sheffield. He explained: 'Well, this is all right – me, an able-bodied man under a shelter, and that woman walking the streets at this time of night to ask if I and many more like me are all right'.[84] The *ARP News* reported in the summer of 1940 that 'air raids have been followed by a rush of volunteers' for civil defence services, although officers warned that 'it is essential to have men and women who trained in advance for their jobs'.[85] Local air raids still had an effect as late as July 1944, when an incident in Handcross, Sussex, 'caused fresh enrolments to come in where previously they had been rather apathetic'.[86]

This trend reflects First World War military recruitment, when 'far from signing up in an initial burst of enthusiasm, the largest single component of volunteers enlisted at *exactly* the moment that the war turned serious'.[87] It also pre-empted one of the biggest challenges facing civil defence recruiters in Britain during the Cold War: recruitment targets were often not met then, as Matthew Grant shows, because many Britons did not envisage the immediate threat of war.[88]

Conclusion: the importance of national, local and personal pressures

Civil defence recruitment in Second World War Britain was shaped by a combination of national, local and personal pressures. Although historians have tended to focus on national government, its publicity was designed to work in combination with local messages, providing a general framework for more targeted appeals. The recruitment publicity produced by these bodies helped to raise awareness of ARP measures and the specific roles involved in civil defence, encouraging people to think about the roles they might fill. Many volunteers, however, required an extra push – whether from an external event, the visibility of civil defence measures or personal persuasion. These factors were particularly significant because they cut across class, gender and age barriers. Where propaganda material reinforced gender divisions, these informal prompts attracted a diverse group of volunteers. Those responsible recognised this and used demonstrations, rallies and canvassing to formalise such influences within the recruitment drive.

The existence of these different pressures makes it difficult to determine the success of recruitment publicity with any real accuracy. Indeed, the decision to volunteer was usually the result of a mixture of factors, which cannot easily be disentangled (see Chapter 14). This was certainly the case for one air raid warden who entered an essay competition on 'Why I became an Air Raid Warden' in a Bristol civil defence magazine. He noted that, although the 'call of National Service' had caused him to '[run] over in my mind what I would like to do', it was a visit from a warden that spurred him on to enrol: 'he was busy, so busy, and like many another at that time was doing the work of a dozen. How then could I defer any longer to at least offer to do what he was doing?'[89] This warden joined at the time of Munich, a full two months before the call for National Service began, and his response reveals one of the most significant impacts of recruitment publicity: it provided a language of active citizenship that chimed with the realities of modern war.

Notes

1 *The Daily Mail*, 'Your Duty: Do It', 7 June 1940.
2 Hansard, HC Debate, 11 June 1941, 372, 281.
3 See, for example, Angus Calder, *The People's War: Britain 1939–1945* (London: Pimlico, 1992, first edition 1969), 67–8; Richard Overy, *The Bombing War: Europe 1939–1945* (London: Penguin, 2013), 141; Daniel Todman, *Britain's War: Into Battle, 1937–1941* (London: Allen Lane, 2016), 489–92.
4 Susan Grayzel, *At Home and under Fire: Air Raids and Culture in Britain from the Great War to the Blitz* (Cambridge: Cambridge University Press, 2012); Lucy Noakes, '"Serve to Save": Gender, Citizenship and Civil Defence in Britain 1937–1941', *Journal of Contemporary History* 47, no. 4 (2012): 734–53.
5 Brendan Maartens, 'To Encourage, Inspire and Guide: National Service, the People's War and the Promotion of Civil Defence in Interwar Britain, 1938–1939', *Media History* 21, no. 3 (2015): 328–41; Lucy Allwright, *The War on London: Defending the City from the War in the Air*, PhD diss. (Coventry: University of Warwick, 2011).
6 Terrance O'Brien, *Civil Defence* (London: HMSO, 1955), 59.
7 Ibid., 107.
8 Ibid., 72.
9 The National Archives (TNA), HO 356/2, Reading to Hoare, 29 April 1938; 'Broad Outlines', 18 May 1938.
10 Mass-Observation Archive (MOA), TC 23/4/A, undated [1938].

112 *Jessica Hammett and Henry Irving*

11 O'Brien, *Civil Defence*, 690.
12 Ministry of Information, *What Britain Has Done* (London: HMSO, 1945), 76; *National ARP Co-Ordinating Committee and ARP & NFS Review Full Report One Day Conference*, 'Opening Session', 25 October 1942, n.p.
13 TNA, HO 186/1, 'ARP General', 5 April 1939.
14 O'Brien, *Civil Defence*, 203–8.
15 Ibid., 347.
16 Ibid., 344.
17 Hansard, HC Debate, 15 November 1937, 329, 43.
18 O'Brien, *Civil Defence*, 548–56.
19 Ibid., 115.
20 TNA, HO 45/17622, untitled script ['The Citizen and Air Raids', 14 March 1938].
21 Sonya Rose, *Which People's War? National Identity and Citizenship in Wartime Britain 1939–1945* (Oxford: Oxford University Press, 2003), 19.
22 Noakes, 'Serve to Save', 735.
23 Hansard, HC Debate, 1 March 1939, 344, 1314; TNA, HO 186/2, 'ARP: Who are "they"?', undated [February 1939].
24 *The Times*, 'A.R.P. Costs to be Reduced', 20 April 1940, 8.
25 *B Twenty-One, Lewisham*, 'Editorial', June 1945, 1.
26 TNA, HO 45/17622, untitled script ['How ARP is Getting On', 23 May 1938].
27 TNA, HO 45/17622, 'Press Statement', 15 March 1938; Home Office and Scottish Office, 'Air Raid Precautions: What You Can Do', March 1938.
28 O'Brien, *Civil Defence*, 128, 163.
29 Maartens, 'Promotion of Civil Defence', 330.
30 TNA, CAB 23/96/9, 'Cabinet Conclusions', 30 November 1938.
31 *The Times*, 'The Call to Service', 28 January 1939.
32 TNA, HO 45/108207, Crutchley to Anderson, 6 February 1939.
33 Maartens, 'Promotion of Civil Defence', 333.
34 TNA, HO 186/319, 'Statement of Publicity Activities', 3 July 1939.
35 *Report of the Select Committee on Estimates* (1938), 273–4.
36 TNA, INF 1/340, Bloxham to Rhodes, 19 December 1940.
37 MOA, FR A24, 'Report on ARP: Survey Carried Out in Fulham by Mass-Observation, April–July 1939', 36. See James Hinton, *The Mass Observers: A History, 1937–1949* (Oxford: Oxford University Press, 2013), 111–12.
38 TNA, HO 186/110, 'National Service Publicity', 19 May 1939.
39 See, for example, TNA, HO 186/2, 'This Is Urgent'.
40 *The Times*, 'National Service Units', 3 July 1939.
41 TNA, HO 186/319, 'Publicity Advisory Panel', 3 July 1939.
42 *The Times*, 'Civil Defence Day', 16 November 1942.
43 TNA, HO 45/17622, 'Bridges to Eady', 17 March 1938.
44 TNA, HO 186/109, 'National Service and Public Relations', 20 February 1939.
45 TNA, HO 186/2, 'Newspaper Advertising'. The Other Cities Were Birmingham, Cardiff, Leeds, Liverpool and Manchester.
46 TNA, HO 186/2, 'A Message from Your Council', August–September 1939.
47 *ARP News*, 'Home Office Lag', July 1938.
48 London Metropolitan Archives (LMA), LCC/CL/CD/1/274, Anderson to Morrison, 8 February 1939.
49 LMA, LCC/CL/CD/1/274, Morrison to Anderson, n.d.; TNA, HO 186/2, unidentified letter to Highet, 15 February 1939.
50 *ARP News*, 'Nation-Wide Appeal for Volunteers', June 1940.
51 *Cheltenham Chronicle*, 'Civil Defence Has Come to Stay', 13 May 1939, 6.
52 TNA, HO 186/110, 'National Service Publicity', 31 March 1939 and 'National Service Publicity', 5 May 1939; *The Times*, 'Civil Defence', 12 April 1939.
53 Allwright, 'War on London', 168–226.

'A place for everyone' 113

54 LMA, LCC/CL/CD/1/274, Morris, 'Demonstration of ARP Services in Kensington', 17 May 1938.
55 TNA, HO 186/319, 'Publicity Advisory Panel', 3 July 1939.
56 MOA, Diarist 5118, 7 January 1940 and 3 March 1940.
57 Catriona Pennell, _A Kingdom United: Popular Responses to the Outbreak of the First World War in Britain and Ireland_ (Oxford: Oxford University Press, 2012), 154.
58 Jay Winter, _The Great War and the British People_ (Houndmills: Palgrave, 2003, 1st edition 1985), 30.
59 _The Siren, A Magazine for Bristol Air Raid Wardens_, 'Letters' 1, no. 1 (January 1940).
60 _ARP News_, 'Flaws in Recruiting', August 1940, 18.
61 LMA, LCC/CL/CD/1/274, 'Minute of an Interview', 31 March 1939.
62 TNA, HO, 207/742, 'House to House Canvass', 26 June 1939.
63 TNA, HO 186/110, 'National Service Publicity', 30 June 1939.
64 _ARP News_, 'Paradox of London's ARP', June 1938. This may be connected to the strong Communist Party element in Poplar.
65 _ARP News_, 'London Calling', August 1938.
66 _ARP News_, 'Recruitment Hampered by Prosperity', May 1940, 15; 'Monthly Notes . . . the Editor', May 1940.
67 TNA, HO 183/316, Mabane, 'To the Personnel of the Civil Defence Services', 23 June 1940.
68 _The Brechin Advertiser_, 'Mainly for Women', 20 June 1939.
69 _ARP News_, 'Hartlepools' Way', October 1938.
70 _Fulham Chronicle_, 'Fulham's Civil Defence Services', 19 July 1940.
71 On the significance of community, see Jessica Hammett, '"The Invisible Chain by Which All Are Bound to Each Other": Civil Defence Magazines and the Development of Community during the Second World War', _Journal of War and Culture Studies_ 11, no. 2 (2018): 117–35.
72 _ARP News_, 'London Calling', August 1938.
73 _ARP News_, 'ARP Parade', December 1938.
74 _The Alert, Plymouth_, 'Chief Warden' 4 (February 1942) and 'Chief Warden' 2 (December 1941).
75 MOA, TC 23/2, 'Fulham ARP Survey Responses', May–June 1939.
76 Ibid.
77 _Coventry Evening Telegraph_, 'Scheme of Co-Operation in Civil Defence', 10 January 1940.
78 _ARP News_, 'Liverpool Pushes Ahead', July 1938.
79 MOA, TC 23/2, Fulham ARP Survey.
80 _ARP News_, 'Portsmouth's Casualty School', July 1941.
81 MOA, FR A24, 'Report on ARP', 44a.
82 _ARP News_, 'Crisis Week Reminiscences', January 1939.
83 O'Brien, _Civil Defence_, 203.
84 _All Clear! Sheffield_, 'Northern "F"', 2 (June 1940), 18.
85 _ARP News_, 'Civil Defence News Digest', August 1940.
86 East Sussex Record Office, CD/8/119, Civil Defence Regional Commissioner to H. S. Martin, County ARP Controller, Lewes, 20 July 1944.
87 Pennell, _Kingdom United_, 145.
88 Matthew Grant, 'Civil Defence Gives Meaning to Your Leisure': Citizenship, Participation, and Cultural Change in Cold War Recruitment Propaganda, 1949–54', _Twentieth Century British History_ 22, no. 1 (2011): 77.
89 _The Siren, Bristol_, 'Why I Became an Air Raid Warden', 1, no. 4 (April 1940).

Part II

Recruitment at a Time of Cold War

8 'It's like a good school, only better'

Recruiting boys to the British armed forces under the first Attlee government, 1946–50

Brendan Maartens

Abstract

Historians have generally been kind to the post-war Labour governments. Responsible for a series of pioneering reforms that included the establishment of a National Health Service and the roll-out of universal national insurance, the Attlee administrations have been credited with a progressive brand of social democracy that prioritised wealth redistribution and egalitarianism within the parameters of a mixed-market capitalist economy. Labour also, however, pursued an expansionist foreign policy to try to shore up Britain's dwindling status as a post-war 'great power', and this policy both required and eventually occasioned a series of major mobilisation campaigns. This chapter will analyse these campaigns, focusing in particular on those aimed at schoolchildren and school-leavers. Drawing on governmental, newspaper and film archives, it will consider the strategies used to attract minors to the Services and their broader legacy as well.

The post-war Labour governments are usually credited with founding the British welfare state.[1] Under their tenure, Britons enjoyed universal national insurance and a National Health Service for the first time. Labour also presided over a major house-building programme, nationalised the railways, electrical utilities and coal and steel industries and established the UK's first national parks. The extent of their reforms and the fact that they were carried out at a time of dire economic straits can explain why Clement Attlee, the man who led Labour in this period, was voted Britain's most successful Prime Minister in three recent historians' surveys.[2] Credited with a progressive brand of social democracy that prioritised wealth redistribution and egalitarianism within the parameters of a mixed-market capitalist society, Attlee is held in high regard because of the 'consensus' his governments reputedly introduced to British polity.[3]

Judged on leadership and a capacity to deal with crises, Attlee certainly ranks high in the pantheon of British Prime Ministers. Yet the struggle to valorise his legacy has diverted attention from other aspects of Labour's project. The Attlee governments were hawkish by post-war standards. Though Labour promised 'Peace for the People' in its 1945 general election manifesto,[4] following that pledge with cuts to Navy expenditure within two years of taking power,[5] it also continued Britain's atomic weapons programme and deployed almost 100,000 troops to Korea in the first major conflagration of the Cold War. Its participation in that war and the 'Atlanticist' orientation of its foreign policy alienated many on the Labour left, who organised themselves into a 'Third Force' which opposed conflict with the Soviet Union and accused the party leadership of kowtowing to 'American imperialism'.[6]

Labour's commitment to the Cold War had many consequences, the most important of which, for young men at least, was the continuation of the wartime draft. The 1948 National Service Act compelled all British males aged 17 to 21 to undertake some form of military service.[7] This ensured a steady stream of manpower (no women were conscripted after 1945) for the Army, Navy and Air Force, but large numbers of volunteers were still required to train the annual influx of conscripts and to occupy the more senior positions within each force. This presented British boys and men with a choice: they could either enrol as conscripts, where they would typically languish at the bottom rungs of the force they joined, or enlist as volunteers, where they would enjoy better pay and promotion prospects but serve for a longer period of time. Most opted for conscription, but hundreds of thousands of males, together with a much smaller number of adult females,[8] still joined up voluntarily in the 1940s and 1950s, with the Attlee governments enticing them to do so using voluntary recruitment campaigns from 1946.

This chapter will explore these campaigns and those aimed at schoolchildren and school-leavers in particular. Minors could enlist as regulars in all three services from the age of 17 and a half. Yet they could also enrol as cadets, which gave them preferential status when undertaking conscripted or volunteer service in any of the three services later in life, join a military school or college to undertake pre-service training in a variety of technical, logistical or support roles, or enlist as an Apprentice in the Army or Air Force or as a Boy Seaman in the Navy from the age of 15 years. Bestowing what one journalist called a 'mental, moral and physical training' that promoted 'patriotism and good citizenship' among the young,[9] such schemes were central to post-war recruiting efforts. Indeed, while a range of 'bounty' programmes was used to lure veterans back into the tri-service after 1945, the lion's share of volunteers was drawn from the under-21 age group, with a majority of those appearing to be under 18 when they signed up.[10] This chapter assesses the strategies used to encourage them to do so but also reflects on the broader post-war legacy of Labour's policies.

Government communications, military recruitment and the start of the Cold War

The recruitment campaigns explored in this chapter occurred at a time of high political drama in Britain. Few prophesied Labour's general election victory in the run up to July 1945, and fewer still believed that this victory would be as comprehensive as it was. Labour gained 296 seats, the Conservatives lost 189, and the swing from one party to the other has remained the largest in British electoral history to this day.[11] It gave Labour a mandate to enact extensive reforms, and no time was lost in exploiting the opportunity. The most sweeping changes have already been mentioned, but others that had a bearing on military recruitment included the establishment, in 1946, of a Central Office of Information (COI), a government communications bureau that provided advertising, public relations and market research services to any department that required them, and the creation of a Ministry of Defence (MOD), an umbrella body whose Minister represented the Services in Cabinet, in 1947.

These bodies allowed for a greater degree of centralised control over military recruitment and for control over spending on paid advertising campaigns in particular, which, for much of the post-war era, were organised jointly by the Service departments, the MOD and the COI. Announcing the creation of the latter department in 1945, Attlee described it as an 'information unit' that would provide 'common technical and production functions' to other government departments.[12] Carefully weighted, his words masked the fact that the COI 'closely resemble[d]' the wartime Ministry of Information and even retained 'many of its personnel and . . . production divisions'. On behalf of its departmental clients, these divisions produced an extensive array of promotion, including posters, leaflets, films and newspaper and magazine advertisements, with the COI also designing opinion polls, organising public exhibitions and circulating press releases using a news distribution service known as the 'COI Run'.[13]

In the first two years of peace, reconstruction consumed much of the information office's resources.[14] In 1948, escalating global tensions prompted a shift in the government's communications strategy, an increase in expenditure on armed forces and the revival of a national network of civil defence. From the second half of that year, more money was also spent on recruitment, with the *proportion* of government funding given to recruiting also increasing when compared to that allocated to non-military departments. The government spent millions of pounds on newspaper advertising each year, with a series of powerful committees determining how much money each department received. In 1946, the tri-service was never given more than 15% of total official advertising expenditure, but by 1950, that figure (which was allocated on a monthly basis) had increased to a low of 28.56% and a high of 56.74%.[15]

In practice, this meant that the Army, Navy and Air Force were given greater prominence in the press than other government departments. Yet pay increases for all three services in 1948 and 1950 also meant that recruiters had more to work *with*, in the way of inducements. The second increase may have been historically unprecedented. The pay of minors who joined the Navy as Seamen, the Army as Privates or the Air Force as Airmen rose from £1.8.0 a week to £2.9.0, an increase of 61%,[16] with the public informed of the scheme through a broadcast address delivered by Attlee and a series of newspaper advertisements which described the revised pay structure in Rooseveltian terms as a 'New Deal for the Fighting Forces'.[17]

These appeals seemed to have the desired effect. Within a week of the announcement, the War Office reported a four-fold increase in applications. The figure for the Air Ministry was even higher, amounting to 500%.[18] The rates were lower

120   Brendan Maartens

when long-term analyses were conducted but still impressive, with the Army enlisting 'about 100 per cent' more recruits than it did before the scheme was introduced and the Air Force witnessing enrolments grow by 235%.[19] In one COI survey of public opinion, pay was described as the 'strongest incentive of general appeal attracting [male] workers to a job or volunteers to the Services'.[20] Yet it was not the only incentive used to attract youngsters to the military. Travel, adventure, pensions, leave entitlements and education were also used by post-war recruiters, who used promotion, to quote one official, to counteract minors' 'very great ignorance of life in the services'.[21]

The 'product' and the 'sales team': organising the campaigns of 1946–50

A single body was tasked with organising the campaigns of 1946–50. Chaired by Sir Robert Fraser, Director General of the COI, the Services Recruiting Publicity Committee (SRPC) was comprised of representatives of each force, the COI and, from 1947, the MOD. Established in mid-1946, it met continuously from that point until the summer of 1949, when it ceased to operate for a time before being reconstituted in 1950 as the Defence Publicity Committee.[22]

The records of these committees, which have informed this chapter, provide a useful overview of the shifting priorities of recruiters and the challenges they faced while mobilising opinion. Chief among these was competition for recruits between the armed forces, nationalised industries and commercial employers. When leaving school, young males had several options. They could go to university and defer National Service until graduation or complete their service before enrolling as a student. They could join the armed forces as a conscript or a Regular, or seek employment in one of the industries which exempted them from military service. The armed forces were not the only organisations trying to entice young people down a given career path, and they found it particularly difficult to compete with private industry, which typically offered better pay and a greater degree of personal freedom.

Shortages of newsprint, ink, photographic paper and flashbulbs represented another obstacle, with the lack of the first two resources particularly damaging to recruiters, who regarded print media as central to their recruiting efforts.[23] A fuel crisis in the winter of 1946–47 made matters worse, further depleting supplies of many raw materials, precipitating the closure of some publications and compelling the government to impose reductions in the physical size of newspapers in the summer of 1947. Thereafter, tabloids usually comprised only four pages apiece, with broadsheets and Sunday titles declining to an average of seven pages each.[24]

Smaller papers meant less space for paid advertising and a threat from publishers (never, in the event, carried out) to boycott government advertisements. It also made journalists less likely to *report* favourably on recruitment, another problem highlighted repeatedly in SRPC minutes. 'The main gap to be closed', the committee agreed unanimously in June 1947, 'lay in the . . . arrangements to secure the better treatment of the recruitment problem in the Press'. To achieve this, occasional meetings were held between the Service departments, the MOD and the Newspapers Proprietors Association.[25] Fraser also recommended monthly press conferences to tell the 'story' of recruitment by providing updates on enrolment rates and issuing press releases or 'handouts' that contained content considered appropriately newsworthy.[26]

Newspapers were prioritised by recruiters for two reasons: they attracted audiences of millions, with the *People*, Britain's leading title, selling upwards of 4.5 million copies per day by 1947,[27] and they were believed to attract certain *kinds* of readers who could be stratified into socio-economic, political or geographical groups. The apparent correlation between reading habits and social class made newspapers particularly valuable to commercial advertisers, who used tabloids to sell mass-market consumer goods and broadsheets to promote more expensive, up-market fare. In the mid-twentieth century, the pages of British newspapers were filled with advertisements for confectionary, detergents, alcohol, cars and other items,[28] but recruiters used the same methods to 'sell' service, combining newspapers with posters (exhibited on as many as 60,000 government-owned hoardings), pamphlets, films and a series of broadcast announcements on the BBC, some of which were 'keyed' to monitor audience responses by encouraging listeners to contact an official identified in the appeal.[29]

The individuals responsible for this work were described by Fraser as a '"sales force"' whose primary goal was to advertise the '"product"' of military service.[30] In the domain of regular recruitment, this 'product' was sold principally through the material rewards it allegedly conferred to the individual. Indeed, while older applicants to auxiliary and reserve forces did their soldiering, according to Major-General Ralph Edgeworth-Johnstone, the War Office's Deputy Director of Public Relations, 'in their own spare time and for very little material return', youngsters joined regular forces because they 'wished to adopt soldiering as a career, and the recruiting appeal [used to attract them] was therefore one of self-interest . . . [and was not therefore] based on such abstract things as patriotism, the duty of a citizen, comradeship, etc.'.[31]

The dichotomy between self-interest and the 'abstract things' of patriotism and civic duty is revealing, suggesting as it does that those who made a career out of service were not motivated by the kinds of ideals they were stereotypically thought to represent. The Secretary of State for War, Jack Lawson, made a similar point when announcing the resumption of voluntary recruitment in a press conference on 16 May 1946. Claiming the military appealed less to 'patriotism and [an] urge for adventure of the young' and more to individuals' 'good sense when choosing a *career*', Lawson claimed that the tri-service offered a 'really attractive, healthy, interesting, useful and properly paid *career*, which will bear comparison with anything civil life can offer . . . [and is] not only interesting but profitable to the enterprising young man'.[32] Such 'profitability' was conveyed in several ways, which will now be explored.

Having a 'man's time' in military: newspaper advertising and the sale of service

Recruiters spent more money on newspapers than any other medium and placed financial and professional rewards at the heart of their promotion. Such rewards were expressed in terms of the pay new recruits received and the allowances for

122 *Brendan Maartens*

food, clothes and accommodation that supplemented their pay, in opportunities for travel, adventure, sports and recreation, and in occasional references to health and well-being. In one advertisement released in the summer of 1947, for example, the Navy claimed to offer a 'life of travel and adventure . . . good food, pay and [career] prospects'.[33] In another displayed the following year, the Air Force enticed individuals to serve with promises of 'full employment, good food, sport, comradeship and travel'.[34] In a 1946 advertisement, the Army said that all soldiers benefitted from '[p]lenty of sports and games to keep [recruits] gloriously fit . . . Good pay and generous leave on full pay. . . . A steady job . . . [and a]mple leisure and relaxation [time]'.[35]

Such advertisements did occasionally reference 'abstract' inducements like comradeship, but the training new recruits received and the 'trades' they learned were highlighted more frequently. Every boy, one advertisement claimed in September 1947, could 'BECOME A SKILLED CRAFTSMAN By enlisting in the Royal Air Force in one of the wide variety of trades for which they will receive the best possible training'.[36] 'In the Army', another advertisement declared in February, 'every soldier is a specialist . . . given specialised training to fit him for his job in the Corps of his choice'.[37] The Navy, which placed less of an emphasis on specialisation in its promotion, did nevertheless offer readers the chance to become electricians, stoker mechanics or even writers in an advertisement released in November.[38]

Such jobs did have counterparts in industry, and recruiters made sure to point this out, sometimes to underscore apparent similarities between military and civilian occupations, sometimes to draw favourable comparisons between them, and sometimes to portray service as a prerequisite to a career in industry.[39] As one 1947 Army appeal declared, military training gives you 'something extra . . . [i]n bearing and character' which makes you the 'sort of man industry needs now and in the future'.[40] As another Navy advertisement released in 1948 suggested, the 'Navy gives a man intensive, interesting training to fit him for a worthwhile job . . . £9 million is being spent on Naval Research. . . . For men interested in modern science and engineering this is a great opportunity'.[41] In a rare reference to war, the Air Force took a different tack, claiming 1939–45 had 'strengthened the bonds of understanding between the "regulars" and their counterparts in civilian life', with many 'realising that the Royal Air Force offers conditions of employment comparable with the best that "Civvy Street" can offer.[42]

The emphasis on employability, transferrable skills, science and technology was also a feature of a large Navy advertisement that appeared in the *Daily Mirror* in 1947. 'Modern equipment and continual scientific development', the copy read, have opened up many new and interesting jobs in engineering, flying and communications'.[43] In its promotion, the Army referred to itself as the 'Modern Regular Army',[44] while the Air Force made regular, prophetic references to the future, telling readers in one case that enlistment 'MAKES YOUR FUTURE SECURE with PAY AS YOU LEARN' and in another that service will 'BETTER YOUR FUTURE'.[45]

The vast majority of these appeals were not classified but display advertisements written in a concise and to-the-point diction. A handful of larger, illustrated advertisements was nevertheless commissioned. Occasionally depicting scenes of work and service but more commonly portraying sailors, soldiers and pilots

'It's like a good school, only better' 123

enjoying time off when *not* serving, these advertisements tended to be more rhetorically ambitious than the smaller pieces and often brought together the myriad appeals mentioned into a single body of writing. In August 1946, for example, the Army released a series of advertisements that contained portraits of soldiers smiling, imploring young people to join up for the 'healthiest, happiest career'. New recruits would enjoy, according to these appeals, 'Good pay with no fares to work, no doctor's or clothing bills. . . . Generous increased pensions for long service. . . . Good prospects on return to "civvy street" . . . Ample leisure time. . . . [and] Free education in a vast number of subjects'.[46]

Many of these appeals were aimed at both minors and adults, with distinctions between the two groups often only appearing towards the end of advertisements, if they appeared at all. Some exhortations, however, targeted young people exclusively, such as one for the Suffolk Army Cadet Force, which offered boys a 'man's time in their spare time' and lured them in with promises of free uniforms and camping.[47] Another advertisement for the Air Force asked readers if they were 'Leaving school?' before offering them a 'chance of a life-time!' in the form of 'highly technical and administrative' vocational training programmes. More than 4000 'young men [sic] between the ages of 15 and 17½' had enrolled on these programmes and reputedly managed to secure 'commissions and top jobs in industry' after graduating.[48] Using a scene of a boy speaking to his former schoolmaster, the Navy emphasised the easy transition from civilian to military life in one advertisement. Dressed in full military attire and smoking a cigarette, the boy faced the man, smiled and gave a glowing testimonial of service:

> Yes, the Navy *is* a good life and the prospects *are* good. I joined for the adventure, Sir, and a chance to see the world. I'm getting these all right, but I'm also getting on. Thanks to you I had a good education at school. Instead of forgetting half of it as soon as I left, I carried straight on with my studies in the Service.[49]

The blithe dismissal of formal education and the notion that military training *continued* one's education are worth highlighting and were repeated in an Air Force appeal released in March 1948, which offered prolonged 'education' to new recruits through 'Regular Service'.[50] In another Navy advertisement circulated in 1947, another fictitious testimonial was given, this time by a boy shown helping his mother in the kitchen. Also smiling, the boy declares:

> Gosh!
> Mum.
> . . . I'm glad I joined the Navy.
> Don't I look well? That's what four good meals a day and plenty of games can do. Uncle Bill was right. It's like a good school, only better. And we're paid to go there. Everything's free, too, so I can afford to send home quite a bit of pay.
> I'll say I'm still sticking to my studies. I'm in the advanced class.[51]

124 *Brendan Maartens*

The day-in-the-life character of this exchange and the domestic setting in which it occurred belied the actual conditions of service boys encountered in the military. Compelled to remain on base until they were granted leave, they may have been paid and educated, but they lacked the freedom many of their peers enjoyed and were also, crucially, compelled to undertake some form of active service *after* they completed their courses. This aspect of military life was conspicuous by its absence in post-war print advertising, some of which even targeted children through their parents, in one case by emphasising the money serving sons could send home:

> TO PARENTS!
> The ROYAL NAVY offers a career to your sons, which gives them a fine training and worth while occupation with excellent opportunities at *no cost* to yourselves.
> From the day of entry your son is well clothed, well-fed, educated and paid. He gets periodical holidays and an allowance towards his upkeep whilst on holiday. He can also make an allotment to his parents if he so desires.[52]

Such 'allotments' were clearly designed to appeal to those struggling to make ends meet, and this suggests a deliberate targeting of the poor.

Fashioning 'news pegs': press conferences, press releases and public exhibitions

Paying for space in newspapers represented one method of attracting readers' attention. Another involved generating coverage of recruitment in news itself. Press conferences were an important means of doing so. Organised by civil servants, they were usually hosted by Ministers or high-ranking officers. In 1949, for example, Felicity Hanbury, Air Commandant of the Women's Royal Air Force, chaired one conference; the year beforehand, Vice-Admiral Sir Wilfred Patterson, commander of the Navy Reserves, led another.[53] Chosen for their capacity to speak with authority on military affairs, these individuals were tasked with delivering prepared speeches to the press and with fielding any questions reporters might have following their speeches. The information they supplied often found its way into print in the form of quotations attributed to named sources, which was described in official memoranda as a matter of fashioning 'news peg[s]' for journalists' stories.[54] The following example, published the day after Lawson's announcement, gives a sense of how such 'pegs' were incorporated into an article in the *Aberdeen Press and Journal*, Scotland's oldest newspaper:

> Launching a campaign to get 250,000 recruits to the Services by the end of the year, three political Service chiefs in London yesterday emphasised that Britain's youth, who answered the time-honoured call now, would follow a career which would leave them well equipped for return to civilian life.
> Said the Secretary for War, Mr Jack Lawson – 'All three Services are highly technical and provide a far better technical preparation for subsequent civil employment has been the case hitherto.

'Unlike the pre-war recruiting appeals, this one is directed not only to the spirit of adventure and the patriotism of young men but also their hard common-sense'.[55]

Quoted matter of this nature does not appear to have been critically evaluated in the British press in 1946–50. On the contrary, it was often used to *substantiate* the claims made by reporters, whose own credibility could be bolstered by quotes attributed to prominent sources.

Moreover, though officials had voiced concern over the apparently poor treatment of voluntary recruitment in the press, many newspapers ran feature articles and opinion pieces that were avowedly pro-recruitment in both tone and outlook. In one front-page piece in Ulster's *Northern Whig* in 1946, for example, readers were treated to a description of service that would not look out of place in an advertisement. The Services, the anonymous author of this article claimed, were 'out for quality', and were especially interested in those with 'energy, ability and character' who could bring such 'goods' to a 'first-class market' for employment. If the commercial metaphor was familiar, so too were the references to pay, which 'compared very well indeed with most jobs in civilian life', the 'opportunities for sport and adventure', and the 'sound training which men would find invaluable when they returned to civil life'.[56]

A positive spin on official recruiting efforts was also given in the *Coventry Evening Telegraph*, which claimed in one leader in 1948 that: 'On the young men and women, on the boys and the apprentices to whom they were now calling, depended the future of the R.A.F. – and on them, too, the future of our way of life might well depend'.[57] In an opinion piece in *The Scotsman*, another major Scottish daily, the author (again anonymous) argued that the 'principal medium' for recruiting should not be newspapers, but the 'spoken word'.

> Let Service speakers . . . take a leaf out of the Communist and Fascist book. Let them address . . . various boys' clubs and other youth organisations. The very fact of membership of a youth organisation suggests a desire for something better than a dead-end occupation or one of the drab varieties of employment [found elsewhere].[58]

The Services had historic ties to several national youth organisations, most notably the Boy Scouts, which were created by the Army officer Robert Baden-Powell in 1908.[59] In the late 1940s, they also participated in annual schoolboys' exhibitions, which became part of the scholarly calendar from 1948 and gave recruiters the opportunity to speak to minors directly at events intended to showcase the many career options available to boys as they approached the end of school. Hosted in school halls, convention centres and other large buildings, the Services sent teams of recruiters to these exhibitions, invited attendants to quiz them on the 'pay and conditions' they received in the military and distributed recruiting literature.[60]

Reports of these events suggest they were frequently characterised by spectacle and pageantry. In one exhibition in Plymouth in 1949, recruiters piqued students' interest with displays of military artefacts, the Admiralty dispatching a 'modern torpedo gyro, a radar set, a torpedo engine, [and] divers' equipment', the War Office a 'working model of a car, a guardsman in full dress, and an exhibition of ancient small arms' and the Air Ministry 'bomb aiming equipment, model aircraft, air-sea rescue equipment, a model airborne life-boat, navigational equipment, and dummy bombs'.[61] In another exhibition in the New Horticultural Hall in Westminster in December 1948, displays of artefacts were combined with a speech delivered by the physicist Sir John Cockcroft, who won a Nobel Prize for splitting the atom in 1951, and a question-and-answer session with an Air Force test pilot. Billed as a festival of 'Supersonics and Atoms', this exhibition also involved a talk by unnamed 'stage and film actors and authors' and bands, parades and a guard of honour.[62] A third exhibition held in the same month in Belfast, dubbed a 'Schoolboys' Paradise' in one article, exposed children not just to a 'certain measure of propaganda . . . for it is organised primarily to inspire interest in the Navy, Army and Royal Air Force, as offering careers for adventurous youth', but to a selection of toys as well, including gliders, model railways, stamp collections, caged butterflies and new games'.[63]

Displaying toys and games at these stalls conflated the act of serving with gaming and may have given the impression to young people that service was akin to recreation.

'What lies beyond the horizon'? Visualising military life on the silver screen

It is important to note that recruiters were not the first to associate enlistment with vicarious enjoyment. Short stories, comic strips, films, board games and postcards had long performed the same function, teaching young Britons (and young boys especially) to view the individuals who waged wars as brave, chivalrous and quintessentially masculine.[64] The state had exploited films for recruiting purposes since the Second Boer War (see Chapter 2), and had capitalised on the mass appeal of film in 1939–45 with big-budget productions like *In Which We Serve* (1941).[65] Nothing as ambitious was commissioned in the post-war era, but several small-scale productions were bankrolled. Most of these were instructional shorts used to train those who had already enlisted,[66] but some were given theatrical releases to try to increase interest in service. *A Sailor Is Born* (1949), for example, told the story of a teenage boy who enlisted in the Navy.[67] *Wonders of the Deep* (1949), described by one reviewer as a 'scientific film', showcased 'startling under-water pictures' filmed by Navy divers.[68] *British Army at Your Service* (1950), finally, used cartoons to depict the 'British soldier throughout history'.[69]

In addition to these shorts, the services also commissioned an unspecified number of 'trailers'. No more than two minutes in length, these items were designed for inclusion in newsreels and were ostensibly factual in nature. *Fighting RAF* (1946), for example, contained footage of Mark Hart, a champion boxer and pilot, training. *Join the Navy* (1946) included scenes of Alexandria, Malta, Sydney and Hong Kong. *Royal Army Ordnance Corps* (1950), for its part, showed men working in warehouses and laboratories. Though they might be considered vaguely newsworthy, such trailers were actually closer to television commercials than conventional news items, advertising recruitment transparently, with the RAF using Hart as a poster boy for the 'battling RAF' and the Army trailer describing the Ordnance Corps in commercial overtones as 'one of the biggest and most up-to-date business houses in the world' which offered applicants a 'job to suit them on the commercial or technical side [of service]'. The Navy took a more oblique approach, asking 'What lies beyond the horizon? This question has always inspired the adventurous. . . . If you want to take the rough with the smooth, you go to sea'.[70]

Released in the decade in which UK cinema attendance reached its all-time peak, these items would have been seen by large numbers of cinemagoers, including many minors, though it is impossible to say how many prospective recruits viewed them and if they responded positively while doing so.

Reviewing the campaigns of 1946–50: a critical assessment

The Attlee governments may have been the first in the post-war era to systematically target schoolchildren and school-leavers for military service. Yet they were not the last. Recruiting for minors continued apace in the 1950s and 1960s,[71] with the policy enjoying broad cross-party support ever since then. Minors as young as 16 are still able to join the British armed forces today, with the Army permitting boys and girls to sign pre-contract agreements from the age of 15 years and 7 months. This gives Britain the dubious distinction of being the only country in Western Europe to recruit child soldiers. The United Nations Committee on the Rights of the Child, Child Soldiers International and Forces Watch are among the organisations that have critiqued this policy, drawing attention not only to the scale of mobilisation efforts – in 2007, 32% of all new recruits to the tri-service were minors[72] – but to their moral implications as well. 'An armed forces career', the critic David Gee wrote in 2008, 'involves ethical questions associated with the justification of killing, the risk of civilian casualties and the political purposes of military action' that children are simply incapable of comprehending. Nor are prospective recruits supplied with accurate *information* on service careers to allow them to make an informed choice to begin with. On the contrary, British recruiters in 2006–7 gave a notably warped portrayal of military life, emphasising putative benefits like 'comradeship, the active lifestyle, travel and training opportunities' but omitting or obscuring potential shortcomings, including the 'radical change from a civilian to a military lifestyle . . . risks to physical and mental health, [and] the legal obligations of enlistment'.[73]

Sixty years earlier, recruiters also took liberties with the truth and seemed equally oblivious to the implications of their actions. The emotional and psychological trauma that service could inflict on combatants, a trauma that many adults experienced firsthand in wartime, was never recorded in official meetings and memoranda and rarely raised in Parliament. With a nod to historical presentism, one could argue that recruiters in 1946–50 were operating in a different social reality, a time when adulthood began earlier in the legal and practical senses of

128 *Brendan Maartens*

the word. Yet the rights of children were enshrined in contemporary legislation, with the 1948 Children Act, for example, compelling local authorities to provide care to all minors (defined as anyone under the age of 18) whose parents neglected them. This begs the question of why all three forces were permitted to enrol those as young as 15 and why they routinely conscripted 17-year-olds. The fact that the Army seemed successful at attracting orphans or children cared for by single parents raises additional questions that do not appear to have been asked at the time.[74]

If there is a conclusion to be drawn from the campaigns of 1946–50, it is that no civilised society permits children to serve in armed forces. Minors, as any parent will attest, are both vulnerable and impressionable and, even when supplied with the information they need to make an informed choice tend to lack the maturity to make the *right* choice. Many grow up regretting decisions made earlier in life, and a considerable number end up in occupations ill suited to their talents. Promotion of the kind explored here was designed to influence young people at a crucial, formative period in their lives and did so in a way that both stylised and sanitised service. The fact that this work was sanctioned by a government which prided itself on its 'socialist' credentials is more than a little paradoxical. Labour's social revolution, clearly, had limits.

Notes

1 But not, crucially, with founding state-sanctioned welfare. Derek Fraser, *The Evolution of the British Welfare State: A History of Social Policy Since the Industrial Revolution* (London: Macmillan, 2009).
2 'Rating British Prime Ministers', Ipsos MORI: www.ipsos.com/ipsos-mori/en-uk/rating-british-prime-ministers; 'Academics Vote Brown One of Britain's Worst Post-War Prime Ministers', University of Leeds: www.leeds.ac.uk/news/article/867/academics_rate_brown_one_of_the_worst_post_1945_pms; 'Cameron Rated Third-Worst Prime Minister Since the End of World War Two', Independent: www.independent.co.uk/news/uk/politics/david-cameron-worst-prime-minister-ranking-third-since-ww2-a7358171.html, all (accessed 8 May 2019).
3 This is consensus is usually regarded as a product of wartime exigency and the social levelling that accompanied it. See Paul Addison, *The Road to 1945* (London: Pimlico, 1994).
4 '1945 Labor Party Election Manifesto', Labor Party: www.labour-party.org.uk/manifestos/1945/1945-labour-manifesto.shtml (accessed 8 May 2019).
5 Peter Hennessy, *Never Again: Britain 1945–51* (London: Penguin, 2006), 91.
6 Mark Pythian, *The Labor Party, War and International Relations* (London: Routledge, 2007), 27; Roy Douglas, *The Labor Party, Nationalism and Internationalism, 1939–1951* (London: Routledge, 2004), 228–9.
7 Miners, farmers and sailors in the merchant navy could avoid service if they worked for a number of years. The act only came into force in 1949, but it applied to all individuals aged 17 to 21, which ensured all boys who grew up in the 1940s were liable for the call-up.
8 Women were prevented from joining up until they reached the age of 18, which is why their story has not been told here.
9 *Milngavie and Bearsden Herald*, 21 August 1948. All newspaper citations have been sourced from the British Newspaper Archive: www.britishnewspaperarchive.co.uk/.
10 The services do not appear to have kept detailed records of volunteers organised by age group, but two-thirds of new recruits to the Army were reputedly drawn from the under-20 age group, boy seamen were regarded as the 'backbone' of the Navy, and, in one year at least, 19,000 out of an intended 58,000 volunteers for the RAF came from the under-18 age group: almost a third of the intake. N[ational] A[rchives], INF 12/71: Notes of a

Meeting (19 December 1947); CAB 134/359: Home Information Services: Estimated Expenditure, 13 November 1950; AIR 2/11578, Cooks to Smith, 21 June 1952.

11 NA, CAB 134/359, Home Information Services: Estimated Expenditure, 13 November 1950.

12 Brendan Maartens, 'From Propaganda to "Information": Reforming Government Communications in Britain', *Contemporary British History* 30, no. 4 (2016): 542.

13 Martin Moore, *The Origins of Modern Spin: Democratic Government and the Media in Britain, 1945–51* (Basingstoke: Macmillan, 2006), 18, 35.

14 William Crofts, *Coercion or Persuasion? Propaganda in Britain after 1945* (London: Routledge, 1989).

15 A detailed breakdown of funding can be found in NA, INF 12/321.

16 Hansard, fifth series, House of Commons, 12 September 1950 (vol. 478), cc. 955–6; *Daily Mirror*, 1 September 1950.

17 *Liverpool Echo*, 4 September 1950; *Daily Mirror*, 1 September 1950; *The People*, 10 September 1950.

18 Hansard, fifth series, House of Commons, 12 September 1950 (vol. 478), 957.

19 NA, CAB 134/359: Home Information Services: Estimated Expenditure, 13 November 1950.

20 NA, RG 23/159: National Service and Enlistment in the Armed Forces, January 1951.

21 NA, INF 12/321: Notes of a Meeting, 29 September 1950.

22 The second committee was given a more expansive brief than its predecessor, combining recruiting with a 'continuous flow of information and explanation which will help understanding and goodwill between the forces and the general public which they serve'. This aspect of its work falls outside the scope of this study. NA, CAB 134/359: Defence Publicity Programme 1950–51, 17 June 1950.

23 The armed forces did not use television for recruiting until the 1960s. Brendan Maartens, 'Modernizing the Military: Promoting a New "Brand Image" of the British Army, Navy, and Air Force in the Post-National Service Era, 1957–63', *War in History* 26, no. 3 (2019): 416.

24 Crofts, *Coercion or Persuasion?*, 22–4.

25 This London-based organisation had a long association with Britain's D-notice censorship system. See Nicholas Wilkinson, *Secrecy and the Media: The Official History of the United Kingdom's D-Notice System* (London: Routledge, 2009).

26 NA, INF 12/71: Robert Fraser to Francis Williams, 14 March 1947; INF 12/71: Minutes of a Meeting, 7 March 1947.

27 Adrian Bingham and Martin Conboy, *Tabloid Century: The Popular Press in Britain, 1896 to the Present* (Oxford: Peter Lang, 2015), 14.

28 Sean Nixon, 'The Advertising Industry in the Age of Affluence', in *Hard Sell: Advertising, Affluence and Transatlantic Relations, c. 1951–69* (Manchester: Manchester University Press, 2013), 16–35.

29 Much of this promotion was aimed at adults, and I have explored aspects of it in Brendan Maartens, 'Your Country Needs You? Advertising, Public Relations and the Promotion of Military Service in Peacetime Britain', *Media, War & Conflict* 3, no. 2 (2020): 213–33.

30 NA, INF 12/71: Notes of a Meeting, 20 June 1947.

31 NA, INF 12/71: Notes of a Meeting, 19 December 1947.

32 NA, PREM 8/281: Broadcast Speech by the Secretary of State for War, 16 May 1946.

33 *Burnley Express*, 13 August 1947.

34 *Cheltenham Chronicle*, 14 August 1948.

35 *Londonderry Sentinel*, 14 September 1946.

36 *Chelmsford Chronicle*, 26 September 1947.

37 *Sligo Champion*, 22 February 1947.

38 *Coventry Evening Telegraph*, 27 November 1947. 'Writers' may have been secretaries.

39 *Chelmsford Chronicle*, 25 April 1947.

40 Ibid., 26 September 1947.

41 *Nottingham Evening Post*, 19 April 1948.

42 *Tamworth Herald*, 8 February 1947.

43 *Daily Mirror*, 20 December 1947.

44 See, for example, *Coventry Evening Telegraph*, 13 August 1946; *Liverpool Echo*, 15 June 1946; *Northern Whig*, 10 August 1946.

45 *Chelmsford Chronicle*, 22 November 1946; *Bucks Herald*, 16 January 1948.

46 This advertisement appeared in, among other titles, the *Belfast Telegraph, Liverpool Echo, Yorkshire Evening Post* and *Coventry Evening Telegraph* in mid-August 1946.

47 *Suffolk and Essex Free Press*, 1 April 1948.

48 *Daily Herald*, 15 November 1948.

49 *The Scotsman*, 18 October 1946.

50 *Airdrie and Coatbridge Advertiser*, 27 March 1948.

51 *Hartlepool Northern Daily Mail*, 3 March 1947.

52 *Milngavie and Bearsden Herald*, 25 May 1946.

53 *The Yorkshire Post and Leeds Intelligencer*, 27 January 1949; *The Scotsman*, 24 September 1948.

54 NA, INF 12/71: Robert Fraser to Francis Williams, 14 March 1947.

55 *Aberdeen Press and Journal*, 17 May 1946.

56 *Northern Whig*, 27 July 1946.

57 *Coventry Evening Telegraph*, 2 October 1948.

58 *The Scotsman*, 21 March 1949.

59 Michael Rosenthal, *The Character Factory: Baden-Powell and the Origins of the Boy Scout Movement* (London: Pantheon, 1986).

60 *Chelmsford Chronicle*, 15 July 1949.

61 *Western Morning News*, 29 December 1949.

62 *The Scotsman*, 20 December 1948.

63 *Belfast News-Letter*, 13 December 1948.

64 Michael Paris, *Warrior Nation: Images of War in British Popular Culture, 1850–2000* (London, Reaktion, 2000), 9.

65 Produced in collaboration with commercial production companies, this film told the story of the sinking of the fictional HMS *Torrin*. John Ramsden, 'British Society in the Second World War', in P. Taylor (ed.), *Britain and the Cinema in the Second World War* (Hampshire: Macmillan, 1988), 26.

66 In 1946, new Army recruits were reputedly obliged to watch as many as 50 instructional films as part of their basic and corps training. Films were preferred to pamphlets, according to one report, because of the 'painfully high proportion' of 'semi-literate' new recruits. *The Sphere*, 9 March 1946.

67 Sponsored by the COI and the Admiralty, this film was produced by Editorial Productions, a company that worked on a range of public information films in the 1950s.

68 *Gloucester Echo*, 8 March 1950.

69 NA, INF 6/784: British Army at Your Service (1949–50).

70 'Fighting RAF' and 'Join the Navy', British Pathe Historical Collection: www.britishpathe. com/video/fighting-raf and www.britishpathe.com/video/trailer-join-the-navy/query/ join+the+navy (accessed 8 May 2019); 'Royal Army Ordnance Corp', British Pathe YouTube Channel: www.youtube.com/watch?v=vom5nt1ywq0 (accessed 8 May 2019).

71 NA, WO 32/16185: Recruitment of Borstal boys into Army: policy and procedure (1952–62); BN 29/2100: Procedure for the enlistment of boys: memorandum, correspondence and draft letter (1969–1970); T 225/3644: Recruitment into the armed forces: Report of the Committee on Boy Entrants and Young Servicemen, chaired by Lord Donaldson (1969–70).

72 Report on Convention of the Rights of the Child, United Nations Committee on the Rights of the Child, 49th session: https://tbinternet.ohchr.org/_layouts/TreatyBodyExternal/ Countries.aspx?CountryCode=GBR&Lang=EN (accessed 8 May 2019).

73 David Gee, *Informed Choice? Armed Forces Recruitment Practice in the United Kingdom* (Joseph Rowntree Charitable Trust, 2008), 8, 3.

74 In 1950, the Army reputedly drew as many as 39% of its volunteer intake from this category of youth. NA, RG 23/159: National Service, 1950.

9 Eastern Europe's reluctant soldiers

Recruitment to the armies of the Warsaw Pact, 1956–1991

Roger R. Reese

Abstract

In the communist Eastern Bloc nations between 1956 and 1991, there was virtually no effort to recruit volunteers. All the armies of the Warsaw Treaty Organization (WTO) were conscript armies, and the vast majority of men aged 20–24 served in the armed forces whether they wanted to or not. Despite the obligatory nature of service, the WTO regimes all sought to gain youths' willing compliance and to minimize draft evasion by inculcating within them support for military service through indoctrination by the communist parties, the various young communist leagues, the national education systems, the respective militaries, and dedicated pre-induction military training organisations. The superiority of the socialist system, the threat of capitalist aggression, and the unity of the peoples of the Union of Soviet Socialist Republics and the Eastern Bloc were prominent themes of pre-induction indoctrination. Above all, military service was portrayed as fulfilment of their civic duty. More than just for national defence, the pre-service preparation and active service were intended to generate loyalty to the idea of socialism, subordination to the one-party state, and acceptance of the need to maintain the Soviet bloc. All WTO nations failed to achieve this goal.

This chapter argues that the pre-conscription preparation in the Warsaw Treaty Organization (WTO) was a monumental waste of time and resources in that it did not generate voluntary enlistment, loyalty to the political system, or to defence of socialism or even offer substantial preparation for military service. Ultimately, it was the legitimacy of the state and its powers to enforce conscription that compelled Soviet and Eastern European youth to serve. The scholarship on recruitment to the armies of the WTO is exceedingly thin. What little work there is on the WTO was done during the Cold War primarily as analyses of current events. There are virtually no published primary sources on the topic. Access to military archives only became available in the former Eastern Bloc after the collapse of communism, yet scholars in the former Eastern Bloc have yet to turn their attention to their national militaries in the communist era. The Ministry of Defence archives of the former Union of Soviet Socialist Republics (USSR) remain closed to foreigners. Due to these factors, there are no historical debates on recruitment in the WTO.

132   *Roger R. Reese*

All the Warsaw Pact countries relied on conscription to man their armies; consequently, they had no expectation of voluntary enlistment. Despite the involuntary nature of military service, the WTO armies did attempt to get their youth to look forward to their service as more than an obligation. They wanted the youth to serve willingly and gladly in ways that would adhere them to the communist regimes. To this end, the regimes sought to prepare their young men physically and psychologically for service well before they turned draft age. The common thread of recruitment among all the WTO armies was the attempt to persuade conscripts to see themselves as part of the continuum of their countries' military history. To this end, the communist parties, the various young communist leagues, the national education systems, and the respective militaries all had a hand in promoting the necessity and supposed privilege of military service. The preparation for service was especially focused on the last two or three years of secondary education, and included compulsory pre-conscription military training.

Although all the WTO armies conformed to the Soviet model of conscription, the content of their pre-conscription indoctrination differed along distinct national lines. How closely the various armies adhered to the Soviet line on the meaning of the WTO, its relation to the USSR, and their different national interests varied widely. The German Democratic Republic (DDR) was slavishly loyal to the USSR, while Romania was at the opposite end of the spectrum, adopting independent military policies and a nationalist orientation. The major themes used to prepare young men for service were nationalism and national unity, socialist internationalism to convince them to support the WTO and the alliance with the USSR (in which their countries were obviously subordinate), and pride in Marxist-Leninism as the superior economic and social system that was threatened by the capitalist West. The problems with these themes were that each WTO nation, other than the USSR, had a long tradition of nationalism founded on anti-Russian histories reinforced by recent experiences that generated anti-Soviet attitudes. Attempts to convince future soldiers that socialism was a superior system ran into two stumbling blocks: they focused young people's attention on their quality of life, which seldom matched the promises made, and they exposed them to a brand of *Soviet* socialism that was imposed by an alien and malignant power. The attempt to generate fear and hatred of the West clashed with the longstanding tradition of Eastern Europe's cultural identification with the West. Nevertheless, the youth of Eastern Europe and the USSR dutifully, though reluctantly, answered the call to serve until the late 1980s, when the legitimacy of the Soviet system was called into question and their governments lost broad societal support.

The establishment of the Warsaw Treaty Organization and the politics of recruitment

When the governments of the USSR, Bulgaria, the DDR, Czechoslovakia, Hungary, Romania, and Poland signed the Treaty of Friendship, Cooperation and Mutual Assistance that established the WTO in May 1955, all but the DDR had standing armies based on conscription. These armies had a history of conscription that dated back to the nineteenth century within either the Russian, German, or

Austro-Hungarian empires, which the new governments that emerged in the aftermath of the First World War continued. Therefore, imposing conscription to man their new armies after the Second World War met little to no protest.

Initially, from 1956 to 1967, the term of conscript service was the longest in the Soviet army, with three years for the ground forces and four years each for the navy and air force. The length of service was reduced by one year in 1967. Bulgaria, Czechoslovakia, and Poland required service for two years, Hungary and East Germany for eighteen months. Romania conscripted men for only sixteen months. The constitutions of all the WTO nations declared military service to be obligatory for all adult males at some point between their eighteenth and twenty-seventh birthdays. Service was variously described as being an honour, a privilege, and a sacred obligation.[1]

All the WTO armies granted educational deferments for students in higher education. However, none allowed exemption from service on the grounds of conscientious objection. The East German and Hungarian armies did, however, provide for alternative, non-combatant service in construction units for conscientious objectors. In Hungary, Nazarenes, Jehovah's Witnesses, and Seventh Day Adventists could choose to perform alternative non-combat service. Initially, East Germany did not allow for conscientious objections to service, but reacting to public pressure in 1964, it allowed conscientious objectors to serve in construction units called *Baueinheiten*. The term of service here was eighteen months, as it was for regular soldiers. Annually, approximately 250 men opted for the *Baueinheiten* until the 1980s, when it rose to about 1000 per year.[2]

All WTO nations subjected draft evaders and those who refused to serve in any capacity on religious grounds to harsh punishment. In the USSR, draft evaders or refusers could be imprisoned for up to seven years; in the other WTO nations, the maximum was five years.[3] In Hungary, in 1988, 158 men were in prison for refusing to serve, including in unarmed status. It is estimated that perhaps as many as 2000 men went to prison for refusing to serve on religious grounds in the DDR between 1964 and 1976.[4] Other than these examples, there is virtually no evidence available to determine the levels of resistance to conscription. Anecdotal evidence suggests a high degree of compliance in all WTO armies until the late 1980s. It is known that in the USSR, men faked illnesses and used *blat* or *protektsiya* (influence of important people) to secure exemptions from service. Others enrolled in higher education just to secure an exemption.[5] A study conducted in the 1980s concluded that 'efforts at service avoidance increased steadily throughout the post-World War II period', and 'that those who illegitimately avoided service in the Soviet military did so largely through individual initiative and resourcefulness'.[6] It was common knowledge that a bribe of 1,000–2,000 rubles could purchase a medical exemption.[7]

Pre-conscription ideological indoctrination and military training: the Soviet model

With the introduction of the 1967 Law on Universal Military Service, the USSR and subsequently over the years the WTO nations all mandated compulsory pre-conscription military training for male youth in their last two or three years of

134   *Roger R. Reese*

secondary school, which usually meant from the ages of fourteen to eighteen years old. The total instruction time amounted to 140 hours.[8] Pre-conscription military training and accompanying ideological indoctrination had been instituted in the USSR in the 1920s and in Eastern Europe with the formation of the WTO. However, only in the late 1960s and 1970s did it become mandatory. After the time in service had been reduced in the USSR to two years (which it had always been in the Eastern European armies), the army claimed that it needed to ensure conscripts would already possess basic military knowledge and skills. This represented the ostensible rationale for the mandatory instruction, but a more likely explanation is that the Soviet regime, and the East European communist parties as well, were insecure about the loyalty of their youth and sought to intensify the indoctrination of young people to get them to adhere to the tenets of Marxism-Leninism, accept the need for compulsory service, and be patriotic citizens.[9] In effect, the regimes saw military service as the school of the nation and pre-induction instruction as the 'pre-school' of the nation. Actual schools, the young communist leagues, and specially formed pre-conscription organisations cooperated to provide such instruction.

The All-Union Voluntary Society for Assistance to the Army, Air Force, and Navy (DOSAAF) was the Soviet pre-conscription organisation. Subordinated to the Ministry of Defence, it had roots going back to the 1920s. After the introduction of the 1967 Law on Universal Military Service made pre-conscription training mandatory, it took five years (1968–1972) to create basic military courses in nearly 80,000 schools. For youth graduating before completing the 140-hour program, the DOSAAF struggled to create instruction points at tens of thousands of collective farms and industrial enterprises.[10] The Ministry of Defence inadequately funded DOSAAF for its entire existence. As a consequence, DOSAAF required schools to pay the salaries of the instructors, many of whom were reserve or retired officers. DOSAAF also sought donations from industrial enterprises to help pay for instruction points in their factories. Beyond that, DOSAAF went into business for itself, charging membership fees (from a largely captive audience), running a lottery, and pursuing money-making operations by renting out its facilities and selling its newspaper, *Sovetskii Patriot.*[11]

Twenty years on, the DOSAAF leadership admitted that their organisation still had not lived up to its potential. They could not claim that it was either well organised or run by conscientious people. Each union republic ran its own DOSAAF organisation. The Russian Soviet Federative Socialist Republic provided the most comprehensive training while the Central Asian and Baltic republics provided the least. Although tens of millions of youth were members at any given time – many joined due to social pressure rather than innate interest in military service – there was no way to compel attendance at training or other activities. Officially, one had to finish the whole 140-hour program to graduate from high school and go on to higher education, but this was not rigorously enforced. The directors of schools, enterprises, and farms were legally responsible for seeing to it that the young people under them received proper military instruction, but they had other priorities and often ignored DOSAAF and left instructors to their own devices.

One Western source estimated in 1980 that only half of all conscripts actually had the mandated DOSAAF experience.[12]

Besides basic military instruction, DOSAAF also sponsored optional sports programs. Prepared for Labour and Defence of the USSR was its physical fitness program, which taught cross-country running, swimming, and several Olympic sports. The so-called military-technical sports programme included parachuting, skiing, scuba diving, glider piloting, motorcycling, automotive mechanics and driving, radio operating and electronics, and seamanship. The ultimate awards were the Ready for the Defence of the Motherland badge and the opportunity to compete at regional, all-union, and international competitions.[13]

General preparation for military service and pre-conscription training in the Eastern European countries generally followed the Soviet model, though recent history made youth sceptical of the pro-Soviet, pro-socialist, and anti-Western rhetoric. Most obviously, Polish and Hungarian youth were strongly anti-Soviet because of the upheavals of 1955–1956, during which the potential for a Polish–Soviet war were quite real and the population of Hungary was left angry and resentful following the invasion by the Soviet army. The Soviet invasion of Czechoslovakia in 1968, supported by East Germany and Hungary, turned an otherwise pro-Soviet population against the USSR and the WTO and pushed the Romanian government to adopt foreign and military that were policies increasingly un-Soviet and independent of the WTO.

Nevertheless, the countries' respective communist youth and pre-conscription training organisations delivered the party line in an effort to indoctrinate and prepare young men for service. Czechoslovakia's version of DOSAAF, *Svaz pro spolupraci s armadou* (the Association for Cooperation with the Army) was thought by Western analysts to be 'a huge (and prosperous) sports and recreational organisation, only "paramilitary" in the broadest sense of the word'.[14] It did not transmit a convincing pro-Soviet message, and in the 1970s and 1980s, the Czechoslovak population felt so humiliated and burdened by the Soviet occupation that the indoctrination of pre-conscript youth proved to be very problematic. As it turned out, Poland's *Liga Oborony Kraju* (League of Defence of the Country) and the *Zwiazek Harcerstwa Polskiego* (Polish Scouts Association), Poland's largest youth organisation, besides promoting Polish nationalism, were under extreme pressure by the anti-socialist and anti-Soviet movements of the 1970s and 1980s, an era marked by mass unrest, strikes, demonstrations, and the rise of the *Solidarity* movement, which, among other things, demanded the democratisation of the army. In those years, the Polish United Workers Party felt very unsure of the loyalty of the youth and of the ability of the pre-conscription programmes to influence them.[15]

The other Eastern Bloc countries all adapted pre-conscription training to fit their national character. Of particular difference between the East European countries and the USSR was their use of history to promote loyalty to the communist regimes on the basis of nationalism. By the 1950s, the USSR was relying nearly exclusively on the experience of the Great Patriotic War, the term used to describe Soviet engagements during the Second World War, to justify loyalty and appeal to patriotism to motivate youth to willingly submit to conscription, with occasional references to the

136 *Roger R. Reese*

superiority of the socialist system and the threat from the capitalist West. Because they either had been on the wrong side during the Second World War or crushed by Nazi invasion early on, Eastern European countries could not use the war experience to generate patriotism. In addition, national pride and communist international-ism were contrary concepts that had to be handled delicately. The histories of the Eastern European countries had been decidedly un-socialist, and internationalism smacked of subordination to the Soviet Union. History, then, had to be recast and reinterpreted from a Marxist-Leninist viewpoint. The DDR went so far as to rein-terpret the roles of Martin Luther, Frederick the Great, and even Otto von Bismarck to support 'socialist patriotism'. Romania reached back to its Daco-Roman roots, Vlad the Impaler, and Stephen the Great. Bulgaria looked back to Cyrill and Metho-dius.[16] Czechoslovakia, Bulgaria, and Hungary had no easily useable military his-tory.[17] The Marxist reinterpretations of history strained credulity, reminded people that their governments were rewriting history to please the Soviets, and underscored national differences between WTO states.[18]

'We will never take up weapons': East Germany as a case study in contrasts

The DDR was the only nation that did not immediately introduce conscription in the aftermath of the Second World War as East European nations created new armies (Poland and Czechoslovakia) or transitioned the armies left over from old regimes to new socialist-oriented nations (Bulgaria, Hungary, Romania). Instead, the DDR attempted to recruit on a voluntary basis. The East German case was unique in that it did not have a government until 1949, did not have an army until 1956, had a means for youth to avoid conscription by easily fleeing to the West until 1961, and for nearly thirty years, many Germans in both East and West saw the division of the country as temporary and thus saw the DDR as only quasi-legitimate. Under these circumstances, East Germans showed a deep-seated reluctance to volunteer. Due to the aforementioned circumstances, volun-tary recruitment was largely unsuccessful. Immediately after the Berlin Wall went up, the regime felt secure in introducing conscription because East German males could no longer flee to avoid it.

When the *Nationale Volksarmee* (NVA) was established in 1956, the East Ger-man regime decided to man it on a voluntary basis, correctly guessing that with the open border in Berlin it would be impossible to enforce conscription on an unwilling population. Recruitment drives launched in the years immediately fol-lowing the founding of the NVA triggered emigration waves among the affected age cohorts. Between 4 February 1952 and 31 December 1959, 234,157 men between the ages of 18 and 24 registered as refugees in West Germany or West Berlin. The regime suspected that some young men temporarily left for the West just so that they would thereafter be considered politically unfit for service upon their return. In attempts to compel 'voluntary' enlistment, the regime made ser-vice in the military a prerequisite to university admission, threatened to reduce the wages of working youth, and blocked promotions for skilled workers who refused to enlist. Nevertheless, recruitment drives consistently returned disappointing results.[19]

The recruitment drive of the autumn of 1961 after the wall was built produced no better results. Military-aged men told recruiters: 'I'll only join the army when conscription is introduced'; 'We won't shoot at other Germans'; and 'We will never take up weapons'.[20] Although the number of men who signed declarations that they would enlist rose significantly during the weeks following the announcement of the 'Defence Law' on 20 September 1961 (which was the first step towards the subsequent introduction of universal male conscription), it was clear that the increase was the result of coercion by recruiters, which included threats of dismissal from one's workplace, fines, or even arrest. As it turned out, in the region of Erfurt, only 181 of the 1,432 youths who had agreed to enlist actually did so. In Magdeburg, recruitment authorities noted that only 209 youth out of 1,835 reported for duty as they promised. Civilian employers were no fans of military service; defying the regime, many factory managers reportedly attempted to keep their young and productive employees at work by raising their pay or helping them obtain various deferments and exemptions. Building the Wall and then introducing the law on universal male obligation to serve further alienated a great many East German youth. In the weeks following the building of the Wall, more than 300,000 youth quit the *Freie Deutsche Jungend* (FDJ), the DDR's Komsomol, or communist youth organisation, in protest.[21] Once it became the law of the land, however, East German youth fell into line and reluctantly began to report for duty.

Indoctrinating the youth of the DDR proved to be particularly challenging given the historical and contemporary events that shaped their thinking. The brutal Soviet conquest and occupation, the workers' uprising in 1953 bloodily crushed by the Soviet army, the imposition of Marxist-Leninist ideology, and the slow economic recovery all worked against convincing youth that they should serve an army seen by many as an extension of the Soviet army. As in the USSR, the school system taught patriotism and hate for the capitalist West, yet the better part of Germany now lay in the West. The DDR's equivalent of the Young Pioneers of the USSR, the *Pioneerorganisation 'Ernst Thälmann'*, enrolled children aged six to fourteen years old, subjected them to political indoctrination, and led them in age-appropriate military training exercises. At age fifteen, youth graduated to the FDJ. According to historian Alan Nothnagle:

> The FDJ adopted the hiking and folkloristic activities of the *Wandervögel*, the uniforms and rhetoric of the pre-war communist and socialist youth movements, the organisational forms and ideology of the Soviet *Komsomol*, and even the belligerent street style of the Hitler Youth.[22]

The *Gesellschaft für Sport und Technik* (Society for Sport and Technology or GST), the equivalent of the DOSAAF, overlapped with the FDJ. The regime wanted the GST to 'prepare young people of pre-conscript age for their military

138   *Roger R. Reese*

service in such a way that they come to see this as a class duty and acquire the necessary [martial] skills in their pre-military training'.[23]

In grades eight to ten in secondary schools, so-called Hans Beimler Contests (*Hans-Beimler-Wettkämpfe*) were the main element in the system of socialist military education organised by the FDJ, with different programs for different groups and ages. These contests included events with a military angle, such as cross-country and obstacle course racing, hand grenade throwing, marksmanship with air rifles, forced marches, trekking, and the like. A 100-hour curriculum for ninth and tenth graders was established in 1973 (60 hours for ninth graders and 40 hours for tenth graders), which concentrated on marksmanship, field exercises, self-defence, and medical training. This usually took place one afternoon for four hours every other week. Although it was declared to be mandatory in 1978, many teens avoided it.[24]

The GST had a four-year course of instruction divided into basic military training and specialised training for NVA careers. Basic training began after the tenth grade and consisted of 85 hours of instruction. A GST member could complete the course by attending at least 80 per cent of the instruction, qualifying as a marksman, and finishing five of the eight subject areas of instruction. For field instruction, GST members wore NVA military uniforms to make them feel and look like soldiers.[25]

In the end, the efforts at indoctrination, which were more thorough in the DDR than anywhere else in the WTO, failed to adhere East German youth to the regime when the opportunity for change arose. The case of the DDR raises the questions that if youth of the other WTO nations had had the opportunity to easily flee their country to avoid service, would they have, and could any of the Eastern European nations have sustained armies based on voluntary service?

An 'ingrained aversion to all uniforms': youth attitudes towards service

For the first twenty years after the founding of the WTO, the general attitude towards being forced to serve in the military among East European youth was one of reluctance and resignation. No evidence has yet surfaced revealing widespread draft evasion prior to 1989, though there were always a few who sought exemptions that they were not entitled to or claimed conscientious objections. The legal right and power of the state to compel service was broadly accepted, and few wished to spend more time in prison than they would in uniform. Therefore, to a large degree, the efforts at indoctrination were unnecessary and, as the events of the 1980s would prove, completely ineffective. In the mid-1970s, with the growth of the dissident movement, people began to question the legitimacy of the communist regimes. East Europeans began to question the need for large armies and the necessity of manning them by conscription. Questions of legitimacy also surfaced among the many nationalities of the USSR, especially in the Baltic republics and the Caucasus. Russians too, questioned the need for so many young men to be taken away for military service.

Eastern Europe's reluctant soldiers 139

It is impossible to say if the growing manifestation of resistance to service in the 1970s was something new or just the result of the new-found confidence of the peoples of the USSR and Eastern Europe in expressing their viewpoint. Ample reasons existed for young men to avoid service apart from the obvious interruption of their lives. In all the armies, the quality of life for recruits was harsh and austere. As Ellen Jones writes, 'In short, military life for the Soviet draftee is physically rigorous, sometimes boring, often unpleasant and lonely, and largely divorced from civilian society'.[26] Beginning sometime in the 1960s, the practice of hazing new recruits (labelled *dedovshchina* in the Soviet army) became pervasive throughout the WTO armies and could be especially brutal when directed against the national minorities in the Soviet army.[27] Future conscripts were well aware of the practice, having heard about it from older relatives and friends who had done their service.[28] WTO armies experienced thousands of desertions, suicides, and murders every year as a result of hazing.

Another disincentive to serve was the merely token pay. In the Soviet army, pay was 3 to 5 rubles per month, or 2.6 per cent of the average monthly wage of 190 rubles in the USSR at the time. Soviet families routinely sent money to their sons to help them get by. Although NVA conscripts were paid better than their Soviet counterparts, the wages were still a rather paltry 120 marks per month – 14 per cent of the 839 marks the average East German employee earned.[29] The other WTO armies paid their soldiers just as poorly.

A number of things set the populations of the USSR and Eastern Europe into open opposition to their governments' military policies that eventually radicalised society and turned youth against conscription. The first was the dissident movement in the Soviet Union that promoted democratic and anti-socialist ideas, which dated from the late 1960s and grew rapidly in the early 1970s with the founding of Helsinki Watch and the Russian offices of Amnesty International. Second was the Soviet invasion of Afghanistan in December 1979. Anti-nuclear protests in Eastern Europe, beginning in 1983, were the third factor. Gorbachev's reforms – *glasnost* – in particular, which took hold in 1986, constituted the fourth and final factor.

Although efforts to avoid service had existed on a minor scale long before the Soviet invasion of Afghanistan in December 1979, the invasion sparked an anti-war movement, which galvanised Soviet mothers in defence of their sons, increased the number of government and party elites who used their influence to get exemptions for their sons, and demoralised future conscripts who saw how the Soviet state neglected its wounded and traumatised veterans. When *glasnost* reduced censorship and allowed for near-complete freedom of expression, the anti-war movement exploded and spilled over into anti-militarism in both the USSR and Eastern Europe. Dodging the draft became a problem for the Soviet army during the war in Afghanistan and continued to increase once the war was over. By 1988, evading conscription and desertion came to be seen by young men as normative behaviour. Students, supported by faculty, staged protests against both the war and lack of deferments for university students in numerous institutions of higher education in the course of 1988. Komsomol officials, disenchanted with

140   Roger R. Reese

the excessive militarisation of the regime, gradually came to unofficially endorse draft evasion, and many law enforcement authorities tacitly accepted it.[30] Pacifist and anti-military attitudes became manifest in youth in the USSR under Gorbachev. Soviet Admiral Egorov admitted in 1988 that only 2 to 3 per cent of university students participated in DOSAAF; the rest 'sit and watch television or go to discos'. Simultaneously, societal support for conscription and pre-conscription training waned significantly. Many considered that the skills imparted by military training would be useless or ineffective against weapons of mass destruction. Some employers, both in the Soviet Union and in the Eastern Bloc, who were responsible for providing training at their enterprises, gave the instruction only lip service and looked for ways to excuse conscripts from participating.[31]

Anti-militarism received another boost when the United States announced that it was going to position intermediate-range nuclear missiles in Western Europe. The Soviet Union countered that it would deploy its own missiles to Eastern Europe. The prospect of the USSR basing missiles and their nuclear warheads in the DDR and Czechoslovakia led the East German and Czechoslovak publics to fear that they would become targets of North Atlantic Treaty Organization (NATO) nuclear strikes. In Czechoslovakia, anti-Soviet street protests against the deployments erupted in 1983 and 1984. Christian clergy spoke out against the Soviet missiles. Secondary school students, on the threshold of becoming conscripts, participated in the protests. Students in Hungary staged anti-nuclear protests inspired by the Peace Group for Dialogue, which proposed making Europe a nuclear free zone and advocated the withdrawal of foreign troops – US and Soviet. The Soviet-sponsored Prague Peace Assembly in June 1983, designed to turn the people's anger against NATO, backfired when Charter 77, the nascent peace movement in Czechoslovakia endorsed by the Catholic Church, received wide attention for its anti-nuclear message aimed at both superpowers.[32] The result of these movements was the inculcation of pacifist and anti-military attitudes in pre-conscript–age youth that communist youth organisations were unable to counter.

The protests were not simply against nuclear weapons but were part of a broader societal discontent with the apparent failure of socialism to deliver on its economic promises at the cost of political and personal freedoms. Religious revivals in all the Eastern European countries and the USSR further undermined faith in the socialist regimes. The churches, focusing on youth ages fourteen to twenty years old, directly challenged the states' young communist organisations and pre-conscription training organisations, in a call for peace and human rights. Generational change also played a role; East European youth were prone to pacifism, first as result of the Second World War and later because of the spectre of nuclear holocaust. They were especially critical of the presence of Soviet troops in their countries and dismayed by the lack of economic opportunity and political freedoms. Czech nuclear physicist František Janouch observed that generations coming of age after August 1968 had an 'ingrained aversion to all uniforms – just like my generation's aversion to the green-grey uniforms of the Wehrmacht', an attitude they handed down to the generation that followed, which duly questioned the excessive militarisation of socialism.[33] The growth of nationalism in Eastern

Eastern Europe's reluctant soldiers 141

Europe and within the Soviet Union, with its anti-Soviet or anti-Russian connotations, served to embolden protesters. All of these factors contributed to youth willingness to defy their governments' call for conscripts. In the DDR, the number of conscripts who opted for non-military construction duties or simply refused to serve at all rose from approximately 700 per year in the 1960s and 1970s to more than 10,000 in 1983.[34]

In the face of massive street demonstrations, Soviet domination of Eastern Europe and the power of the East European communist governments began to unravel very quickly beginning in 1989. Hoping to satisfy public pressure to demilitarise their countries, all the WTO governments reduced the size of their armies, thus reducing the number of conscripts. In 1989, all the East Bloc armies immediately announced that they would reduce the size of their armies by at least 10,000 men in the next draft cycle, Poland by 55,000. (Poland even went so far as to release 22,000 men from duty early and introduced legislation to allow for alternative service for conscientious objectors.) Simultaneously, the time of conscripted service was shortened from two years to eighteen months or even less.[35] Finally, acknowledging the vast latent antipathy to the presence of Soviet soldiers in Eastern Europe, Poland, Hungary, and Czechoslovakia appealed to nationalism when they insisted on the complete withdrawal of all Soviet troops rather than just a reduction in their numbers, as suggested by Gorbachev. Only the DDR did not call for the removal of all Soviet troops, and this led to pent-up anti-Soviet sentiments to burst out in violence. In 1990, East Germans held demonstrations against the presence of the 363,000 Soviet soldiers and their families and, more ominously, began shooting at them (and killing several), beating up soldiers, and hurling rocks and bottles at their barracks and officers' housing.[36]

Public pressure to end or modify conscription increased dramatically. Within the USSR, as early as 1987, the pacifist group Trust openly protested against compulsory military service. Encouraged by their communities, in 1990, thousands of young men, especially those from Estonia, Latvia, Lithuania, Georgia, and Armenia began to avoid conscription. The Estonian leadership petitioned Moscow for major changes in how their people would serve and included calls for alternative service for conscientious objectors and the abolition of military training in schools. Latvians simply stopped registering for the draft. By 1990, the overall rate of draft evasion in the USSR was estimated to be 26 per cent but was higher in the earlier-mentioned republics, ranging from 46 per cent in Estonia to 92 per cent in Armenia. Roughly 400,000 men failed to report for duty in 1990. Of considerable alarm to the authorities was the degree to which society sympathised with draft evaders, thought to be largely due to the knowledge of and the extent of *dedovshchina*. It was clear that Soviet society as a whole, including the Russians, no longer supported the military and in fact blamed it for many of the USSR's problems.[37]

The situation was worse for the armies of the Eastern Bloc. In 1990 and 1991, thousands of potential East German conscripts fled to the West through Hungary, which had opened its border with Austria. Scores of soldiers defected to West Germany, and some even joined the West German army. In 1991, 6000 men

142 Roger R. Reese

illegally left Bulgaria to avoid the draft. Another 3,500 failed to report for duty.[38] The failure of the pre-conscription Marxist-Leninist, patriotic, and military indoctrination had become all too clear.

Conclusion: the relationship between service and strife in the communist East

During the Cold War, the vast majority of Soviet and East European men obeyed their countries' laws to report for duty, many having first been exposed to pre-conscription political indoctrination and military training. They did so unenthusiastically, accepting their governments' right to draft them, although not necessarily the need. It is important to note that the WTO governments and armies offered no incentives to volunteer or to re-enlist. The pay was insultingly low and conditions often miserable. There were no post-service benefits regarding education or employment. Young men understood that they had a choice: prison or military service. Overall, military service in the WTO was an unrewarding experience, so when governmental legitimacy was cast into doubt by the failure to deliver the quality of life promised by socialism, and when the prospect of war with NATO diminished following Gorbachev's rapprochement with the West, the youth of the USSR and Eastern Europe rebelled against conscription. They realised that their governments' ability to punish them for evading the draft was gravely weakened and believed that their governments could no longer justify drafting them. They were also, however, exposed to a different type of recruiting appeal to that circulated in the capitalist West during the same period. While youth in Eastern Europe and the USSR were taught to view service as a duty, an honour, and a privilege, their counterparts in Britain (see Chapter 8) and the US (see Chapter 10) were generally exposed to more materialistic inducements. This, together with a lack of actual material rewards for service in the East, might explain why so many served reluctantly.

Notes

1 Mark N. Kramer, 'Civil-Military Relations in the Warsaw Pact: The East European Component', *International Affairs* (Royal Institute of International Affairs 1944) 61, no. 1 (1984): 50.
2 Stephen R. Burant, *Hungary: A Country Study* (Washington, DC: Library of Congress, 1990), 246; Thomas M. Forster, *The East German Army: The Second Power in the Warsaw Pact*, trans. Deryk Viney (Cologne: Markus-Verlagsgesellschaft, 1980), 47; Henry Krisch, 'German Democratic Republic', in Daniel N. Nelson (ed.), *Soviet Allies: The Warsaw Pact and the Issue of Reliability* (Boulder and London: Westview, 1984), 24.
3 Lawrence Klippenstein, 'Exercising a Free Conscience: The Conscientious Objectors of the Soviet Union and the German Democratic Republic', *Mennonite Life* 40, no. 3 (September 1985): 23.
4 Janes Information Group, *The RUSI Soviet Warsaw Pact Yearbook 1989* (Surrey, UK: Jane's Defence Data, 1989), 220; Krisch, 'German Democratic Republic', 25–6.
5 William Zimmerman and Michael L. Berbaum, 'Soviet Military Manpower Policy in the Brezhnev Era: Regime Goals, Social Origins and "Working the System"', *Europe-Asia Studies* 45, no. 2 (1993): 287, 288, 296, 297.

Eastern Europe's reluctant soldiers 143

6 Ibid., 285, 290.
7 Ellen Jones, 'Social Change and Civil-Military Relations', in Timothy J. Colton and Thane Gustafson (eds.), *Soldiers and the Soviet State: Civil-Military Relations from Brezhnev to Gorbachev* (Princeton, NJ: Princeton University Press, 1990), 256.
8 David M. Gist, 'The Militarization of Soviet Youth', *Naval War College Review* 30, no. 1 Special Issue (Summer 1977): 125.
9 Dimitri K. Simes, 'The Military and Militarism in Soviet Society', *International Security* 6, no. 3 (Winter 1981–1982): 136–7; *The RUSI Soviet Warsaw Pact Yearbook 1989*, 57–9.
10 Ellen Jones, 'Manning the Soviet Military', *International Security* 7, no. 1 (Summer 1982): 115; Robert G. Wesson, 'The Military in Soviet Society', *The Russian Review* 30, no. 2 (April 1971): 139.
11 William E. Odom, 'The Soviet Military-Educational Complex', in Dale R. Herspring and Ivan Volgyes (eds.), *Civil-Military Relations in Communist Systems* (Boulder, CO: Westview, 1978), 93, 94; Herbert Goldhammer, *The Soviet Soldier: Soviet Military Management at the Troop Level* (London: Leo Cooper, 1975), 41, 42.
12 Simes, 'The Military and Militarism in Soviet Society', 140; Raymond E. Zickel, *Soviet Union: A Country Study* (Washington, DC: Library of Congress, 1991), 742; *The RUSI Soviet Warsaw Pact Yearbook 1989*, 57–9; Gist, 'The Militarization of Soviet Youth', 126.
13 Gist, 'Militarization of Youth', 124.
14 Ihor Gawdiak, *Czechoslovakia: A Country Study* (Washington, DC: Library of Congress, 1989), 245.
15 'Speech by Stanislaw Kania at Meeting of Party and State Leaders of the Warsaw Pact', 5 December 1980, *History and Public Policy Program Digital Archive*, ANIC, Central Committee of the Romanian Communist Party, chancellery, No.5257, 9.12.1980. CWIHP Document Reader, vol. 2. 'Romania and the Warsaw Pact, 1955–1989': https://digitalarchive.wilsoncenter.org/document/112068; 'Memorandum Regarding the Meeting between Comrade Leonid Ilyich Brezhnev, Erich Honecker, and Gustav Husak in the Kremlin', May 16, 1981, *History and Public Policy Program Digital Archive*, SAPMO-BArch ZPA, vorl.SED 41559 https://digitalarchive.wilsoncenter.org/document/112630.
16 Nothnagle, 'From Buchenwald to Bismarck', 107; Walter M. Bacon, Jr., 'The Military and the Party in Romania', in Herspring and Volgyes (eds.), *Civil-Military Relations in Communist Systems*, 167; Volgyes, 'Bulgaria', 118.
17 Václav Šmidrkal, 'Abolish the Army? The Ideal of Democracy and the Transformation of the Czechoslovak Military after 1918 and 1989', *European Review of History: Revue européenne d'histoire* 23, no. 4 (2016): 624.
18 'Information on the 20th Session of the Committee of the Ministers of Defence of Warsaw Pact Member States', 30 November 1987, *History and Public Policy Program Digital Archive*, Archives of the Ministry of National Defence, No.: 033438–84/1987 https://digitalarchive.wilsoncenter.org/document/110290.
19 Corey Ross, 'East Germans and the Berlin Wall: Popular Opinion and Social Change before and after the Border Closure of August 1961', *Journal of Contemporary History* 39, no. 1 (January 2004): 33; Forster, *The East German Army*, 61.
20 Ross, 'East Germans', 38.
21 Ibid., 38, 39.
22 Alan Nothnagle, 'From Buchenwald to Bismarck: Historical Myth-Building in the German Democratic Republic, 1945–1989', *Central European History* 26, no. 1 (1993): 102.
23 Forster, *East German Army*, 51, 52, 152.
24 Ibid., 54; H. Hurwitz, S. O. Crane and W. P. Davison, 'Political Opinion in the Soviet-Occupied Zone of Germany', in *In Brief* (Santa Monica, CA: Rand Corporation, 1959), 39; Krisch, 'German Democratic Republic', 172.
25 Forster, *The East German Army*, 155–6.
26 Jones, 'Social Change and Civil-Military Relations', 239.

144 *Roger R. Reese*

27 Teresa Rakowska-Harmstone, 'Baltic Nationalism and the Soviet Armed Forces', *Journal of Baltic Studies* 17, no. 3 (Fall 1986): 191; Natalie Gross, 'Youth and the Army in the USSR in the 1980s', *Soviet Studies* 42, no. 3 (July 1990): 481.

28 Bruce D. Porter, *Red Armies in Crisis* (Washington, DC: The Center for Strategic & International Studies, 1991), 35–7.

29 Zickel, *Soviet Union: A Country Study*, 745; Forster, *The East German Army*, 297; Mikhail Tsypkin, 'The Conscripts', *The Bulletin of Atomic Scientists* (May 1983): 32.

30 Jeffrey Simon, *Warsaw Pact Forces: Problems of Command and Control* (Boulder, CO: Westview, 1985), 157–63; Gross, 'Youth and the Army in the USSR in the 1980s', 483; Porter, *Red Armies in Crisis*, 39; *The RUSI Soviet Warsaw Pact Yearbook 1989*, 60.

31 Robert English, 'Europe's Doves', *Foreign Policy*, no. 56 (Autumn 1984): 47–50, 51, 56; Julian Cooper, 'The Military and Higher Education in the USSR', *The Annals of the American Academy of Political and Social Science* 502, Universities and the Military (March 1989): 115–17; Gawdiak, *Czechoslovakia: A Country Study*, 245; *The RUSI Soviet Warsaw Pact 1989*, 56.

32 English, 'Europe's Doves': 45; Krisch, 'German Democratic Republic', 174–6; Gawdiak, *Czechoslovakia: A Country Study*, 245.

33 Šmidrkal, 'Abolish the Army?', 626.

34 English, 'Europe's Doves', 57, 58; Ferenc Koszegi and E. P. Thompson, 'The New Hungarian Peace Movement', *History and Public Policy Program Digital Archive*, END Special Report, European Nuclear Disarmament and the Merlin Press, 1982: https://digitalarchive.wilsoncenter.org/document/113738.

35 Dale R. Herspring, 'Reassessing the Warsaw Pact Threat: The East European Militaries', *Arms Control Today* 20, no. 2 (March 1990): 8, 9; Porter, *Red Armies in Crisis*, 20; *The RUSI Soviet Warsaw Pact Yearbook 1989*, 245.

36 Ray Moseley, 'In East Germany, Soviet Soldiers Pay for Overstaying Welcome', *Chicago Tribune* (20 September 1990); Prokop Tomek, 'Life with Soviet Troops in Czechoslovakia and after Their Withdrawal', 106: https://doi.org/10.7592/FEJF2017.70.tomek; Evgeny V. Volkov, 'German Democratic Republic of the 1970s-1980 through the Eyes of Soviet Officers (Oral Stories)': https://doi.org/10.7592/FEJF2017.70.volkov.

37 Walter R. Iwaskiw, *Estonia, Latvia, and Lithuania: Country Studies* (Washington, DC: Library of Congress, 1996), 77, 160; David Holloway, 'State, Society, and the Military under Gorbachev', in Alexander Dallin and Gail W. Lapidus (eds.), *The Soviet System: From Crisis to Collapse* (Boulder, CO: Westview, 1995), 550, 553; Stephen M. Meyer, 'How the Threat (and the Coup) Collapsed: The Politicization of the Soviet Military', *International Security* 16, no. 3 (Winter 1991–1992): 17, 18, 21–2, 24; Zickel, *Soviet Union: A Country Study*, 743; Jones, 'Social Change and Civil-Military Relations', 256–7.

38 Dale R. Herspring, *Requiem for an Army: The Demise of the East German Military* (Lanham, MD: Rowman & Littlefield, 1998), 43, 48; Nothnagle, 'From Buchenwald to Bismarck', 91; Glenn E. Curtis, *Bulgaria: A Country Study* (Washington, DC: Library of Congress, 1993), 253; Porter, *Red Armies in Crisis*, 40, 41.

10 'The Army just sees green'
Utopian meritocracy, diversity, and United States Army recruitment in the 1970s

Jessica L. Ghilani

Abstract

In 1973, in the wake of the Civil Rights, Women's Rights, and anti-war movements, the United States Department of Defense (DOD) overhauled its recruitment strategy from a partly conscripted military to an 'all-volunteer' force. To meet recruitment goals, DOD officials increased the US army's budget for advertising and publicity. Army advertisements rebranded military service to dazzle audiences with patriotic imagery depicting the benefits of enlistment. The corresponding copy incorporated pro-equality discourses that had been popularised through social movement rhetoric. Advertisements positioned service itself as a meritocratic utopia, in which one's demographic status as a racial or ethnic minority or woman of any racial or ethnic background would not be a barrier to success and fulfilment. To do so, advertisements co-opted the language of social movements and targeted racial and ethnic minorities as well as women more so than ever before. This chapter uses archival records, including advertising tear sheets, internal advertising agency memos, transcripts from oral history interviews, and other materials held within the corporate archives of N. W. Ayer & Son, the advertising firm that worked for the Army, to examine the promise of merit in selling military enlistment to diverse audiences in the 1970s.

In 1973, the United States armed forces underwent a dramatic transition. Conscription was replaced with a voluntary model, and the American military has filled the ranks with volunteers ever since. In the early years of the transition, the biggest branch of the armed forces, the Army, was afforded the largest recruitment budget to assist with the change.[1] The Army's ranks outsized all others in number, so it faced significant challenges in transitioning from a partly-conscripted to an all-volunteer force. Economists and military sociologists who were advising the Department of Defense (DOD) through the transition argued that the most efficient strategy to spur volunteer recruitment was to invest in advertising.[2] Advertising promised cost efficiency and broad audience reach. Substantial changes to individual enlistment incentives would have been costlier.[3] Numerous scholars, including Bernard Rostker, Beth Bailey, and Melissa Brown, have studied the American military's use of advertising toward the transition to a volunteer era.[4] This chapter builds on that work by looking closely at archival records and

146 *Jessica L. Ghilani*

advertisement tear sheets to understand the strategies and practices of commercial military recruiting advertising in action. Ads put forth a social utopia that positioned merit first and foremost, borrowing the rhetoric of the civil rights and women's rights movements along the way. But first, I will provide background on the decision to go all volunteer.

Prominent economists such as Milton Friedman and Allen Greenspan were members of President Richard Nixon's Gates Commission, assembled in the late 1960s to explore the viability of a volunteer force. They concluded that a market-driven model of military enlistment would be feasible, particularly due to high demands for job training, salary, money for college, healthcare benefits, etc. offered through military service. Neoliberal economic theory guided their thinking, and in their final report, they even likened conscription to taxation:

> Conscription is . . . a tax-in-kind. A mixed force of volunteers and conscripts contains first-term servicemen of three types – (1) draftees (2) draft-induced volunteers and (3) true volunteers. Draftees and draft-induced volunteers in such a force are coerced into serving at levels of compensation below what would he required to induce them to volunteer. They are, in short, underpaid. This underpayment is a form of taxation.[5]

Further into the report, the taxation metaphor continues as the authors explain what they viewed as the hidden costs of conscription. They called conscription a regressive tax because it removed viable labour from the private, civilian workforce, where they would see market-rate compensation and grow the US economy. They reasoned that the volunteer force might require an increase to the DOD budget, but the overall costs to the federal government are less than they seemed when subtracting the economic growth resultant from the change.[6]

But rather than raising salaries for volunteers substantially, they argued for expanding the practice of using skilled, salesman-like recruiters in conjunction with advertisements distributed via mass media, including print magazines, direct mail, radio, and television. Advertisements could emphasise the existing benefits of enlistment, carrying messages widely across audiences targeted according to demographics. The advertising efforts would focus on reaching those for whom economic incentives would be most persuasive. In other words, such advertising campaigns aimed to reach economically disadvantaged groups with less potential for higher, market-rate wages.

Demographically speaking, due to the intersections of race, class, and gender, this also meant that ads tried more than ever before to resonate with audiences of racial and ethnic minorities and women. Racial and ethnic minorities and women were more likely to encounter unconscious bias and discrimination in hiring and promotion practices, creating barriers to high wages.[7] When the US military shifted to an all-volunteer system, ads highlighted service as a venue for accessing equal opportunities. Army recruitment appropriated the rhetoric of the civil rights and women's rights movements in framing the armed services as a utopian meritocracy, where gender, race, or ethnicity or the intersection of these identity

The Gates Commission, the Army, and the beginning of the 'volunteer' era

President Nixon was careful to appoint Gates Commission members with varied views regarding the viability of a volunteer force so that the question could be explored in depth and without a predetermined conclusion.[8] The chairman of the commission, Thomas Gates Jr., was actually against the idea of a voluntary system.[9] Rostker writes that although the deck was not stacked with members who were in favour of a volunteer military, it was intellectually stacked with prominent economists, Milton Friedman and Allen Greenspan, who supported the idea.[10]

The Commission's goal was 'to develop a comprehensive plan for eliminating conscription and moving toward an all-volunteer force'.[11] It sought to do so by 'study[ing] a broad range of possibilities for increasing the supply of volunteers for service, including increased pay, benefits, recruitment incentives and other practicable measures to make military careers more attractive to young men'.[12] The economic concept of supply and demand was important to the rationale about whether the volunteer military would succeed. The steady supply of soldiers throughout the armed forces would sustain the volunteer military. Advertising could help cultivate the supply. But the volunteer army, in particular, faced significant challenges because it had the largest ranks to fill and suffered from the lowest reputation and status among the armed forces.[13] To compensate, the volunteer army's 1973 recruitment budget exceeded those of the other branches.[14]

Print and television commercials for the volunteer army implemented individualism, promising recruits access to opportunities rather than framing service as a civic duty.[15] In the 1970s, emphasis on individualism and individuality in the army's recruitment tactics reflected economic liberalism supported by economists on the Gates Commission.[16] Together with the senior military personnel also on the committee, they assembled a report offering a plan for eliminating the draft. The commission was convened by President Nixon in 1969[17] and published a report the following year that asserted:

> A return to an all-volunteer force will strengthen our freedoms, remove an inequity now imposed on the expression of the patriotism that has never been lacking among our youth, promote the efficiency of the armed forces, and enhance their dignity. It is the system for maintaining standing forces that minimizes government interference with the freedom of the individual to determine his own life in accord with his values.[18]

The report highlighted mechanisms that would enable the transition, placing advertising in central focus. Specifically, 'more advertising in mass media will be both required and rewarding once an all-volunteer force has been instituted, for the elimination of conscription will coincide with improved incentives in the

148   *Jessica L. Ghilani*

military'.[19] While ads were not the only strategies discussed, and the military has relied upon numerous methods to engage and integrate with the civilian public, advertising was listed prominently alongside mentions of recruiters particularly skilled in salesmanship and public relations.[20]

Still, the Commission's recommendation did not come without scepticism from academics as well as military personnel. Military sociologist Charles Moskos argued that 'The abandonment of conscription (in the US) has jeopardized the nation's dual-military tradition, one half of which . . . is the citizen soldiery'.[21] Morris Janowitz, another sociologist, feared that a volunteer force would lead to 'a predominantly or even all Negro enlisted force in the army', because of economic hardships that disproportionately harm underprivileged racial minorities.[22] He believed the demography of the army should reflect the demography of the broader nation. Anthropologist Margaret Mead argued in favor of a national service system because it, 'would provide an opportunity for young adults to establish an identity and a sense of self-respect and responsibility'.[23] Citing socioeconomic inequality, the then-president of Saint Xavier College in Chicago, Harry Marmion, wrote that a volunteer concept was undemocratic. He charged that self-interest guided many of the arguments for ending the draft, and posited that an 'all-volunteer army would liberate the middle class from the legal necessity of serving but commit others to compulsory service by economic circumstance . . . in effect, forcing the poor and the less fortunate into the armed forces'.[24] Even the word 'volunteer' was problematic because it signified un-coerced, uncompromised free will. Economic incentives promised to enlistees through recruitment communications ensure that those most in need are drawn to service.

As political scientist Ronald Krebs observed: 'Leading scholars of civil-military relations often argue that the installation of the volunteer force in 1973 marked the end of, or even . . . severed the link between citizenship and military service'.[25] Bailey writes that some high-ranking military members of the Gates Commission were concerned about ending conscription.[26] Military personnel worried about the potential for lowered standards of admission should service demands not meet the supply of volunteers.[27] Advertising functioned as public relations in trying to assuage all of these concerns across audience groups.

Consumer research practices from marketing and business enabled military recruiters to craft individualised recruitment appeals, issuing calls to serve through otherwise mundane channels of passive entertainment and advertising in popular magazines and on popular television and radio programmes. Recruiters sought to use these channels to bring persuasive messages that portrayed service as a meritocratic utopia. The work would be hard, but you would be judged and rewarded based on your abilities and earned success, not because of who you knew or what you looked like.[28]

The print ads from this period were the product of a much larger financial commitment to recruiting advertising and warrant close examination. Some of the ads were even in Spanish and were subcontracted to the Sosa & Associates agency, which worked with Ayer to create Spanish-language versions of the English-language campaigns.[29] Spanish-language ads began to appear during the Vietnam

War but expanded as an area for targeted recruitment after the end of conscription.[30] The Vietnam War's impact on public opinion of the military presented a major challenge for Ayer and the DOD in their recruitment messaging.

'Be all you can be': the N. W. Ayer–Army partnership

The military hired private advertising agencies to produce recruiting campaigns. For the bulk of the twentieth century, J. Walter Thompson worked with the Marine Corps and N. W. Ayer & Son held the Army account. These agencies bid competitively for contracts from the DOD, pitching their ideas in the hope of being awarded a lucrative government contract.

During the time of transition from conscription to volunteer recruiting, Philadelphia-based N. W. Ayer & Son held the Army account. It had worked with the Army before – during the 1940s and then again in the 1960s – and worked with it in the 1980s as well. A prominent ad firm in the US, its client roster included AT&T, DeBeers, Ford, R.J. Reynolds, Philip Morris, United Airlines, Nabisco, Burger King, and Morton's Salt.[31] The agency was responsible for many famous slogans including, 'A diamond is forever', 'I'd walk a mile for a camel', 'When it rains, it pours', and 'Reach out and touch someone'. It was named *Advertising Age*'s Agency of the year in 1978 and was the eighteenth-largest agency worldwide in 1985.[32]

However, despite pioneering many eventual industry standards, the agency was reluctant to innovate strategies in order to maintain a competitive edge. Archivist Mimi Minnick writes that 'The inherent conservatism of Ayer left the agency vulnerable to the "creative revolution" of the 1960s and 1970s, the restructuring of the 1980s, and the economic recession of the early 1990s'.[33] Although Ayer folded in 2002, its imprint on the history of advertising endures.[34] Responsible for the Army's renowned 'Be all you can be' slogan, which *Advertising Age* ranked at number 18 in its Top 100 advertising campaigns of the twentieth century, its work for the army continues to earn it recognition from within and beyond the industry.[35]

The advertising campaigns Ayer produced for the Army involved multi-media promotion coordinated simultaneously for maximum clarity, synthesis, reach, and impact. Print advertisements formed part of these campaigns and were placed in general as well as niche-interest magazine publications. Although recruitment ads appeared in newspaper classified sections that primarily offered contact information for nearby recruiters, glossy display ads were assumed to be more effective and therefore were prioritised.[36] Television and radio commercials were implemented as a trial, with $10 million of the 1971 fiscal year recruitment budget allocated for them specifically.[37] Television commercials had been used at various points prior to this, but they ran primarily during undesirable time slots when the broadcast networks offered free advertising time for public service announcements.[38] TV spots aired during college football games and during other sporting events.[39] Beth Bailey writes that 'The young men inclined to volunteer, according to research, were more likely to watch television than to read magazines. Thus prime-time television offered the best targeting of "good prospects"'.[40] During this time, the television industry in the United States comprised three big broadcast networks: the National Broadcasting Company, the American Broadcasting Company, and the Columbia Broadcast System (renamed 'CBS' in 1974). As the term 'broadcast' suggests, these networks reached audiences spread widely across demographics and geographies. It is difficult to access detailed information about ratings during the airing of particular ad spots, but due to the limited choices in broadcast networks, audiences were far less fragmented and diffuse than they became in the decades that followed.

Nevertheless, rather than mirror the targeted campaigns from print by featuring diverse racial, ethnic, and gender representations of the ranks, the clips gave a whitewashed portrayal of the branch, using mostly white male actors and, whenever possible, enlisted service personnel as protagonists. The same cannot be said for the agency's print work, where representations of diverse racial, ethnic, and gender identity positions took centre stage.[41]

It is unsurprising that the medium of print featured more plentiful representations of diversity. The broad range of titles and profusion of niche and speciality publications enabled advertisers to strategically target messages based on characteristics like age, race, gender, hobby, interest, profession, and more. This was not yet the case for television. In the early 1970s, cable television was still a fledgling industry with very few subscribers. Television commercials were also costlier to make and distribute than print ads. Because of broadcast dominance, the big networks could command even higher advertising rates from sponsors. Sponsors knew they would be casting a broad net to reach audiences. Ayer mimicked what most television ads of the period were representing by featuring white men in their Army commercials.

Advertising and reality are often out of alignment. John Berger writes about advertising as a medium that attempts to simulate reality while also putting forward that to which to aspire.[42] Jean Baudrillard writes that simulations of the real will always be diminished. Ads can never do more than mimic reality.[43] It is common practice for advertising to present a utopia, in that it is an ideal place but also a place that does not truly exist.[44] Advertising is relegated to simulation in that regard. Sir Thomas More first wrote of *Utopia* in the sixteenth century, and the Greek etymology translates to 'no-place' or 'nowhere'.[45] Utopia is in perpetual tension as a place that is ideal and yet unattainable, very much like the worlds put forth in advertising. The concept of utopia functions specifically in many of the targeted Army advertisements, representing opportunities and benefits for economically disadvantaged racial and ethnic minorities as well as women, regardless of race. The decision to recruit for a volunteer force required marketing toward economically disadvantaged groups. This was implicit to arguments made by members of the Gates Commission.[46]

'Today's Army wants to join you': utopia in recruitment advertising

The Vietnam War loomed large in public consciousness in the early 1970s. It was the first televised 'living-room war', meaning that Americans could see and access military content in more complete and complex ways than during prior US military interventions. Michael Mandelbaum writes about the role of television during this time, indicating that 'When Americans could only read about war, they could contemplate it with dispassion. When they could see and hear it in their living rooms, they turned against it'.[47] The military had less control over how audiences encountered news information, and news coverage was more comprehensive and timely than that witnessed during the Second World War and the Korean War.

The Gates Commission noted the impact that mass media had on civilian and military culture during the Vietnam War, stating: 'There is now significant interaction between the military and the rest of society. The military is not isolated from the mass media which permeate all walks of life'.[48] Because advertising presents an idealised simulation, many of the challenges to military representation in civilian news media could be subverted by offering curated messages. Advertising is not news and not easily confused with news outside of publicity stunts, which are typically regarded as a staple of public relations, a different but related profession. Advertising has no responsibility to convey information about civilian casualties, military injuries, failed missions, military misconduct, and soldier deaths, but it did offer a form of escapism from such 'reality'.

Advertising is a realm that sometimes uses and relies upon notions about utopia. There is an inherent tension between advertising and reality just as there is an inherent tension between utopia and real life. Both advertising (in many cases) and utopia envision an idealised but largely impossible reality. Many commercial advertisements depict a consumerist utopia, in which problems are easily solved through buying products. Advertising also offers a materialistic utopia in which life can be fulfilled via the procurement of the 'right' material goods. Scholars and historians of advertising have used the concept of utopia toward this purpose. Roland Marchand writes that advertising strives to articulate the American Dream for audiences, creating aspirational messages about what one's goals should be in a particular cultural moment.[49] Michael Schudson has said that advertising does not claim to picture 'reality as it is but reality as it should be – life and lives worth living'.[50] Marsha Richins has written that advertisements invite social comparisons, at least in part because audiences recognise the implicit messages about social norms contained within these brief glimpses of consumer utopia.[51] Gib Prettyman has argued that brands use advertising to put forth their messages about the utopia awaiting consumers upon making 'good' consumer choices.[52] A prevailing theme of advertising promises that utopia becomes one's reward for being a good consumer.

Advertising often puts forth a kind of consumerist utopian vision wherein everyone has equal opportunities and resources to buy products that solve everyday problems. A utopian framework is used in many different kinds of advertising for traditional as well as non-traditional commodities. The same agencies that created campaigns to sell soap, cars, sodas, and other commercial goods were tasked with selling military service to the American public.

Advertising also made economic sense for the Army. A member of the 1978 President's Commission on Military Compensation named K. A. Goudreau wrote that 'In increasing the overall [DOD] end-strength, it would appear to be most cost effective to put more money into recruiting and advertising than into higher wages'.[53] Although this conclusion was drawn regarding the future of the volunteer force at the five-year mark, similar sentiments were established in the 1970 Gates

152   *Jessica L. Ghilani*

Commission report. The comment underscores the logic behind advertising as an entrusted venue for recruitment: it is believed to be cost-effective when compared to the cost of increased wages, it is efficient, and it can be distributed widely on a massive scale. Advertising also can help shape broader public conceptions about the armed force branches. Although the setting of an unpopular war is not anyone's ideal, the Vietnam War–era advertisements that targeted women presented a softened version of the challenges Women's Army Corps (WAC) and Nurse Corps members faced. Kara Dixon Vuic discusses recruitment in her history of the Nurse Corps during Vietnam.[54] Because nurses were needed in Vietnam, the ads recruiting nurses referenced the war directly, in ways that WAC ads otherwise avoided.

On the whole, Ayer's WAC recruitment conveyed military service as a carefree, exciting way to forge new experiences and make new friends.[55] In many ways, the process of recruiting women functioned as a test case for the volunteer era.[56] Policy shifts at the federal level removed a cap that had kept female enlistment figures below 2 per cent of the overall soldier population. According to military sociologists, Janowitz and Moskos, the utilisation of women as military personnel was 'essentially token,' at least before the Vietnam War. In 1964, 1.1 per cent of uniformed military personnel were female, but by 1974, the figure had more than tripled to 3.5 per cent.[57] Ads aimed at women made all sorts of promises. Some ads for the WAC claimed that military service was a great way to meet male suitors as well as acquire useful skills and job training. The protagonist portrayed in Figure 10.1, Amy, looked every bit as stylish and charming as Marlo Thomas, star of the popular late-1960s proto-feminist television sitcom *That Girl*.[58]

Amy is shown leaning in to listen to her handsome, well-dressed partner in conversation. Although the audience is not informed of the content of their exchange, the body language speaks volumes. Her bright, engaged smile and comfortable closeness suggest flirtation. Her hand clutches a bouquet of flowers meant to signify a romantic gift. Audiences were told that 'Amy is an expert in psychological warfare', which conveyed a subtle flirtation and implicit sexism, as if to warn about her potential to manipulate as well as entice.[59] Her black gloves, mod 1960s trench coat, and scarf evoked the stylized spy films of the era. If the text was swapped out and replaced, this ad could have just as easily sold toothpaste, shampoo, or perfume. But it was selling enlistment in the WAC. The 1968 ad ran in the April issue of *Time Magazine College Edition* and the May issue of *Mademoiselle*, just in time to be read by senior students anticipating their impending graduations.[60] A series of similar ads ran over the following two years, all of which focused on women's potential for professional as well as personal growth through military service. Figure 10.1's protagonist appears fun and enviable. The ad's narrative depicts a breezy, modern attitude: 'No gal Friday job for her . . . Army jobs available to gals like Amy: like communications, public relations, management consulting, finance, personnel management'. The pursuit of a career dovetailed with the repeated referencing of the modern protagonist as gal, signalling loudly to all the similarly modern women she represented or inspired. Without the copy, ad photographs depicting attractive, stylish, feminine young women could be mistaken for commercials selling gum, yogurt, or feminine hygiene products.[61]

'The Army just sees green' 153

Figure 10.1 'Amy's an Expert in Psychological Warfare'

Source: AAARS, 'Psychological Warfare', SIL. The 1968 ad ran in the April issue of *Time Magazine College Edition* and the May issue of *Mademoiselle*. Whenever possible, I include publication information from archives, but records do not always permit this.

154   *Jessica L. Ghilani*

There were many ads like this from the era. Their use of gendered tropes varied. Ads created a framework for recruitment that was built during the volunteer era. Representing social and meritocratic utopia was possible in the late 1960s and early 1970s because the advertisements also began to employ ideas that were increasingly widespread thanks to social and countercultural movements.[62] The influence of the civil rights movement and the second wave of feminism were evinced in the shifting language choices of army advertisements during the 1970s. Embedded within the messages of these advertisements was a notion that if there was no place in civilian life where one's identity would be treated separately from one's talent, you could enlist in the Army. The army saw only the colour of your uniform. 'The Army Sees Green' was the title of one such ad that championed the military as a place where hard work and ability were paramount and the colour of your skin was irrelevant.[63]

But not all ads of the period adopted social movement language. Many relied on deep-seated American ideology to convey utopia. Rather than using a meritocratic tone, one ad (see Figure 10.2) offered a nod to American exceptionalism and individuality. In this ad, the gifts of liberty and choice were bestowed on targets for recruitment. This ad still posited a kind of utopia.

In Figure 10.2, the protagonist and the recruiter are shown together, smiling. In terms of design and page layout, the people in the ad take up a fraction of space. But they appear to be harmonious and amicable. The ad was a part of a campaign called 'Today's Army Wants to Join You'. The slogan was an inversion of James Montgomery Flagg's iconic First World War propaganda poster, 'I Want YOU for the US Army'. The title of this text-heavy ad read, 'Now that you don't have to go into the Army, here's why you should'. The copy emphasised benefits, opportunities, and individual advantages. Many early volunteer-era ads sought to put distance between the draft and the new market-driven military. This ad confronted the topic directly. Aimed at young men who managed to avoid the draft lotteries that defined the Vietnam War but found themselves graduating from high school during an economic downturn, the ad parroted youthful slang: 'With only a high school diploma and no work experience, the jobs aren't that *hot*'.[64] Ambivalence and uncertainty permeated the ad to try to capture the emotional complexity of being post-adolescent: 'You know you'd like more time. Time to think about what you've learned in school. Time to try different things, visit other places, meet new people, or just plain get to know yourself'.[65] Job training, salary, promotions, fringe benefits, experiences, travel, independence, and adventure were also mentioned, but at the core of the appeal lay individual *choice*. The army offers a 'choice of over 200 job-training courses', the ad claimed: 'Jobs you can learn and pursue in the Army or in civilian life'.[66] To convey this message, a young, floppy-haired man in a sweater stands with a recruitment officer. Both smile. In the liminal space between job and college, the army became a detour from either. Delay your decision between them, or enable yourself to have a choice in the first place by enlisting.

After the draft's overturn in 1973, ads became even more explicit in signalling utopia to target audiences through the use and appropriation of civil rights and women's rights rhetoric. The 'Today's Army Wants to Join You' campaign was launched in 1971 and followed in 1973 by the campaign titled, 'Join the People Who've Joined the Army'. This campaign featured more racial, ethnic, and gender

'The Army just sees green' 155

Figure 10.2 'Now That You Don't Have to Go'
Source: AAARS, 'Now That You Don't Have to Go', SIL; emphasis added

156 Jessica L. Ghilani

Figure 10.3 'Lead the People Who've Joined the Army'

diversity in the advertising. In one ad, helmeted men wielded guns as they stood near a tank in the background that featured a racially diverse circle of men examining a map together.[67] The leader stood apart from the group with his helmet on his knee and pencil in his hand. And the ad itself guaranteed elite leadership experience while still evoking an inclusive, democratised appeal conveyed in the

'The Army just sees green' 157

slogan itself. It was significant to depict an African American male as the leader of the racially diverse cadets shown in the ad. Ads from this period situated military service as both competing with and complementing other sectors of the job market.

Another 'Join the People Who've Joined the Army' ad featured a female protagonist with the headlining title of 'Specialist' (see Figure 10.3).[68] The ad ran in February 1978 issues of *Senior Scholastic* magazine. *Senior Scholastic* magazine was Scholastic Inc.'s first magazine, launched in 1920.[69] The female 'Specialist,' the text tells us, aspired to a medical career but worked in the Army repairing helicopters. Shown in three photographic vignettes, she repaired a helicopter, lunched with girlfriends in civilian clothing, and flew in one of the aircraft she repaired. Her quiet determination in the first and last scenes was offset with a disarming display of happiness in the centre of the ad. In first-person narration, she mentioned that her confidence grew upon enlistment and that she relished mastering a skill that 'few other people can' master. Although the text contained no direct references to feminism, the ad offered a tempered, approachable version of it. Readers saw a confident, happy, capable, feminine, and strong woman thriving through her military service. The caption described information about pay and benefits. Being paid while learning what ultimately became one's specialty may have been an attractive offer for women eager to join the workforce but possibly unsure of where to start.

Conclusion: idealised simulations in military service in recruitment advertising

In numerous advertisements examined during the time frame covered by this chapter, the concept of utopia was employed to convey an idealised simulation of the reality of military service. Advertisements function as cultural barometers and can offer insight into popular trends of historical time periods. After the draft was overturned, broad public awareness of the civil rights movement and the women's rights movement enabled some incorporation of social movement rhetoric in advertising, principally to appeal to audiences from disenfranchised groups, such as people of colour and women. In other ads, the version of utopia advertised free choice and individuality or a respite from the responsibilities and pressures of adult life. In all cases, utopia functions in correspondence with the goals of advertising: namely, to present an idealised simulation of what *could* be. As John Berger writes: 'Advertising images belong to the moment in the sense that they must be continually renewed and made up-to-date. Yet they never speak of the present. Often, they refer to the past and always they speak of the future'.[70] In advertising, the future is brimming with possibilities and goodness. It offers an escape from a life we are not yet ready to lead or a chance for an opportunity that the world had previously closed off. Although it is not the only variable deserving credit, the use of utopia in military recruitment advertising has facilitated the enduring success of the volunteer military concept in the United States.[71]

Notes

1 Derek Thompson, 'War and Peace in 30 Seconds: How Much Does the Military Spend on Ads?', *The Atlantic*, 30 January 2012: www.theatlantic.com/business/archive/2012/

158 *Jessica L. Ghilani*

01/war-and-peace-in-30-seconds-how-much-does-the-military-spend-on-ads/252222/ (accessed 31 October 2019).

2 K. A. Goudreau, 'Draft: Seminar on Recruiting Research, 1/30/1978', Accession Number 94–074, Box 5, Folder 1, in Smithsonian Institution Assistant Secretary for the Sciences, Manpower Research and Advisory Services Records, S[mithsonian] I[nstitution] L[ibrary].

3 Bernard Rostker, *I Want You! The Evolution of the All-Volunteer Force* (Santa Monica, CA: Rand Corporation, 2006); Beth Bailey, *America's Army: Making the All-Volunteer Force* (Cambridge, MA: Harvard University Press, 2009); and Melissa T. Brown, *Enlisting Masculinity: The Construction of Gender in US Military Recruiting Advertising during the All-Volunteer Force* (New York: Oxford University Press, 2012). See also Samuel W. Black (ed.), *Soul Soldiers: African Americans and the Vietnam Era* (Pittsburgh: Senator John Heinz Regional History Press, 2006); Rachel Brett and Irma Specht, *Young Soldiers: Why They Choose to Fight* (Boulder: Lynne Rienner Publishers, 2004); and Peter A. Padilla and Mary Riege Laner, 'Trends in Military Influences on Army Recruitment: 1915–1953', *Sociological Inquiry* 71, no. 4 (2001): 421–36.

4 Ibid.

5 Thomas S. Gates, Jr., *The Report of the President's Commission on an All-Volunteer Armed Force* (Washington, DC: United States Government Printing Office, 1970), 23–4.

6 Ibid.

7 Rakesh Kochhar and Anthony Cilluffo, 'Income Inequality in the US Is Rising Most Rapidly among Asians', *Pew Research Centre Social and Demographic Trends*, 12 July 2018: www.pewsocialtrends.org/2018/07/12/income-inequality-in-the-u-s-is-rising-most-rapidly-among-asians/; see also Patricia Hill Collins, 'Black Feminist Thought in the Matrix of Domination', in *Black Feminist Thought: Knowledge, Consciousness, and the Politics of Empowerment* (Boston: Unwin Hyman, 1990), 221–38.

8 Rostker, *I Want You!*, 66–7.

9 Ibid.

10 Ibid. See also Beth Bailey, 'The Army in the Marketplace', *Journal of American History* 94, no. 1 (2007): 47–74.

11 Gates, Jr., *Report of Commission*, vii.

12 Ibid.

13 See Bailey, *America's Army*, 69–71; and Richard W. Stewart, ed., *American Military History Volume II: The United States Army in a Global Era: 1917–2003* (Washington, DC: Centre of Military History, 2005), 370–1.

14 Goudreau, 'Draft – Seminar', SIL.

15 Ibid.

16 Economic liberalism emphasises the primacy of free markets, individualism, and governmental deregulation. Pierre Bourdieu writes extensively on economic neoliberalism in *Acts of Resistance: Against the Tyranny of the Market* (New York: New Press, 1999).

17 Evans, 'The All-Volunteer Army', 40–6.

18 Gates, Jr., *Report of Commission*, 6.

19 Ibid., 84–5.

20 Ibid.

21 Charles C. Moskos, 'From Citizens' Army to Social Laboratory', *Wilson Quarterly* 17, no. 1 (1993): 85.

22 Morris Janowitz, 'The Logic of National Service', in S. Tax (ed.), *The Draft: A Handbook of Facts and Alternative* (Chicago: University of Chicago Press, 1967), 67.

23 Margaret Mead, 'A National Service System as a Solution to a Variety of National Problems', in Tax (ed.), *The Draft*, 105.

24 Harry A. Marmion, *The Case against a Volunteer Army: Should America's Wars by Fought Only by the Poor and the Black?* (Chicago: Quadrangle Books, 1971), 46.

25 Ronald R. Krebs, 'The Citizen-Soldier Tradition in the United States: Has Its Demise Been Greatly Exaggerated?', *Armed Forces and Society* 36, no. 1 (2009): 153–74.

26 Bailey, *America's Army*, 26–7, 29.

27 Janowitz, 'Logic of Service'; see also Mead, 'National Service System', 105.

'The Army just sees green' 159

28 For an example of this kind of advertisement, see the A[yer] A[dvertising] A[gency] R[ecords], 'Specialist', SIL. This ad ran in *Senior Scholastic Magazine* in 1978.

29 AAARS, 'Cartography Profession', SIL. To read about the background of Hispanic advertising pioneer, Sosa & Associates, see Randall Rothenberg, 'Sosa Takes the Off Path to Success', *New York Times*, 29 May 1990.

30 AAARS, Army Account Advertising Tear Sheets, SIL.

31 Mimi L. Minick, 'N.W. Ayer & Son, Inc.', in *Advertising Age's Encyclopaedia of Advertising, Volume 1, A-E* (Chicago: Fitzroy Dearborn, 2002), 125–30.

32 Ibid., 128.

33 Ibid., 125.

34 For a history of Ayer, see Anonymous, *Ayer: 125 Years of Building Brands* (New York: Ayer Worldwide, 1994); Bart Cummings (ed.), *The Benevolent Dictators: Interviews with Advertising Greats* (Chicago: Crain, 1984); Deanne Dunning and Blake Hunter, 'The New Ayer', *Communications Arts* 12, no. 1 (1970); and Stephen Fox, *The Mirror Makers: A History of American Advertising and Its Creators* (New York: Morrow, 1984).

35 It was also the only military campaign in the list. See Bob Garfield, 'The Advertising Century: Top 100 Advertising Campaigns', *Advertising Age*, 29 March 1999: http://adage.com/article/special-report-the-advertising-century/ad-age-advertising-century-top-100-campaigns/140918/ (accessed 15 January 2020).

36 Mimi L. Minick, Vanessa Broussard Simmons and Katie Richards, Unpublished, *N W Ayer Advertising Agency Collection, 1849–1851, 1869–2001: History* (Washington, DC: National Museum of American History Archives Centre Library, 2004).

37 Beth Bailey, 'The Army in the Marketplace', 60.

38 Rostker has written about television ads in *I Want You*, 153. During the 1950s, the ad firm Dancer Fitzgerald Sample created for the Army at least one television commercial and perhaps print ads too. In the 1950s, recruitment funds were frozen by the DOD, and it is unclear how and how much the agency was paid. The research is conflicting. But according to an archived issue of *Billboard Magazine*, a list of 'The Billboard Scoreboard: TV Film Commercials in Production' indicated that the firm was working for the Army as late as 1955. 'The Billboard Scoreboard: TV Film Commercials in Production', *Billboard Magazine*, 15 January 1955.

39 Bailey, 'The Army in the Marketplace', 63.

40 Ibid.

41 Ayer's archives also contain many more print ads than television commercials. See Minick, Simmons and Richards, 'N W Ayer'.

42 John Berger, *Ways of Seeing* (London: BBC Enterprises, 1972), 129–54.

43 Jean Baudrillard, *Simulacra and Simulation* (Ann Arbor: University of Michigan Press, 1994).

44 The rise of anti-advertising in the middle part of the century was a response to the ubiquity of advertising's unrealistically sunny portrayals of reality. See Thomas Frank, *The Conquest of Cool: Business Culture, Counterculture, and the Rise of Hip Consumerism* (Chicago: University of Chicago Press, 1997).

45 Thomas More, *Utopia*, trans. Paul Turner (New York: Penguin, 2003).

46 Gates, Jr., *Report of Commission*.

47 Michael Mandelbaum, 'Vietnam: The Television War', *Daedalus* 111, no. 4 (Fall 1982): 161.

48 Gates, Jr., *Report of Commission*, 138.

49 Roland Marchand, *Advertising the American Dream: Making Way for Modernity, 1920–1940* (Berkeley: University of California Press, 1985).

50 Michael Schudson, *Advertising, the Uneasy Persuasion: Its Dubious Impact on American Society* (New York: Basic Books, 1984), 215.

51 Marsha L. Richins, 'Social Comparison and the Idealized Images of Advertising', in *Journal of Consumer Research* 18, no. 1 (June 1991): 71–83.

52 Gib Prettyman, 'Advertising, Utopia, and Commercial Idealism: The Case of King Gilette', in *Prospects* 24 (1999): 231–48, 'Utopian Audiences: How Readers Locate

Nowhere', *American Literary Realism* 38, no. 2 (2006): 179–80 and 'Gilded Age Utopias of Incorporation', *Utopian Studies* 12, no. 1 (2001): 19–40.

53 Goudreau, 'Draft – Seminar', SIL.

54 Kara Dixon Vuic, *Officer, Nurse, Woman: The Army Nurse Corps in the Vietnam War* (Baltimore: Johns Hopkins University Press, 2010); see also Jessica L. Ghilani, 'Glamour-Izing Military Service: Army Recruitment for Women in Vietnam-Era Advertisements', *American Journalism* 34, no. 2 (2017): 201–28.

55 Ghilani, 'Glamour-Izing Military Service', 2017.

56 See Morris Janowitz and Charles C. Moskos, 'Report on Five Years of the Volunteer Force: 1973–1978 in January 1979', in Manpower Research and Advisory Services Records 1971–1994, box 5 folder 8, SIL.

57 Martin Binkin and Shirley J. Bach, *Studies in Defence Policy: Women and the Military* (Washington, DC: Brookings Institution, 1977), 12–13.

58 For a theoretical analysis of Thomas's *That Girl* character, Ann Marie as a safe, single, protofeminist girl, see: Moya Luckett, 'Sensuous Women and Single Girls', in Hilary Radner and Moya Luckett (eds.), *Swinging Single: Representing Sexuality in the 1960s* (Minneapolis: University of Minnesota Press, 1999), 293–4; see also Katherine J. Lehman, *Those Girls: Single Women in Sixties and Seventies Popular Culture* (Lawrence: University Press of Kansas, 2011).

59 Ibid.

60 Ibid.

61 See Debra Merskin, 'Adolescence, Advertising, and the Ideology of Menstruation', in *Sex Roles* 40, nos. 11–12 (June 1999): 941–57; see also Kate Kane, 'The Ideology of Freshness in Feminine Hygiene Commercials', *The Journal of Communication Inquiry* (1990): 1483–92.

62 For a history of the Women's Rights Movement in the US during the mid-twentieth century, often referred to as the second wave of feminism, see Estelle Freedman, *No Turning Back: The History of Feminism and the Future of Women* (New York: Ballantine, 2002). For context about the legacy of chattel slavery, rise of Jim Crow laws during reconstruction, and the Civil Rights Movement see '1619 Project', *The New York Times Magazine*, 14 August 2019.

63 AAARS, 'The Army Sees Green', SIL.

64 AAARS, 'Now That You Don't Have to Go', SIL; emphasis added.

65 Ibid.

66 Ibid.

67 AAARS, 'Lead the People Who've Joined the Army', SIL. The ad ran in the late 1970s in *Ebony Magazine* and possibly elsewhere.

68 AAARS, 'Specialist', SIL. This ad ran in *Senior Scholastic Magazine* in 1978.

69 *Senior Scholastic* was succeeded by *Scholastic Update* magazine and eventually *New York Times Upfront* in 1999, which continues to be published. *New York Times Upfront* has a tagline that reads, 'The news magazine for high school'. This Scholastic Inc. publication aims broadly toward high school student readers in the United States. Each issue includes corresponding curricular content and a 'teacher's edition' so that the magazines can integrate into high school classrooms easily. See 'The Media Business: Times and Scholastic Plan Magazine for Teen-Agers', *New York Times*, 18 March 1999.

70 Berger, *Ways of Seeing*, 130.

71 Utopia continues to be used as a strategy in advertising. For readings on how advertising uses the notion of utopia, see Richins, 'Social Comparison of Advertising', 71–83; Prettyman, 'Advertising, Utopia', 'Utopian Audiences', and 'Gilded Age'; T. J. Jackson Lears, *Fables of Abundance: A Cultural History of Advertising in America* (New York: Basic Books, 1994); Marchand, *Advertising American Dream*; John McDonald Hood, *Selling the Dream: Why Advertising is Good Business* (Westport: Praeger, 2005).

Part III
Recruitment in the digital age

11 Canadian military public affairs and recruitment in an age of social media platforms

Tanner Mirrlees

Abstract

This chapter provides a holistic overview of the Canadian Department of National Defense and Canadian Armed Forces' public affairs publicity and recruitment practices in the twenty-first century. Giving a snapshot of the government offices, policies and personnel responsible for promoting military service to the public, it highlights some of the most significant paid and unpaid publicity events and recruitment campaigns they organised and promoted across a wide variety of media forms, including pop culture, news, television advertisements, and social media platforms. It also considers the role Canadian military promotion and recruitment play in militarising Canadian media and culture, constructing Canadian national identity, selling military service, and bringing about a collaborative relationship between the Canadian military and US social media platforms.

In the lead-up to and first year of the First World War, the Canadian Army launched a recruitment campaign. With rousing public speeches and carefully placed newspaper editorials, the Army encouraged young men to join 'the boys' on the front lines to secure Canada and the British Crown against the threat of the 'Hun'. Especially significant to the mobilisation campaign was the printed poster, which targeted potential enlistees with messages such as 'Here's YOUR chance, It's MEN WE WANT', 'Help the boys to keep them [the Germans] running' and 'Fight for her'. The Army paid for the posters, which were affixed to walls by some hands and ripped down by others.[1]

More than one hundred years have passed since these devices were used to recruit for the 'Great War', and though military recruitment has continued in the twenty-first century the media environment has changed. Militaries still, of course, wield the spoken word and printed poster for recruitment pitches, but their campaigns flow through many media venues and platforms: pop culture, in-cinema commercials, radio, television and online advertisements, and Facebook, Twitter and YouTube. In the 'digital age', militaries frequently pay public relations and advertising companies to create and produce multi-media recruitment campaigns, and once produced, reproduce and spread them far and wide in assemblages of binary code via the Internet and World Wide Web, at little to no additional cost. Also, due to Web 3.0's convergent digital technologies, the people targeted by multi-media military recruitment campaigns are not a passive 'mass' audience of the kind depicted in critiques of 1914–18 propaganda but rather interactive users of laptop computers, smartphones, websites and software who produce and consume (or 'prosume') appeals in ways that may both support and challenge a military's public affairs and recruitment goals.

Attentive to the new twenty-first century communications and digital media environment of military recruitment, this chapter probes the public affairs office, policies, publicity and recruitment practices of the Canadian Department of National Defense (DND) and Canadian Armed Forces (CAF). To this end, the chapter's first section contextualises Canadian military public affairs and recruitment with regard to the larger geopolitical context that shapes it by presenting an overview of Canadian foreign policy in the twenty-first century. The second section focuses on the structure, policy and practice of the DND and CAF public affairs office and then probes some salient twenty-first-century publicity events and recruitment campaigns it organised to promote the military and military service to civilians. The third section shows how public affairs and recruitment have entered the 'digital age' with a look at the DND and CAF's Internet and social media policy, presence and practices, especially across the world's most significant (American) social media platforms. The conclusion takes the CAF's growing dependence upon US social media platforms for publicity and recruitment to be the latest expression of Canada's economic, military and technological integration with the US and a salient example of the current power of US platform imperialism.

Studies of the Canadian military organisations, policies and practices that produce and circulate positive stories and images of military service to drum up civilian support for military operations and enlist new recruits to the ranks are needed. So are studies of how military self-promotion and recruitment are being redesigned for social media platforms, which arguably represent 'the future of recruitment'.[2] This chapter's holistic overview of Canadian military public affairs and recruitment in the digital age is a preliminary contribution to this scantly developed area of research in Canadian communications studies. The CAF's military operations have persisted and grown over the past two decades, and at present, the CAF is deployed in nearly forty missions that spread across North America, Central and South America, Europe, Africa, the Middle East and Asia-Pacific.[3] Yet few scholars have examined the Canadian military public affairs offices, policies and practices that mobilise and militarise Canadian media and culture in the attempt to sell military service to civilians. Furthermore, while researchers have examined a Canadian military recruitment advertising campaign made for the media of television and cinema,[4] there is a dearth of research on the Canadian military's integration of the Internet and social media platforms into their public affairs and recruitment arsenals. In this regard, the chapter's look at the CAF's recent attempts to interact with, inform, influence and recruit civilians through social media platforms is novel. It shows how the Canadian military has integrated with US social media platforms for self-promotion and recruitment and addresses the benefits and drawbacks of this digital dependency.

Recruitment in an age of social media   165

Canada's foreign policy, the Department of National Defence and the Canadian Armed Forces in the twenty-first century

The DND and CAF implement Federal Government decisions concerning the security and defence of Canada's national interests at home and abroad. The DND is headquartered in Ottawa, and the current Minister of National Defense is Sarjat Singh Sajjan. CAF bases are spread across the country, while CAF personnel serve on sea, land, and in the air with the Navy, Army, Air Force and Special Forces. As it expands operations around the world, the DND is trying to increase its personnel to 125,000 members, including 71,500 regular CAF members, 30,000 reservists and 25,000 civilian employees.[5]

In the twenty-first century, the story often told about Canada's role in the world – about Canadian foreign and defense policy – is a positive one. Canada, a benign and benevolent country, projects free markets, liberal democracy and multiculturalism and uses its military and diplomatic personnel to protect peace, stability and human rights in each country it intervenes in and trades with. This feel-good foreign policy story is routinely produced and consumed with great enthusiasm by officials. It is conveyed by the speeches of Conservative and Liberal party prime ministers. It intertwines with research studies published by Canada's strategic think tanks such as the Canadian Global Affairs Institute and the Canadian Defence & Foreign Affairs Institute. It interlinks with press releases crafted by the Department of Foreign Affairs and International Trade, as well as the DND and CAF. It is often carried by the mainstream news media, in their frames of Canadian foreign policy, and is also 'prosumed' by users across social media sites.

The story of Canada as home to a military committed to peacekeeping and a diplomat corps geared to conflict mitigation is part of Canada's 'soft power' arsenal,[6] and this 'liberal internationalist' position (established by former president Lester B. Pearson) has long been a popular way of distinguishing Canada's way in the world from the US's.[7] Canada, we are told, makes allies by multi-laterally making peace. The US, by contrast, makes enemies by waging unilateral wars.

Pervasive as it is, this story is dubious, for it relies upon a somewhat idealised image of Canada's past and present conduct in the world. Far from being a 'peaceable kingdom,' Canada has a long history of war.[8] For example, when Great Britain declared war on Germany, Canada, subordinate to the British Empire, was compelled to enter the First World War. Of 600,000 Canadians deployed, 60,000 were killed and 170,000 wounded. In the Second World War and Korean War, Canadian forces fought alongside their British and American allies. Canada projected a position of 'neutrality' during the Cold War, but its foreign policy was integral to the broad anti-Soviet aims of the US and North Atlantic Treaty Organization (NATO). After all, Canada was a founding member of NATO. It played a key role in drafting the original treaty and inserting a clause into the treaty that emphasised military alliance *and* economic collaboration between members. After the Cold War, Canada joined the United Nations (UN) Security Council–backed and US-led international military coalition against Iraq with air and naval forces but no troop deployments till the aftermath (1990–1991). Canadian forces also took part in the Somali Civil War (1992–1995), the Bosnian War (1992–1995) and the Kosovo War (1998–1999).

In the 1990s, Canada forged a UN peacekeeper profile, but following the September 11, 2001, terrorist attacks Canadian military and political elites aligned with the world's sole military superpower in its Global War on Terror, explicitly playing down Canada's old peacekeeper brand and playing up one that emphasised combat readiness and war fighting.[9] Canada joined the US-led NATO war in Afghanistan to eliminate al-Qaeda and neutralise the Taliban. The Liberal governments of Jean Chrétien and Paul Martin oversaw the CAF's role in this war until 2006. The Conservative government of Stephen Harper extended the CAF's deployment to 2014. During the nine-year government of Harper's Conservatives (2006–2015), the CAF's peacekeeping capacities, 'including negotiation, conflict management, and an understanding of UN procedures and capabilities, were deemphasised in favour of trainings better suited to combat missions'.[10] Forty thousand Canadians fought in the war in Afghanistan, and 158 were killed. One in ten Afghanistan war veterans suffered post-traumatic stress disorder, and more than seventy of these had committed suicide by December 2017. Despite the billions spent and officials emphasising NATO's progress in securing Afghanistan, Canada and its NATO allies did not accomplish their mission in Afghanistan. As a *Maclean's* headline put it: 'Canada utterly failed in Afghanistan'.[11]

After CAF exited Afghanistan in 2014, the bright young Liberal Party leader, Justin Trudeau, campaigned in 2015 with a promise to 'renew Canada's commitment to peacekeeping operations' via the UN. When elected prime minister of Canada, Trudeau declared that 'Canada is Back' as a peacekeeper, yet there was a notable gap between Trudeau's rhetoric and the government's foreign policy practice.[12] Months after his announcement, Trudeau turned down multiple UN peacekeeping requests. To prepare Canada for future wars, the Trudeau government's 2017 defense doctrine, dubbed 'Strong, Secure, Engaged', proposed a 70 per cent defense spending increase between 2016 and 2026 to pay for new warships and jet fighters, drones for airstrikes and surveillance and new cyberwarfare systems to give CAF the resources it needs to be even more active beyond Canada's borders. The doctrine framed the CAF's role as defending Canada, helping secure the continent and making more 'concrete contributions' to NATO's global operations. It also called for increasing the size of the regular force from 68,000 to 71,500, the reserves from 27,000 to 30,000 members and civilian employees from 24,000 to 25,000.[13] Recruiting more women and people from diverse ethnic and cultural backgrounds represented an additional objective, and the CAF is currently engaged in a wide variety of missions, including the NATO war against the Islamic State of Iraq and the Levant (ISIL) and the Global Coalition Against Daesh.

For nearly two decades, successive Canadian governments have put boots 'on the ground' in combat missions. The Canadian government has organised media events and recruitment advertising to recruit the personnel required for these missions, and it is to that topic that we will now turn.

The Canadian military's public affairs office, militarising media events and recruitment advertising

The Government of Canada's main office for military public affairs (including recruitment advertising) is the Assistant Deputy Minister Public Affairs (ADM-PA). In the years following 9/11, the ADM-PA office expanded. By 2011, it boasted 575 officers and an annual budget of about $40 million. Approximately $15 million of that sum goes to recruitment advertising.[14] The ADM-PA also provides, in its own words, 'communications advice, guidance, services and products in support of the Government of Canada and its defence priorities'.[15] More specifically, it is 'committed to leading and enhancing defence communications' by 'understanding the views of Canadians and defence stakeholders through public opinion research and consultations', 'designing, developing and implementing strategic communications plans and products', 'leading defence internal and external communications channels including the web and social media' and 'monitoring, analysing and responding to the [news] media'.[16]

The ADM-PA's work is guided by the Defence Administrative Orders and Directives 2008–0 Public Affairs Policy, which defines 'public affairs' in informational terms as all the 'activities related to informing internal and external audiences' as well as 'research and analysis, communications advice and planning, and the delivery of information programs'.[17] According to this policy, the goal of ADM-PA 'is to promote understanding and awareness among Canadians of the role, mandate and activities of the CAF and DND and of the contributions that the CAF and DND make to Canadian society and the international community'.[18] The policy claims that by promoting understanding and awareness of 'how the CAF and DND make a difference at home and abroad,' 'public support for the CAF and DND' will develop.[19] The policy furthermore frames CAF and DND public affairs activities as committed to the ethical principle of veracity – telling the truth. It claims public affairs officers work 'to inform the public' of 'policies, programs, services, activities, operations, and initiatives in a manner that is accurate, complete, objective, timely, relevant, understandable, and open and transparent within the law'.[20] However, Canadian military public affairs may also engage in the work of engaging, influencing and persuading and may be less about passively reflecting war and military service and more about actively representing these things in partial and selective ways. In any case, the ADM-PA is a significant part of the government of Canada's 'publicity state',[21] which derives its strategies and tactics from public relations and advertising and sells defense policies and military service to the public.

The ADM-PA's public affairs officers train for their jobs at the DND's Public Affairs Learning Centre in Gatineau, Quebec. By enrolling in and completing a six-month course, these CAF experts acquire 'the knowledge and skills required to advise a Commander on public affairs, create communications products and tools, conduct media relations, public affairs planning and internal communications, coordinate a media event, foster community relations, support public affairs operations, and manage the production of audio-visual products'.[22] The role of the CAF public affairs officer is 'to provide sound communications advice at the tactical, operational and strategic levels' and advise CAF commanders 'on all aspects of external and internal communications' while 'developing, executing and evaluating communications approaches designed to inform the public of CAF roles, activities and work'.[23] Furthermore, the public affairs officer works to 'Analyse and evaluate attitudes in the national and international media' toward the CAF, 'Contribute to policy development', 'Gather and provide information internally and externally' and 'Communicate with journalists, special interest groups and individuals regarding Defence'.[24] While public affairs officers work 'in a modern office setting,' they may also undertake their communicative labour from 'major bases and various headquarters across Canada and abroad' and be 'required to deploy anywhere in the world to support CAF operations during times of conflict'.[25]

The Ancient Greek dramatist Aeschylus famously said 'In war, truth is the first casualty,' and in 1916, the British Labour politician and socialist Philip Snowdon made a similar remark: 'Truth, it has been said, is the first casualty of war'.[26] From 1914–18 to the present day, governments throughout the world have actively concealed the hard and often ugly truths of wars, using a combination of censorship and propaganda to try to engineer consent.[27] In the twenty-first century, US officials lied to or misled the public about the reasons for and outcomes of the wars in Afghanistan.[28] In Canada, even though the motto for the badge of the CAF's Public Affairs branch is Veritas (Latin for 'Truth'), governmental, military, corporate and media organisations constructed a military-friendly media and cultural environment that glorified the CAF's actions and lionized its personnel to the public.[29] In the post-9/11 period, and in conjunction with Canada's role in the war in Afghanistan, military public affairs officers collaborated with private organisations to create militarising media events that rebranded Canada as a 'warrior nation' and placed war and military service before the public in a positive light[30] and 'militaris[ed] Canadian national identity'.[31]

Their work has been extensive and wide ranging. In 2007, the government renamed the MacDonald-Cartier Freeway in Ontario the Highway of Heroes to encourage drivers to remember and venerate Canada's fallen soldiers. Citizens often line the route driven by the hearses carrying deceased soldiers back to their home bases. In the same year, Tim Horton's, Canada's largest coffee and donut chain, set up quick-service outlets in Afghanistan while also giving free coffee to uniformed CAF members at stores across Canada. Military-themed entertainment products such as *Afghanada* (2006–2011), an award-winning Canadian Broadcasting Corporation radio drama, and *Passchendaele* (2008), a First World War film featuring Afghanistan War vets that increase the prestige of military service, were also supported by the CAF.[32] To further embed the military in popular culture and mesh militarism with the maple leaf, CAF personnel routinely appeared at national sporting events. Militarised halftime shows and CAF appreciation games at minor and major league hockey, baseball, basketball and football franchises, meanwhile, allowed them to show their 'support [for] the troops'.[33] Following a public-sector initiative in 2009, citizens affixed yellow ribbons to their automobiles, doors, and lapels to convey their support of the troops.[34] To bridge the military–civilian gap, the CAF launched a public affairs program called Operation

Connection, which linked soldiers with civilians at big national events, such as the Canadian National Exhibition, the Calgary Stampede, the Pacific National Exhibition and the Winnipeg–Saskatchewan Labour Day Canadian Football League game. The CAF's public affairs officers also targeted news media with the goal of setting the agenda of public discussions. In 2015, Chief of Defence Staff General Jonathan Vance proposed to 'weaponise public affairs' when dealing with journalists.[35] To generate free publicity, public affairs officers sourced 'good news' stories to journalists deemed friendly to the CAF while excluding journalists who wrote critical stories.[36] Under the Liberal government, the CAF continued 'to operationalise military public affairs' in this (weaponised) way by combining aggressive media sourcing with limits to media access.[37]

These governmental public affairs practices portrayed military service as the ultimate act of patriotism, a heroic and virtuous expression of one's love of country and self-sacrifice for its security. Frequently embraced by private media organisations, they fostered a media and cultural milieu in which Canada's history of war and present warfighting capabilities were showcased and, of course, coupled with CAF-supported recruitment advertising campaigns.

In the early 2000s, with many CAF personnel retiring, the number of people exiting the CAF was projected to exceed the number of people entering it. Due to a low youth unemployment rate, public scepticism about Canada's role in the war in Afghanistan and negative views of work in the CAF, the CAF had difficulties enlisting Canadians for twenty-first-century wars. In response, the CAF ratcheted up its recruitment advertising. Working with commercial public relations firms, it built an attractive new brand for itself which helped it meet personnel quotas for a younger and more diversified force. In 2018, the government spent $6.5 million on recruitment advertising.[38] When recruiting, the CAF searches out and aims to enlist qualified personnel into its ranks, and to do so, its recruitment ads deploy a combination of enlistment appeals. Sometimes, the CAF's ads appeal to the patriotism of audiences and frame military service as a way for citizens to perform their allegiance to and sacrifice for the well-being or security of the nation. Other times, CAF ads appeal to the individual career goals of their subjects and frame military service as a way for individuals to secure a good job or acquire skills for a civilian job in the future.

Two major CAF recruitment ad campaigns exemplify this. The first was called *Fight*, a response to a recruitment downturn and an attempt to reframe the meaning of the CAF in 2006–2008. The CAF hired one of the world's largest advertising companies, Publicis, and paid it $3 million to create the campaign, which was comprised of three TV broadcast and in-cinema ads: 'International Security and British Columbia Search and Rescue', 'Disaster Relief in Canada and Rescue at Sea' and 'Drug Bust and Hard Landing'. Civilians were exposed to *Fight* ads while watching TV shows in their homes during commercial breaks and during Hollywood films at local theatres during previews. The target audience for these ads was (mostly male) 17- to 34-year-old viewers, who were urged to 'Fight Distress, Fight Fear, Fight Chaos – Fight with the Canadian Forces'.[39]

Fight ads represented CAF personnel as mostly white and male. '[P]articipating in dangerous, fast-paced, internationally oriented combat missions', it cast these personnel as 'helpful heroes focused not on the action of combat, per se, but

170 *Tanner Mirrlees*

instead on helping civilians'.[40] Reportedly allowing the CAF to exceed its recruitment quota,[41] *Fight* also helped 'political and military elites to re-brand the image' of the CAF as a 'combat-capable institution', toughened 'the image of the CAF' in the public mind and resolved the 'tension between elite aspirations to redirect Canadian foreign policy towards combat-assertive activities and the longstanding public desire for the military to focus on "traditional" peacekeeping'.[42] *Fight* ads were part of a larger 'discursive regime in which political elites signalled to the Canadian public that peacekeeping (as traditionally understood) was no longer a viable foreign policy option and that increasingly combat-oriented operations would (re)define Canada's foreign affairs'.[43] These ads recast the CAF as being constituted by 'helpful heroes' who sacrifice themselves for the security of Canada and of civilians around the world.

The CAF's second major recruitment advertising campaign was called *Dare to be Extraordinary*. This campaign was created by the Montreal branch of Ogilvy, another leading agency, and launched in the summer of 2017, after the end of the CAF's combat mission in Afghanistan. Like its predecessor, *Dare to be Extraordinary* represented a response to a shortfall in new recruits.[44] Lieutenant General Charles Lamarre, Commander, Military Personnel Command, said the campaign 'kick-start[ed] efforts to ensure that we have a dedicated, motivated and highly skilled CAF, to defend Canada and promote Canadian values and interests at home and abroad'.[45] According to the CAF, this campaign was designed to 'speak directly to millennials' and 'provide them with a sense of the many advantages of life in the military – paid education, travel, humanitarian assistance – and inspire them to find out more'.[46] It was also intended to speak to people from social groups historically underrepresented in the CAF, such as women, non-white minorities and indigenous people. The ads mostly used women, including women of colour, as CAF personnel, with each ad being narrated by a woman.

While *Fight* represented CAF personnel as mostly male heroes deployed in dangerous combat missions, *Dare to Be Extraordinary* portrays feminised personnel doing non-violent service jobs as cooks, technicians, divers and health care providers. CAF personnel here are not represented as part of a 'warrior nation' securing Canada against terrorists, nor are they depicted as 'helpful heroes' saving the world. Instead, they are career-oriented individuals. The taglines for each ad, shared on YouTube and elsewhere in three different versions, are telling: 'Dare to be extraordinary with the Canadian Armed Forces: Apply for 1 of over 100 full and part-time careers and acquire sought after skills and training that will serve you everywhere';[47] 'Dare to be Extraordinary with the Forces and acquire skills that will serve you everywhere';[48] and 'Dare to be extraordinary, with training that will serve you everywhere'.[49] These ads rebrand the image of the CAF as something more akin to a vocational college than a combat institution. Even though the nation is at war, the ads portray military service as a combat-free yet extraordinary experience that empowers people to upskill and land cool careers. These ads do not frame Canada as a peacekeeper or a warfighter but instead depict Canadian women and people of colour serving in the military as a way to achieve stable employment or to acquire skills related to future employment.

Like *Fight, Dare to Be Extraordinary* deployed television and in-cinema commercials, but what was unique about the campaign was its presence on social media platforms. When *Fight* launched in 2006, only some Canadians were using social media platforms such as Facebook (launched in 2004), YouTube (launched in 2005) and Twitter (launched in 2006). *Fight* was not designed to be a social media recruitment campaign. *Dare to be Extraordinary*, however, was launched at a time when a majority of Canadians were online, using smartphones and social media platforms to interact with one another, businesses and even government. What are social media platforms? How has the CAF integrated these into its publicity and recruitment toolkits? What Internet and social media policies guide its digital interactions with civilians?

The Canadian Armed Forces' social media platforms, policies and practices

In the early twenty-first century, social media platforms interweave with contemporary economics, politics and cultures. Some of the world's most prominent media platforms and apps encompass social networking services (Facebook), micro-blogging services (Twitter), video-sharing services (YouTube), cross-platform messaging services (WhatsApp) and photo-sharing services (Instagram). Most of the world's most populated and profitable platforms are owned and operated by US corporations that stretch across many countries around the world. Over the past decade, the CAF has increased its Internet presence and carved out a space on the World Wide Web for its promotional and recruitment activities,[50] and it sees social media platforms as valuable tools for interacting with, informing and influencing civilians and prospective personnel.

As of 15 January 2019, the CAF's Facebook page, entitled CanadianForces, was liked by 267,836 people and followed by 270,387 people. The page's 'Our Story' section invites visitors to 'Join the Canadian Armed Forces!' and, to potentially expedite enlistment, includes a convenient link to the CAF's online recruitment portal.[51] The CAF's Facebook page links to its other CAF social media sites, as well as to pages for 'posts', 'reviews', 'videos', 'photos', a 'community' discussion forum, a page about how to join the forces and a page for recruitment events.[52]

The CAF is on Twitter as well, using the @CanadianForces handle and followed by 113,300 people. From Twitter, the CAF tweets and retweets photos of CAF personnel, recruitment ads, defense speeches by officials, commemorative and ceremonial stories, calls to 'Support our Troops', updates about activities in Iraq, light-hearted videos of soldiers shooting cannons into snowbanks and morale-boosting stories about how the CAF empowered a woman to achieve her dream of becoming a doctor. On Twitter, the CAF uses hashtags such as #CAF, #MyCAF and #CdnForces to help users search for and find tweets about the CAF.[53]

The CAF's YouTube site has 32,500 subscribers. It displays hundreds of CAF-produced videos spread across categories such as Defence Team News, CAF stories, Commemorations and History, Military Science and Technology, Popular

172   *Tanner Mirrlees*

Uploads, Jobs in the Forces, Operations and Exercises. The videos on the CAF's YouTube site have a total of 18,884,808 views.[54]

The CAF is followed by 161,000 users on Instagram, and its 1,853 Instagram posts display headshots of retired and active-duty personnel, glossy images of military hardware (jets, helicopters, battleships, boats, tanks and guns) and CAF personnel aiming or firing weapons (rifles, machine guns and cannons) and engaged in daring activities (jumping out of planes, skydiving and parachuting).[55]

Last but not least, the CAF is also on the employment networking site LinkedIn, where its 59,122 followers receive daily updates about CAF jobs.[56]

Evidently, the CAF's public affairs office has marked out its territory on the Internet and is nowadays promoting its personnel, policy and practices across, as well as recruiting from, major social media platforms. At the same time, the comments sections of the CAF social media sites enable civilians to interact with CAF personnel and one another. In response to an image of a soldier in a helicopter, Facebook user Paige Runolfson posted: 'It's a bird, It's a plane, no it's the real superheroes'. As this example indicates, the civilians once on the receiving end of military public affairs and recruitment pitches may now affirmatively add to these campaigns through their own online interactions. Through social media platforms, military public affairs and recruitment seem to merge 'top-down' government-to-civilian communication with 'bottom-up' civilian-to-government communication. While large-scale governmental and military media organisations produce and circulate military promotions and recruitment campaigns, civilians are increasingly using social media platforms not only to receive the messages and imagery from official campaigns but also to create and impart their own military-themed messages and images. For example, civilians may virtually socialise on these CAF sites (by, for example, chatting with a friend who lives many miles away about the CAF), 'lurk' (by watching what another user is writing and posting about the CAF but without them ever knowing) and act in relation to existing content (by sharing or commenting on a story or image posted by the CAF). But what are the limits to and drawbacks of the CAF's social media platforms and the interactivity they afford? The CAF's social media policy (its Internet 'Terms and Conditions' and 'Section 8: Social Media Notice')[57] give a clue as to what the CAF social media platforms may give to and take from their users.

First, the CAF policy claims its 'use of social media serves as an extension of its presence on the Web' but notes that 'Social media accounts are public and are not hosted on Government of Canada servers'. In that regard, 'Users who choose to interact with US via social media should read the terms of service and privacy policies of these third-party service providers and those of any applications you use to access them'. This social media policy seems to balance the politics of CAF public affairs with the economics of 'platform capitalism'.[58] After all, social media platforms are not just a means for the CAF to communicate but part of a 'new business model, capable of extracting and controlling immense amounts of data'.[59] When users sign up to use the services afforded by these social media platforms and click 'I agree' to the terms of service and privacy policies such use is precipitated by, they grant the corporations that own these platforms the right

Recruitment in an age of social media 173

to collect, process, commoditise and sell their data (or access to user attention) to advertisers.[60] So while the CAF extends itself through social media platforms and utilises this ostensibly 'free' means of self-promotion and recruitment, it opens itself (and its followers) to the data-extractive infrastructure of platform capitalism. The CAF does not pay Facebook, Twitter, YouTube or Instagram to operate its pages, handles and profiles, nor does it pay to place its content before the networked public. But the CAF's use of these platforms implies consent to dataveillance practices, and so it arguably pays companies with data about what it (and those it interacts with) do and express each day. In this regard, the CAF's use of social media platforms for publicity and recruitment supports platform capitalism by attracting new users to the sites, generating fresh content that becomes monetisable as data and keeping the ad clients that pay to access users happy.

Second, the CAF policy says it uses social media platforms to directly interact with, inform and influence users: 'We use our social media accounts as an alternative method of sharing the content posted on our website and interacting with our stakeholders. By following our social media accounts (by 'following', 'liking' or 'subscribing'), you can expect to see information about CAF operations, programs and initiatives'.[61] By spreading its public affairs and recruitment content through social media platforms that are integrated into the daily lives of millions of Canadians, the CAF may become less reliant on traditional or 'legacy' media venues for communicating with the public. While the CAF once had to pay TV networks and theatre chains to place recruitment ads before the public and had to negotiate the gatekeeping powers and filters of professional news organisations and curry the favour of their journalists to earn positive coverage, social media platforms enable the CAF to speak directly to civilians in whatever way it chooses, whenever it wants. Social media platforms enable CAF public affairs officers to directly attract and interact with civilian users of these services. They seem to transform CAF publicity and recruitment into a military-to-civilian affair, intermediated by the private infrastructure of Silicon Valley firms. Technological optimists initially framed Web 2.0 social media platforms as putting communicative power in the hands of the people *at the expense* of big and powerful organisations, but the CAF social media platforms suggest that even bigger organisations like militaries are integrating with the world's biggest technology corporations to interactively influence publics.

Third, the CAF policy expresses censorship powers over user expressions on its social media platforms. It stipulates its power to prohibit, limit and remove content deemed 'inappropriate' from sites. Censorship is the repression of expressions that government and corporate organisations deem to be objectionable or dangerous, and the CAF exercises censorship powers over the content that the users, followers, visitors and subscribers to its sites create. Section 8.4 of its policy, 'Comments and Interaction,' for example, indicates that DND and CAF personnel will 'read comments and participate in discussions when appropriate' but stipulates that user 'comments [must] be relevant and respectful' and asserts 'the right to delete comments that violate this notice' and 'block' the user and report them to 'authorities' to 'prevent further inappropriate comments'.[62] The

174   *Tanner Mirrlees*

meaning of 'inappropriate' user comment seems to be quite broad, as the CAF policy reserves 'the right to edit or remove comments'[63] that:

- Contain personal information.
- Are contrary to the principles of the Canadian Charter of Rights and Freedoms.
- Express racist, hateful, sexist, homophobic, slanderous, insulting, or life-threatening messages.
- Put forward serious, unproven or inaccurate accusations against individuals or organisations.
- Are aggressive, coarse, violent, obscene, or pornographic.
- Are offensive, rude, or abusive to an individual or an organisation.
- Are not sent by the author or are put forward for advertising purposes.
- Encourage illegal activity.
- Contain announcements from labour or political organisations.
- Are written in a language other than English or French.
- Are unintelligible or irrelevant.
- Are repetitive or spam.
- Do not, in our opinion, add to the normal flow of the discussion.

Furthermore, Section 8.4 qualifies that 'Comments used for political party purposes will not be published' and further warns that the DND and CAF 'will take seriously and report to the proper authorities any threats to the DND and CAF, their employees, agents, other users or the federal government'.[64]

In sum, the CAF is promoting itself through, recruiting from and exercising censorship powers over social media platforms. But what might be the consequence of the CAF's integration with American firms?

Conclusion: Canadian military digital dependence in the age of US platform imperialism

Over the past three decades, Canada's business class, military brass and political officials have pushed to ensure that Canadian national interests sync with Wall Street, the Pentagon and Washington. Currently, Canada and the US are top military allies. They continue to be partners in NATO, the North American Aerospace Defense Command and the Global Coalition Against Daesh. Over the past two decades, the US and Canadian security states have integrated. Canada is also intertwined with the US economy, and the two countries form the globe's largest trading partnership. Canada and the US share a $1.4 trillion bilateral trade and investment partnership, and billions in trade flow between these countries each day. The US is Canada's largest export market and accounts for nearly 73 per cent of total annual Canadian exports. Also, Canada is the US's largest foreign supplier of oil, natural gas and electricity. Furthermore, US corporations are the primary sources of foreign direct investment in Canada. Because Canadian prosperity, GDP and jobs depend in part upon the strength of the US economy, Canada works through the International Monetary Fund, the World Trade Organisation

Recruitment in an age of social media   175

and the World Bank to protect and promote a North America–centric global trade order that supports the interests of Canadian and US capital alike. What was once known as the 'Washington Consensus' is Canada's as well: diplomats push neo-liberalism and new technologies around the world.

Given Canada's military and economic integration with the US, it is not surprising that the CAF now relies upon American-owned and -operated social media platforms for its online publicity and recruitment campaigns. The US is the globe's leading 'platform imperialist', because US corporations own the lion's share of the digital age's hardware and software, intellectual property rights and user data.[65] In this regard, the CAF's integration with US social media platforms for self-promotion and recruitment is yet another example of how deeply integrated Canada is with the US Empire, which has long relied upon developments in communications technologies and new media forms to expand and buttress its global economic, military and cultural power.[66]

In the digital age, the CAF has harnessed the power of social media platforms, but this reflects the subordinate position of Canada to the US. After all, these social media platforms are not Canadian or totally subject to Canada's own digital legal, policy and regulatory frameworks. Given this context, the CAF's reliance upon American social media platforms to promote itself and recruit for wars initiated by the US perpetuates a US-centered platform imperialism and Canada's ongoing digital dependence.

Notes

1 Jeff Hershen, *Propaganda and Censorship During Canada's Great War* (Edmonton: The University of Alberta Press, 1996). Ontario Ministry of Government and Consumer Services, 'Canadian Posters from the First World War', 12 March 2020: www. archives.gov.on.ca/en/explore/online/posters/index.aspx.
2 Tamara Spitzer, 'Using Social Media to Tackle Recruiting Shortages in the Armed Forces', *CDA Institute*, 7 March 2019: https://cdainstitute.ca/ using-social-media-to-tackle-the-recruiting-shortages-in-the-armed-forces/.
3 Government of Canada. National Defense and the Canadian Armed Forces, 'Canadian Armed Forces Current Operations Map', 15 February 2019: www.canada.ca/en/department-national-defence/services/operations/military-operations/current-operations/list.html.
4 Janis Goldie, 'Fighting Change: Representing the Canadian Forces in the 2006–2008 Fight Recruitment Campaign', *Canadian Journal of Communication* 39, no. 2 (2014): 413–30.
5 Government of Canada. National Defense and the Canadian Armed Forces, 'Mandate of National Defence and the Canadian Armed Forces', 15 February 2019: www.forces. gc.ca/en/about-us.page.
6 Evan H. Potter, *Branding Canada: Projecting Canada's Soft Power through Public Diplomacy* (Toronto: McGill-Queens University Press, 2010).
7 Roland Paris, 'Are Canadians Still Liberal Internationalists?', *OpenCanada*, 25 September 2014: www.opencanada.org/features/are-canadians-still-liberal-internationalists/.
8 Jack Granatstein, *Canada's Army: Waging War and Keeping the Peace* (Toronto and Buffalo: University of Toronto Press, 2004).
9 Ian McKay and Jamie Swift, *Warrior Nation: Rebranding Canada in an Age of Anxiety* (Toronto: Between the Lines, 2012).
10 Stewart Patrick, 'Is Canada Back? Trudeau's Peacekeeping Promises are Not Enough', *Council on Foreign Relations*, 29 May 2018: www.cfr.org/blog/canada-back-trudeaus-peacekeeping-promises-are-not-enough.

176 *Tanner Mirrlees*

11 Scott Gilmore, 'Canada Utterly Failed in Afghanistan: Why Can't We Say This Out Loud', *Maclean's*, 11 December 2019: www.macleans.ca/opinion/canada-utterly-failed-in-afghanistan-why-cant-we-say-this-out-loud/.

12 Walter A. Dorn and Joshua Libben, 'Unprepared for Peace? The Decline of Canadian Peacekeeping Training (and What to Do about It)', *Canadian Centre for Policy Alternatives/Rideau Institute on International Affairs*: www.policyalternatives.ca/publications/reports/unprepared-peace.

13 Government of Canada. National Defense and the Canadian Armed Forces, 'Mandate of National Defence and the Canadian Armed Forces'.

14 David Pugliese, 'Veteran DND Public Affairs Staff Quitting over Interference: Report', *National Post*, 25 September 2011: http://news.nationalpost.com/2011/09/25/veteran-dnd-public-affairs-staff-quitting-over-interference-report/.

15 Government of Canada. National Defense, 'Assistant Deputy Minister (Public Affairs)', 3 October 2017: www.canada.ca/en/department-national-defence/corporate/organizational-structure/assistant-deputy-minister-public-affairs.html.

16 Ibid.

17 Government of Canada. National Defense, 'DAOD 2008–0, Public Affairs Policy', 19 March 2017: www.canada.ca/en/department-national-defence/corporate/policies-standards/defence-administrative-orders-directives/2000-series/2008/2008-0-public-affairs-policy.html.

18 Ibid.

19 Ibid.

20 Ibid.

21 Kirsten Kozolanka (ed.), *Publicity and the Canadian State: Critical Communication Perspectives* (Toronto: University of Toronto Press, 2014).

22 Government of Canada. Canadian Armed Forces, 'Public Affairs Officer', 2 January 2019: https://forces.ca/en/career/public-affairs-officer/.

23 Ibid.

24 Ibid.

25 Ibid.

26 Philip Snowdon, 'Introduction' to *Truth and War, Edmund Dene Morel* (London: National Labour Press, 1916), vii.

27 Susan L. Carruthers, *The Media at War* (London: Palgrave Macmillan, 2010); Andrew Hoskins and Ben O'Loughlin, *War and Media* (Cambridge: Polity, 2011).

28 Peter Beaumount, 'US Lies and Deception Spelled Out in Afghanistan Papers' Shocking Detail', *The Guardian*, 9 December 2019: www.theguardian.com/world/2019/dec/09/afghanistan-papers-military-washington-post-analysis.

29 Jody Berland and Blake Fitzpatrick (eds.), *Cultures of Militarization* (Sydney, Nova Scotia: Cape Breton University Press, 2010).

30 McKay and Swift, *Warrior Nation*.

31 A. L. McCready, *Yellow Ribbons: The Militarization of National Identity in Canada* (Toronto: Fernwood Publishing, 2013).

32 David Mutimer, 'The Road to Afghanada: Militarization in Canadian Popular Culture during the War in Afghanistan', *Critical Military Studies* 2, no. 3 (2016): 210–25.

33 Tyler Shipley, 'The NHL and the New Canadian Militarism', *Canadian Dimension*, 6 August 2013: https://canadiandimension.com/articles/view/the-nhl-and-the-new-canadian-militarism.

34 McCready, *Yellow Ribbons*.

35 David Pugliese, 'Chief of the Defence Staff Gen: Jon Vance and the "Weaponization of Public Affairs"', *Ottawa Citizen*, 21 September 2015: https://ottawacitizen.com/news/national/defence-watch/chief-of-the-defence-staff-gen-jon-vance-and-the-weaponization-of-public-affairs.

36 Ibid.

37 David Pugliese, 'Governor General Gets New Advisor: A Public Affairs General Who Specializes in Information Warfare', *Ottawa Citizen*, 26 April 2018: https://ottawacitizen.

com/news/national/defence-watch/governor-general-gets-new-advisor-a-public-affairs-general-who-specializes-in-information-warfare.

38 David Akin, 'Canada's Armed Forces, Struggling to Hit Diversity Goals, Turns to New Digital Recruiting Tools', *Global News*, 14 September 2018: https://globalnews.ca/news/4450927/canada-armed-forces-diversity-goals-digital-recruiting/.

39 Norman Ramage, 'Advertising is War', *Marketing Mag*, 2 October 2006: http://marketing mag.ca/news/marketer-news/advertising-is-war-19941.

40 Goldie, 'Fighting Change', 413.

41 Ibid.

42 Nicole Wegner, 'Militarisation in Canada: Myth-Breaking and Image-Making through Recruitment Campaigns', *Critical Military Studies* 2, no. 3, 4 (2018): 67–85.

43 Ibid., 6.

44 CTV News Staff, 'Canada Aims to Grow Military with New Ad Campaign', *CTV News*, 18 February 2016: www.ctvnews.ca/politics/canada-aims-to-grow-military-with-new-ad-campaign-1.2783143.

45 Mishall Rehman, 'Government of Canada Launched New CAF Recruiting Campaign', *Canadian Military Family Magazine*, 21 June 2017: www.cmfmag.ca/duty_calls/government-of-canada-launches-new-caf-recruiting-campaign/.

46 David Pugliese, 'New – and Bland – Military Recruiting Campaign Focused on Offering Millennials a Job', *Ottawa Citizen*, 21 June 2017: https://ottawacitizen.com/news/national/defence-watch/new-and-bland-military-recruiting-campaign-focused-on-offering-millen nials-a-job.

47 Canadian Armed Forces, 'Dare to Be Extraordinary', *YouTube*, 10 August 2017: www.youtube.com/watch?v=VBLnz2pT9Tc [one minute and sixteen seconds].

48 Canadian Armed Forces, 'Dare to Be Extraordinary', *YouTube*, 2 May 2018: www.youtube.com/watch?v=S81NF5TXGuE [fifteen seconds].

49 Canadian Armed Forces, 'Dare to Be Extraordinary', *YouTube*, 19 August 2017: www.youtube.com/watch?v=npPdgXTthdg [thirty seconds].

50 Government of Canada, 'Train for Your True Calling: The Canadian Armed Forces': https://forces.ca/en/ (accessed 15 February 2020).

51 Ibid.

52 Canadian Armed Forces, *Facebook*: www.facebook.com/CanadianForces/ (accessed 15 February 2020).

53 Canadian Armed Forces, *Twitter*: https://twitter.com/CanadianForces (accessed 12 March 2020).

54 Canadian Armed Forces, *YouTube*: www.youtube.com/user/CanadianForcesVideos (accessed 15 February 2020).

55 Canadian Armed Forces, *Instagram*: www.instagram.com/canadianforces/ (accessed 15 February 2020).

56 Canadian Armed Forces, *LinkedIn*: https://ca.linkedin.com/company/canadian-forces (accessed 15 February 2020).

57 Government of Canada. National Defense and Canadian Armed Forces, 'Internet Terms and Conditions', 9 December 2019: www.forces.gc.ca/en/terms-conditions.page.

58 Nick Srniceck, *Platform Capitalism* (London: Polity Press, 2016).

59 Ibid., 6.

60 Christian Fuchs, *Social Media: A Critical Introduction* (London: Sage, 2019).

61 Government of Canada. National Defense and Canadian Armed Forces, 'Internet Terms and Conditions'.

62 Ibid.

63 Ibid.

64 Ibid.

65 Dal Yong Jin, *Digital Platforms, Imperialism and Political Culture* (New York: Routledge, 2015).

66 Tanner Mirrlees, *Hearts and Mines: The US Empire's Cultural Industry* (Vancouver: University of British Columbia Press, 2016).

12 'Life is wonderful because of the military'

People's Liberation Army recruitment campaigns in contemporary China

Orna Naftali

Abstract

This chapter examines recruitment campaigns for the Chinese military under the current leadership of Xi Jinping in the context of China's ongoing attempts to modernise and professionalise its army. Reviewing the conscription challenges the People's Liberation Army (PLA) faced in the 2000s and the steps taken to address these challenges, it analyses a series of promotional videos produced in 2013–18. Drawing on Chinese government, military and media sources, it explores the form and content of such videos and the ways in which they sought to attract new recruits to the PLA. The analysis shows that alongside traditional appeals to recruits' sense of patriotism and collective duty, the PLA's contemporary advertisements also promote military service as a vehicle for self-fulfilment and personal development. Disseminated through social media sites, this new marketing message attests to the PLA's ability to adapt to new civilian sensibilities and to adapt its propaganda accordingly. Yet it also carries considerable risks for the PLA's recruitment goals and its public standing in China.

In an article published in early 2019, the director of the Propaganda and Cultural Centre at the Political Work Department of the People's Liberation Army (PLA) described the centre's mission as a 'life-and-death contest' in the field of public opinion. To win this battle, the Director said, the PLA must 'borrow ships to go to sea' – in other words, to adopt the tactics of commercial entities to remain relevant in the digital age.[1] How has the PLA implemented this new strategy in its recent conscription campaigns, and what are the broader implications of the strategy for the army's efforts to professionalise its personnel and construct a favourable public image? This chapter addresses these questions while drawing on the analysis of conscription and publicity videos produced by the PLA in 2013–18[2] and on Chinese-language government, military, and media publications.

As the discussion reveals, distinct demographic trends, economic liberalisation, and the growing influence of a new consumer ethos among internet-savvy Chinese millennials pose obstacles for the PLA's recruitment goals. To overcome these obstacles, the PLA's propaganda videos, which are now available on social media sites, promote not only the traditional tropes of patriotism and collective duty but

Life is wonderful because of the military   179

also the idea of the military as a site of opportunity and as a means to fulfil recruits' personal ambitions. The adoption of this marketing ploy, which has been used by other armies worldwide, attests to the PLA's crucial ability to adapt and innovate in the digital age. This tactic also carries considerable risks, however, due to contradictions in the videos' messages and discrepancies between the fantasy they promote and the realities of military life. The deployment of recruitment films on social media sites which allow user interaction further exacerbates these risks and can damage not only the PLA's conscription efforts but also its moral clout.

From a guerrilla force to a modern army: a history of the People's Liberation Army

As a political and cultural entity, 'China' stretches back two millennia. Yet modern Chinese nationalism emerged only in the late nineteenth century in response to foreign imperialism, and the first Chinese republic was established in 1912 following a revolution which overthrew the last imperial dynasty. The PLA itself has existed for less than a century. Initially referred to as the 'Red Army', the PLA is not a national institution but rather the military arm of the Chinese Communist Party (CCP). Established in 1927, the army spent much of its first two decades fighting the Nationalists led by Chiang Kai-shek during the intermittent Chinese Civil War as well as the Japanese during the Second World War (referred to in China as the War of Resistance Against Japan). During this period, the PLA constituted a low-tech infantry force mainly engaged in guerrilla campaigns.[3]

Led by Mao Zedong, the CCP declared victory over the Nationalists in October 1949. That same year, the PLA expanded to include the PLA Navy and the PLA Air Force and began its first attempts at modernisation along Soviet lines. While the PLA remained technologically inferior to Western militaries, China's leaders readily employed its forces against the United States in Korea and Vietnam. During the Maoist period (1949–76), the PLA was also one of the primary means through which the CCP maintained its control over the country in accordance with Mao's dictum that 'political power grows out of the barrel of a gun'.[4]

The political upheavals of the Great Leap Forward (1958–60) and the Cultural Revolution (1966–76) nonetheless derailed the PLA's modernisation efforts. From the mid-1960s to the mid-1970s, domestic political struggles became the overriding priority, and PLA officers effectively had little to no training or even basic education.[5] As a result, at the end of the Mao era, the PLA lacked the same combat power that other large armed forces possessed. The failure to achieve comprehensive modernisation during Mao's rule was brought home during the 1979 conflict between China and Vietnam, when the PLA's performance exposed grave weaknesses.[6]

After Deng Xiaoping's assumption of power in 1978, national defence was included as the fourth of China's four 'modernisations' (the others being industry, science and technology, and agriculture). As China launched its first wave of market reforms and the Open Door policy in the 1980s, Deng also declared that the most likely military challenge that China faced was no longer 'early, major, and nuclear war' (as foreseen by Mao), but rather 'local, limited war'.[7] National defence was therefore accorded the lowest priority, which carried implications for military funding and development. Nonetheless, in the 1980s, China's military began to study contemporary foreign, particularly Western, military operations, undertook considerable reductions of unnecessary personnel, and reintroduced military ranks after a 25-year hiatus.[8]

In 1989, PLA units intervened on behalf of the CCP to suppress political demonstrations in Tiananmen Square, which considerably damaged the PLA's domestic and international image. World events in 1991, including the US military's performance in the Persian Gulf War, further shook CCP leaders' confidence in the PLA. As a result, in the early 1990s, China again altered its military doctrine, concluding that the most likely conflict the country would face would be a 'local war under high-technology conditions', later amended to 'conditions of informatisation', a reference to warfare in the digital age. This approach differed markedly from the Maoist paradigm of luring an enemy into China to fight a 'people's war' with regular troops, irregular (guerrilla) forces, and the general populace.[9]

Entering the twenty-first century, China's leaders recognised a number of factors that led them to expand the scope and quicken the pace of PLA modernisation: China's growing global economic and political interests; rapid technology-driven changes in modern warfare; and perceptions of increased strategic-level external threats, including to China's maritime interests in the East and South China Seas.[10] In 2004, then-President Hu Jintao outlined plans for the PLA to transition away from a force bound only to defending China's immediate territorial and sovereign interests to a force that could assume a global role. Subsequent PLA activities, such as counter-piracy operations in the Gulf of Aden, international training and exercises, non-combatant evacuations in Libya and Yemen, and expanded peacekeeping operations in Africa under United Nations (UN) auspices, have all been part of China's increasingly ambitious vision. China's establishment of its first overseas military base in Djibouti in 2017 – overturning Beijing's insistence from its first defence white paper issued in 1998 that China 'does not station troops or set up military bases in any foreign country' – is the latest development in this progression towards fulfilling a greater international role.[11]

Nonetheless, the main danger to China's national security today appears to be domestic. The most pressing threat is posed by extremists in China's westernmost province, Xinjiang, where the Turkistan Islamic Group, a terrorist outfit, is active. Tibetan separatism is regarded as another potential threat, while the unresolved political status of Taiwan also poses a strategic risk.[12] Notably, the PLA's growing professionalism in the past few decades has not diminished its role in supporting the political agenda of the CCP. Aside from regularly contributing to the CCP's propaganda efforts, for instance, through the Patriotic Education and the National Defence education campaigns, China's military also takes part in disaster-relief operations and in poverty-alleviation programs run by the Communist Party. PLA political commissars at the grassroots level can also access financial and other state resources to fund developmental projects, in some cases even cooperating with commercial joint ventures.[13]

To enable the PLA to fulfil these various missions, China has increased the military's budget by an average of 10 per cent per year from 2000 to 2016. During the

2000s, Beijing further instituted scientific and technical programs to improve the defence-industrial base, placing greater emphasis on operations in outer space and cyberspace.[14] Since President Xi Jinping's ascension to power in 2012, these trends have continued, with a greater focus on the theme of party rule over the military.[15] In 2015, Beijing unveiled the most substantial PLA reforms in at least 30 years. The reforms sought to clarify command authorities, integrate China's military services for joint operations, facilitate transition from peace to war, and improve the quality of military personnel.[16] The last goal, as we shall see, has proved particularly challenging.

Volunteers and 'involuntary conscripts': the challenges of recruiting in the twenty-first century

China has 2 million service personnel, with approximately 915,000 active-duty personnel in combat units, which makes it the largest armed force in the world.[17] The Military Service Law (adopted in 1984, amended in 2011) states that all male citizens have the obligation to perform military service, that China 'practices a military service system which combines conscripts with volunteers', and that the duration of service is two years. Women are not required to register for military service, but they can providing they are at least eighteen years of age.[18]

Although the PLA does not publish statistics regarding the percentage of 'volunteers' versus 'involuntary conscripts', it is estimated that approximately 10 to 11 million males turn 18 each year in China. Only about 3 per cent of them are required to provide the 300,000 to 400,000 recruits needed annually.[19] As supply exceeds demand, there is no need for all youths reaching the age of enlistment to join the armed forces. Thus, while obligatory by law, in practice, China's military recruitment system is rather selective.[20] Experts further agree that the Chinese military engages in active recruitment and that entrance into military service is often a competitive process, which in some instances involves bribery. The PLA and official media in China have acknowledged cases of unqualified personnel paying their way into the services, attempts to avoid conscription by feigning health problems, and attempts to bribe government officials to keep certain qualified recruits out of the military.[21]

The PLA's main challenge, however, has been to attract the best talent in an era of major economic growth. Under Maoist ideology, soldiers were listed as one of the three 'purest proletarian classes', ranked alongside workers and peasants, and were portrayed in official media as role models for all Chinese citizens. This notion has faded since the beginning of economic reform in 1978.[22] Although the public image of soldiers and veterans remains positive in mainstream media, high-school graduates, particularly in urban areas, prefer to pursue higher education rather than join the military, and those who fail college entrance exams (or cannot enrol for financial reasons) usually opt to work in industry instead.[23] While those born in the 1990s and 2000s may possess strong patriotic sentiments, they increasingly subscribe to ideals of self-fulfilment, personal development, and the pursuit of a comfortable lifestyle.[24] These ideals, needless to say, clash with military service, which involves danger, high-intensity training, strict discipline, and remote postings where hardship can be a part of life. Male recruits often find it hard to find a wife, and those who are married may experience family difficulties.[25] Notably, the PLA has also encountered widespread dissatisfaction among active and retired personnel regarding their (anticipated or actual) post-service employment and benefits.[26]

Under these circumstances, military service in China continues to be more attractive to poor rural residents than to wealthier urban youth. However, rural recruits often have relatively limited education and training and insufficient exposure to advanced technologies to master and maintain complicated equipment. For an army that seeks to become a world-class force that can fight wars under 'conditions of informatisation', this constitutes a major problem.[27]

Demographic factors also pose an obstacle. Although China's One Child Policy ended in 2015, it has (and will continue to have) a lingering effect on the PLA. Parents, particularly in urban areas, are reluctant to allow their only sons to choose a non-lucrative path that would require prolonged family separation and potentially endanger their child's safety. Another problem relates to the distinct features of the One-Child generation. According to Chinese media and academic publications, the One Child policy and dramatically improved standards of living in cities have created a 'culture of entitlement' among urban recruits of the post-1990s generation.[28] This has allegedly led to problems of poor physical fitness, a 'refusal to take orders from superiors . . . lack of mental preparation for hardship, inability to deal with frustration, lack of real-life experience, self-centredness, unwillingness to sacrifice themselves for national defence, and poor discipline'.[29] According to Chinese media reports, PLA military instructors have in recent years faced arguments with recruits about whether it was necessary to fold quilts neatly as well as complaints against encroachments on recruits' 'right to privacy'.[30] In one case, recruits even offered to pay to have their own rooms during training.[31]

To address these issues, and to attract and retain more graduates of colleges and universities, the PLA has in the past two decades begun to reform its recruitment procedures.[32] Notable measures include a reduction of service from four to two years to alleviate the hardships placed on families who have only one son;[33] recruiting civilian college graduates to become enlisted personnel without first having to spend two years as conscripts;[34] raising the age limit for conscription to 24 to allow college graduates to enlist; lowering the physical examination criteria; adjusting the timing of the conscription intake to coincide with college graduation;[35] and employing a system of preferential treatment, according to which student conscripts have their tuition fees paid, among other benefits.[36] Media tactics have also changed.

Strengthening the 'brand' and the 'packaging': media campaigns in the age of Web 2.0

The rise of a market economy and of a more open and connected society in the past several decades poses a daunting challenge for PLA recruiters. In the Mao period, propaganda work was characterised by overt appeals to mass audiences based on a one-size-fits-all approach. Publicity work in the era of market reforms, particularly in the 2000s, has been more difficult, with the PLA vying with international broadcasts, films, websites, online games, mobile applications, and commercial ads for the attention of young, especially urban, consumers.[37]

Although traditional recruitment methods, such as public posters and banners and the deployment of recruiting sergeants to campuses and local communities, remain in use, the PLA's conscription apparatus has acknowledged the need to 'strengthen its brand', pay more attention to 'packaging',[38] and create publicity products with greater appeal and 'strong emotional content'.[39] To achieve this goal, China's military has begun to rely on 'brand planning teams' comprised of civilian PR experts and media consultants, copywriters, analysts of user experience, product designers, and professionals from various creative industries.[40] In the course of the 2000s, the PLA introduced regular press briefings by army spokespeople, published a variety of defence-related magazines, and invested in the production of military-themed TV shows, films, animation, music videos, computer games, and toys, often in collaboration with commercial companies.[41]

Diagnosing 'online public discourse as a high-priority risk to ideological security', the CCP leadership has recognised the Internet as 'the main battlefield of public opinion struggle'.[42] The PLA's recent campaigns have reflected this shift in priorities. In the summer of 2013 (just in time for August 1, National Military Day), the PLA launched its first online game, co-developed by the Nanjing Military Area Command of the PLA and Giant Interactive Group Inc. Reportedly modelled on *America's Army* (2002–2019), the PLA's game, *Glorious Mission* (*Guangrong shiming*), was initially developed and distributed among army troops with the aim of honing soldiers' combat skills in 2011. According to official media, the game was subsequently distributed publicly to attract 'adolescent gamers' and increase appeal of the military and 'national defence education' among them.[43]

The PLA also released its first-ever online conscription video in 2013.[44] Entitled *Thanks to You, China Is Strong!* (*You ni, Zhongguo qiang!*), the video aired on TV, cinema screens, public transport media systems, government and commercial websites, and the military's Weibo and WeChat accounts. Weibo and WeChat are two of China's most popular social media networks, and prospective recruits were encouraged to visit them to view motivational clips, receive information (in some cases through live chat), and register online for military service.[45] Heeding the rising popularity of reality TV programming in China, the PLA also experimented with online media formats that involve user feedback and user-generated content, inviting soldiers and civilians to create their own conscription materials through competitive submissions or casting votes for their 'favourite conscription video' in online polls.[46]

Contributing to 'national rejuvenation': the Chinese conscription video

While the format and distribution methods for PLA campaigns have changed, so too has their content. Examining motivational videos publicly available on the PLA website, Chinese Military Network (*Zhongguo jun wang*), this section will show how. Formerly the online version of the *PLA Daily* (*Jiefangjun ribao*), the military's official newspaper, the website was revamped in 2017 to include micro-videos, blogs, and interactive features. The site currently holds more than a hundred publicity and conscription videos of various lengths produced by the PLA since 2013. For the purposes of this chapter, the discussion will focus on 21 'conscription videos' (*zhengbing pian*) that are typical of the available selection. Employing both content and discourse analysis, the discussion identifies the main themes and formats of these videos while noting recurrent messages and marketing ploys.

According to the PLA's online guidelines for potential recruits, citizens engaged in active service 'must love the Chinese Communist Party, love the socialist motherland, love the people's army, abide by the law, have good moral character . . . [and be] determined to fight heroically to resist aggression and defend the motherland'.[47] In line with this statement, PLA videos produced in 2013–18 appeal to audiences' sense of patriotism while underscoring soldiers' collective duties and responsibilities. Such messages are reflected in slogans such as 'Join the military to protect the nation and its borders'; 'safeguard China's interests against foreign incursions'; 'fight for China's dignity'; 'heed the call of the motherland at any time'; 'joining the army to protect the country is the highest form of glory'; and 'contribute to China's national rejuvenation' (the latter a slogan widely touted by the CCP under Xi Jinping's leadership). As a 2018 clip further intones: 'In wearing military uniform . . . I sign up to serve my country without regrets. I am a soldier of the people, I am the guardian of a beautiful life'.[48] The imagery backing this and similar appeals commonly includes soldiers saluting the national flag and the PLA flag or swearing an oath of allegiance to the CCP and footage from recent national military parades exhibiting the full range of China's weaponry.

Notably, explicit references to 'war' or images of battle also appear in some of the videos and are more prevalent than allusions to 'peace' or PLA disaster-relief efforts at home or abroad. The theme of war is conspicuous, for instance, in the animated clip *Entering the Military Camp, Dreaming to Sail*, produced by the Beijing Municipal Recruitment Office in 2015.[49] The clip begins with a famous quote from Sunzi's (Sun Tzu) *The Art of War (Bingfa)*: 'The art of war is of vital importance to the State. It is a matter of life and death, a road either to safety or to ruin'. It then shows images of renowned warriors throughout Chinese history while casting viewers as heirs of this rich military legacy. In another video, entitled *Battle Declaration (Zhandou xuanyan)* (2016), a hip-hop tune accompanies images of China's latest armaments – aircraft carriers, ballistic missiles, stealth jet fighters, and spaceships – and the soldiers, marines, and pilots who use them in battle or anti-terror operations. The lyrics of the song are explicit:

> There will always be a mission in our minds, there will always be enemies in front of our eyes / the battle can start at any time / Are you ready?
>
> Even if the bullet passes through my chest, the mission is still engraved in my heart / Born on this soil, I swear to protect this territory.
>
> Roar with animal spirit, from the centre to the border. Let's go to war, let's fight to win!
>
> There is no time to waste, the moment of life and death has arrived / you are not afraid / just wait for the command to kill! Kill! Kill![50]

Written and performed by army veteran Zhang Wei, the lyrics of the song were reportedly inspired by actual slogans used by PLA soldiers during training sessions. In a media interview, the video's editor, described as a member of the post-1990s generation in China, said, 'I wanted to make a video that I personally like, one that soldiers would like. I wanted it to be a video that can make people feel excited'.[51] It created a stir on Chinese social media, racking up more than 100,000 comments on Weibo within days of its release. Two years later, the PLA released another music video boasting a similarly belligerent message. Entitled *Decisive Battle*, this text depicted seemingly realistic scenes of combat backed by a fast-paced rock song performed by the (civilian) singer Li Jianke. 'Winning', viewers were informed, 'is my battle declaration':

> If you are arrogant . . . and dare to attack / I will fight you through 'till the end / if you attack my China, no matter how far away you are, I will not be polite / I will kill, kill, kill any great power / Kill, kill, kill, and launch a fatal counterattack.[52]

Reminiscent of the combative rhetoric of Mao-era propaganda, the videos' hostile tone reflects Beijing's recent shift to a more assertive security policy.[53] While some are clearly bellicose, however, many invoke a different type of message that highlights individual rather than collective benefits and advances the idea that service is about not merely duty but opportunity.

'Fulfil your personal dream of military life': the use of aspirational appeals

Recognising that military service is a choice rather than an obligation, PLA videos portray service as a means of helping recruits 'fulfil their personal dreams and ambitions', 'broaden their horizons', and 'free their imaginations'. For instance, in the 2015 video *Life iIs Wonderful Because of the Military! (Rensheng yin congjun er jingcai!)*, produced by the Henan Province Recruitment Office, a recent high school graduate is shown leaving an exam centre wearing a crestfallen expression before returning to his rural hometown to work in the fields. 'That year, I failed the college entrance examination', the narrator sadly intones, 'and gave up my dream to enter college. But I wasn't satisfied with being a farmer'. The man is then shown working at an urban construction site ('I also wasn't happy with the life of a migrant worker') and subsequently in front of the TV watching a military-themed show at night. He is then pictured wearing army uniform while the narrator states: 'Then I joined the military, and finally found a purpose to my life',[54] an acknowledgement that recruiters knew that military service was not the first choice of many targeted in this commercial.

A 2014 animated clip titled *Join the Military, Fulfil Your Personal Dream of Military Life! (Canjun ba, yongyou ziji de junying meng!)* boasts a similar message by showing an urban college student talking to a mother of a current PLA soldier. She assures the young man that 'joining the military not only serves the

186 *Orna Naftali*

Motherland, but also contributes to your personal development', before proceeding to discuss the PLA's preferential policies for college students and graduates.[55] Another ad, produced by the Beijing Municipal Recruitment Office in 2015, claims military service 'now involves the use of advanced high-tech weapons' and training for 'informationised warfare', which can help recruits gain a 'strong body and healthy lifestyle' and 'knowledge' that can improve their overall 'quality' (*suzhi*), allow them to become 'more creative', and 'soar to the skies' while 'leaving the competition' behind.[56]

Most of the ads also advance the idea that army service can help recruits acquire desirable psychological traits, including 'self-discipline', 'organisation skills', 'ability to withstand hardship', 'courage', 'determination', 'independence', and 'maturity'. Maturity, it is worth noting, is often defined as and conflated with masculinity, in common with military recruitment campaigns waged elsewhere around the world. In PLA ads, masculinity is depicted in images of bare-chested, muscular fighters and articulated in slogans such as 'army service has made me into a manly man (*dingtianlidi nanziahan*)'; 'always remember that a man should strive to perform immortal feats!'; 'fighting in the battlefield, like a man should!', and 'harden yourself in the military to become a courageous man!'. A few of these clips further allude to the development of strong male camaraderie, showing scenes of male soldiers helping each other during training exercises and participating in arm-wrestling competitions.

The social benefits of service and male and female soldiers coming together in social gatherings are recurrent themes, most notably in the music video *Motherland! I'm Coming* (*Zuguo! Wo lai le*), produced by the Shanxi Provincial Recruitment Office in 2014.[57] This text uses the popular song '*Xiao pingguo*' (Little Apple), performed by the Beijing-based duo the Chopstick Brothers (*Kuaizi xiongdi*) and originally written for the 2014 musical *Old Boys: The Way of the Dragon* (*Laonanhai meng longguo jiang*).[58] Appropriated by the PLA, this song makes no mention of national dignity or the idea of military service as a collective duty but repeated allusions to romance, suggesting 'Life is short, but I'll love you forever / I'll never leave you / You are my little apple'. It is juxtaposed, rather strangely, with scenes of planes performing exhilarating aerial manoeuvres, rockets exploding, and soldiers shooting at cardboard targets. Midway through the clip, conventional combat imagery is replaced with male and female soldiers collectively singing the lyrics of 'Little Apple' while performing the song's choreographed dance moves (widely available on Chinese video-sharing sites). The ad won first place in an online poll organised by the website *Chinese Military Network*. According to Chinese media reports, it was not only 'well received among netizens' but also 'attracted a large number of young people to join the army' after its release.[59]

While it is difficult to substantiate the latter claim, one thing is clear: the video and other recent online ads surveyed here signal a shift in the Chinese military's approach to conscription work. Rather than merely attempting to mobilise citizens to serve the country and 'fight for China', as was previously the case, the PLA now promotes soldiering as an exciting experience or one that is crucial for personal development and the achievement of an idealised (male) maturity.

Conclusion: military recruiting in an era of market liberalism

This chapter has shown that in an attempt to counter the unfavourable image of military service, particularly among educated youth, the PLA has adopted new media formats and new types of messaging. The conscription videos it produced in 2013–18 portray service not only as a collective duty but also (and increasingly) as an individualistic consumer fantasy similar to the kind frequently promulgated by commercial entities in China. It is worth noting that this strategy is not unique to the PLA, having been adopted by other military organisations around the world in the past few decades.[60] Yet it has represented a significant departure in recruiting practices in China, which used to be modelled on a version of Soviet authoritarianism but now embrace the doctrines and principles of free-market capitalism. The shift may have worked. According to official Chinese sources, there has been an increase in the numbers of college students and graduates joining the PLA in recent years, with Chinese media reports linking this trend to recent amendments in conscription procedures but also, crucially, to the PLA's innovative publicity methods.[61] However, since the PLA does not make the demographic composition of its personnel public, it is difficult to assess the validity of such claims.

Whether accurate or not, promoting military service as a means of fulfilling personal ambitions carries considerable risks for those who do decide to enrol in response to these campaigns. It also has complex political and moral ramifications. The touting of military service as a fun experience which may help young people, and men especially, fulfil their personal desires obfuscates the realities of service life, which is characterised by strict hierarchy and discipline, arduous training, and risks to personal safety if war is declared. It also highlights internal contradictions within the ruling Communist Party, which continues to tout the benefits of 'socialism' even as it encourages individual competition and market entrepreneurship among the current generation of Chinese youth. The reliance on an individualistic ethos in PLA conscription ads may attract young recruits but might also therefore bolster the same materialistic ethos which has led many elite youth to avoid military service to begin with.

The PLA's shift in tactics poses another danger. Chinese video-sharing sites allow users to express their approval or disapproval of official promotion with a push of a button. They also permit users to comment, interact with others, or share content across a range of platforms. These features can be a boon for the PLA's propaganda efforts insofar as they can help to exponentially increase audience exposure to such propaganda. Yet there is a trade-off: the ability of the PLA to control online discussion of its propaganda is limited. Indeed, anecdotal evidence suggests that audiences express both positive and negative reactions to the PLA's ads. For example, a video extolling the heroism and sacrifices of Chinese soldiers posted on National Military Day in 2018, which to date has amassed more than 300,000 views and 35,000 'likes' on the popular Chinese video-sharing site Bilibili,[62] also garnered the following response from a (self-identified) male user:

> we are not great men, we are not saints. . . . We are concerned about our lives. We feel unsure about our futures. We feel tired after working hard. We receive a negligible salary, and spend our days with strangers instead of

188 *Orna Naftali*

our parents, children, and wives. The daily life of the troops includes boring training and boring classes. There is not much entertainment, and there is not much time to rest. We do all this not for a greater goal or because of our 'youthful enthusiasm'. We do it just because we happen to be soldiers.[63]

This candid portrayal of army life, posted 15 minutes after the original ad appeared, received close to 8000 positive votes, making it the most popular comment on the ad and the most visible one at the time of writing. It has not yet been censored, though China's government can and does employ extensive online censorship tools.[64] A systematic analysis of user responses to the PLA promotion is beyond the scope of this chapter and merits a separate study. That said, it could be argued that the PLA's attempts to adapt to contemporary tastes and sensibilities of Chinese youth and extend its messages into online spaces that allow citizens to 'talk back' may well lead the Chinese army into a PR battle it will find difficult to win.

Notes

1 Yang Wang, '*Cong "xin" kaishi, dazao lujun xuanchuan wenhua xin pinpai*' [Starting from "New", Creating a New Brand of Army Propaganda Culture], *Junshi jizhe* [Military Reporter], 20 February 2019: www.81.cn/jsjz/2019-02/20/content_9430535.htm (accessed 26 December 2019).
2 In this chapter, I employ the term 'conscription videos' (in Chinese, *zhengbing xuanchuan pian*), since the PLA itself uses this term to describe its propaganda materials. However, although all men in China are legally liable for military service, in practice, recruitment is voluntary in most or all cases. The unique features of China's military recruitment system are discussed in detail in what follows.
3 US Defense Intelligence Agency (USDIA), 'China Military Power: Modernizing a Force to Fight and Win', 3 January 2019, 1: www.dia.mil/Portals/27/Documents/News/Military%20Power%20Publications/China_Military_Power_FINAL_5MB_20190103.pdf (accessed 10 April 2019); Roy Kamphausen, Andrew Scobell and Travis Tanner, 'Introduction', in Roy Kamphausen, Andrew Scobell and Travis Tanner (eds.), *The 'People' in the PLA: Recruitment, Training, and Education in China's Military* (Carlisle, PA: Strategic Studies Institute, US Army, September 2008), 3.
4 Dennis J. Blasko, *The Chinese Army Today: Tradition and Transformation for the 21st Century* (London: Routledge, 2012), 6.
5 Kamphausen, Scobell and Tanner, 'Introduction', 4.
6 USDIA, 'China', 2, 16; Blasko, *Chinese Army*, 4.
7 Blasko, *Chinese Army*, 5.
8 Ibid., 2; see also David Shambaugh, 'The People's Liberation Army and the People's Republic at 50: Reform at Last', *The China Quarterly* 159 (September 1999): 665.
9 USDIA, 'China', 2; James Char and Richard A. Bitzinger, 'Introduction: A New Direction in the People's Liberation Army's Emergent Strategic Thinking, Roles and Missions', *The China Quarterly* 232 (December 2017): 850; 'China's National Defence in the New Era', *State Council Information Office of the PRC* (July 2019): www.xinhuanet.com/english/2019-07/24/c_138253389.htm (accessed 2 August 2019).
10 Bernard Cole, 'The People's Liberation Army in 2020–30: Focused on Regional Issues', in R. Kamphausen and D. Lai (eds.), *The Chinese People's Liberation Army in 2025* (Carlisle, PA: US Army War College Press, July 2015), 172.
11 USDIA, 'China', 4; Char and Bitzinger, 'Introduction', 855–6.
12 Char and Bitzinger, 'Introduction', 355–6; Juliette Genevaz, 'China's People's Liberation Army: The Politico-Military Nexus' (EU Institute for Security Studies, March 2015), 4:

Life is wonderful because of the military 189

www.iss.europa.eu/content/china%E2%80%99s-people%E2%80%99s-liberation-army-%E2%80%93-politico-military-nexus (accessed 10 January 2019); David Johnson et al., 'Preparing and Training for the Full Spectrum of Military Challenges: Insights from the Experiences of China, France, the United Kingdom, India, and Israel' (Santa Monica, CA: RAND Corporation, 2009), 39.

13 Genevaz, 'China's People's Liberation Army', 2; Sofia K. Ledberg, 'Analysing Chinese Civil: Military Relations: A Bottom-Up Approach', *The China Quarterly* 234 (June 2018): 378; Juntao Wang and Anne-Marie Brady, 'Sword and Pen: The Propaganda System of the People's Liberation Army', in Anne-Marie Brady (ed.), *China's Thought Management* (London: Routledge, 2012), 142.

14 Char and Bitzinger, 'Introduction', 851; Kamphausen, Scobell and Tanner, 'Introduction', 5.

15 USDIA, 'China', 4.

16 Ibid., 5.

17 Donghua Zhang and Guoshun Liu, 'China Launches Preparation for 2019 Conscription Campaign', *China Military Online*, 9 January 2019: http://eng.chinamil.com.cn/view/2019-01/09/content_9400648.htm (accessed 20 March 2019); USDIA, 'China', 7, 61.

18 Military Service Law of the PRC (PRC State Council, 2011): http://eng.mod.gov.cn/publications/2017-03/03/content_4774222.htm (accessed 21 March 2019).

19 Johnson et al., 'Preparing', 26, 34.

20 Shumei Wang, *The PLA and Student Recruits: Reforming China's Conscription System* (Stockholm-Nacka: Institute for Security and Development Policy, January 2015), 7: http://isdp.eu/content/uploads/publications/2015-wang-the-PLA-and-student-recruits.pdf (accessed 22 April 2019); see also Kenneth Allen and Morgan Clemens, 'The Recruitment, Education, and Training of PLA Navy Personnel' (China Maritime Studies Institute US Naval War College [CMSI], Red Books 10, Newport, Rhode Island, 2014), 15–17: https://digital-commons.usnwc.edu/cmsi-red-books/10 (accessed 20 April 2019). As Allen and Clemens further note, the fact that all 'recruits' continue to be referred to as 'conscripts' (in Chinese, *yiwubing*) demonstrates the contradictory nature of the system and suggests a reluctance on the part of the Communist Party-state to abandon the term for political or practical reasons.

21 Allen and Clemens, 'The Recruitment', 17; Dennis Blasko, 'PLA Conscript and Non-commissioned Officer Individual Training', in Kamphausen, Scobell and Tanner (eds.), *The 'People' in the PLA* (Strategic Studies Institute, US Army, September 2008), 105; Roger Cliff, *China's Military Power: Assessing Current and Future Capabilities* (Cambridge: Cambridge University Press, 2015), 111.

22 Chunni Zhang, *Military Service and Life Chances in Contemporary China, Population Studies Centre Research Report 14–829* (Ann Arbor, MI: Institute for Social Research, University of Michigan, September 2014), 5.

23 Wang, 'PLA', 16.

24 Elina Sinkkonen, 'Nationalism, Patriotism and Foreign Policy Attitudes among Chinese University Students', *The China Quarterly* 216 (2013): 1045–63; Alex Cockain, *Young Chinese in Urban China* (London: Routledge, 2012); Yan Yunxiang, *The Individualization of Chinese Society* (Oxford: Berg Publishers, 2009); Orna Naftali, *Children in China* (Cambridge: Polity Press, 2016), 95–124.

25 Wang, 'PLA', 16; Wang and Brady, 'Sword', 135.

26 Michael Chase et al., 'Weaknesses in People's Liberation Army Organization and Human Capital', in *China's Incomplete Military Transformation: Assessing the Weaknesses of the People's Liberation Army (PLA)* (Santa Monica, CA: RAND Corporation, 2015), 53–4: www.jstor.org/stable/10.7249/j.ctt13x1fwr.10; Neil Diamant, 'Veterans, Organization, and the Politics of Martial Citizenship in China', *Journal of East Asian Studies* 8 (2008): 119–58.

27 Cliff, *China's Military*, 104–5; Wang, 'PLA', 14–16.

28 Cited in Peter Wood, 'The Spirit of Xu Sanduo: The Influence of China's Favorite Soldier', *China Brief* 23, no. 15 (26 July 2013): 16.

190 *Orna Naftali*

29 Cited in Cliff, *China's Military*, 112; see also: Chase et al., 'Weaknesses', 60; Blasko, 'PLA Conscript', 12.
30 Orna Naftali, 'Marketing War and the Military to Children and Youth in China: Little Red Soldiers in the Digital Age', *China Information* 28, no. 1 (2014): 3–4.
31 Cited in Wood, 'The spirit', 16.
32 John Corbett, Edward O'Dowd and David Chen, 'Building the Fighting Strength: PLA Officer Accession, Education, Training, and Utilization', in Kamphausen, Scobell, and Tanner (eds.), *The 'People' in the PLA*, 151.
33 Blasko, *Chinese Army*, 49.
34 Cliff, *China's Military*, 112.
35 Ibid.; Wang, 'PLA'; Zhang and Liu, 'China Launches Preparation'; see also 'Chinese Military to Open Online Enlisting Service', *China Daily*, 9 January 2019: www.chinadaily.com.cn/a/201901/09/WS5c35b2c0a31068606745fc1a.html (accessed 10 January 2019).
36 Wang, 'PLA', 9, 12, 15.
37 Ashley Esarey, 'Winning Hearts and Minds? Cadres as Microbloggers in China', *Journal of Current Chinese Affairs* 44, no. 2 (2015): 71; Wang and Brady, 'Sword', 135–8.
38 Yunlong Wang, 'Zuo hao xin shidai wanghshang yulong gongzuo' [Do a Good Job in the New Era of Online Public Opinion], *Junshi jizhe* [*Military Reporter*], March 2019: www.81.cn/jsjz/2019-03/01/content_9436757.htm (accessed 31 July 2019).
39 Li Liu and Jin Guo, 'Meiti ronghe huanjing xia de junshi wenhua chuanbo chuangxin' [Military Culture Communication Innovation in the Environment of Media Convergence], *Junshi jizhe*, 1 March 2019: www.81.cn/jsjz/2019-03/01/content_9436775 (accessed 10 August 2019).htm; Longquan Yang and Dongming Wang, 'Gongyi xuanchuan pian: Baba, wo zhangda le ye yao dang bing' [Public Information Clip: Dad, I Too Want to Be a Soldier When I Grow Up], *Xinhua*, 10 July 2018: jz.chinamil.com.cn › jssp › content › content_8084702 (accessed 19 May 2019).
40 Yang, 'Cong "xin" kaishi'; Peng, Li, 'Jun bao pi lu "zhandou xuanyan" xijie: Junying rap you 54 jituan jun shibing chuangzuo' [Military Newspaper Reveals the Details behind 'Combat Declaration': Military Rap Was Created by Soldiers from the 54th Army], *Jiefang ribao* [*Liberation Army Daily*], 13 May 2016: www.thepaper.cn/news Detail_forward_1468666 (accessed 10 February 2019).
41 Tai Ming Cheung, 'Engineering Human Souls: The Development of Chinese Military Journalism and the Emerging Defence Media Market', in Susan L. Shirk (ed.), *Changing Media, Changing China*(Oxford: Oxford University Press, 2011), 129; Chase et al., 'Weaknesses', 66; see also Naftali, 'Marketing'; Annie Nie Hongping, 'Gaming, Nationalism, and Ideological Work in Contemporary China: Online Games Based on the War of Resistance against Japan', *Journal of Contemporary China* 22, no. 81 (2013): 499–517.
42 Wang '*Zuo hao*'; Rogier Creemers, 'Cyber China: Upgrading Propaganda, Public Opinion Work and Social Management for the Twenty-First Century', *Journal of Contemporary China* 26, no. 103 (2017): 87–8; Lianrui Jia, 'What Public and Whose Opinion? A Study of Chinese Online Public Opinion Analysis', *Communication and the Public* 4, no. 1 (2019): 32.
43 Yu Fu, 'Military Online Game to Open to Public in China', *Xinhua*, 31 July 2013: http://english.cri.cn/6909/2013/07/31/2941s778931.htm (accessed 30 August 2019). In 2017, the commercial Internet giant, Tencent, released a mobile version of the game.
44 Ying Lan, 'Zhongguo zhengbing xuanchuan gaobie kongdong shuojiao junying ban xiao pingguo bei zan zui meng' [China's Conscription Propaganda Bids Farewell to Empty Preaching, Military Version of 'Little Apple' Praised for its Cuteness], *Xinhua*, 19 June 2015: www.xinhuanet.com/mil/2015-06/19/c_127932782.htm (accessed 29 August 2019).
45 Liu and Guo, 'Military'; Yang and Wang, 'Public'.
46 Yang, 'Starting'.
47 *China Conscription Network* [*Zhongguo zhengbing wang*], 'College Students' Enlistment Policy', 1 August 2018: www.gfbzb.gov.cn/zbbm/zcfg/dxsrw/201808/20180801/1710941292.html (accessed 29 August 2019).

48 *Zhongguo junshi wang* [China Military Network], 'Wo he jundui de bu jie zhi yuan gun -"wo shi Zhongguo junren", xianli jian jun 91 zhounian' [My Indissoluble Bond with the Army – "I am a Chinese Soldier": A Gift Presented on the Occasion of the PLA's 91st Anniversary], *video*, 02:23: http://tv.81.cn/jlwyx/2018-08/01/content_9238508.htm (last modified 1 August 2018).

49 *Beijing shi zhengbing ban* [Beijing Recruitment Office], 'Zoujin junying, mengxiang qi hang' [Entering the Military Camp, Dreaming to Sail], *Zhongguo junshi wang* [China Military Network], animated video, 01:49: www.81.cn/2015zb/2015-08/12/content_6625987.htm (accessed 21 August 2019).

50 *Zhongguo junshi wang* [China Military Network], 'Zhongguo jun wang fabu 2016 zhengbing xuanchuan pian: Zhandou xuanyan' [China Military Network Releases 2016 Recruitment Video: Battle Declaration], video, 03:11: http://tv.81.cn/sytj-tupian/2016-04/28/content_7028467.htm (last modified 28 April 2016).

51 Li, 'Military'.

52 *Zhongguo junshi wang* [China Military Network] website, 'Zhongguo jun wang fabu 2018 nian kai xun MV "juezhan"' [China Military Network Releases 2018 Music Video, "Decisive Battle"], video, 03:00: http://tv.81.cn/jlwyx/2018-01/03/content_7894471.htm (last modified 3 January 2018).

53 Char and Bitzinger, 'Introduction', 842.

54 *Henan sheng zhengbing ban* [Henan Province Recruitment Office], 'Rensheng congjun er jingcai!' [Life Is Wonderful Because of the Military (Because of Military Service)!], video, 03:42, *Zhongguo junshi wang* [*China Military Network*] website: www.81.cn/2015zb/2015-08/06/content_6616861.htm (accessed 20 April 2019).

55 *Yunnan sheng renmin zhengfu zhengbing bangongshi* [Recruitment Office of the People's Government of Yunnan Province], 'Donghua: canjun ba, yongyou ziji de junying meng!' [Join the Military, Fulfil Your Personal Dream of Military Life!], *Zhongguo junshi wang* [*China Military Network*] website, animated video, 00:59: www.81.cn/2014zbxcp/2014-07/31/content_6072331.htm (accessed 12 August 2019).

56 *Beijing shi zhengbing ban*, '*Zoujin junying*'.

57 *Shanxi sheng renmin zhengfu zhengbing bangongshi* [Recruitment Office of the People's Government of Shanxi Province], 'Zuguo! Wo lai le!' [Motherland! I'm Coming], *Zhongguo junshi wang* [China Military Network] website, video, 03:40: www.81.cn/2014zbxcp/2014-07/25/content_6063292.htm (accessed 12 August 2019).

58 In an ironic twist, this film tells the story of two brothers who leave China to chase their dreams in New York. Yang Xiao and Wang Taili, dirs. 2014; LeVision Pictures, Youku Tudou and Ruyi Films, PRC.

59 Lan, 'China's conscription'.

60 See, for example, Beth Bailey, 'The Army in the Marketplace: Recruiting an All-Volunteer Force', *Journal of American History* (June 2007): 50.

61 Xiubao Li, 'Zuo junshi meiti ruohe xiang zongshen fazhan de kaita zhe' [Be a Pioneer in the Development of Military Media], *Junshi jizhe*, 2 April 2019: www.81.cn/jsjz/2019-04/02/content_9465890.htm (accessed 12 August 2019); see also Wood, 'PLA', 15.

62 '*Wo shi shei? Wo shi Zhongguo junren, wo shi renmin zidi bing!*' ['Who Am I? I Am a Chinese Soldier, I Am a Soldier of the People!'], *Bilibli* website, video, 02:20, 08:37: www.bilibili.com/video/av28243234/ (last modified 1 August 2018).

63 *Buzheng jing de e h* ['Unkind'], 'Wo xiang shuo yi xia, women bu shi weiren' [I Want to Say That We Are Not Great Men], user comment, *Bilibli*, posted on 1 August 2018, 08:52: www.bilibili.com/video/av28243234/.

64 See Gary King, Jennifer Pan and Molly E. Roberts, 'How Censorship in China Allows Government Criticism but Silences Collective Expression', *American Political Science Review* 107, no. 2. (2013): 326–43.

13 The caliphate wants you! Conflating Islam and Islamist ideology in Islamic State of Iraq and Syria recruitment propaganda and Western media reporting

Halim Rane and Audrey Courty

Abstract

Having declared its caliphate in mid-2014, the militant group known as the Islamic State of Iraq and Syria (ISIS) effectively utilised Islamic terminology, texts and narratives to recruit thousands of Muslims globally to join its ranks in the conquest of territory in Iraq and Syria and to commit acts of terrorism in numerous cities around the world. This chapter will examine ISIS recruitment propaganda carried in its online magazines Dabiq *and* Rumiyah. *Of particular focus will be the extent to which the militant group draws on the religion of Islam as a recruitment strategy in the service of its Islamist politico-military ideology and objectives. This will be addressed in relation to the scholarly debate over the relationship between Islam and Islamism. The chapter examines the appeal of ISIS among significant, albeit relatively small, numbers of discontented Western Muslims and the extent to which Western media organisations have been complicit in ISIS recruitment through a tendency to conflate Islam and Islamism and frame the group in ways that are consistent with its own propaganda material.*

Almost a century after the Ottoman caliphate was abolished by the Republic of Turkey, the world witnessed the rise and fall of a new entity claiming the title of caliphate. The Salafi-jihadist group known as the Islamic State of Iraq and Syria (ISIS) ruled extensive territory across Iraq and Syria from 2014 until the end of 2017. This chapter focuses on the time period between 2014 and 2017, with some discussion of events prior to the emergence of ISIS and following the collapse of the group's caliphate in 2017, when it lost control of its territory.

Although short-lived, ISIS has had a transformative impact on perceptions of Islam in the West and relations between Muslim communities and Western states and societies. This chapter focuses on ISIS's strategy of conflating the religion of Islam with its own Islamist political agenda to recruit thousands of discontented Muslims to not only join its armed forces, but also become citizens of its 'state'. It highlights ISIS's religio-political appeal and how the group exploited Western media to amplify its propaganda messages directed at Western audiences. With the collapse of ISIS's caliphate, the group is now almost entirely focused on its propaganda efforts to promote a civilisational clash between Islam and the West by promoting acts of terrorism, against its Muslim and non-Muslim enemies, as an Islamic religious obligation.

'Caliphate' is derived from the Arabic word *khilafa*, referring to an Islamic state under the leadership of a caliph, and is understood to be an 'Islamic' political system. However, the term *khilafa* is not used in the Quran, and no details of a political system are provided by the Prophet Muhammad. The word *caliph* is used in the Quran not in reference to a political leader but to human beings in general as inheritors of the earth entrusted with its wellbeing.[1] The idea of a caliphate as an Islamic political system emerged in the centuries after the death of the Prophet Muhammad in 632 AD.[2] Other related terms, also central to ISIS propaganda, like *hijra* (migration), *jihad*[3] and *shariah*[4] are used by the group in ways that appeal to Muslim audiences but are also inconsistent with their original meaning in the Quran and in classical Islamic scholarship.[5] For instance, ISIS's consistent use of the term *shariah* as an Islamic legal code has some consistency with classical Islamic jurisprudence, but it is inconsistent with the use of the term in the Quran and the fact that *shariah* was not used by the Prophet Muhammad or his companions in reference to a legal code.[6]

Since the fall of the Ottoman caliphate and especially in the aftermath of Muslim-majority countries acquiring independence from European colonial rule, influential movements developed in Muslim-majority countries championing the establishment of an Islamic state. These movements, which are broadly classified as Islamist, sought a return to the political order of the classical Islamic era or some modified form of it. The term 'Islamist' is addressed in what follows, but in brief, it refers to individuals, groups and movements engaged in activities to establish a social or political order based on an interpretation of Islam. For some Western Muslims, ISIS represented a formidable, seemingly religiously legitimate response to their grievances with Western military interventions in Muslim-majority countries and also appealed to their sense of powerlessness and marginalisation in their own societies. The group's achievements in battle and propaganda spoke to their longing for a return of Islam's glory days as a dominant military and political power. Massive death tolls and destruction caused by Western military interventions in Muslim-majority countries have created conditions that have produced militant groups such as ISIS and reinforced their recruitment propaganda,[7] while Western media coverage and political discourses that conflate Muslims with terrorism and Islam with politicised violence[8] have contributed to the alienation and radicalisation of some Muslims targeted in ISIS's recruitment propaganda.

The origins of the Islamic State of Syria and Iraq and its propaganda network

As with any state or non-state actor, ISIS is by no means an autonomous entity and did not emerge in a vacuum. The catalysts for its emergence include the Saudi

Wahhabist ideology and interpretation of Islam, which has spread among Muslim communities globally, with varying degrees of acceptance, since the latter half of the twentieth century, and the US-led invasion and occupation of Iraq in 2003. Its genesis can be traced to Abu Musab al-Zarqawi's formation of Jamaat al-Tawhid wa-l-Jihad (Organisation of Monotheism and Jihad) in post-Soviet Afghanistan and his pledge of *bay'ah* (allegiance) to his one-time financier Osama bin Laden in 2004. Al-Zarqawi was subsequently appointed as bin Laden's man in Iraq.[9] After al-Zarqawi's death in 2006, the group continued to evolve under the successive leaderships of Abu Omar al-Baghdadi,[10] Abu Ayyub al-Masri[11] and eventually its current leader Abu Bakr al-Baghdadi. This occurred against a backdrop of takeovers and alliances that saw the creation of the Mujahideen Shura Council, the Islamic State of Iraq and the merger with parts of the Syrian al-Nusra Front, which in turn led to ISIS.

The formation of ISIS, however, created a rift between al-Baghdadi's ISIS and the al-Qaeda leadership. Having similar goals as al-Qaeda – the promotion of a civilisational clash between Islam and the West and establishing a caliphate – the two groups vied for supremacy as the defender of 'Islam' against the 'Crusader enemy' and ultimately competed for the same audience. By all accounts, ISIS was the more successful of the two, partly due to its superior use of communication technology as an intrinsic component of its politico-military campaign. In a 2016 ISIS document entitled *Media Operative, You Are a Jihadi, Too* – a rare articulation of the group's propaganda doctrine – ISIS glorifies 'information warfare' in a manner that is seemingly unparalleled by any other Islamist-jihadist group.[12] The 55-page monograph emphasises the importance of propaganda by framing it as part of 'a battle', as 'more than half of this battle is taking place in the battlefield of the media'.[13] Indeed, quoting Saudi cleric Hamud bin Uqla al-Shuaybi, the authors explain:

> The media offers a fine way to spread news of Muslim victories over the enemy, support the mujahidin [jihad fighters], demonstrate their courage and extoll their virtues. These matters are critical in terms of their potency for sustaining the mujahidin's steadfast pursuit of victory for the Muslims and defeat for their enemies.[14]

Taking this idea further, the authors suggest the creation and dissemination of ISIS propaganda is tantamount to fighting in the caliphate's army or conducting terrorism in its name:

> To every media operative brother in the Islamic State, you should know and be convinced of the following fact, [that] the media is a jihad in the way of Allah [and that] you, with your media work, are therefore a mujahid in the way of Allah.[15]

In this manner, the document repeatedly glorifies propaganda activism as an aspirational act, claiming even that 'verbal *jihad*' can sometimes be 'more important than *jihad* of the sword'.[16] Although *Media Operative* is a propaganda document in itself, the great lengths the authors go to in branding ISIS's 'information warfare' as a legitimate and logical part of *jihad* demonstrates the centrality of propaganda operations to the group. Testimonies of ISIS detractors appear to confirm this, as they reveal senior media operatives were treated as 'Emirs' of equal rank to their military counterparts.[17]

However, since ISIS shrouds its information and recruitment activities in secrecy, much of what is known in the academic literature is derived from ISIS propaganda itself. While former ISIS recruits testify to having consumed ISIS propaganda prior to enlisting,[18] there is yet to be any empirical study of the efficacy of ISIS propaganda for recruitment. This chapter concentrates on ISIS's English-language publications *Dabiq* and *Rumiyah* in order to explain the ways in which the group *attempted* to recruit Western (Anglophone) audiences. The observations presented here do not necessarily align with the approaches identified in other forms of ISIS propaganda, including periodicals published in other languages.

'A state for all Muslims': recruiting using *Dabiq* and *Rumiyah*

The goal of establishing a caliphate is shared by many Islamist-jihadist groups, including al-Qaeda and Jemaah Islamiyah, as well as some ostensibly non-violent groups like Hizbut Tahrir. None has been as successful, in terms of acquiring territory and attracting fighters and citizens, as ISIS. Within a few years of its inception as an offshoot of al-Qaeda, ISIS rapidly expanded, took control of extensive territory in Iraq and Syria, and amassed revenue estimated at around US$2 billion.[19] Additionally, through its appeals to such concepts as caliphate, migration and armed struggle, which have significance in mainstream Islamic teachings, ISIS was able to attract fighters from all over the world, estimated at between 10,000 and 100,000.[20]

The key to ISIS's success may be its use of internet-based communications technology and its religiously oriented multi-lingual propaganda. Reflecting the group's diverse national and linguistic composition, ISIS produced recruitment propaganda in Arabic, English, French and German. However, as this chapter's focus is on the recruitment of Western English-speaking Muslims, our analysis is confined to the English-language versions of *Dabiq* and *Rumiyah*.

ISIS's flagship publications include the digital magazines *Dabiq*, which ran for 15 issues from 2014 to 2016, and *Rumiyah*, which included 13 issues between 2016 and 2017. While the identities of the people who produced and translated *Dabiq* and *Rumiyah* are not publicly known, news reports suggest ISIS recruited 'as a headhunting firm would, people with a background in graphic design and production and with media degrees'.[21] Given the high production quality and language fluency of the magazines, it is reasonable to assume they were created by professionals who are native or proficient English speakers.

Dabiq and *Rumiyah* reflect the changing fortunes of ISIS on the ground and its recruitment potential. While the names of both magazines are derived from places mentioned in apocalyptic prophecies, the former refers to the town of Dabiq in

Syria, and the latter is an Arabised reference to Rome and the 'West' more generally. Reflecting ISIS's relative strength between 2014 and 2016, *Dabiq* emphasises the religious legitimacy of the caliphate and a call to Muslims globally to migrate to the territory of the Islamic State. As described in one study, it 'brings together ISIS's military, governance, and religious activities into one united outreach effort . . . to integrate military and governance actions to support a coherent religious vision'.[22] In contrast, *Rumiyah* was published during ISIS's decline and loss of territory, including the town of Dabiq, which prompted a shift in content from military recruitment and governance in Iraq and Syria to an emphasis on encouraging supporters to launch attacks on their own homelands.[23]

The latter represents a different type of recruiting exhortation to that considered elsewhere in this volume. In conventional military recruiting, individuals are enticed to serve in armed forces that are either deployed to a foreign country or based at home for defensive purposes. *Rumiyah* encouraged prospective recruits to take up arms by themselves, independently of any existing military, and launch terrorist attacks on their countries of residence.

US intelligence officials have not publicly indicated who controls ISIS's propaganda strategy, though it was presumed to be led by the group's main spokesman, Abu Muhammad al-Adnani, in 2015.[24] One analyst counted a network of as many as 48 official media offices, including affiliates in Yemen, Libya, and West Africa, and nine additional, centrally administered outlets.[25]

One of the main tasks of these bodies is to establish ISIS's legitimacy vis-à-vis Islam. In particular, *Dabiq* emphasised the religious obligation of Muslims to migrate (*hijrah*) to the Islamic state as well as *jihad* to establish the caliphate and implement *shariah* law:

> The State is a state for all Muslims. The land is for the Muslims, all the Muslims. To Muslims everywhere, whoever is capable of performing hijrah to the Islamic State, then let him do so, because hijrah to the land of Islam is obligatory.[26]

ISIS also used the threat of eternal damnation to motivate Muslims to join the Islamic state, telling readers that if you cannot migrate or express public or private allegiance to ISIS, your 'belief that the Islamic State is the [Caliphate] for all Muslims will be sufficient to save you from the warning mentioned in the hadith [or sayings of the Prophet]'.[27]

A key strategy of ISIS recruiters is to convince its target audience to prioritise support for the caliphate over other commitments and obligations, in particular education. 'Every Muslim professional', one *Dabiq* article claimed, 'who delayed his jihad in the past under the pretence of studying [Islamic law], medicine, or engineering, etc., claiming he would contribute to Islam later with his expertise, should now make his number one priority to repent and answer the call to hijrah'. Students were treated to a similar plea, the author warning of 'abandoning the obligation of the era', an obligation more 'urgent than spending an unknown number of years studying while exposed to doubts and desires that will destroy their religion'.[28]

However, under circumstances where travel to the Islamic state was not possible, ISIS shifted the obligation to committing acts of terrorism in one's homeland, as exemplified in the quote that follows concerning an attack in Sydney in 2014:

> This month, an attack was carried out in Sydney by Man Haron Monis, a Muslim who resolved to join the mujahidin of the Islamic State in their war against the crusader coalition. . . . It didn't take much; he got hold of a gun and stormed a café taking every-one inside hostage. Yet in doing so, he prompted mass panic, brought terror to the entire nation, and triggered an evacuation of parts of Sydney's central business district. The blessings in his efforts were apparent from the very outset.[29]

As a recent study of Muslim Australians convicted of terrorism offences highlighted, so-called 'Islamic' beliefs and obligations propagated by ISIS were key motivations for waging or planning attacks. Most of the more recently convicted offenders had been prevented from travelling to the Islamic state and subsequently directed their 'jihad' against fellow citizens.[30]

Over time, attacks in one's homeland against Western citizens became more pronounced in ISIS propaganda, with one issue of *Dabiq* claiming

> If you can kill a disbelieving American or European – especially the spiteful and filthy French – or an Australian, or a Canadian, or any other disbeliever from the disbelievers waging war . . . then rely upon Allah, and kill him in any manner or way however it may be. Do not ask for anyone's advice and do not seek anyone's verdict.[31]

This shift in focus from joining the Islamic State to committing acts of terrorism at home is more apparent in *Rumiyah*, though the theme of using the religion of 'Islam' to justify bloodshed remained consistent across both publications. As the first issue of *Rumiyah* stated, Islam is a 'religion of sound principles, providing the perfect foundations upon which the solid structures of justice and glory are built'. One such principle is that 'all people must be fought until they accept Islam or come under an [Islamic legal] covenant'.[32]

Another key aspect of the effectiveness of ISIS recruitment propaganda concerns how it positions its audiences in relation to those it defines as outsiders. One study, for instance, explains that '*Dabiq* appeals to its audiences by strategically designing in-group identity, Other, solution and crisis constructs which it leverages via value-, crisis- and dichotomy-reinforcing narratives'.[33] In so doing, ISIS is able to 'shape its readership's perceptions, polarise their support and drive their radicalization'.[34] The main divisions that ISIS seeks to exploit are between the Islamic State and the West and between the so-called 'true' Sunni Muslims and other Muslims and non-Muslims.[35] *Rumiyah* articulates these divisions in terms of a 'battle' of creed between camps of 'believers' and 'unbelievers' and emphasises that 'any slogan raised for any battle between us and them, other than the slogan of religion, is an utter lie and deception'.[36] Muslims who do not subscribe

198   *Halim Rane and Audrey Courty*

to ISIS's 'religion' are subsequently excluded from the camp of 'believers', and attacks are called upon them:

> Those Muslims residing in the West, in particular, have an opportunity to terrorize the Crusaders themselves as well as the imams of [disbelief] allied to the Crusaders. These [apostate] imams have fabricated a false religion of apostasy from elements of democracy, nationalism, liberalism, pacifism, and pluralism, doing so in servitude of their Crusader masters.[37]

Central to ISIS's recruitment strategy is its effective use of Islamist narratives and appropriation of Islamic concepts to appeal to marginalised Muslims. As one study states:

> The various master narratives employed by ISIS are powerful tools in the recruitment process because they give its propaganda a degree of legitimacy reinforced by the historical experiences of Islam. ISIS uses these narratives to exacerbate historical and political grievances and to harness feelings of personal victimisation and discrimination experienced by Western Muslims (long considered to be key components in the radicalisation process). Feelings of victimisation and isolation within these countries can create a foundation for the rejection of Western values and instigate what they perceive to be a return to an Islamic identity. By evoking the higher authority of Islam over modern state-imposed versions of legality and ethics, ISIS is able to appeal to otherwise vulnerable Muslims living in Western countries.[38]

Mahood and Rane identify three master narratives – crusader, ignorance, and hypocrites – as central to ISIS propaganda intended to reinforce the group's 'Islamic' self-presentation.[39] The crusader narrative was found to be the most extensively used by ISIS, framed in relation to a view of the West as harbouring a deep-rooted hatred of Islam. The ignorance and hypocrites narratives are used to delegitimise Western societies vis-à-vis Islam and to legitimise the targeting of non-Muslims and Muslims who oppose ISIS. We suggest that all three narratives are intended to encourage ISIS supporters to disassociate themselves from societies, communities, neighbours, family and friends who do not conform to its ideology. This doctrine of in-group loyalty and out-group disavowal, central to Wahabbism and Salafism,[40] is reputedly a defining characteristic of Muslims convicted of terrorism offences,[41] and it has appeal because it seems to be derived from and have legitimacy within Islam.

Islam, Islamism and the use of religion in mobilisation promotion

Islam and Islamism are not the same thing. The former is a faith, the latter an ideology that borrows from the religion of Islam for its legitimacy.[42] Mozaffari contends that 'Islamism is more than merely a "religion" in the narrow sense of theological

The caliphate wants you! 199

belief, private prayer and ritual worship, but also serves as a total way of life with guidance for political, economic and social behaviour'.[43] Islamism selectively uses the teachings of Islam to form the sets of ideas that comprise the ideology, which it reproduces as legitimate religious obligations.[44] Islamists, as one leading scholar of political Islam puts it, are 'Muslims who are committed to political action to implement what they regard as an Islamic agenda'. The content of that agenda and its pursuit, meanwhile, is Islamism.[45] Others have defined Islamists as 'Muslims with Islam-based political agendas . . . who reject the separation of religious authority from the power of the state . . . and seek to establish some version of an Islamic political and legal structure'.[46] Yet their definition does not account for pro-democracy political Islamists, such as Tunisia's En-Nahda Party and Turkey's Justice and Development Party, that advocate political secularism.[47]

Although we use the term 'Islamist' in order to be consistent with the academic literature, not all Islamists are violent; in fact, most advocate non-violent means, including democratic elections, to achieve their vision of an Islam-based political agenda.[48] However, research on the prevalence of Islamism among Western Muslim youth gives some reason for concern. Goli and Rezaei, for instance, found that half of the young Danish Muslims included in their study adhere to some form of Islamism, including those that they categorised as fundamentalists (27 per cent), radical Islamists (18 per cent), and militants (6 per cent).[49] Radical Islamists who advocate the use of violence to achieve national or transnational political goals are often referred to as Islamist jihadists or simply jihadists.[50] Rabasa et al. point out that 'radical Islamism has been an enduring problem for many nations, but it became a prominent international priority only after the 9/11 attacks'.[51]

Like its forerunner al-Qaeda, ISIS represents a distinct form of Islamism that incorporates Salafist-jihadism and Saudi Wahabbism as its religious ideology. Salafist-jihadism is essentially a religio-political ideology that seeks to overthrow near enemies (Muslim nation-states) and cause the destruction of far enemies (Western nation-states) to establish a caliphate and implement *shariah* law.[52] While other Salafist groups do not necessarily advocate violence in pursuit of political goals and many remain apolitical, Salafi-jihadists consider *jihad* a religious duty. Salafists also discriminate against non-Sunni Muslims, particularly Shiites, and advocate the subjugation and even the enslavement of non-Muslims.[53] Wahhabism is a form of Salafism developed and disseminated by Saudi Arabia based on the teaching of Muhammad ibn Abdul Wahhab (d. 1792), a key ally of Ibn Saud, founder of the first Saudi state in 1744. It is characterised by its exclusivism, literalism, ultra-conservatism and intolerance, especially in relation to the rights of women, non-Muslims, and non-Sunnis.

Such tenets are reflected in ISIS's brand of Islamism, as described in one issue of the *Rumiyah* magazine that defines Islam in accordance with the ideas and terminology well established in the Salafi movement and Wahhabism in particular. There is a clear rejection of Western political systems and ideas, including democracy and nationalism. This has particular appeal for Muslims who feel modern Muslim and Western nation-states have failed them socially, politically and economically and who feel nostalgia for what they imagine to be a glorious, powerful

200 *Halim Rane and Audrey Courty*

Islamic polity of the past. This also relates to ISIS's rejection of the borders of the modern Middle Eastern nation-states, which were not determined by the people of the region but established by European colonial powers. In this piece, ISIS condemns systems of governance and laws outside of the Islamic context as oppressive and idolatrous – the antithesis of Allah's will and of Islam itself.

The same piece also condemns alternate Islamic approaches to politics and governance, specifically that of the Muslim Brotherhood, which it attacks with a play on words by referring to the group as 'Murtadd', meaning apostate. ISIS also affirms its association with the Salafism and the Wahhabi ideology as the true Islam by invoking such terms as *tawhid* (monotheism), *Shariah* (Islamic law), *wala* and *bara* (loyalty to Muslims and disavowal of non-Muslims) and jihad. The use of these terms in relation to Islamist-jihadism is addressed elsewhere,[54] but it is important to note, with the exception of *wala* and *bara*, their potency comes from their prominence in mainstream Islamic thought. Such a propaganda strategy blurs the line between Islam and ISIS, making it difficult for vulnerable Muslims without sufficient Islamic education to discern between the two. A study of 20 foreign fighters recruited by ISIS confirms this, suggesting:

> interactions with these individuals were so heavily mediated by religious discourse it seems implausible to suggest that religiosity (i.e., a sincere religious commitment, no matter how ill-informed or unorthodox) is not a primary motivator for their actions. Religion provides the dominant frame these foreign fighters use to interpret almost every aspect of their lives, and this reality should be given due interpretive weight.[55]

Finally, the cited quote from *Rumiyah* also refers to ISIS's enemies as Crusaders in order to evoke historic memory of Western non-Muslim invaders of Muslim lands. This narrative is likely to be intended to prevent Western Muslims from forming a Western Muslim identity in which they feel accepted in their country of birth or residence. As noted in what follows, feelings of marginalisation and alienation among Western Muslims were ripe for exploitation, especially when combined with highly pejorative Western media reporting on Islam and Muslims.

ISIS's hatred for non-Muslims and fellow Muslims, who do not accept its ideology, was manifested in brutal violence and atrocities that meant the actions of the group would be newsworthy, particularly for a Western media that has for decades adopted a formula of covering Islam through a prism of conflict and crises.[56] This, combined with the Western media's limited frame of reference to Islam, audience appetite for sensational reporting and lack of information about ISIS allowed the organisation to largely set the media agenda.

Giving terrorists the 'oxygen of publicity': Western media reporting

Bolstering ISIS's politico-military campaign is its insidious ability to become part of Western news cycles and exploit mainstream media to amplify its propaganda. Indeed, while ISIS is effective in transmitting its deeds and messages using its own communication channels, it depends on Western media reporting for amplification and legitimacy. This is consistent with the idea, first articulated by British Prime Minister Margaret Thatcher, that terrorists rely on the 'oxygen of publicity' to influence the attitudes and perceptions of international audiences.[57]

To this end, ISIS deliberately manipulates Western media by tailoring the 'production and release of its propaganda material to the needs of media outlets'.[58] Developing high-quality media content that is easily accessible and reproducible by mainstream outlets is another strategy.[59] As Semati and Szpunar describe, 'the media to which [ISIS] is intricately tied is often accompanied by the adjective "Western" . . . it is "slick", it speaks "our" language', and it shares a similar journalistic style.[60] Williams claims that ISIS often releases 'high-impact' images and videos of its brutality after military setbacks or during lulls in international news.[61] The group does this, she contends, to detract from potentially negative coverage and to ensure it continues to dominate international agendas.[62] In so doing, it can be argued that ISIS is using Western media coverage to help build its 'brand'. It is certainly, as one US intelligence official remarked, 'very image-conscious, much like a corporation'.[63]

Systematic studies of ISIS propaganda output suggest the group targets international audiences with the aim of demoralising and intimidating its opponents, as well as agitating and polarising Western societies.[64] Courty et al. organise this propaganda into two main categories: 'formidable foe' and 'clash of civilisations'.[65] The first category of propaganda focuses on the group's brutal exploits and triumphs in order to enhance public perceptions of its strength and success and legitimise its institutions. The second category advances the notion that the world is engaged in a civilisational war between the two camps ISIS classifies as 'Muslims' and 'non-Muslims'. This manipulates audiences' worldview to divide Western societies along religious lines, which has manifested in a rise of anti-Islam sentiments as well as right-wing groups and political parties with an explicit anti-Islam agenda.[66] Combined, the formidable foe and clash of civilisations narratives are designed to convey an image of a Western world intent on destroying Islam, in which true Muslims do not belong, and of ISIS as the saviour of Muslims.

This divisive rhetoric is fundamental for ISIS's attraction of foreign recruits. As one *Dabiq* article declared: 'Muslims in the West will quickly find themselves between one of two choices': 'either apostatize [convert] . . . or [migrate] to the Islamic State and thereby escape persecution from the crusader governments and citizens'.[67] Courty et al. found in some instances Western media supported this notion of a civilisational clash by repeatedly linking Muslim communities to terrorism and failing to meaningfully distinguish the Islamic faith from Islamist ideology.[68] For example, *The Daily Mail*'s sensationalist reporting of the 2015 Paris attacks repeatedly conflated Islam and Islamism and portrayed the wider Muslim community as a potential threat to Western societies.[69] The British tabloid deliberated on the role of 'Islamic' doctrine, and its more provocative headlines warned of 'the enemy within'.[70]

Courty et al. also found that although more responsible outlets like *The New York Times* and the *Times* were comparatively more discerning and controlled in their reporting of ISIS, official sources overwhelmingly dominated the way ISIS is represented and understood.[71] The claims and actions of officials, particularly

202 *Halim Rane and Audrey Courty*

government leaders and representatives, were therefore uncritically accepted and consequently shaped public dialogue about counter-terrorism policies.[72] This is significant because it allowed alarmist, inflammatory and divisive political rhetoric to roam unchecked in the media, and it's ironic because it ultimately benefitted ISIS. By omitting alternative and more reasonable voices, news media reinforced ISIS's claim of persecution of Muslims, which is so crucial to their ability to prey on disaffected and marginalised Muslims in Western societies.[73]

Moreover, sensationalist reporting, which overstated the threat posed by ISIS and glorified its fearsome image, was harnessed by the group as part of its own propaganda strategy. In *Dabiq*, for example, ISIS used the 'words of the enemy' to derive legitimacy for its actions. This regular feature of the online magazine would highlight Western news and political commentary that supported ISIS's propaganda claims of military and tactical prowess. In particular, *Dabiq* would feature stand-alone quotes from Western analysts and politicians who emphasised ISIS's victories and conquests and confirmed the threat posed by the group. In its first issue, for instance, *Dabiq* referred to an article written by two American counter-terrorism experts about the state of ISIS in 2014. It featured comments by the authors which described ISIS as a 'de facto state' and 'a real, if nascent and unrecognized, state actor' and compared its 'multi-ethnic army' to 'a foreign legion'.[74] The recognition of ISIS as a legitimate 'state actor' bolstered its claims of maintaining a caliphate as a legitimate 'Islamic' political entity.

In summary, the Western media's uncritical acceptance of ISIS as Islamic rather than Islamist left non-Muslim audiences with a limited capacity to reject the group's claims of legitimately manifesting the teachings of Islam and gave disenfranchised Muslims a long-awaited champion that seemed to seriously challenge Western dominance.

Conclusion

Estimates vary, but it is generally agreed that ISIS was far more successful than its predecessors in recruiting Muslims from around the world to join its cause. Much has been written about the group's effective use of communication technology to disseminate its recruitment propaganda. This chapter has highlighted some examples of Islamic terminology, texts and narratives used by ISIS in its flagship publications, *Dabiq* and *Rumiyah*. The main point of this chapter is that the key to ISIS's military recruitment strategy was an ability to link militant Islamist goals with the religion of Islam. While this is not a strategy unique to ISIS, setting the group apart was its more effective use of digital media technologies, its willingness to communicate to audiences in their native languages, and its exploitation of Western media. Not only was Western media reporting on the group a regular feature in ISIS's *Dabiq* magazine, the group's notoriety as a formidable foe and the notion of a clash of civilisations were reinforced by Western media reports. This chapter argues that by conflating Islam with ISIS's Islamist propaganda, the Western media contributed to the legitimisation of ISIS propaganda as 'Islamic'.

This chapter discussed some recent scholarship from the field of Islamic Studies which challenges ISIS's use of such concepts as caliphate, *jihad* and *shariah* for its Islamic narrative, but we were not able to identify such critical analysis in Western media reporting of ISIS. Rather, ISIS's claims of Islamic legitimacy tended to be uncritically accepted, which contributed to its own propaganda. This reporting was an important aspect of ISIS's recruitment of discontent Western Muslims whose anti-Western sentiments had been driven in part by images of death and destruction in Muslim-majority countries in the aftermath of Western military interventions as well as the religious extremism of Saudi Wahhabism and Salafism more generally. These audiences were predisposed to support entities that Western media reporting and political discourses framed as the enemy, especially a formidable, 'Islamic' one like ISIS. This ultimately served the central goals of ISIS, and others such as al-Qaeda, which were to establish a caliphate as rival political entity to other Western and Muslim systems of governance, disrupt and destroy the peaceful coexistence of Islam in the West and to convince Muslims and non-Muslims of the inevitability of their mutual enmity.

At the time of writing this chapter, the president of the United States, Donald Trump, announced the death of the ISIS leader Abu Bakr al-Baghdadi in a US-led operation in Syria. While this may represent a blow to the group, this chapter contends that the key to destroying ISIS is to undermine support for its ideology among Muslims around the globe, which was weak to begin with and has eroded over time. This could be most effectively achieved through more critical rejections of ISIS's claims of Islamic legitimacy, including by Western media organisations. Additionally, more critical engagement from Islamic religious authorities and an attempt to promote Islam's teachings concerning religious pluralism and inter-faith relations are likely to be decisive in diminishing ISIS's recruitment potential.

Notes

1 Halim Rane, '"Cogent Religious Instruction": A Response to the Phenomenon of Radical Islamist Terrorism in Australia', *Religions* 10, no. 4 (2019): 246–68.
2 Halim Rane, 'Democracy and Muslims', in Mark Woodward and Ronald Lukens-Bull (eds.), *Handbook of Contemporary Islam and Muslim Lives* (Berlin: Springer, 2018), 1–22.
3 The term *jihad* literally means to strive or struggle in reference to the exertion of spiritual, intellectual, charitable or physical efforts, which may include defensive armed struggle. However, the term evolved to be used in reference to defensive and offensive armed struggle.
4 The term *shariah* literally refers to a path that leads to water but has a meaning in the Quran of a life path towards salvation in this world and the afterlife. In the classical era of Islam's history (from the eighth to the 13th centuries), *shariah* came to be used as the term for the Islamic law developed by the classical era Islamic jurists and legal scholars.
5 Halim Rane, '"Cogent Religious Instruction"', 246.
6 Mohammad Omar Farooq and Nedal El Ghattis, 'In Search of the Shari'ah', *Arab Law Quarterly* 32, no. 4 (2018): 315–54.
7 Samantha Mahood and Halim Rane, 'Islamist Narratives in ISIS Recruitment Propaganda', *The Journal of International Communication* 23, no. 1 (2017): 15–35.
8 Audrey Courty, Halim Rane and Kasun Ubayasiri, '"Blood and Ink: The Relationship between Islamic State Propaganda and Western Media', *The Journal of International Communication* 25, no. 1 (2019): 69–94.

204   *Halim Rane and Audrey Courty*

9 Aaron Y. Zelin, 'The War between ISIS and al-Qaeda for Supremacy of the Global Jihadist Movement', *The Washington Institute for Near East Policy Research Notes* 20 (June 2014): 1–11: www.washingtoninstitute.org/uploads/Documents/pubs/Research Note_20_Zelin.pdf (accessed 27 October 2019).
10 Joseph Felter and Brian Fishman, *Al-Qa'ida's Foreign Fighters in Iraq: A First Look at the Sinjar Records* (New York: Combatting Terrorism Center at West Point, 2007): 1–31.
11 Brian Fishman, *Dysfunction and Decline: Lessons Learned from Inside Al-Qa'ida in Iraq* (New York: Combatting Terrorism Center at West Point, 2009): 1–36.
12 Charlie Winter, *Media Jihad: The Islamic State's Doctrine for Information Warfare* (London: The International Centre for the Study of Radicalisation and Political Violence, 2017): 1–28: https://icsr.info/wp-content/uploads/2017/02/ICSR-Report-Media-Jihad-The-Islamic-State's-Doctrine-for-Information-Warfare.pdf (accessed 27 October 2019).
13 Winter, *Media Jihad*, 11.
14 Ibid.
15 Ibid., 13.
16 Ibid., 21.
17 Greg Miller and Souad Mekhennet, 'Inside the Surreal World of the Islamic State's Propaganda Machine', *The Washington Post*, 20 November 2015: www.washington post.com/world/national-security/inside-the-islamic-states-propaganda-machine/ 2015/11/20/051e997a-8ce6-11e5-acff-673ae92ddd2bstory.html (accessed 27 October 2019).
18 Ibid.
19 Martin Chulov, 'ISIS: The Inside Story', *The Guardian*, 11 December 2014: www.the guardian.com/world/2014/dec/11/-sp-isis-the-inside-story (accessed 27 October 2019).
20 Carol K. Winkler, Kareem El Damanhoury, Aaron Dicker and Anthony F. Lemieux, 'The Medium Is Terrorism: Transformation of the about to Die Trope in *Dabiq*', *Terrorism and Political Violence* 31, no. 2 (2019): 224–43.
21 Krishnadev Calamur, 'ISIS's Newest Recruiting Tool: Regional Languages', *The Atlantic*, 24 April 2019: www.theatlantic.com/international/archive/2019/04/isiss-newest-recruiting-tool-tamil-and-regional-languages/587884; Miller and Souad, 'Inside the Surreal World'.
22 Harleen Gambhir, *Dabiq: The Strategic Messaging of The Islamic State* (Washington, DC: Institute for the Study of War, 2014): 2: https://undestandingwar.org/sites/default/ files/Dabiq%20Backgrounder_Harleen%20Final_0.pdf (accessed 27 October 2019).
23 Tyler Welch, 'Theology, Heroism, Justice, and Fear: An Analysis of ISIS Propaganda Magazines Dabiq and Rumiyah', *Dynamics of Asymmetric Conflict* 11, no. 3 (2018): 186–98.
24 Miller and Mekhennet, 'Inside the Surreal World'.
25 Charlie Winter and Jordan Bach-Lombardo, 'Why ISIS Propaganda Works', *The Atlantic*, 13 February 2016: www.theatlantic.com/international/archive/2016/02/isis-propaganda-war/462702/ (accessed 27 October 2019).
26 'The Return of Khilafah', *Dabiq* no. 1 (10 October 2014): 10: https://clarionproject. org/docs/isis-isil-islamic-state-magazine-Issue-1-the-return-of-khilafah.pdf.
27 'The Flood', *Dabiq* no. 2 (10 October 2014): 4: https://clarionproject.org/docs/isis-isil-islamic-state-magazine-Issue-2-the-flood-.pdf.
28 'The Call to Hijrah', *Dabiq* no. 3 (10 October 2014): 26: https://clarionproject.org/ docs/isis-isil-islamic-state-magazine-Issue-3-the-call-to-hijrah.pdf.
29 'Al-Qa'idah of Waziristan: A Testimony From Within', *Dabiq* no. 6 (10 October 2014): 3: https://clarionproject.org/docs/isis-isil-islamic-state-magazine-issue-6-al-qaeda-of-waziristan.pdf.
30 Rane, 'Cogent Religious Instruction', 246.
31 'Al-Qa'idah of Waziristan', 4.
32 'Issue 1', *Rumiyah*, 10 October 2014, 35: https://clarionproject.org/wp-content/uploads/ Rumiyah-ISIS-Magazine-1st-issue.pdf.

33 Haroro J. Ingram, 'An Analysis of Islamic State's Dabiq Magazine', *Australian Journal of Political Science* 51, no. 3 (2016): 458.
34 Ingram, 'Dabiq Magazine', 458.
35 'Issue 2', *Rumiyah*, 10 October 2014, 18–19: https://clarionproject.org/wp-content/uploads/Rumiyah-ISIS-Magazine-2nd-issue.pdf.
36 Ibid.
37 'Issue 2', 3.
38 Mahood and Rane, 'Islamist Narratives', 31.
39 Ibid., 15–35.
40 Uriya Shavit, 'Can Muslims Befriend Non-Muslims? Debating Al-Walā' Wa-Al-Barā' (Loyalty and Disavowal) in Theory and Practice', *Islam and Christian – Muslim Relations* 25 (2014): 67–88.
41 Rane, 'Cogent Religious Instruction', 246.
42 Bassam Tibi, *Islamism and Islam* (London: Yale University Press, 2012), vii.
43 Mehdi Mozaffari, 'What Is Islamism? History and Definition of a Concept', *Totalitarian Movements and Political Religions* 8, no. 1 (2007): 22.
44 Mozaffari, 'What Is Islamism?', 17–33.
45 Piscatori in Richard C. Martin and Abbas Barzegar, *Islamism: Contested Perspectives on Political Islam* (Stanford: Stanford University Press, 2009), 27.
46 Angel Rabasa, Stacie L. Pettyjohn, Jeremy Ghez and Christopher Boucek, *Deradicalizing Islamist Extremists* (Santa Monica: Rand Corporation, 2010), 2: www.rand.org/pubs/monographs/MG1053.html (accessed 27 October 2019).
47 Halim Rane, *Islam and Contemporary Civilization: Evolving Ideas, Transforming Relations* (Carlton: Melbourne University Press, 2010); Rane, 'Democracy and Muslims', 1–22.
48 Martin and Barzegar, *Islamism*.
49 Marco Goli and Shahamak Rezaei, 'Radical Islamism and Migrant Integration in Denmark: An Empirical Inquiry', *Journal of Strategic Security* 4, no. 4 (2011): 81–114.
50 Tibi, *Islamism and Islam*.
51 Rabasa et al., *Islamist Extremists*, 37.
52 Rane, 'Cogent Religious Instruction', 246.
53 Adis Duderija, 'The Salafi Worldview and the Hermeneutical Limits of Mainstream Sunni Critique of Salafī-Jihadism', *Studies in Conflict & Terrorism* (2018): 1–17.
54 Rane, 'Cogent Religious Instruction', 246.
55 Lorne Dawson and Amarnath Amarasingam, 'Talking to Foreign Fighters: Insights into the Motivations for Hijrah to Syria and Iraq', *Studies in Conflict & Terrorism* 40, no. 3 (2017): 192.
56 Edward Said, *Covering Islam: How the Media and the Experts Determine How We See the Rest of the World* (New York: Random House, 1981); Halim Rane, Jacqui Ewart and John Martinkus, *Media Framing of the Muslim World: Conflicts, Crises and Contexts* (London: Palgrave Macmillan, 2014).
57 Bruce Hoffman, *Inside Terrorism* (New York: Columbia University Press, 2006).
58 Lauren Williams, *Islamic State Propaganda and the Mainstream Media* (Sydney: Lowy Institute for International Policy, 2016), 1: https://lowyinstitute.org/sites/default/files/islamic-state-propaganda-western-media_0_0.pdf (accessed 27 October 2019).
59 Ibid., 6.
60 Mehdi Semati and Piotr M. Szpunar, 'ISIS Beyond Spectacle: Communication Media, Networked Publics, Terrorism', *Critical Studies in Media Communication* 35, no. 1 (2018): 2.
61 Williams, *Islamic State Propaganda*.
62 Ibid.
63 Miller and Mekhennet, 'Inside the Surreal World'.
64 Daveed Gartenstein-Ross, Nathaniel Barr and Bridget Moreng, *The Islamic State's Propaganda Strategy* (Hague: International Centre for Counter-Terrorism, 2016), 1–84; Williams, *Islamic State Propaganda*; Charlie Winter, *The Virtual 'Caliphate': Understanding Islamic State's Propaganda Strategy* (London: Quilliam, 2015), 1–51.

65 Courty et al., 'Blood and Ink'.
66 Geoff Dean, Peter Bell and Zarina Vakhitova, 'Right-Wing Extremism in Australia: The Rise of the New Radical Right', *Journal of Policing, Intelligence and Counter-Terrorism* 11, no. 2 (2016): 121–42.
67 'From Hypocrisy to Apostasy', *Dabiq*, no. 7, 62: https://clarionproject.org/docs/islamic-state-dabiq-magazine-issue-7-from-hypocrisy-to-apostasy.pdf (accessed 27 October 2019).
68 Courty et al., 'Blood and Ink'.
69 Ibid.
70 Ibid.
71 Ibid.
72 Ibid.
73 Bibi van Ginkel and Eva Entenmann, *The Foreign Fighters Phenomenon in the European Union* (The Hague: International Centre for Counter-Terrorism, 2016), 1–149.
74 'The Return of Khilafah', 33.

Conclusion

14 Narratives of service, sacrifice and security

Reflecting on the legacy of military recruitment

Brendan Maartens

Abstract

Attempts to persuade people to fight are as old as conflict itself and have taken many different forms over the course of recorded history. Public spectacles, cultural artefacts and monoliths were among the first discussed in this book and were complemented by the spoken and written words and by appeals carried in and across mass and digital media. The military recruitment campaign, as it has been explored in this book, is a product of such historical forces. Merging ancient traditions of military pageantry and iconography with the persuasive strategies and techniques of the modern advertising, public relations and media industries, it has become an intrinsically mediated *phenomenon that is central to war and representations of it. This chapter will draw some broader conclusions about the legacy of such campaigns. Beginning with a review of recruiting exhortations, it seeks to answer a question posed at the outset of this book – were similar appeals used to encourage civilians to serve in different countries, regions and periods? – and then considers whether such appeals were actually effective. The final sections consider potential future avenues of scholarly research and what the future might have in store for us all as we approach a critical juncture in human history.*

'Successful propaganda', the American political scientist Harold Lasswell wrote in 1938, 'depends upon the adroit use of means under favourable conditions. A means is anything which the propagandist can manipulate; a condition is anything to which he [sic] must adapt'.[1] Recruiters, as we have seen, turned to a range of means to sell service during the twentieth and twenty-first centuries and adapted their work to suit an equally diverse array of conditions. Yet they did more than just manipulate. They also created what Lasswell called 'streams of suggestions': tailor-made appeals carried in and across communications channels to achieve specific objectives at given moments in time.[2] Writing of Great War propaganda from a comparative, international perspective, Lasswell contended that certain 'streams' appeared time and again, such as the idea of a war of self-defence waged by governments whose only concern was protecting citizens against unchecked foreign aggression, the idea of a satanic enemy whose 'sins' included the execution of prisoners and the wounded and '[l]ooting, arson, rape and murder' and the idea that war could help preserve 'cordial relations among allies'.[3]

210 Brendan Maartens

Central to the process of priming populations for war, some of these tropes have featured in the more targeted military recruitment promotion explored in this book. The Islamic State of Iraq and Syria (ISIS), for example, used online magazines to castigate certain foreigners as 'Crusaders' and to portray ISIS as a defender of its own distorted interpretation of Islam (see Chapter 13). The All-Union Voluntary Society for Assistance to the Army, Air Force, and Navy, a pre-conscription pressure group that operated throughout the Union of Soviet Socialist Republics during the Cold War, sponsored sporting events that conferred Ready for the Defence of the Motherland badges to participants (see Chapter 9). Drawing on long-standing aspirations to construct an enlarged state from the rump of surrounding Ottoman territories, Greek recruiters in 1915 portrayed enlistment as a means of defending *their* motherland by checking possible Bulgarian aggression (see Chapter 4).

These examples share two things in common: the construction of an *idea* of a nation-state, which is 'imagined' in the sense in which Benedict Anderson deployed the term many years ago,[4] and the attempt to define that nation, state and the people who comprise it in opposition to *other* nation-states and peoples. This process of Othering and the 'almost unconditional and overpowering sense of in-group sameness and out-group difference' that it entails is crucial to modern warfare.[5] Yet it is also a marked feature of much recruitment promotion, which draws on ideas of national distinction when pitching service to prospective recruits. One method of doing so is to use allegorical figures like Columbia and Uncle Sam, widely deployed, as we have seen, to mobilise troops in the United States in 1917–18 (see Chapter 6). Another is to use living human beings, as the British did during the same war with portrayals of Lord Horatio Herbert Kitchener, a man regarded by many at the time as the country's finest living soldier.[6] A third is to use national flags and insignia,[7] as the Chinese did a century after their American and British counterparts by using both the national Chinese flag and the flag of the People's Liberation Army to promote an idea of 'national rejuvenation' (see Chapter 12).

Such 'streams' help to sustain the very notion of a nation-state but also encourage recruits to view themselves as participants in grander national projects – 'people's wars'. Fought for and by the people, these wars have become enduring motifs in recruitment promotion, particularly in times of conflict, and are advantageous from the point of view of enlistment because they seem to suggest that military organisations are classless entities that welcome all regardless of status, gender or creed. The problem, of course, is that almost every army, navy or air force that has operated in recent times has been anything but inclusive, with institutional hierarchies enshrined in ranking systems and enforced through oppressive codes of disciplinary conduct. There is a glaring contradiction here between the depiction of service in recruitment promotion and the actual lived experiences of servicemen and servicewomen. The rank and file see it when commanded by officers, and women see it when excluded from frontline service and most senior command positions. Historically under-represented in armed forces, women also occupied a subsidiary role in the civil defence services Britain maintained during

Narratives of service, sacrifice and security 211

the Second World War, being encouraged to bear the 'burden of caring for the sick and the wounded' while men engaged in more active work during their country's 'moment of need' (see Chapter 7).

While notions of collective sacrifice cannot paper over ingrained structural inequalities, much less change them, they have an enduring allure in many societies, particularly militarised ones. The same can be said for ideals like duty, heroism and honour. Used by recruiters as binding, universal qualities, these ideals were deployed so widely during the Great War that they were subsequently lampooned as 'Big Words' that had been completely stripped of substance and meaning. Such 'grand abstractions', as one literary critic has described them,[8] surface frequently in recruitment promotion, with residents of the Union of South Africa in 1914–18, for instance, encouraged to enlist because of '[c]onscience, duty, [and] honour'[9] (see Chapter 3), and their counterparts in Australia implored to do so to ensure they had done their 'duty' to keep the nation's 'promise' to supply more men to the Allied camp in Europe (see Chapter 5). The evidence presented in each case suggests that they were at least partially successful.

These exhortations will not surprise historians of propaganda, who have become accustomed to the use of nationalism and patriotism in large-scale mobilisation campaigns. In some senses, the strain that wars place on the social fabric compels governments to pander to such 'grand abstractions'. Though wars are fought and ultimately won with manpower, womanpower, munitions and money, they have become, in the words of one theologian, something of an 'institution' that has taken on an important *moral* quality. Preserving 'virtues that would otherwise be lost', they appeal to notions of 'self-sacrifice . . . [a] sense of cooperation . . . [and] devotion to a higher cause',[10] qualities that are essential to a functioning military but not to the capitalist individualism that dominates most of the globe.

There is a tension here between individualist and collectivist conceptions of social organisations, and this tension can be mapped in recruitment promotion, which tends to pander to 'Big Words' in times of war and crisis and different ideals when no threat to a nation or people can be identified. These ideals include the pay new recruits receive and their capacity to rise through the ranks to more lucrative positions after enrolling. The research presented in this book, and in other published studies that have helped to inform it,[11] confirms this. In Britain in the immediate post-war period, for example, pay was central to recruiting drives, partly because it was increased by upwards of 60 per cent but also because it was perceived to be a more compelling inducement to serve than patriotism. The War Office's Deputy Director of Public Relations admitted as much, suggesting that 'recruiting appeal[s]' that exploited the 'self-interest' of prospective recruits carried more weight in peacetime than 'such abstract things as patriotism, the duty of a citizen, [and] comradeship'. The Secretary of State for War, for his part, talked not of service but of 'careers' (see Chapter 8).

Militaries, of course, do offer careers. Yet there is a subtle but significant difference between promoting the military as a career and promoting it as a civic duty. Appeals to duty imply *sacrifices* on the part of prospective recruits, while appeals to careers pander to individuals' sense of fulfilment and satisfaction – *rewards*.

212   *Brendan Maartens*

The sociologist Charles Moskos made a similar point in an oft-cited structural analysis of the US Army published in the late 1970s. Reflecting on the period when the US was engaged in hostilities in south-east Asia in the earlier part of that decade, Moskos suggested that the Army had been presented to the American public as an 'institution . . . legitimated in terms of values and norms, i.e., a purpose transcending individual self-interest in favour of a presumed higher good'. After the US withdrawal from Saigon in 1975, however, the Army started to resemble an 'occupation . . . legitimated in terms of the marketplace, i.e., prevailing monetary rewards for equivalent competencies'.[12]

Moskos did not write about military recruitment advertising, public relations or propaganda, but his model has been applied by other scholars to explain how the Belgian, American and Israeli armed forces have promoted themselves in recent years.[13] The Canadian armed forces, as shown in Chapter 11, can be added to this list. Their recent *Dare to Be Extraordinary* campaign emphasised skills and training that would not just benefit recruits in service but also potentially aid them if or when they decided to leave the service and return to civilian life. This campaign, as we have seen, rebranded the Canadian military as a kind of vocational college, portraying new recruits not as 'helpful heroes' but as career-orientated individuals.

This, too, implies a different kind of service to that associated with war. When attracting new recruits to the military with promises of training, pay and promotion prospects, recruiters are essentially appealing to them as *individuals*. When pandering to a person's sense of duty, patriotism or honour, recruiters ultimately encourage individuals to affirm their membership of *collectives*. In the first case, rewards – material, financial, educational – represent the primary inducements; in the second, though recruits can be said to gain certain things, such as the respect of their peers, and although they are also rewarded with salaries and other perks like travel, they are expected to make sacrifices to gain those things in the first place.

Reviewing the campaigns examined in this book, it is clear that military organisations tend to define themselves as 'institutions' when engaged in combat, presumably because the collective ideals associated with such institutions are deemed essential for maintaining *esprit de corps*. In times of peace, 'occupational' inducements emphasising individual gratification are more common. There are obviously exceptions to this rule, which is by no means hard and fast, but it is worth bearing in mind when exploring recruitment promotion between and within nations. The evidence from Britain, indeed, suggests that recruiters have oscillated between these two categories of appeal for much of the twentieth century, adapting their appeals according to how active the nation's armed forces were.[14]

What conclusions might be drawn from these 'streams of suggestions'? One observation worth making concerns the relationship that military recruiting shares to other, non-military forms of promotion. We have already seen how commercial advertising and public relations experts are hired by recruiters to exhort civilians (see Chapter 2). What we have not yet considered are the *similarities* between commercial and military promotion. The literature on commercial advertising can be instructive here. Corporations, Douglas Goodman reminds us, are fond of portraying their goods and services as solutions to problems. Some of these problems are 'personal . . . [like] halitosis, shyness or physical unattractiveness', but others are 'social . . . such as oppression or inequality'.[15] The trick here is to portray a brand or company as an agent of positive social change, a trick that recruiters themselves have learned to play. In one case explored here (see Chapter 10), recruiters portrayed enlistment as a means of resolving the broader concerns articulated by the feminist, civil rights and anti-war movements in the US in the 1970s. Elsewhere, enlistment in times of war and peace is routinely depicted as a means of redressing injustice, loneliness or endemic poverty.

A second observation concerns representations of war and conflict in recruitment promotion. Given the work that soldiers, sailors and pilots actually do, one might expect to see depictions of battle taking centre stage in the material explored in this book. In most case studies, however, scenes of combat and fighting are conspicuous by their absence, and in those that do feature such representations, the portrayal of conflict has taken on a game-like appearance that sanitises service. One could, I suppose, contend that the horrors of war are too explicit to make an appearance in recruitment campaigns. Yet the absence of death, injury and other occupational hazards in recruitment promotion clearly does new recruits a disservice, since they give them an entirely unrealistic portrayal military life. The same might be said for discipline. One of the biggest bugbears of enlisted personnel, it rarely if ever features in official promotion. The dearth of realism in such promotion raises important ethical questions that need to be addressed, not least because recruiters aggressively and proactively target young people who lack a real understanding of what military life actually entails.

Measuring the impact of campaigns: the factors and effects of enlistment

Did civilians line up outside recruiting depots in response to these campaigns? Governments have historically sought to answer this question by comparing enrolment rates before, during and after mobilisation efforts. This approach is appealing because it seems to give an accurate measure of the impact recruiters had on their target audiences and because such a measurement requires only basic arithmetic to make. It is also an approach used widely in the corporate world, where fluctuations in sales are commonly used as a yardstick for judging the efficacy of a company's advertising or public relations.

While there is an inherent simplicity to it, however, there is also a fundamental problem: other variables can and invariably do influence a person's behaviour. Whether one buys shoes, perfume or a holiday abroad or decides to sign up to serve in an armed or unarmed force, one's decision making is not governed by a single factor but many. Some of these factors are *internal*, which is to say they relate to a person's values, attitudes and beliefs, while others are *external*, incorporating such things as socio-economic status, disposable income, and place of residence.[16] An entire subfield of marketing is devoted to exploring how such factors shape consumer behaviour, with research indicating that customers weigh

214 *Brendan Maartens*

up the pros and cons of purchases by considering external variables like price, value for money and past experiences (if any) of the brand or seller in relation to their own personal, internal perceptions. Research has also shown that consumers devote little thought to 'frequently purchased, low-cost items' but 'extensive' time and intellectual effort to 'unfamiliar, expensive or infrequent purchases'.[17]

For most people, military service will remain an unknown quantity and may therefore be treated with the same degree of caution that an expensive or infrequent purchase is. Yet the decision to sign up carries more weight, in terms of the impact it has on a person's life, than almost any purchase a consumer can make. When enrolling, volunteers are usually given a short grace period during which they are allowed to withdraw from the military. However, once that period has lapsed, they are compelled to serve, and if they refuse to do so, they run the risk of a military tribunal – a court martial. New recruits, particularly those who sit on the bottom rungs of military hierarchies, are also given little choice as to *where* they serve and can be deployed from one part of a country to another or from one part of the world to another on a moment's notice. When compared to conventional civilian employment, these impositions make service unappealing to many and might explain why most armed forces struggle to attract volunteers.

On this basis, we might therefore say that comparisons between purchase decisions and enlistment are misleading. However, we actually know relatively little about recruits' motivations for enlisting and certainly a great deal less than we know about consumer purchase intentions. Of the research that has been published, most has concerned the United States in the all-volunteer era,[18] and though some general observations can be drawn from this body of scholarship, these observations may not, needless to say, be universally applicable.

Dominique Hanssens and Henry Levient authored one of the first papers, an econometric analysis of recruitment to the US Navy that compared the influence of 'environmental and marketing variables' on lead generation and enrolment rates in 1983. Environmental variables included 'economic factors such as unemployment rate and civilian income, sociodemographic variables such as urbanisation . . . and local youth attitudes toward the Navy'. Marketing variables amounted to 'national advertising expenditures in seven media, local advertising expenditures, [and] recruiter strength'.[19] The authors found that while both environmental and marketing variables had 'significant impact on variations in recruiting performance over time and across recruiting districts', environmental variables had 'more drastic' effects, with local and national unemployment rates the most important of all factors.

> [T]he national average advertising/sales ratio (total media advertising divided by total contracts) was \$41 in 1976, \$76 in 1977 and \$96 in 1978. During that period, unemployment declined from 7.2% to 6.2% to 5.7% and the total numbers of [service] contracts written were about 104,000, 83,000 and 68,000. These figures illustrate that increased marketing spending does not fully compensate for a more difficult recruiting environment . . . [characterised by] a declining unemployment rate.[20]

Narratives of service, sacrifice and security 215

Tom Reichert, Joo Young Kim and Ignatius Fosu also wrote on US Naval recruitment in 2007, arguing that exposure to television 'commercials results in more favourable behavioural beliefs' towards service but that such favourability did not necessarily translate to increased *interest* in service or indeed an increased *likelihood* of individuals serving. Where recruitment promotion did curry favour, the authors claim, was in the values and beliefs of 'important others', especially parents, who held sway in a prospective recruit's life. Such people have a 'stronger influence on military recruitment than advertising – unless that advertising is directed toward the parents and others whose opinions are valued by the recruited', in which case it can, the authors argue, stimulate recruitment but only indirectly.[21]

Florian Drevs and Markus Müller unearthed similar findings, though their 2015 study concerned Germany, not the United States, and was described as an investigation of all 'safety-critical' organisations, including police and fire services, although the authors appear to have only surveyed recruitment for the German armed forces. Suggesting that 'social circles, especially parents, are among the strongest influences on youth career decisions', they claim that effective promotion must 'take into account the role of close friends and family in individuals' enlistment decisions', and that 'ads that tap into patriotic motives [for serving] through highlighting the societal contribution of enlisting positively affect the support intentions of close friends and family', which can in turn translate into increased enrolment.[22]

Each of these studies focuses on the recent past, but historians of the early and mid-twentieth century have also made insightful observations. In his analysis of recruitment to the New Armies raised in Britain on the outbreak of the First World War, Peter Simkins uses eye-witness testimony to contest the argument, beloved of inter-war and post-war critics, that millions of volunteers 'came forward in the spirit of romantic idealism'. Though this was certainly an impetus for some, the 'prospect of adventure and the opportunity to escape from poverty, dreary surroundings or a tedious job [also] played their part in drawing men to recruiting offices'. The factors that 'impelled so many to enlist' were, indeed, as 'diverse as the recruits themselves', with 'only a small number [having] a single overriding motive for enlistment [and] most recruits being driven to join by a combination of external pressures and personal desires and loyalties'.[23] In her study of the post-war Auxiliary Territorial Service, a branch of the same Army staffed by women, Lucy Noakes has drawn attention to a similar range of motivations but has also found that many volunteers served because of ambitions to build careers, a prospect that may have been denied to them elsewhere in civilian life.[24]

Whether it is an ambition for a successful career, the influence of one's family or friends, the prospect of travel or adventure, the need for food and board or a deep-seated conviction in the value of public service, recruits join up for a variety of reasons, and any assessment of mobilisation campaigns needs to take account of them. Recruits are also more likely to join up when social and economic conditions favour service. Focusing on just one variable, whether that is a poster campaign, a programme of public events or a social media drive, may be convenient but can run the risk of 'inappropriate media centrism and an artificial

216 *Brendan Maartens*

de-contextualization of media use and consumption'[25] which relies on a very simplistic and reductive understanding of persuasive communications.

While single variables rarely drive the kind of change implied in studies of media effects, this does not mean, nevertheless, that campaigns have no effects to speak of. Recruiters, to paraphrase the political scientist Bernard Cohen, may not be capable of telling people what to think, but they are capable of influencing what they think *about*.[26] Bombarding the public with appeals in print, broadcast, film and digital media, recruiters ensure that military values and institutions are never far from view and always part of the cultural and political zeitgeist. They do so in different ways. When dealing with the press, recruiters help to tell the 'story' of service by acting as 'primary definers': spokespersons whose status and access to 'more specialised information on particular topics than the majority of the population' afford them a privileged role in the newsgathering process.[27] When producing advertising or propaganda, recruiters construct narratives of service that can entertain or captivate audiences and that may sustain the cultures of machismo that have long characterised military organisations. Armed forces, as Alessia Zaretti reminds us, like to '"build" men'[28] and use promotion to portray service as a means of proving one's manliness. Women, for their part, are usually treated to more ambiguous portrayals, which, as Melissa Brown has noted in her study, reinforce traditional 'gender divisions . . . even as [they] help to broaden definitions of femininity'.[29]

Central to popular understandings of service, these tropes may not convince people to serve, but that does not mean they hold no sway over people's *perceptions* of service. Drawing from cultural historians Graham Dawson and Michael Paris, we might suggest that these tropes help to sustain a 'pleasure culture of war' which involves a 'reconstruction of conflict as entertainment' and helps to 'resolve moral uncertainties about the use of violence'.[30]

Looking ahead: future avenues of scholarly research

This book represents the first international study of military recruitment promotion and is best read as an initial foray into an emerging field rather than a comprehensive dissection of that field. It has considered recruitment work around the globe from the First World War until the present day and has featured more than twenty countries in eleven case studies. This is a respectable haul, but many parts of the world receive no direct coverage here, with some receiving no mention at all. How did recruiters socialise conscripts into military service in Apartheid South Africa? How does the Israeli Defence Force use ideas of Jewishness to promote voluntary enlistment? Were there similarities in recruiting practices and approaches in Nazi Germany and imperial Japan? Did the Argentinian dictator Jorge Videla and his Philippine counterpart Ferdinand Marcos adopt contrasting strategies for mobilising men in the 1970s? These are just some of the questions that could be asked in future studies, and they are questions that are worth asking. The world, as noted in what follows, does not appear to be getting any safer, and studies of military recruitment can help scholars understand how governments mobilise populations and how populations in turn respond to such mobilisation efforts.

Narratives of service, sacrifice and security 217

However, they are not the only questions that can be asked. We have already seen how some recruiting appeals emphasised material rewards while others pandered to abstract ideals like duty, sacrifice and honour. Making distinctions between such appeals is useful, but large-scale content analyses are required to test their validity. Allowing scholars to quantitatively map patterns in large samples of media texts, content analyses have been applied to studies of war propaganda since the 1930s.[31] Yet I could only find two studies that assess military recruitment in this way: an unpublished doctoral dissertation completed in 2013 and a journal article published in 2017.[32] Both explore recruitment promotion in the United States, a country that spends far more on recruitment promotion (and on the military per se) than any other. However, other countries could also be explored, and when multiple national case studies have been completed, more substantive conclusions could be drawn about the nature of military recruitment. If a correlation between 'institutional' appeals and conflict is proven, scholars might, for example, be better able to predict when nations are gearing up for war.

Media texts have been central to many of the case studies explored in this book, and much can be made of them. Yet it is equally important to study the individuals who produced them. Where possible, contributors to this volume have cited recruiters' testimony, but cultures of secrecy and confidentiality within many military organisations and a dearth of archival evidence have not always permitted this. It is important to hear from recruiters not only because they preside over recruitment campaigns but also because they frequently *speak* to prospective recruits. They do so at public events of the kind explored in several chapters in this book but also at recruiting depots, which typically provide the first point of contact between a prospective recruit and the military and which are staffed with individuals specially trained to exhort those who visit these places. Ethnographic studies that shed light on the work that goes on in these depots and the rhetorical strategies that recruiters deploy within them would add colour to the field, and scholars could also make great mileage out of interviews, focus groups and surveys to explore what recruiters actually believed they achieved while recruiting.

Similar methods could, of course, be applied to study the individuals recruiters target with their appeals. Recruits risk their lives to serve in armed forces and are often (despite claims to the contrary) paid very little for the privilege. Yet their stories are rarely heard in studies of communications, which devote more space to representations of war than to the experiences of those who actually fight in them. Why do some people enrol while others do not? Are the experiences of those who serve consistent with the representation of service conveyed in recruitment promotion? What, for the want of a better word, are the 'real' values of service?

Some significant strides have been made in recent years to address these questions and others. In one study of female service personnel in the US, the authors suggest two main inducements draw women to service: the 'opportunity' enlistment provides for the career-minded and the 'calling [women] feel to serve their country'.[33] In another paper, this time concerning the life experiences of male soldiers in the UK, the authors draw attention to formative experiences in veterans' lives, and in particular to violent upbringings, that help to condition them for conflict in uniform and in civilian life.[34] In a third, an exploration of the processes

218   *Brendan Maartens*

of socialisation that accompany conscripted service in Israel, the authors suggest that despite the prevailing belief that conscription serves as a great social leveller, 'militarised socialisation is still a major mechanism that maintains a hierarchical social order' in contemporary Israeli society. The very 'image of the combat soldier as the "good citizen"', the authors claim, 'helps to reproduce and legitimise . . . [Israel's] hierarchical class structure'.[35]

Positioning recruits' voices and experiences at the heart of scholarly discussions, such interventions represent a useful counterpoise to the exaggerated and unrealistic portrayals of service found in recruitment promotion. Yet they are just one of many potential future avenues of research that scholars could and perhaps should consider in the years to come.

Looking ahead: military recruitment in an unstable world

'The future', Nicholas Rescher contends, is an 'object both of curiosity and of intense practical concern'. Predictions are our only 'access to it', but 'even the most rigorous of observers' can abandon 'common sense' when mustering the courage to make them.[36] This book makes no grand promises about what will transpire in the months and years to come. What it has tried to do is make sense of what *has* happened and what *is* happening, and to use these things to draw some more substantive conclusions about the nature of military service and the values and ideals that have come to be associated with it. This has not, needless to say, been light work.

It is not easy to explore the same topic across time and space, and to do so from different disciplinary perspectives and approaches. Contributors to this volume have been drawn from a wide range of scholarly backgrounds, with some social or military historians, others media or cultural studies academics and others disciplinary nomads who travel from one field to another without ever settling on a single place to call home. Each of us has brought our own interpretation to bear, and though there have been similarities in the conclusions we have drawn, there have also been differences. These differences are important. Underscoring the complexity of military recruitment promotion, they check the temptation to make sweeping generalisations and bold statements. Revealing how diverse vantages provoke different readings of the same phenomenon, they can foster inter-, multi- and trans-disciplinary exchanges.

Encouraging such exchanges represented a primary objective of this book when it was first pitched to Routledge in the summer of 2018. The world has not gotten any safer since then. If anything, it has become more unstable, more unpredictable and more unforgiving. Armed conflicts of one sort or another rage on all continents bar Antarctica. The war in eastern Ukraine has taken the lives of more than 13,000 civilians and soldiers. The civil war in Yemen, 3000 kilometres to the south, has consumed about eight times that amount, with the Mexican Drug War (a war in both name and reality) taking more lives than the first two conflicts combined.[37] Entire regions have become inherently volatile, with the Middle East the most combustible of all, and António Guterres, the United Nation's Secretary-General, has described the flow of weapons into this region and other areas marred by armed conflict as a 'wind of madness that is sweeping the globe'.[38] This wind, unfortunately, shows no sign of abating and brings more than just conflict with it.

Narratives of service, sacrifice and security   219

Refugees from Afghanistan, Sudan and Syria continue to cross the Mediterranean in search of a better life in Europe. They are among the 70.8 million people who have been forcibly displaced by war, violence or famine in the past decade and whose number keeps rising with each passing year, thanks in part to outbreaks of violence and persecution in Myanmar, Somalia and other places.[39] There are more refugees now, in fact, than there have been at any point since the Second World War. If another global conflict erupted tomorrow, the human cost would be so great as to be almost incalculable; it is already, in any case, indefensible.

If this represents a genuine cause for concern, the climate crisis is a threat more dangerous than any war that does not involve the complete annihilation of the human race. Scientists have been warning about the dangers of rising global temperatures since the 1970s.[40] These warnings have been heeded by many but are not being treated with the seriousness they clearly deserve in the upper echelons of business and government. Climactic instability increases food insecurity, and food insecurity often precipitates conflict.[41] Rising sea levels imperil all humans who live near coastlines, and longer and more powerful storms, together with more droughts and heat waves, endanger us all to varying degrees. The systematic exploitation of the world's natural resources and the wholesale extinction of plant, animal and insect life that has accompanied it only makes matters worse. Indeed, as resources decline, as food becomes scarcer, and as more parts of the world become uninhabitable, wars become more likely.

The only way to solve these problems is to work towards long-term, collaborative solutions. Yet the political and economic systems that shape our world are ill suited for this very purpose. Forty years of neoliberal orthodoxy have eroded the ideals of collective action, and there is too much money in war and fossil fuels to convince the powerful (elected and otherwise) to forgo the pursuit of both. The resurgence of neo-fascism and ethno-nationalism in many parts of the world and the return of the presidential Strong Man in some makes a peaceful resolution even more elusive and increases the likelihood of conflict, both between and within nations, further. Jair Bolsonaro, Viktor Orbán and Donald Trump are really the last leaders humanity needs in this hour, and yet they enjoy enough domestic support to remain in power.

None of this should be taken lightly, and it has been mentioned for a reason. Though no one can predict the future with complete accuracy, educated guesses about what might happen can be made. Those who forget the mistakes of the past, the old adage goes, are destined to repeat them, and it is the responsibility of all those who have a voice in higher education to ensure that this does not happen. Clarion calls of this kind might seem out of place in an edited collection, but they have to be made to be heard. With a bit of luck, they will be.

Notes

1 Harold Lasswell, *Propaganda Technique in the World War* (New York: Peter Smith, 1938), 185.
2 Ibid.
3 Ibid., 47, 85 and 114.

220 *Brendan Maartens*

4 Anderson draws a distinction between official and popular nationalist movements, though space does not exist to examine this here. Benedict Anderson, *Imagined Communities: Reflections on the Origins and Spread of Nationalism*, revised ed. (London: Verso, 1991).

5 Siniša Malešević, *Identity as Ideology: Understanding Ethnicity and Nationalism* (Basingstoke: Palgrave, 2006), 54.

6 Keith Surridge, 'More than a Great Poster: Lord Kitchener and the Image of the Military Hero', *Historical Research* 74, no. 185 (2001): 298–313.

7 Flags, it is worth noting, predate the formation of nation-states by millennia, being 'mentioned extensively in the Old Testament and . . . attached to the carved wooden standards of the Egyptians some 3000 years before Christ'. Terence Wise, *Military Flags of the World in Colour* (Poole: Blandford, 1977), 16.

8 Randall Stevenson, *Literature and the Great War, 1914–18* (Oxford: Oxford University Press, 2013), 48.

9 Anne Samson, 'South Africa and the First World War', in T. Paddock (ed.), *World War I and Propaganda* (Leiden: Brill, 2014), 124.

10 Alessandro Rovati, 'War Is America's Altar: Violence in the American Imagination', in F. Gursozlu (ed.), *Peace, Culture, and Violence* (Leiden: Brill Rodopi, 2018), 205.

11 See, for example, Beth Bailey, *America's Army: Making the All-Volunteer Force* (Cambridge, MA: Harvard University Press, 2009) and my own study of Britain around the same time, Brendan Maartens, 'Modernizing the Military: Promoting a New "Brand Image" of the British Army, Navy, and Air Force in the Post-National Service Era, 1957–63', *War in History* 26, no. 3 (2019): 406–29.

12 Charles Moskos, 'From Institution to Occupation: Trends in Military Organization', *Armed Forces & Society* 4, no. 1 (1977): 41 and 42.

13 Beth Bailey, *America's Army: Making the All-Volunteer Force* (Cambridge, MA: Harvard University Press, 2008); Phillipe Manigart, 'Risks and Recruitment in Postmodern Armed Forces: The Case of Belgium', *Armed Forces & Society* 31, no. 4 (2005): 559–81; Yagil Levy, 'The Essence of the "Market Army"', *Public Administration Review* 70, no. 3 (2010): 378–89.

14 Brendan Maartens, 'Your Country Needs You? Advertising, Public Relations and the Promotion of Military Service in Peacetime Britain', *Media, War & Conflict* (February 2019), doi: 10.1177/1750635219828774.

15 Douglas Goodman, *Consumer Culture: A Reference Handbook* (Santa Barbra: ABC Clio, 2004), 49.

16 David Kurtz, Herb MacKenzie and Kim Snow, *Contemporary Marketing*, 2nd ed. (Scarborough, Canada: Nelson Education, 2009), 130.

17 Charles Lamb, Joe Hair and Carl McDaniel, *Essentials of Marketing* (Mason: South-Western Cengage, 2009), 174.

18 See, for example, P. L. Brockett, W. W. Cooper, S. C. Kumbhakar, M. J. Kwinn, Jr. and D. McCarthy, 'Alternative Statistical Regression Studies of the Effects of Joint and Service Specific Advertising on Military Recruitment', *The Journal of the Operational Research Society* 55, no. 10 (2004): 1039–48; James Dertouzos and Steven Garber, 'Effectiveness of Advertising in Different Media: The Case of U.S. Army Recruiting', *Journal of Advertising* 35, no. 2 (2006): 111–22.

19 Dominique Hanssens and Henry Levient, 'An Econometric Study of Recruitment Marketing in the U.S. Navy', *Management Science* 29, no. 10 (1983): 1167.

20 Ibid., 1181.

21 Tom Reichert, JooYoung Kim and Ignatius Fosu, 'Assessing the Efficacy of Armed-Forces Recruitment Advertising: A Reasoned-Action Approach', *Journal of Promotion Management* 13, no. 3–4 (2007): 409.

22 Florian Drevs and Markus Müller, 'Public Service Motivation as Driver of Social Support to Apply for Safety-Critical Organizations? An Empirical Study in the Context of German Military Service', *Journal of Nonprofit & Public Sector Marketing* 27 (2015): 135–54.

Narratives of service, sacrifice and security 221

23 Peter Simkins, *Kitchener's Army: The Raising of the New Armies, 1914–1916* (Barnsley: Pen & Sword, 2007), 185.
24 Lucy Noakes, "'Gentle in Manner, Resolute in Deed": Women in the Postwar Army', *Women in the British Army: War and the Gentle Sex, 1907–1948* (London: Routledge, 2006), 146.
25 David Deacon and Emily Keightley, 'Quantitative Audience Research: Embracing the Poor Relation', in V. Nightingale (ed.), *The Handbook of Media Audiences* (Oxford: Wiley-Blackwell, 2011), 314.
26 Cohen was referring to the capacity of the press to influence readers, though the same principle can be applied to recruitment. Bernard Cohen, *The Press and Foreign Policy* (Princeton, NJ: Princeton University Press, 1963), 13.
27 Stuart Hall, Chas Critcher, Tony Jefferson, John Clarke and Brian Roberts, *Policing the Crisis: Mugging, the State and Law and Order* (London: Macmillan, 1978), 58. For a wide-ranging review of the relationship between journalists and their sources, see Bob Franklin and Matt Carlson (eds.), *Journalists, Sources and Credibility: New Perspectives* (New York: Routledge, 2011).
28 Alessia Zaretti, 'Lesbian Gay Bi-Sexual Transgender (LGBT) Personnel: A Military Challenge', in G. Caforio (ed.), *The Handbook of the Sociology of the Military*, 2nd ed. (Cham: Springer, 2018), 396.
29 Melissa Brown, "'A Woman in the Army Is Still a Woman": Representations of Women in US Military Recruiting Advertisements for the All-Volunteer Force', *Journal of Women, Politics & Policy* 33, no. 2 (2012): 151.
30 Graham Dawson, 'Playing at Soldiers: Boy-Hood Fantasies and the Pleasure Culture of War', in *Soldier Heroes: British Adventure, Empire and the Imagining of Masculinity* (Oxon: Routledge, 1994), 233–58; Michael Paris, *Warrior Nation: Images of War in British Popular Culture, 1850–2000* (London: Reaktion, 2000), 44.
31 The method was also used at this time to explore how African Americans were 'presented in the Philadelphia press . . . how US textbooks described wars in which the United States had taken part . . . and how nationalism was expressed in children's books published in the United States, Great Britain, and other European countries'. Klaus Krippendorff, 'History', *Content Analysis: An Introduction to Its Methodology* (Thousand Oaks: Sage, 2004), 7.
32 Wen Cheng Fu, *Persuasive Strategies of the United States Military Television Recruitment Advertising during the All-Volunteer Force Era*, unpublished doctoral dissertation (University of Illinois, 2013): http://hdl.handle.net/2142/44396 (accessed 27 February 2020); Sejin Park, Jinhee Lee and Jin Seong Park, 'Evaluating the Message Strategy of U.S. Army Advertising: With Focus on Information Needs and Motivational Cues', *Journal of Promotion Management* 23, no. 2 (2017): 303–19.
33 Mariann Mankowski, Leslie Tower, Cynthia Brandt and Kristin Mattocks, 'Why Women Join the Military: Enlistment Decisions and Postdeployment Experiences of Service Members and Veterans', *Social Work* 60, no. 4 (2013): 322.
34 Jeffery Banks and Katherine Albertson, 'Veterans and Violence: An Exploration of Pre-Enlistment, Military and Post-Service Life', *European Journal of Criminology* 15, no. 6 (2018): 730–47.
35 Gal Levy and Orna Sasson-Levy, 'Militarized Socialization, Military Service, and Class Reproduction: The Experiences of Israeli Soldiers', *Sociological Perspectives* 51, no. 2 (2008): 368.
36 Nicholas Rescher, *Predicting the Future: An Introduction to the Theory of Forecasting* (Albany: State University of New York Press, 1998), 11.
37 These figures have been sourced from Sweden's Uppsala University, which has been compiling global conflict mortality rates since the mid-1980s. These rates are published online at 'Uppsala Conflict Data Programme', *Uppsala Universitet*: https://ucdp.uu.se/ (accessed 11 March 2020).
38 Orlando Crowcroft, 'U.N. Chief Warns of "Wind of Madness" over Global Conflict, Climate Change', *Euronews*: www.euronews.com/2020/02/04/u-n-chief-warns-of-wind-of-madness-over-global-conflict-climate-change (accessed 23 February 2020).

39 UN Global Trends: Forced Displacement in 2018, *United Nations High Commissioner for Refugees*: www.unhcr.org/uk/statistics/unhcrstats/5d08d7ee7/unhcr-global-trends-2018.html (accessed 23 February 2020).
40 Bert Bolin, *A History of the Science and Politics of Climate Change: The Role of the Intergovernmental Panel on Climate Change* (Cambridge: Cambridge University Press, 2007), 33.
41 Marc Cohen and Andersen Per Pinstrup, 'Food Security and Conflict', *Social Research* 66, no. 1 (1999): 375–416.

Index

Note: Page numbers in *italic* indicate a figure on the corresponding page. Page numbers followed by 'n' indicate a note.

26th Air Squadron 41
1912 Defence Force Act 41
1915 Native Followers Recruitment
    Ordnance 36
8 Children Act 128
1967 Law on Universal Military Service
    133, 134

Aberdeen Press and Journal 124
ability to withstand hardship 186
Aderente, Vincent 83, *84*
administrators 34–5, 37, 38, 41, 44;
    see also colonial administrators
advertising/advertisements 18–21,
    40–2, 146; commercial 7, 9, 79; craft
    20; display 20; film 20; Internet 20;
    military recruitment campaigning
    6–9; newspaper 20–1, 39; novel 20,
    26; online 163; profusion of 19; radio
    20; responsibility 151; technology 20;
    television 21; tripartite 19; types of 18;
    uses 17–28; utopia and 151
Advertising Age's Agency of the year 149
Advertising Division 79
Aeschylus 168
Afghanada 168
Afghanistan 139, 166, 168–9
Africa 11–12, 27, 33–6, 39, 42, 164
African Americans 13, 157
African black 33, 37
African People's Organisation 41
agencies 18–21
agents 20
Agricultural Implement Makers 66
Airman Challenge 24
Air Raid Precautions (ARP) 96, 99, 107

Air Raid Precautions Act 98, 99, 104
Air Raid Precautions Gazette (Doncaster)
    109
'Air Raid Wardens Wanted' poster *102*
al-Adnani, Abu Muhammad 196
al-Baghdadi, Abu Omar 194
Albanian state 50
Alexandria 126
Allied Army ('Armée d'Orient') 50
Allied blockade 56
Allied forces 51, 54, 56
Allied military 53
Allied victory 57
Allied war 22
all-volunteer Army, United States 6
al-Masri, Abu Ayyub 194
al-Qaeda 166, 194, 195
al-Shaybani, Muhammad ibn al-Hasan 4
al-Shuaybi, Hamud bin Uqla 194
Altheide, David L. 78
al-Zarqawi, Abu Musab 194
Amazon Warrior 81
American Broadcasting Company 150
American Civil War 10
American Committee on Public
    Information 12
American imperialism 118
American Office of War Information 22
America's Army 183
'Amy's an Expert in Psychological
    Warfare' *153*
Ancient Egypt 10
Ancient Greece 17
Ancient Greek 168
Anderson, John 38, 98, 99–100, 104–5,
    108

224 *Index*

Anglosphere 6
Anschluss 99
anti-militarism 140
anti-nuclear protests 139
anti-Soviet movements 135
appeals 7, 13
Aquinas, Thomas 4
Arabs 35
Aragon 38
archetypes 19
Aristotle 3, 17, 28n2, 78, 93
Armee de Terre YouTube channel 24
Armenia 141
Army 118–23
Army bands 40–2
Army Council 39
Army Life; or How Soldiers Are Made 21
Army's Signal Corps' Pictorial Service 22
Arnoldi's Scouts 42
ARP News 104, 107, 109–10
Arsenal Football Club 106
art of war 3
Art of War (Bingfa), The 184
Asante 37
Ashanti 37
Asia 12, 34
Asia Minor 51
Asia-Pacific 164
Assistant Deputy Minister Public Affairs
    (ADMPA) 167
Athens 50, 55
atrocity stories 40–2
AT&T 149
Attlee, Clement 117
Australia 27; coercion 65–8; conscription
    65–8; duty and patriotism to 64;
    publicity in First World War 62–5;
    recruiting in 61–72
Australian community 63
Australian Imperial Force (AIF) 61, 63,
    64–5, 69
Australian Worker 67
Austro-Hungarian empires 133
Auxiliary Fire Service 104

Baden-Powell, Robert 125
Bailey, Beth 6, 42, 145, 148–9
Balkan Peninsula 53
Balkans 49, 53
Balkan Wars 6, 50, 52, 55
Ballina Recruiting Association 66
Baltic republics 138
Bamford, Frederick 66
bands *see* Army bands

Banta, Martha 82
bara 200
Barnum, P. T. 26
Battle Declaration (*Zhandou xuanyan*) 184
Battle of Britain 108
Baudrillard, Jean 150
Baueinheiten 133
Beaumont, Joan 62, 64
Beijing 181, 185
Beijing Municipal Recruitment Office 184,
    186
Bemba villages 40
Bendigo Trades Council, Victoria 66
Benson, Krystina 77
Berger, John 150
Berlin Wall 23
Bernard of Clairvaux 10
biennium 1915–1917 50–1
Big Picture, The 22–3
Birmingham 104, 108
Bishop Weston of Zanzibar 36
Bismarck, Otto von 136
Bivins, Tom 12, 19
black Africans 11
Blaulicht 23
Blaxland Shire 61
Blitz 101, 108–9
Boorstin, Daniel 26
Bosnian War 166
Boy Scouts 125
Boy Seaman 118
Brechin Advertiser, The 108
Brigade HQ 39
Brigade of Guards 103
Brisbane Industrial Council 66
Britain 11–13, 26, 34, 40, 41, 64
British Africa 8, 33
British Air Force 72
British armed forces 21
British Army 6, 12, 21, 63
British Army at Your Service 126
British Army Council 64
British Broadcasting Corporation's (BBC)
    99, 103, 121
British civil defence 20, 96–111; *see also*
    civil defence
British Crown 163
British East Africa (BEA) 35, 38
British Empire 11, 33–44, 165
British forces 39
British Government 42, 64
British impressment 38
British Navy 12
British regiments 41

Index 225

British South African Police 34
British territories 38
British War Office and Admiralty 42
Britons 35, 110, 126
broadcast media 48
Broken Years, The (Gammage) 63
Brown, Melissa 145
Brunello, Anthony R. 77, 78
Bulgaria 50–1, 53, 133, 136
Bulgarian advance 55, 57
Bulgarian mobilisation 53
Burger King 149
Burgess 61

cable television 150
Calgary Stampede 169
caliph 193
caliphate 193
Call to Arms 62–9
Cameroon 34, 37–8, 41, 42; *see also*
    German Cameroon
Cameroon campaign 38
campaigning/campaign: of 1946–50 120–1,
    128; in boroughs and cities 104–7;
    National Service 99–100, 104, 110; in
    towns 104–7
Canada 13, 163, 166
Canadian Armed Forces (CAF) 21, 164–9,
    170–4; Facebook page 171; LinkedIn
    172; personnel retiring 169; policies
    and practices 171–4; public affairs
    office 172; second major recruitment
    advertising campaign 170; social media
    platforms 171–4; supported recruitment
    advertising campaigns 169; in twenty-
    first century 165–6; on Twitter 171;
    YouTube site 172
Canadian Army 163
Canadian case study 13
Canadian communications studies 164
Canadian Defence & Foreign Affairs
    Institute 165
Canadian foreign policy 163, 165–6
Canadian Global Affairs Institute 165
Canadian military public affairs 164;
    Canada's foreign policy 165–6;
    Department of National Defence (DND)
    165–6; militarising media events 167–71;
    overview 163–4; and recruitment 163–75;
    recruitment advertising 167–71
Canadian National Exhibition 169
Capell, A. E. 34
Cape Town 36
case studies 11–13

Casey, Ralph D. 76
Catholic Church 17, 140
Catts, James H. 67, 71
Caucasus 138
Central Africa 36, 38
Central America 8, 12, 164
Central Asian and Baltic republics 134
central Bureau of the Postmaster's Office
    (Dead Letter Office) 67
central committee 69
Central Office of Information (COI)
    119–20
Central Power 50–1, 54, 57
challenges of recruiting 39–40
Chamberlain, Neville 100
Chelsea 106
Cheltenham 105
Chiang Kai-shek 179
China 8, 10, 13, 22, 178–87
China's One Child Policy 182
Chinese Civil War 179
Chinese Communist Party (CCP) 180,
    183–4
Chinese conscription video 183–5
Chinese Military Network (*Zhongguo jun
    wang*) 183, 186
Chrétien, Jean 166
Christians 4, 10
Christy, Howard Chandler 80, 86, *87, 90*
Christy Girl 81, 86
'Citizen and Air Raids, The' 100
Citizen to Soldier (Dawes and Robson) 62
civil administration 39
civil conflict 51
civil defence 96; administrative framework
    97–9; analysis of 97; campaigning
    104–7; challenge 99; Lewisham 100;
    local events 106; in London 97; national
    network of 119; recruitment campaign
    101; *see also* British civil defence
Civil Defence Day 103
civilianisation 27
civilian-to-government communication
    172
civilisations of antiquity 9
Civil Rights 13
Civil War 25, 83
Civvy Street 123
Clarke, Frank 70
Coca-Cola 22
Cockcroft, John 126
Coercion 37, 65–8
COI Run 119
Cold War 12, 110, 118–19, 131, 165

226 *Index*

Colombo 7
Colonel Sandford 65
colonial administrators 37
Colonial and War Offices 38
Colonial Office 35
Colosseum 9
Coloured community 34
Columbia 82–4, 86, 92
Columbia Broadcast System (CBS) 150
Columbia Calls 83, *84*
Columbia/Liberty *84*, 88
commercial advertising 7, 9, 79
Committee for Finland 6
Committee of Imperial Defence Sub-
    Committee 97
Committee on Public Information (CPI)
    76, 79–80, 83, 88
communications: civilian-to-government
    172; corporate 18; governmental 18;
    government-to civilian 172; mass media
    5; networked 13; online 24; persuasive
    5; promotional 19; revolution 7; twenty-
    first century 164
Communist Party 180
community: Australian 63; South African
    Coloured 41
compulsory labour 36
concomitant fluctuations 6
conflict 5, 9; civil 51; direct 12; future
    97; Greek neutrality 50; internecine
    9; military conscription in 36; painful
    civil 49
conscription 36–8, 65–8, 146
Constantine, King 50–1, 52, 53–4, 57;
    see also National Schism
Corax 17
corporate communication 18
County Hall 105
courage 186
Courty, Audrey 13, 24, 201
Coventry Evening Telegraph 125
CP Crewe 41
creative revolution 149
Creel, George 76, 80–1
Crusades 10
Crutchley, Ernest 100
Cuba 27
Cultural Revolution 179
cultural transformations 4
Cunningham, Stanley B. 78
Czechoslovakia 133, 136, 140–1

Dabiq 195–8, 202
Daily Mail, The 96, 111n1, 201

Daily Mirror 122
Dardanelles campaign 50
Dare to be Extraordinary 171
Darling Downs Gazette 67
Dawes, J. N. I. 63
Dā'ish 8
DeBeers 149
Decisive Battle 185
dedovshchina 141
Defence Administrative Orders 167
Defence Law 137
Defence Publicity Committee. 120
Defence Team News 171
Deng Xiaoping 179
Department of Defence (DOD) 69, 145–6,
    151
Department of Foreign Affairs and
    International Trade 165
Department of National Defence (DND)
    13, 165–6, 167, 174
Derby, Lord 64
determination 186
Deutscher Fernsehfunk 23
direct conflict 12
Directives 2008–0 Public Affairs Policy
    167
display advertisements 20
display advertising 19–20
diversity 28, 33, 42, 149–50, 155
Division of Pictorial Publicity (DPP) 80–1
DND's Public Affairs Learning Centre in
    Gatineau, Quebec 167
Duffy, Gavin 66, 70
Dumenil, Lynn 79

Eady, C. W. G. 100
East Africa 33–42
East Africa Mounted Rifles 42
East Bloc 141
Eastern Bloc 131, 135, 140, 141
Eastern Europe 8, 132, 134, 141
Eastern European 131
Eastern Europe's reluctant soldiers 131–42
Eastern Freemantle 68
Eastern Macedonia 51, 57
East German 141
East Germany 133, 135, 136–8
East Twenty-Third Street, New York
    City 83
economic necessity 4
Edgeworth-Johnstone, Ralph 121
Edinburgh 104
Egypt 3, 34
Ellul, Jacques 77

Index 227

Elmslie, George 68
Engels, Frederick 4
England 34, 39
English 37–8, 77
English language campaigns 148
English press 41
English troops 53
Entente 50, 51, 54
Entente alliance 53
Entente assistance 53
Entente forces 54
esprit de corps 9, 103, 212
Estonia 141
Estonian leadership 141
ethnicity 36–8
Eugenius III 10
Europe 9, 12, 34–8, 41, 49, 69, 86, 164
European recruitment 35
events 25–7
exhortations 8
experienced officer 41
experiences of enlistment 39–40

Facebook 13, 24, 163, 171
fada'il literature 10
fashioning 'news pegs' 124–6
Federación de Mujeres Cubanas
   (Federation of Cuban Women) 27
Federal Government 165
federalism 68–71
Federal Parliamentary Recruiting
   Committee (FPWC) 66–9
Fight ads 170
Fighting RAF 126
Fight or Buy Bonds (Christy) 86, *87*
film 20
Film Division 79
Finlandskommittén (Committee for
   Finland) 6
First Rhodesia Regiment 34
First World War 8, 17, 21, 27, 97, 133;
   America into 79; Britain 107; coherent
   examination of 49; debate on Great Idea
   52; film featuring Afghanistan War 168;
   in Great Britain 62; Greece in 48–59;
   hostilities 56; innovations 81; military
   recruitment 110; mobilisation during
   53–7; propaganda in 51; propaganda
   poster 154; publicity in Australia in
   62–5; Western European countries in 54;
   women in 75–93
Fischer, David Hackett 82
Fisher, Andrew 66
Fisher, Harrison 80

Flagg, James Montgomery 80, 83, *85*, 154
Ford 149
För Nordens Frihet 7
Fort Rupel 54
Fox, Jo 5
France 10, 39, 55
Fraser, Robert 120
Frederick the Great 136
Freetown 40
Freie Deutsche Jungend (FDJ) 138
French Army 24
French refugees 40
French Revolution 82
French territories 40
French troops 53
Freud, Sigmund 76
Friedman, Milton 146, 147
Fulham 103
full-service agencies 21
fundraising events 41
future conflict 97

Gambia Company 37, 39
Gammage, Bill 63
Gates, Thomas 147
Gates Commission 147–8, 151, 152
Gawler South Australia committee 68
Gee, David 127
gender diversity 154–5
General Post Office (GPO) 101
Georgia 141
German Army 50
German-Bulgarian advance 51
German-Bulgarian troops 54
German Cameroon 37; *see also* Cameroon
German Democratic Republic (DDR) 23,
   132–3, 136–40, 141
German military 63, 79
German South West Africa (GSWA)
   34–6, 41
Germany 25, 41, 50, 165
Gesellschaft für Sport und Technik (GST)
   138
Ghilani, Jessica 12, 21
Giant Interactive Group Inc. 183
Gibson, Charles Dana 80, 86, 92, *92*
Gibson Girl 80, 81
Glasgow 104
glasnost 139
Global Coalition Against Daesh 166
Global War on Terror 166
Glorious Mission (Guangrong shiming)
   183
Gold Coast 33, 40, 43

228 *Index*

Gold Coast Ashanti 35
Gold Coast Regiment 40
Gorbachev 140, 141–2
Goudreau, K. A. 151
governmental communications 18, 119
government-to-civilian communication 172
Grant, Matthew 110
Grayzel, Susan 81, 96
Great Britain 55, 62, 165
Great Idea 50, 52
Great Leap Forward 179
Great Patriotic War 135
great propaganda machine 75–6
Great War 6, 11, 16n53, 19, 49–50, 53, 54, 65, 163, 209–10
Greece 8, 11, 27, 49; approach to Great War 50; choice of neutrality 53; Dardanelles campaign 50; Entente camp 50; history of 49; mobilisation 53–7; participation 53; in Peace Conference in Paris 51; press history 51; propaganda in 51–2; public dialogue in 52; rival factions in 54; territorial gains 52; uncertain benefits for 50
Greek army 50–1, 53
Greek communities 55
Greek goddesses 82
Greek historiography 56
Greek-inhabited areas 50
Greek leadership 50
Greek neutrality 50
Greek press 48
Greek public life 52
Greek society 51–2, 56, 57
Greeks of Asia Minor 50
Greek state 55, 60n22
Greek territory 55
Greek–Turkish War 49, 51
Green, Leanne 62
Greenspan, Allen 146, 147
Grey Global 21
grievance 37
Grundlingh, Albert 33
Gulf of Aden 180

Halsted, Frances Adams 83, *84*
Hammett, Jessica 12, 21
Hanbury, Felicity 124
Han China 10
Hans Beimler Contests *(Hans-Beimler-Wettkämpfe)* 138
Harpenden and District Local History Society *106*

Harper, Stephen 166
Harper's Weekly 10
Hart, Mark 127
Hartlepool 108
Hellenic Constitution 53
Henan Province Recruitment Office 185
Herter, Albert *89*
Highet, Alexander 100
Highway of Heroes 168
hijra (migration) 193
Hiley, Nicholas 6–7
Hittites 9
Hizbut Tahrir 195
Hoare, Samuel 98–9, 104
Hodges, Geoffrey 33, 36
Hodsoll, John 107
Hollywood 22
Homo Lector (Poe) 7
Homo Somnians (Poe) 7
Homo Videns (Poe) 7
Hong Kong 126
Hope, Bob 22
Horton, Tim 168
Hughes, Billy 65
Hughes, William 65, 66
Hu Jintao 180
humanity 3, 7
Hungary 22, 133, 136, 141
Hutus 22

idealism 4
Imaging American Women (Banta) 81
Imperial Garrison forces 34
Imperial War Museum *102*
independence 186
India 21
Indian Army 21
Indian Congress 41
Indians 34
Information Division 25
information unit 119
Instagram 24
internecine conflict 9
Internet 20, 163
'In the name of mercy give' (Herter) *89*
In Which We Serve 126
Iran 24
Iran Army 24
Iran Military 24
Iran Military Facebook page 24
Iraq 8, 13, 192–3, 195
Ireland 21
Iron Curtain 23
Irving, Henry 12, 21

Islam 198–200; civilisational clash 193; glory days 193; interpretation of 193; Sunni 4; in West 193
Islamic political system 193
Islamic religious obligation 193
Islamic Republic 24
Islamic State of Iraq 8
Islamic State of Iraq and Syria (ISIS) 13, 24, 193, 210; brand of Islamism 199; caliphate 193; information warfare 195; origins of 193–4; propaganda 193; recruiting using *Dabiq* and *Rumiyah* 195–8; religio-political appeal 192; strategy of conflating religion 192; Western media reporting 200–2
Islamic State of Iraq and the Levant (ISIL) 166
Islamism 199–200
Islamist 193
isolationism 79
Israeli Defence Force's Spokesperson's Unit 27

Jamaat al-Tawhid wa-l-Jihad 194
James, Pearl 86
Janouch, František 140
Janowitz, Morris 148, 152
Japan's Self Defence Force 25
Jehovah's Witnesses 133
Jemaah Islamiyah 195
jihad 193, 195, 199
Johnson, J. M. 78
Join the Navy 126
Jones, A. D. 66
Jones, Ellen 139
Jowett, Garth 5, 77, 78, 93

Kadushin, Charles 25
Kant, Immanuel 4
Kasama 38
Kenny & Co. 21
Kensington High Street 106
Khamenei, Ayatollah Ali Hosseini 24
khaṭībs 9
khilafa 193
Kikamba 37
Kikuyu Missions 36
King's African Rifles (KAR) 35
Kiswahili 37
Knibbs, George Handley 66, 70–1
Koinadugu 38
Korea 118
Korean War 12, 151, 165
Kosovo War 166

Krebs, Ronald 148
Kuang, Xun 4
Kumasi 42
Kya Rosa 41

Labor Party, Australian 65
labour recruitment 37
Laden, Osama bin 194
Lady Liberty 86
Lamarre, Charles 170
Lameroo 71–2
languages: English 37, 77; Kiswahili 37
Larson, Cedric 76
Lasswell, Harold 77
Latin American 22
Latinos 13
Latvia 141
Launceston 70
Lawson, Jack 121, 124
'Lead the People Who've Joined the Army' *156*
Lears, Jackson 18
Leeds 104
Lemonidou, Elli 11, 27
Leo Burnett Solutions 7
Levant 8
Lewisham civil defence 100
Leyendecker, J. C. 88, *91*
Leyendecker, Joseph 80
Liberal Party 166
Liberty bonds 86
Libya 180, 196
Life magazine (Gibson) *92*
Liga Oborony Kraju (League of Defence of the Country) 135
Li Jianke 185
Lincoln, Abraham 4
LinkedIn 172
Lion Cubs in Paradise 7
Lithuania 141
Liverpool 109
London 21, 100, 104
London County Council (LCC) 105, 107
London Fire Brigade 106
London's Hyde Park 103
Lord Privy Seal 98
Lugard, F. 39
Luther, Martin 136

Maartens, Brendan 12, 97
Mabane, William 108
MacDonald-Cartier Freeway 168
Macedonia 53, 55
Macedonian Front 48, 51, 57

230 *Index*

Mackinnon, Donald 63, 69
Mademoiselle 152
Mahābhārata 3
Mahood, Samantha 198
Malta 126
Malthus, Thomas 4
Manchester 104
Mandelbaum, Michael 150
Mandis 38
Man Haron Monis 197
Manifold, Walter 66
Maoist ideology 181
Mao Zedong 179, 182, 185
Marchand, Roland 151
Marine Corps 148
Marmion, Harry 148
Martin, Paul 166
Marxist-Leninist ideology 137
Maryborough 64
Maryborough Chronicle 64
mass-circulation newspaper 7
mass media 37; communications 5; growth
    of 5; military recruitment campaigning
    6–9
Mass-Observation's Fulham Survey 108–9
mass political rituals 25
mass-spectator militarism 26
materialistic utopia 151
maturity 186
McIntyre, Ronald G. 69
Mead, Margaret 148
media 6, 19; broadcast 48; campaigns
    182–3; coverage 25; print 6, 20;
    traditional 13; *see also* specific media
Media Operative 194
Middle Ages 9
Middle East 49, 164
militarisation 7
militarising media events 167–71
military: engagements 7; iconography
    9–11; leadership 50; mobilisation 55;
    organisations 5, 18; pageantry 9–11;
    representation in civilian news media
    150
military recruitment 5, 119; issues and
    reputation 25–7; promotion 8; public
    relations (PR) of 25–7; in times of war
    and peace 11–13
military recruitment campaigning:
    advertising 6–9; global analysis 3–13;
    iconography 9–11; mass media 6–9;
    pageantry 9–11; public opinion 4–6;
    recruitment 4–6; studies of propaganda
    4–6; in times of war 11–13

Military Service Law 181
Minerva 82
Ministry of Defence (MOD) 119–20
Ministry of Home Security 98
Ministry of Information 97
Minnick, Mimi 149
Mirrlees, Tanner 13, 21
mobilisation: of 18 April 1917 54–5; of
    22 January 1918 56–7; of 23 September
    1915 53–4; announcement of 54;
    Bulgarian 53; efforts 8; during First
    World War 53–7; Greece 53–7; of Greek
    army 53; military 55; promotion 198–200;
    scale of 34; studies of 5
mobilising propaganda 48–59
Mock, James 76
Modern Regular Army 122
Montreal 21
Monuments and Maidens (Warner) 82
More, Thomas 150
Morgan, A. E. 101
Morrison, Herbert 96, 104
Morton's Salt 149
Moscow 141
Moskos, Charles 148, 152
Mount Fuji 25
Moyamba 40
Mujahideen Shura Council 194
mukaffirun 4
Munich Agreement 97
Munich Crisis 97–100
Murphy, Dennis M. 83
Muslim Australians 197
Muslim communities 192
Muslim enemies 193
Muslims 10, 37

Nabisco 149
Naftali, Orna 3
Nanjing Military Area Command 183
National ARP Committee 97
national aspirations 48–59
National Broadcasting Company 150
national campaign 99–104
National Committee of Patriotic Societies
    (NCPS) 82
Nationale Volksarmee (NVA) 136–8
National Health Service 117
nationalism, Polish 135
national radio 7
national rejuvenation 184–5
National Schism 50, 52, 54–7;
    see also Constantine, King;
    Venizelos, Eleutherios

Index 231

National Service (guide) *101*
National Service Act 99, 118
National Service campaign 99–100, 104, 110
National Service Committees 98, 105
National Service handbook 107
National Service publicity 101
National Service Week 104
native America 26
Navy 118–23, 125–6
'Navy Needs You, The' (Flagg) 83, *85*
Navy Reserves 124
Nazarenes 133
Near East 9
networked communication 13
New Horticultural Hall 126
News Division 79
New South Wales (NSW) 61, 64, 66–7
newspaper 20, 52
newspaper advertisements 39
newspaper advertising 20–21, 121–4
Newspapers Proprietors Association 120
newsreels 21–2
New York City 20, 80
New York Times 80, 82, 83, 201
Nicholls 61
Nigeria 40
Nixon, Richard 146–7
Noakes, Lucy 96, 99
Nobel Prize 126
non-Muslim enemies 193
Nordic Independence 7
North America 12, 34, 83, 164
North Atlantic Treaty Organization (NATO) 12, 140, 165–6
Northern Rhodesia 38–40
Northern Rhodesia forces 42
Northern Territories 37, 40
Northern Whig 125
North Yorkshire village 110
Nothnagle, Alan 137
Nottingham 103, 104, 106
novel advertisements 26
novel advertising 20
'Now That You Don't Have to Go' *155*
Nuremburg Rallies 25
Nurse Corps 152
N. W. Ayer, New York 21
N. W. Ayer & Son 149–50, 152
Nyasaland 40

O'Donnell, Victoria 5, 77, 78, 93
oeuvre (Taylor, Phillip) 5
Officer Commanding Gold Coast 37

Ogilvy 170
Ogilvy, Montreal 21
Omar, Karima 81
online advertisements 163
online communication 24
Ontario 168
Open Door policy 179
Operation Connection 168–9
Ordnance Corps 127
organisations: military 5; rabid socialist 67; skills 186
Ottawa 165
Ottoman 50–1
Ottoman caliphate 192
Ottoman Empire 6, 50
Overseas Expeditionary Force 36
Oxford 104
Oxford Dictionary 77

Pacific National Exhibition 169
Page, Melvin 33
painful civil conflict 49
Pals Battalions 107
papal bulls 10
Paris 51
Parker, Critchley 69
Passchendaele 168
Patterson, Wilfred 124
Peace Conference, Paris 51
Peace Group for Dialogue 140
Peacock, Alexander 67
Pearce, George 67
Pearce, S. 70
peer-group persuasion 108–9
peithō 17; *see also* persuasion
Penfield, Edward 80
Penshurst 66
pension arrangements 63
People 121
People's Liberation Army (PLA) 13, 22; challenges 181–2; conscription efforts 179; domestic and international image 179; growing professionalism 180; history of 179–80; media campaigns 182–3; modernisation 180; national rejuvenation 184–5; online guidelines 184; propaganda videos 178; recruitment campaigns 178–87; recruitment goals 178; use of aspirational appeals 185–6
Persian Gulf War 180
personal persuasion 108–9
persuasion 6; art of 9; methods of 9; peer-group 108–9; power and limits of

232   Index

62, 107; psychological 77; religious 17;
techniques of 8, 77–8, 93; tools of 10;
types of 17; *see also peithō*
persuasive communication 5
Petri, Alexandra 80
Philadelphia Record 80
Philip Morris 149
Phillip Pretorius 42
Phoney War 97, 110
Pioneerorganisation 'Ernst Thälmann'
137
PLA Daily (Jiefangjun ribao) 183
Poe, Marshall 7
Poland 133, 135, 141
Polish nationalism 135
Polish–Soviet war 135
Polish United Workers Party 135
political confrontation 53
Poplar Borough Council 107
Port August committee 68
Portugal 36
post-Soviet Afghanistan 194
post-war peace negotiations 56
Prague Peace Assembly 140
pre-conscription military training 134–5
press conferences 26, 124–6
press releases 124–6
Pretoria 41
Prettyman, Gib 151
Preventive Service, Gold Coast 33
print media 6, 20
pro-conscription movement 68
pro-Greek propaganda 57
promotion 8, 18
promotional communication 19
propaganda 4–6; channels and content
of 51–2; defined 76–9; efficacy of 78;
First World War 51; great propaganda
machine 75–6; Greece 49, 51–2, 54;
Islamic State of Iraq and Syria (ISIS)
193; mobilising 48–59; newsreels 21–2;
pejorative overtone 17; to promote
service and allegiance 17–28; propriety
of 78; royal 57; support 22; vigorous 71;
war 4–6, 13; women in First World War
75–93
Propaganda and Persuasion (Jowett and
O'Donnell) 78
Prophet Muhammad 193
protecting angel 81, 86–8
Provisional Government of Thessaloniki 55
psychological traits 186
public affairs, defined 167
public exhibitions 124–6

publicity 63–5
public relations (PR) 17–28; activities of
events 63; *see also* military recruitment;
military recruitment campaigning
public speeches 40–2
public 'voyage experiences' 25
purest proletarian classes 181

Qing Dynasty 10
quantum praedecessores 10
Queensland Recruiting Committee
(QRC) 66
Queensland town 64, 67, 69
Quran 193

rabid socialist organisations 67
radio 20
Radio Television Libre des Mille Collines 22
Ramesses II 9
Rane, Halim 13, 24, 198
recruiting/recruitment: agriculture 35;
to armies of the Warsaw Pact 131–42;
Army bands 40–2; in Australia
61–72; boys to British armed forces
117–28; to British civil defence 96–111;
challenges 39–40, 181–2; civilianisation
27; commerce 35; conscription
36–8; economics of 35; ethnicity 36–8;
federalism and 68–71; localisation of
104–7; mining 35
recruitment advertising 150–7
Red Army 179
Red Cross 88, 97
Reese, Roger 12, 23
religious: activities 195; authority 198;
ceremonies 6; in Eastern European
countries 140; extremism 203; harsh
punishment 133; ideology 199; Islamic
authorities 203; Islamic obligation 192;
leaders 43; legitimacy of caliphate
196; legitimate obligations 199; multi-
lingual propaganda 195; obligation of
Muslims 196; pluralism 203; response
193; transformations of 4; vision 196;
Western societies 202
Republic of Turkey 192
Richins, Marsha 151
Richmond 64
rituals 25
R. J. Reynolds 149
Robertson, Emily 11, 27
Robson, L. L. 63
Roman Empire 9
Romania 133, 136

Rostker, Bernard 145
Royal Air Force 118, 122, 127
Royal Albert Hall 100
Royal Army Ordnance Corps 126
royal propaganda 57
Rumiyah 195–8
Russia 6
Russian offices of Amnesty International 139
Russians 138
Russian Soviet Federative Socialist Republic 134
Rwandan genocide 22
Ryan, Victor H. 65, 70

A Sailor Is Born 126
Saint Xavier College in Chicago 148
Sajjan, Sarjat Singh 165
Salafism 198
Salafist-jihadism 199
sales force 121
Salvation Army 77
Samson, Anne 11, 27
Sanskrit 3
Saudi Wahabbism 199
Scandinavian ancestry 7
Scholastic Inc. 157
Schoolboys' Exhibitions 26
Schudson, Michael 151
Scotland 124
Scotsman, The 125
Second Boer War 126
Second Crusade 10
Second World War 6, 12, 21–2, 26, 44, 49, 107, 110, 133, 135–6, 140, 151, 165, 179, 210, 219
Secretary of the State War Council (SWCSA) 67–8, 70
self-discipline 186
sell service 6, 9–11, 12–13, 18, 21–4, 121–4, 209
Semati, Mehdi 201
Senior Scholastic magazine 157
Serbia 53
Serb military forces 53
Services Recruiting Publicity Committee (SRPC) 120
Servicio Militar Voluntario Femenino (Women's Voluntary Military Service) 27
Seventh Day Adventists 133
Shanxi Provincial Recruitment Office 186
shariah 193, 200
sharp political confrontation 53
Sheffield 110

Shover, Michelle 81–2, 88
Sierra Leone 37, 40
Skin Corps 42
Smith, Jessie Wilcox 80
Snowdon, Philip 168
social events 108
socialist patriotism 136
social media platforms 24
Solidarity movement 135
Somali Civil War 166
Somaliland 34
Somalis 35
Sosa & Associates agency 148
South Africa 34–7, 41
South African Boers 35
South African Coloured community 41
South African Department of Native Affairs 38
South African Expeditionary Forces 41
South African Native Labour Corps (SANLC) 38
South America 8, 12, 164
South Australia 65, 67
South-East Africa 38
Southern Rhodesia (Zimbabwe) 34
Southern Rhodesia Volunteers 34
South West Africa 33
Sovetskii Patriot 134
Soviet army 135, 137, 139, 140
Soviet European 131
Soviet model 133–5
Soviet Republic 22
Soviet socialism 132
Soviet Union 118, 140
Spain 25
Spanish Civil War 22
Spanish-language 148
Speakers Division 79
speeches *see* public speeches
'Spirit of America, The' (Christy) 88, *90*
Spirit of War 82
SS *Königsberg* 42
SS *Mendi* 38
Stanley, Peter 62
State Recruiting Committees, Australia 70
State War Council of South Australia 65
State War Councils, Australia 69
St John's Ambulance 97
Suffolk Army Cadet Force 123
Sunni Islam 4
Sunni Muslims 197
Sutton, Peter 23
Swahilis 37
Switzerland 56–7

234   Index

Sydney 126
Syria 8, 13, 192–3, 196, 203, 219
Syrian al-Nusra Front 194
Szpunar, Piotr M. 201

Taiping Heavenly Kingdom 10
Taiwan 180
Taliban 166
Tamil separatists 6
Tasmania 70
Tate and Lyle sugar factory 109
tawhid 200
Taylor, Philip 4–5
TeamAFP 24
television 21
television broadcasting 7
terrorists 199, 201–2
Thatcher, Margaret 201
'Army Sees Green, The' 154
Thessaloniki 51, 53–6
'Third Liberty Loan Campaign'
   (Leyendecker) *91*
Thomas, Marlo 152
Thompson, J. Walter 149
Thutmose III 3
Tiananmen Square 180
Time Magazine College Edition 152
Timini 37
Tisias 17
Togoland 33, 38
Townsend, Alfred 71–2
Trades Hall Council 66
traditional media 13
transformations 4
Transvaal Chamber of Mines 36
Treaty of Friendship 132
Treaty of Sevres 51
Trowbridge 106
Trudeau, Justin 166
Tunisia's En-Nahda Party 199
Turkey's Justice and Development Party 199
Turkistan Islamic Group 180
Tutsis 22
Twitter 13, 24, 163, 171

Uganda Railway 42
Uncle Sam 82, 83
Union Defence Force 42
Union of Soviet Socialist Republics
   (USSR) 12, 131–3, 137–9
United Airlines 149
United Kingdom 110
United Nations Committee 127
United Nations (UN) Security Council 165

United States 6, 80, 82, 86, 140; America
   76, 79; armed forces 145; Army
   recruitment 145–57; German agents and
   saboteurs in 76
US Air Force 24
US Army 13, 22–3
US military 77
utopia 150–7
utopian meritocracy 146

Vance, Jonathan 169
Venizelos, Eleutherios 50–1, 53–7; *see also*
   National Schism
Venizelos–Constantine rupture 54
Veritas 168
Victoria 64, 66–7
Victorian Labor Party 68
Victory Parade of Spotlight Bands 22
Vietnam 179
Vietnam War 13, 149, 151–3, 154
vigorous canvas 63
vigorous propaganda 71
Vogt, George 79
Voluntary Society for Assistance to the
   Army, Air Force, and Navy (DOSAAF)
   134–5, 140
Vörös Riport Film (Red Newsreel) 22
Vuic, Kara Dixon 152
Vyasa 3

Wahabbism 198
Wahhab, Muhammad ibn Abdul 199
wala 200
war: described 4; propaganda 4–6, 13;
   see also specific war
War Census, Australia 64
War Councils, Australia 69, 86
Wardens' Post, The (Middlesbrough) *105*
war events 110
Warner, Marina 82
Warning, The 100, 103, 106
War Office 35, 39, 101, 107, 119, 121, 125
War of Self-Defence, First Report, The 22
War Pensions Bill 63
War Precautions Act 67
Warrant Officers and Non Commissioned
   Officer (WONCO)
Warsaw Pact 12, 132
Warsaw Pact countries 23
Warsaw Treaty Organization (WTO) 12,
   131, 138; constitutions of 133; draft
   evaders 133; educational deferments
   133; establishment of 133
war-time carrier recruitment 36

wartime mobilisations 5
Watkins, Oscar 38
Wavell's Arabs 42
WeChat 13, 183
Weibo 13, 183
Welch, David 5
West Africa 34–7, 42, 196
West African territories 40
West Berlin 136
Western Australia 68
Western Europe 127
Western European countries 54
Western Front 49, 75
Western media reporting 200–2
Western Muslims 193
West Germany 136
White, James F. 83
white officers 35, 37–9
Wi-Fi 23
Wilson, Woodrow 76, 78, 82, 86
Wiltshire 106
Winnipeg–Saskatchewan Labour Day
  Canadian Football League 169
Winter, Jay 107
women: in First World War 75–93; as
  propaganda technique 81; as symbol
  82–7

Women's Army Corps (WAC) 152
Women's Royal Air Force 124
Women's Voluntary Services (WVS) 97
Wonders of the Deep 126
World War I (WWI) *see* First World War
World War II (WWII) *see* Second World
  War
World Wide Web 7, 23, 163
W. S. Crawford 21, 100, 104
Wyeth, N. C. 80

Xenophon 9
'*Xiao pingguo*' (Little Apple) 186
Xi Jinping 181
Xiuquan, Hong 10
Xunzi (Kuang) 4

Yankee Doodle 82
Yemen 180, 196
youth attitudes 138–41
YouTube 13, 163, 171

Zhang Wei 185
Ziino, Bart 62, 66, 68
Zouaragou 40
Zwiazek Harcerstwa Polskiego (Polish
  Scouts Association) 135